T0328929

Music and Ceremonial at British Coronations

Coronations are the grandest of all state occasions. This is the first comprehensive in-depth study of the music that was performed at British coronations from 1603 to the present, encompassing the sixteen coronations that took place in Westminster Abbey and the last two Scottish coronations. Range describes how music played a crucial role at the coronations and how the practical requirements of the ceremonial proceedings affected its structure and performance. The programme of music at each coronation is reconstructed, accompanied by a wealth of transcriptions of newly discovered primary source material, revealing findings that lead to fresh conclusions about performance practices. The coronation ceremonies are placed in their historical context, including the political background and the concept of invented traditions. The study is an invaluable resource not only for musicologists and historians, but also for performers, providing a fascinating insight into the greatest of all royal events.

MATTHIAS RANGE is Research Assistant to DIAMM at the Faculty of Music, University of Oxford, and Associate Lecturer in History at Oxford Brookes University. His areas of research are interdisciplinary, and he has published numerous articles on seventeenth- and eighteenth-century music at royal events, as well as on general cultural history. His research is supported and inspired by his practical experience and activity as a musician: as an organist trained in Germany and as a choral singer at The Queen's College, Oxford. His findings and research outcomes have led to numerous performances, including recordings with HM Chapel Royal.

Music and Ceremonial at British Coronations

From James I to Elizabeth II

MATTHIAS RANGE

CAMBRIDGE
UNIVERSITY PRESS

Shaftesbury Road, Cambridge CB2 8EA, United Kingdom

One Liberty Plaza, 20th Floor, New York, NY 10006, USA

477 Williamstown Road, Port Melbourne, VIC 3207, Australia

314–321, 3rd Floor, Plot 3, Splendor Forum, Jasola District Centre, New Delhi – 110025, India

103 Penang Road, #05–06/07, Visioncrest Commercial, Singapore 238467

Cambridge University Press is part of Cambridge University Press & Assessment, a department of the University of Cambridge.

We share the University's mission to contribute to society through the pursuit of education, learning and research at the highest international levels of excellence.

www.cambridge.org
Information on this title: www.cambridge.org/9781009366120

First published 2012
First paperback edition 2023

A catalogue record for this publication is available from the British Library

Library of Congress Cataloging-in-Publication data
Range, Matthias, 1977–
Music and ceremonial at British coronations : from James I to Elizabeth II / Matthias Range.
    p.   cm.
Includes bibliographical references.
ISBN 978-1-107-02344-4
1. Coronation music – Great Britain – History and criticism.   I. Title.
ML285.R36   2012
781.5'7–dc23

2012015495

ISBN   978-1-107-02344-4   Hardback
ISBN   978-1-009-36612-0   Paperback

For H.M.

Meinen lieben Eltern in Dankbarkeit

Contents

Illustrations and examples

Illustrations

Examples

Tables

Acknowledgements

This book would not have come into existence without the support and encouragement of many institutions and individuals. The first thanks ought, indeed, to go to my parents: from my earliest youth they did whatever they could to support me and my (to them at least) 'bizarre' interests in music and history.

As to the actual project, I am grateful to the Arts and Humanities Research Council (AHRC) and the German Academic Exchange Service (DAAD) for their generous financial and logistic support during my DPhil studies which were the foundation stone of this book.

I have incurred many obligations in the course of writing this study. I feel honoured to be able to head my list of acknowledgements with the name of Her Majesty Queen Elizabeth II by whose gracious permission I was allowed to use material at HM Chapel Royal at St James's Palace. Furthermore, I am grateful to His Grace the Archbishop of Canterbury for allowing me to use the material at the library in Lambeth Palace; to the Royal Collection at Windsor Castle, the British Library, Westminster Abbey, the Royal Academy of Music, the Royal College of Music, the College of Arms (Herald's College) and the Gerald Coke Handel Collection for allowing me to use their sources and for the kind support of their staff. I would particularly like to thank Tony Trowles, the Keeper of the Muniments at Westminster Abbey – discussing my ideas with him always proved most fruitful and he was of great help.

However, most of the time of work on this book I spent in Oxford. Many thanks go to all the staff at the Bodleian Library and at the Music Faculty who were always very helpful and supportive. Furthermore, I wish to thank some Oxford college libraries and librarians: The Queen's College, St John's College, Christ Church, and Brasenose College as well as the Sackler and Taylorian Libraries, Duke Humfrey's, and the Special Collections reading room.

I am grateful to several individuals in particular who brought 'my' music back to life in performances: Andrew Gant at HM Chapel Royal, Owen Rees at The Queen's College, and Stephen Taylor and the choir of Cothill House School. In addition, I have had inspiring discussions with several individuals not otherwise listed: Sir Roy Strong, Prof. Reinhard Strohm, Prof. Donald

Burrows, Dr. H. Diack Johnstone, Dr Ruth Smith, David Baldwin from HM Chapel Royal and James O'Donnell at Westminster Abbey – my thanks to all of them. Special thanks go to the editors at Cambridge University Press who showed confidence in my project and encouraged me to extend my research into a full range book covering all the coronations up to 1953.

Last, but by no means least, my thanks go to John Caldwell; not only did he encourage me to embark on this project in the first place, but he also supervised me for four years when I was writing my thesis on the project. During that time he showed the utmost patience with my changing ideas and my occasional outbursts of enthusiasm. We'd always have a good, fruitful discussion over a freshly brewed cup of coffee – I shall always treasure these fond memories.

In the end I wish to extend my especial gratitude to all those that I may – by mistake! – have forgotten in this list.

Abbreviations and conventions

AM	Acta Musicologica
BJ	The British Journal
EECM	Early English Church Music, published for the British Academy (London: Stainer and Bell).
CJ	The Country Journal, or, The Craftsman
DC	The Daily Courant
DT	The Daily Telegraph
EM	Early Music
f.	(after number): and the next following
ff.	(after number): and the two following
fo.	folio
fos.	folios
FP	The Flying-Post
GM	The Gentleman's Magazine, and Historical Chronicle
GSJ	The Galpin Society Journal
Harmonicon	The Harmonicon, a Journal of Music
HHA	Hallische Händel Ausgabe, published for the Georg-Friedrich-Händel Gesellschaft, Series I–V and suppl. vols. (Leipzig and Kassel, 1955–).
HHB	Walter Eisen and Margret Eisen (eds.), Händel-Handbuch, published by the 'Kuratorium der Georg-Friedrich-Händel-Stiftung', 4 vols. (Leipzig, 1978–85).
HJB	Händel-Jahrbuch, published for the Georg-Friedrich-Händel-Gesellschaft (Halle, 1928–)
JRMA	Journal of the Royal Musical Association
LEP	London Evening Post
LEPC	Lloyd's Evening Post and British Chronicle
LG	The London Gazette
LJ	The London Journal
MB	Musica Britannica: A National Collection of Music (London: Stainer and Bell, 1951–)
ML	Music and Letters
MLAI	The Mirror of Literature, Amusement, and Instruction
MLMS	The Musical Library. Monthly Supplement

MH	*The Musical Herald*
MQ	*The Musical Quarterly*
MT	*The Musical Times* (1844–1902: '*and Singing Class Circular*')
MW	*The Musical World, a weekly record of Musical Science, Literature, and Intelligence*
NG	*The New Grove Dictionary of Music and Musicians*, ed. by Stanley Sadie and John Tyrell, 2nd edn, 29 vols. (London: Macmillan, 2001).
OED	*Oxford English Dictionary* (online edition: http://dictionary.oed.com)
PA	*The Public Advertiser*
PL	*The Public Ledger or, Daily Register of Commerce and Intelligence*
PM	*The Post-Man*
pp.	pages
PS	*The Works of Henry Purcell*, The Purcell Society, 32 vols. (London: Novello, 1878–1965; 2/1961– [Stainer and Bell since 2007])
QMM	*The Quarterly Musical Magazine and Review*
r	(after number) *recto* side of a page; included only if otherwise ambiguous
SJC	*St. James's Chronicle or the British Evening Post*
SJEP	*The St. James's Evening Post*
TO	*The Observer*
v	(after number): *verso* side of a page
WAC	*The Westminster Abbey Chorister*
WEP	*The Whitehall Evening Post or London Intelligencer*

Newspapers

I have relied mainly on the Nichols newspaper collection and other collections in the Bodleian Library, Oxford. Where necessary this has been complemented with the Burney Collection in the British Library, and the newspaper archive in Colindale for more recent titles.

Libraries and Archives

Where convenient I have used abbreviated references for library collections, based on *RISM* sigla (*Répertoire International des Sources Musicales*). Full details are given at the first mention and in the bibliography.

Dates

Until 1752 the Julian Calendar was used in Britain (so-called Old Style/OS). The New Year began on Lady Day, 25 March, and the dates were also a few days behind those of the Gregorian Calendar which was used on the Continent (New Style/NS).[1] To avoid confusion with the dates given in older sources the original dates will be retained, i.e. in Old Style. However, for dates between 1 January and 24 March the year is given in both ways, Old and New Style.

Spelling and Punctuation

Quotations from original sources follow these as closely as possible; any changes are indicated in square brackets.

So as to avoid confusion, the spelling 'choir' is used only for the musical body. For the part of the church building with the same name the traditional spelling 'quire' is used.

Translations

Unless otherwise stated all translations are the author's.

References

Unless otherwise stated all manuscript references refer to Libraries in Great Britain. Details about the manuscripts are, if necessary, given only in the main text, but not in footnotes; they can be found in the bibliography.

For printed sources full references in footnotes are given only when a title appears for the first time; after that a short form is given (usually the surname and short title). The abbreviations 'p.' and 'pp.' for page(s) are given only in cases of ambiguity; 'fo.' and 'fos.' for folio(s) are always given.

---

[1] For details on the change of calendar see N. Merill Distad, 'Calendar Reform (1751)', in Gerald Newman (ed.), *Britain in the Hanoverian Age, 1714–1837: An Encyclopedia* (London: Routledge, 1997), 91.

1 | Introduction: the British coronation and its music

The coronation of a monarch is the prime example of the combination of a great state occasion and an elaborate religious act: the new monarch is presented to and acknowledged by the people and the principle of divine right is manifested by the anointing with holy oil. In the words of Geoffrey Fisher, Archbishop of Canterbury at the coronation of Elizabeth II in 1953, it is 'one of the oldest institutions' in the 'English church and state', and 'the occasion for much splendid pageantry'.[1] This book examines one specific part of this 'splendid pageantry': the music. As observed by two writers in 1911, at the time of the coronation of George V and Queen Mary, 'music is the art which adds most to the grandeur of the ceremony' and it 'helped to make the great solemnity impressive'.[2] In order to understand how exactly music contributes to the ceremony, it is instructive to examine the musical programme at the coronations, its actual performance, its reception and possible interpretations. The music's exact place, and role, in the ceremonial will be addressed – an aspect hitherto largely neglected. In this way the present study will follow up a question formulated by David Cannadine:[3]

If it is the case [. . .] that pomp is of itself a visible form of power, then *precisely what form of power is it?*

Many studies have tackled the issue of pomp, ceremony and ritual as means of power. Nevertheless, the exact nature and character of this 'pomp' and its precise relationship with the ceremonial are all too often neglected. At the same time, Cannadine's understanding of pomp as a visible form of power is

---

[1] 'The Coronation Service. An Introduction by His Grace the Lord Archbishop of Canterbury', in *The Coronation of Her Majesty Queen Elizabeth II, 2 June* 1953. *Approved Souvenir Programme* (London: Odhams Press, [1953]), 30.

[2] Walter G. Alcock, Preface to *The Form and Order of the Service* [. . .] *in the Coronation of Their Majesties King George V and Queen Mary* [. . .] *With the Music to be Sung*, ed. by Sir Frederick Bridge (London: Novello, 1911), iii–vi, here iii; 'Music in the Coronation Service. By our Representative in Westminster Abbey', *MH* (1911), 213–15, here 213.

[3] David Cannadine, 'Introduction: Divine Rites of Kings', in David Cannadine and Simon Rice (eds.), *Rituals of Royalty. Power and Ceremonial in Traditional Societies* (Cambridge University Press, 1987), 1–19, here 17 (emphasis original).

here expanded to include especially the audible aspect: indeed, in many ways the visual and audible part of pomp work closely together to create a ceremonial *Gesamtkunstwerk*.

Liturgically, the coronation service is similar to the consecration of a bishop.[4] It is modelled around the celebration of Holy Communion and a division of the service into two main parts became evident early: the coronation part with all the ceremonies of the investiture of the new monarch, and the celebration of the Eucharist. Some sources describe the second part of the service as the 'Communion Service'.[5] However, strictly speaking, the whole of the service is a communion service. Notably, there was never any sort of congregational communion and one commentator pointed out:[6]

No one communicates with the Archbishop save the King and Queen, the Dean of Westminster who assists in the Administration, and the Bishops Assistant.

From a ceremonial point of view it is a striking that at coronations the monarchs appear always to have received the sacrament in full view of the assembled congregation. In contrast to that, when the monarch took communion in the Chapel Royal, at least until the reign of George III this happened in a special, secluded traverse near the altar.[7]

The 1603 coronation was an important caesura in the history of the ceremony: it was the first fully to follow the rites of the Church of England and it is also the earliest for which some more information on the music survives. Furthermore, this coronation was the first of a *de facto* 'British' monarch, as James I/VI reigned over England with Wales, and Scotland. Since 1066 Westminster Abbey has been the traditional place of the crowning of English monarchs, and, since the Act of Union in 1707, of the monarchs of 'Great Britain'. In addition, in the period of study here there were two coronations in Scotland: those of Charles I in 1633 and of Charles II in 1651. Another 'coronation' ceremony, the investiture of the Prince of Wales, was not celebrated on a grand scale before the investiture of

---

[4] Jocelyn Perkins, *The Crowning of the Sovereign of Great Britain and the Dominions Overseas: A Handbook to the Coronation* (London: Methuen, 1937), 99. See also Ch. 8, fn. 29.

[5] See, for instance, *London, College of Arms (Lca) MS Ceremonials 18*: 'Coronations. Queen Anne. George Ist'. (Steer Catalogue, No. [18]), item 90, Procession and order of service for the coronation of George I in 1714: '[after the Homage] Then follows the Communion Service.'

[6] Perkins, 124.

[7] John Adamson, 'The Tudor and Stuart Courts 1509–1714', in John Adamson (ed.), *The Princely Courts of Europe. Ritual, Politics and Culture under the Ancien Régime 1500–1750* (first publ. 1999 by Weidenfeld and Nicolson, paperback edn, London: Seven Dials, 2000), 95–117, here 104.

the future Edward VIII in 1911.[8] Ifan Kyrle Fletcher described the 1911 ceremony as 'revived with a splendour surpassing any of its predecessors'.[9] However, generally little is known about the individual ceremonies before the twentieth century.[10] Regarding the music, it has been stated that Tallis's English adaptation of his famous forty-part motet 'Spem in alium' ('Sing and glorify heaven's majesty') was sung at the investitures of Prince Henry in 1610, of Prince Charles in 1616, and also at that of the future Charles II in 1638.[11] An eighteenth-century description of such a ceremony contains many general details, but gives no information on the music.[12]

The history and evolution of the coronation service has always generated much interest in Britain. Printed accounts of coronations appeared very early on, and they were soon complemented by comprehensive studies of the ceremony.[13] The situation is similar in other countries in which the coronation was an important state ritual, such as France.[14] In the Holy Roman Empire, the coronations in the sixteenth and eighteenth centuries were commemorated in semi-official 'diaries', or descriptions.[15] In modern

---

[8] For the history of this ceremony see Francis Jones, *God Bless The Prince of Wales. Four Essays for Investiture Year* 1969 (Carmarthen: Lodwick and Sons, 1969). For 1911 see *Ceremonial to be observed at the Investiture of His Royal Highness The Prince of Wales, K.G., Carnavon Castle, 13th July, 1911* ([London:] Harrison and Sons, [1911]). For a more contextual approach to this ceremony see also Krishan Kumar, *The Making of English National Identity* (Cambridge University Press, 2003), 182, and the literature referred to there.

[9] Ifan Kyrle Fletcher, *The British Court. Its Traditions and Ceremonial* (London: Cassell, 1953), 104.

[10] See, for instance, Douglas Macleane, *The Great Solemnity of the Coronation of the King and Queen of England According to the Use of the Church of England, with an introduction by the Lord Bishop of Salisbury* (London: George Allen, 1911), 208f. Macleane refers to 'a description of the investiture of Henry, son of James I., in the Parliament House, June 4, 1610', but no details of this source are given. See also below, fn. 12.

[11] John Morehen, 'The English Anthem Text, 1549–1660', *JRMA* 117 (1992), 62–85, here 66; and Suzanne Cole, *Thomas Tallis and His Music in Victorian England* (Woodbridge: Boydell, 2008), 105.

[12] Johann Christian Lünig, *Theatrum ceremoniale Historico-Politicum, oder Historisch-und Politischer Schau-Platz Aller Ceremonien* [. . .], 2 vols. (Leipzig, 1719–20), vol. II, 1039: 'Beschreibung / mit was vor Ceremonien ein Printz von Wallies creiret wird.'

[13] One of the earliest examples is John Selden's *Titles of Honor* (London, 1614), which includes an edition of the medieval Egbert order with comments. See P.L. Ward, 'The Coronation Ceremony in Medieval England', *Speculum* 14 (1939), 160–78, here 161, fn. 1.

[14] For the French coronations see the bibliography in Josef Johannes Schmid, *Sacrum Monarchiae Speculum. Der Sacre Louis XV. 1722: Monarchische Tradition, Zeremoniell, Liturgie* (Münster: Aschendorff, 2007), xxxii–xxxiv.

[15] Since the coronation of Leopold I in 1658 these were known as *Krönungsdiarium*. See Bernhard A. Macek, *Die Krönung Josephs II. zum Römischen König in Frankfurt am Main. Logistisches Meisterwerk, zeremonielle Glanzleistung und Kulturgüter für die Ewigkeit* (Frankfurt am Main: Peter Lang, 2010), 11f.

times, the interest in coronations is still especially high in Britain; this may be due to the fact that the monarchy is still an integral part of everyday life and that it is the only European country still to have a coronation ceremony.[16] Two of the leading scholars of British coronations were John Wickham Legg and his son Leopold George, who produced several studies at the beginning of the twentieth century, most prominently the extensive *English Coronation Records* (1901) by the latter. A very authoritative volume was Percy Ernst Schramm's 1937 study, which, however, was concerned mostly with the earlier, medieval coronations.[17] Of a more encompassing character was the work of Lawrence Tanner, librarian of Westminster Abbey.[18] A number of more populist contributions, containing little or no original research, appeared throughout the century, especially when there actually was a coronation. The present state of research is summarized in a collection of essays edited by Paul Bradshaw and, most compelling of all, Roy Strong's comprehensive study of the topic.[19] The coronations and their ceremonial specifically in the early modern period have recently also been discussed by Alice Hunt.[20] While these works give a good introduction to the topic of coronations, they deal with the music only marginally. The coronation music itself has been examined in a number of earlier essays.[21] There are two more recent overviews of the music and Jeffrey Richards presented a good, comprehensive introduction to the programme and performance conditions at the twentieth century

---

[16] All the other remaining monarchies (Spain, Benelux and the Scandinavian countries) have, at best, a blessing of the monarch; however, no crowning, or crown-wearing, takes place in these countries. The last papal coronation was that of Paul VI on 30 June 1963.

[17] Percy Ernst Schramm, *A History of the English Coronation*, transl. by Leopold G. Wickham Legg (Oxford: Clarendon Press, 1937).

[18] Lawrence Tanner, *The History of the Coronation* (1952, repr. London: Pitkin, 1953).

[19] Paul Bradshaw (ed.), *Coronations. Past, Present and Future*. Essays by Henry Everett, Paul Bradshaw and Colin Buchanan. Joint Liturgical Studies 38 (Cambridge: Grove, 1997). Roy Strong, *Coronation: A History of Kingship and the British Monarchy* (London: Harper Collins, 2005).

[20] Alice Hunt, *The Drama of Coronation: Medieval Ceremony in Early Modern England* (Cambridge University Press, 2008).

[21] J[ohn] S[outh] Shedlock, 'Coronation Music', *Proceedings of the Royal Musical Association* 28 (1901–1902), 141–60; Frederick J. Crowest, 'Coronation Music', *The Anglo-Saxon Review: A Quarterly Miscellany* 10 (September 1901), 24–37; Janet Leeper, 'Coronation Music', *Contemporary Review* 151 (January/June 1937), 554–62; Anselm Hughes, 'Music of the Coronation over a Thousand Years', *Proceedings of the Royal Musical Association* 79 (1952–1953), 81–100. See also 'Westminster Abbey' in *MT* 48 (1907), 293–301 by F.G. Edwards, the editor of *MT*, published under the pseudonym 'Dotted Crotchet'; and the anonymously published essay 'Coronation Music of the Past', *The Athenaeum*, no. 3871 (1902), 25–7.

coronations.[22] However, several new details can be added to these studies; and generally so far little consideration has been given to the music's place within the overall ceremonial – but it is the exact place of the music within the service that can have significant implications for its composition and performance.

Notwithstanding one or two exceptions, there is often much uncertainty regarding the music at British coronations before the twentieth century. There is not a single coronation for which the complete programme of music can be established with certainty and for which all of the music survives. Many of the pieces that are extant survive in only a few sources, which might furthermore not reflect the original scoring and performance practice.[23] It is only from the 1902 coronation onwards that the music is more fully documented, but still some details have remained obscure. In 1953, Gerald Hayes commented:[24]

It is curious that while the most elaborate records are accessible of the ceremonies, processions, liturgies, clothes and expenses of long-past Coronations, references to the music are very meagre and to composers still slighter.

In the same year another writer summarized that 'State occasions of pageantry are usually feasts only for the eye, with music as a background accompaniment.'[25] However, it will remain to be seen how far such a verdict is generally justified for the coronation music; and while that writer already promulgates an exception for the 1953 event, it appears that also at the earlier coronations the music was much more than a mere 'background accompaniment'.

Apart from the actual scores, one of the main sources for the coronation music, and especially for its place in the ceremonial, are the orders of service. In Britain, the 'form and order of the service of the coronation' has never been fixed obligatorily, as were other special services in the Book of Common Prayer – for example, a thanksgiving service for the monarch's

---

[22] Thomas Robert Schultz, 'Music in the Coronations of the Kings and Queens of England (1603–1953)', unpublished MA thesis, Trenton State College (1992). David Stanley Knight, 'The Organs of Westminster Abbey and their Music, 1240–1908', 2 vols., unpublished Ph.D thesis, King's College, University of London (2001), esp. vol. I, ch. 5: 'The Organs used for Coronation Services 1661–1838, Special Events at the Abbey, and the Music Performed', 102–35. Jeffrey Richards, *Imperialism and Music. Britain 1876–1953* (Manchester University Press, 2001), ch. 4 (pp. 88–151): 'Music for official occasions: coronations and jubilees'.

[23] For details see the individual chapters. See also the author's article '"With Instrumental Musick of all sorts" – The Orchestra at British Coronations before 1727', *AM* 82 (2010), 87–104.

[24] Gerald Hayes, 'Coronation Music', in L.G.G. Ramsey (ed.), *The Connoisseur Coronation Book, 1953* ([London, 1953]), 9–12, here 9.

[25] Evan Senior, [Editor's Preface], *Music and Musicians.* Coronation Number (June 1953), 5.

accession. Therefore, the coronation service is arranged anew for each monarch. In the words of the late Georgian author Robert Huish 'a coronation is the mere creature of precedent, and rests rather upon practice than principle, although the reason of it also may be traced'.[26] The order of service is usually prepared by the Archbishop of Canterbury, who, as the Primate of all England, has the right to crown the monarch. His proposed order is discussed and eventually ratified by the Privy Council, which regulates all matters concerning the accession of a new monarch. While the ceremonial of the church service is arranged by the ecclesiastical authorities, the other ceremonies of the day are regulated by the heralds of the College of Arms under the Duke of Norfolk as the hereditary Earl Marshal, who is responsible for the ceremonial at all the great occasions of state. The clear division of the responsibility for the service and for the rest of the ceremonies is vividly illustrated by an example from 1902. Joseph Armitage Robinson, then Dean of Westminster, wrote to Archbishop Frederick Temple about the printed order of service for the coronation of that year; he pointed out:[27]

I am startled & shocked by the new cover, which introduces the Earl Marshal and the Herald's College – neither of which have anything to do with a Church of England Service. This is a most dangerous precedent, & ought in my opinion to be absolutely quashed. I acquit the Earl Marshal, but the Heralds are full of mischief!

Nevertheless, there was some historic precedent for at least a light collaboration: it is documented that in 1761 the Archbishop of Canterbury had discussed some of the ceremonial aspects with Garter King of Arms before the service.[28]

It is important to remember that sources such as the order of service or ceremonials written by the heralds are merely official guidelines, normally produced before the ceremony and representing an ideal; they do not necessarily report what actually happened. In his manuscript account of the 1727 coronation Stephen Martin Leake, then Lancaster Herald, remarked sharply about the problems when arranging the various processions:[29]

---

[26] Robert Huish, *Memoirs of George the Fourth, Descriptive of the more Interesting Scenes of his Private and Public Life, and the Important Events of his Memorable Reign* [. . .], 2 vols. (London: Thomas Kelly, 1831), vol. II, 311.

[27] Robinson to Temple, 6 April 1902 (*London, Lambeth Palace (Llp) MS 2797*, fo. 143).

[28] See Ch. 6, fn. 8. Close collaboration between these two officials is also documented for the 1937 and 1953 coronations.

[29] *Lca MS S.M.L. 44*, 'Heraldic Annals', vol. I, p. 25.

Another difficulty, that always attends these Grand proceedings, is, That the Great ones, will not observe the directions of the Heralds.

Furthermore, referring to problems at the coronation of George III and Queen Charlotte in 1761, Leake later explicitly stated:[30]

This shows how little Ceremonials are observed, there being thirteen [*sic*] persons, beside the two Bishops Supporters, after Garter who had the Archbishops printed form of the Solemnity, though not one knew where his Majesty was to go upon his Entrance.

Similarly, in respect to printed reports and illustrations it has been observed that some mistakes in fact multiplied themselves and soon became established custom.[31] However, comparison of all the surviving sources – official documents, unofficial reports, pictures, and the music itself – allows the reconstruction of at least part of the musical programme and ceremonial, and to gain new insights into its performance, reception, and possible meaning.

The music of the service is predominantly choral music, consisting of the liturgical music related to the celebration of Holy Communion, and several topical anthems. It has been observed that it was at the 1603 coronation that 'the Anthem first appeared', referring to a setting of a Biblical text in English rather than in Latin, as in the pre-Reformation antiphons.[32] Even though the order of service does not normally include any specific details about the music, crucially, it provides the texts to be sung. Like most of these texts, the music is chosen or written for each coronation individually.

The coronation choir traditionally consisted of the monarch's own choir, the Chapel Royal, and the choir of Westminster Abbey, it being both the coronation church and a royal peculiar. The selection of the music and the overall responsibility for its performance usually lay with the leading musician of the Chapel, and, from the twentieth century onwards, the organist of the Abbey. In the nineteenth and twentieth centuries the choir was augmented by other choirs and selected individuals from different places in Britain and the Empire/Commonwealth. Orchestral accompaniment of the choir, mostly drawn from the royal musicians, is documented from the seventeenth century onwards.

Although there is little evidence of monarchs being personally involved in the planning of the ceremonial, there are several instances of them being

---

[30] *Lca MS S.M.L. 65* 'Heraldic Memorials', vol. II, p. 302.

[31] For a short study of these see Martin Holmes, 'Some Coronation Fallacies', in L.G.G. Ramsey (ed.), *The Connoisseur Coronation Book, 1953* ([London, 1953]), 26–32.

[32] Hayes, 10.

involved in matters concerning the music. This may be due simply to many British monarchs' enthusiasm for music, but it is also a reminder of the fact that the music is one of the most flexible parts of the service.

Music at the coronation: its place

Up to 1661, the coronation included a cavalcade from the Tower of London through the city to the Palace of Westminster on the day before the coronation. Proceedings on the coronation day itself, until the coronation of William IV and Queen Adelaide in 1831, began in Westminster Hall, where the monarch to be crowned was shown the regalia. From there a procession with all the nobility and clergy to Westminster Abbey took place. The participating choirs also walked in this procession and accompanied it with the performance of an anthem. This practice can be traced back to the twelfth century, when the so-called 'Third Recension', a revision of the first order of service for a coronation, came into use; it mentions the choir singing the antiphon 'Firmetur manus tua', 'Let thy hand be strengthened'.[33] The fact that there were also instrumentalists from early on is confirmed by the order for King Stephen's coronation in 1135, which stipulates 'Let him be conducted to the church with sound of trumpets and with chanting.'[34] From the seventeenth century onwards at least, the text of the anthem accompanying this procession was 'O Lord, grant the King a long life'.[35] However, the musicians were so far ahead of the king or queen that their anthem did not directly accompany the royal procession. Furthermore, the singing must have been difficult as the choir was stretched out, and much of the music would surely have been drowned out by the ringing of the Abbey bells and the shouts of the cheering crowds.

Once the procession had reached the Abbey, the royal party was 'received', as it is usually worded in the orders of service, with the entrance-anthem.[36] For the earlier coronations it is not clear exactly when and how this anthem was performed; but from 1685 onwards the reports explicitly

---

[33] See Strong, 42–5. In addition, there is evidence for this processional antiphon at the coronation of Richard I in 1189. See J. Wickham Legg, 'Notes on the coronation of King William and Queen Mary', in J. Wickham Legg (ed.), *Three Coronation Orders* (London: Harrison and Sons, 1900), 129–59, here 135.

[34] See Macleane, 248.

[35] The text then consisted of vv. 6–7 from Ps. 61 and v. 19 from Ps. 132.

[36] Some authors use the term 'introit' for this anthem. However, at least from 1902 onwards this term was used to denote the anthem that marks the beginning of the communion service, and therefore the term 'entrance-anthem' is more appropriate.

describe that it accompanied the procession through the nave to the quire. At earlier coronations its text had been taken from Ps. 84, beginning at verse 9: 'Protector noster' ('Behold, O Lord our protector/defender'), a text which was also used at papal coronations.[37] Since the seventeenth century the text has been a selection of verses from Ps. 122, 'I was glad'. An additional feature at the beginning of the service is the shouting or singing of the *Vivats*, the Latin acclamation 'Vivat Rex NN/ Vivat Regina NN'.[38]

Very little is known of the music at the pre-Reformation coronation service. The service included the *Ordinarium* and *Proprium Missae*, and the additional ceremonies were accompanied by several antiphons and the Te Deum. Indeed, especially the Te Deum, probably the grandest song of praise in the church, features prominently in earlier descriptions of coronations.[39] Some of the earliest surviving coronation music appears to be the *Laudes Regiae* that were sung at medieval coronations.[40] A presumably pre-Reformation manuscript description of 'The maner of Coronations of the Kinges & Queenes of England' includes the names of a few antiphons, but nothing about the respective settings.[41] One copy of this includes at the end some music in score, probably for six parts; however, it is not clear if this music is in any way linked to coronations.[42]

The Reformation did not change the form of the coronation service significantly. The first Protestant coronation in Britain was that of Anne Boleyn, second queen consort to Henry VIII. She was crowned in 1533 by Archbishop Thomas Cranmer who also wrote a description of the event.[43] The first coronation of a reigning monarch after the Reformation was that of Edward VI. Hunt has argued that this event was modified so as to articulate 'a new conceptualization of the authority of coronation and the legitimacy of ceremony'.[44] After only six years, however, Edward VI was succeeded by

---

[37] Andrew Hughes, 'Antiphons and Acclamations. The Politics of Music in the Coronation Service of Edward II, 1308', *The Journal of Musicology* 6 (1988), 150–68, here 164f.

[38] Andrew Hughes, 'Antiphons', 150ff., shows that these had originally been sung at the end of the service, and were moved to its beginning in the 'Fourth Recension', in the early fourteenth century. For the later custom see Ch. 3.

[39] See William Jones, *Crowns and Coronations. A History of Regalia* (London: Chatto and Windus, 1883), 179, 262, and 264ff.

[40] For the history of the early *Laudes* see Herbert Edward John Cowdrey, 'The Anglo-Norman Laudes Regiae', *Viator: Medieval and Renaissance Studies* 12 (1981), 37–78. See also Strong, 40.

[41] *Oxford, Bodleian Library (Ob) MS Rawlinson B 120*, fo. 113.

[42] *London British Library (Lbl) MS Harl. 4848*, fos. 79v–83: 'The maner of Coronations of the Kinges & Queenes / of Englande.', *c.* 1530. The music is on fos. 84v–88.

[43] For details of this coronation see Strong, 162 and 510 (for sources and literature).

[44] Hunt, ch. 3 (77–110); this quotation on p. 79. For details of this coronation see also Strong, 199–211.

his Catholic half-sister, Mary I, who tried to reverse the Reformation. After her short but intense reign Protestantism could not be re-introduced immediately; the coronation of her successor, Elizabeth I, in 1558, was still incorporated into a full Catholic mass.[45] By the time Elizabeth I died, Protestantism was firmly established and the coronation of her successor James I (James VI of Scotland) and his queen in 1603 was a clearly Protestant affair. The ceremonies concerned with the inauguration of the new monarch saw few or no changes and were still combined with the celebration of the Eucharist. From that coronation on they were integrated into the Communion Service according to the Book of Common Prayer and no longer into a full (Roman Catholic) mass. The service continued the pre-Reformation tradition by including a number of special, topical motets, or anthems as they were more commonly called now. Their texts were never fixed and to this day depend solely on tradition; they were normally taken directly or in slightly varied versions from either the Prayer Book or the King James version of the English Bible. As before the Reformation the main stages of the coronation part of the service were punctuated by such anthems:

1. The **Recognition** occurs at the very beginning of the ceremony and symbolizes the affirmation of the monarch by the people. The archbishop proclaims the monarch to the four compass points and the people signify their consent ('recognition') by shouting 'God save the king/queen'. This is followed by the singing of an anthem during which the monarch returns to the Chair of Estate.[46]

2. The **Anointing**, when the archbishop anoints the monarch with holy oil, is the spiritual climax of the service.[47] It begins with the singing of *Veni Creator Spiritus* ('Come Holy Ghost'). This ninth-century Pentecostal hymn has been used at this place in 'every coronation of which a record survives', and the origins of its inclusion at coronations have been seen in its use at the election of popes and the consecration of bishops.[48]

   The *Veni Creator* is followed by the anthem 'Zadok the Priest', a translation of the antiphon *Unxerunt Salomonem*. The text is derived

---

[45] Strong, 208f. For the 1558 music see Timothy Morris, 'Music to Celebrate the Coronation of Elizabeth I', in booklet text to *Coronation of the First Elizabeth*, CD GCCD 4032 (Griffin: 1994), 4–6.

[46] For the history of this anthem see Legg, *Three Coronation Orders*, 136.

[47] Tanner, 30. Cf. Robert Zaller, 'Breaking the Vessels: 'The Desacralization of Monarchy in Early Modern England'', *Sixteenth Century Journal* 24 (1998), 757–78, here 757f.

[48] Ian Bradley, *God Save the Queen. The Spiritual Dimension of Monarchy* (London: Darton, Longman and Todd, 2002), 88.

from the first chapter of the first Book of Kings and describes the anointing of King Solomon by Zadok the Priest and Nathan the Prophet. The antiphon is included in the so-called Pontifical of Egbert which dates from 'around 1000' but was probably 'in use a long time before 900'.[49] The singing of *Unxerunt Salomonem* is reported for the coronation of King Edgar in 973, the first English coronation of which a full order of service and a clear record survive.[50] While there is no evidence that the antiphon was sung in the period between 1100 and 1300, it has been a constant part of the service ever since.[51]

3. The **Crowning**, with the moment of the actual putting on of the crown, has for long been perceived as the ceremonial climax of the service.[52] It is followed by a fanfare, the acclamation of the people within the Abbey, a short prayer, and then an anthem. For the coronations up to the Interregnum, two anthems are mentioned at this place: the *Confortare* ('Be strong and of a good courage') and *Deus in virtute* ('The King shall rejoice'). Later, however, this was reduced to one anthem, the text of which varied.

   Intriguingly, a British coronation means not only the crowning of the sovereign and possibly his consort: after the monarch's coronation, the assembled peers also put on their coronets of rank. This custom seems to be first confirmed for the coronation of Mary I in 1553, but one of the heralds then already described it as 'ancyente'.[53] In later coronations this custom was extended to include also the peeresses and also the bishops with their caps. As will be seen, the anthem at one point had a special, structural role within the ceremonial of this 'multiple crowning'.

4. The **Homage** follows after the monarch's crowning and 'Inthronization', during which the sovereign is 'lifted up into the throne'.[54] Following the

---

[49] Strong, 24ff.   [50] Bradley, 1 and 78. See also Strong, 28f.

[51] Andrew Hughes, 'The Origins and Descent of the Fourth Recension of the English Coronation', in János M. Bak (ed.), *Coronations: Medieval and Early Modern Monarchic Ritual* (Berkley: University of California Press, 1990), 197–216, esp. 197–99. See also Andrew Hughes, 'Antiphons', 153; and Schramm, 108.

[52] Cf. Richard A. Jackson, *Vive Le Roi! A History of the French Coronation from Charles V to Charles X* (Chapel Hill and London: University of North Carolina Press, 1984), 3: 'The French tend to speak of the consecration, the *sacre*, of a king, while the English usually refer to the coronation [...] The French thus emphasize the ecclesiastical and liturgical aspects of the ceremony, and the English emphasize the constitutional aspects.' Cf. also below: Ch. 3, fn. 96; Ch. 4, fn. 17; and Ch. 6, fn. 43.

[53] See Strong, 207.

[54] The archaic term 'Inthronization' was used up to the 1937 coronation and is kept in accordance with the primary sources. For the 1953 coronation it was still used in the draft orders of service (see *Llp Fisher 125*), but for the finally printed version was changed to 'Enthroning'. Some modern literature also uses the alternative 'Enthronement'.

Liber Regalis up to 1838 the procession to the throne was accompanied by the Te Deum. Once enthroned, or 'inthronized', the peers of the realm pay homage to their new sovereign. It has been suggested that up to the coronation of Charles II in 1661 the anthem during this ceremony was at the same time the introit to the ensuing celebration of Holy Communion.[55] However, an anthem at this place was first included in the order of service in 1626. Since 1937 several shorter pieces have been performed at this place. The texts and music for this anthem, or anthems, are chosen for each coronation individually. Up to the nineteenth century much else was going on during the Homage: a General Pardon was proclaimed and the specially minted coronation medals were 'scattered', or thrown amongst the people. An illustration of the Homage at the coronation of William IV in 1831 gives a vivid impression of the tumultuousness of the scene.[56]

This scheme applies to the coronation of either a king alone or a *queen regnant*, a queen who reigns in her own right. A queen's husband is not acknowledged by any special ceremony. However, if a king is married, his wife is usually crowned as well, and since 1603 all coronations of queen consorts have taken place in the service of the king's coronation, following the Homage. The ceremonial of a queen consort's coronation is relatively short: there is no Recognition, the Anointing and Crowning closely follow each other, and the Investiture includes fewer items. An anthem for the queen's coronation, sung during her inthronization, is first recorded for the 1685 coronation, but the custom was discontinued after 1831. The order of service is generally very flexible, with anthems being added or omitted quite freely.

These ceremonies related to the inauguration of the monarch are followed by the celebration of Holy Communion. Regarding the music, the Agnus Dei had been omitted from the second Book of Common Prayer in 1552; at the same time the Kyrie had been replaced by the Responses to the Ten Commandments and the Gloria had been moved to the end of the service. Hence, the liturgical pieces of the coronation service from 1603 onwards consisted only of the Responses, the Creed, the Sanctus (without

[55] See Arthur Taylor, *The Glory of Regality: An Historical Treatise of the Anointing and Crowning of the Kings and Queens of England* (London: R. and A. Taylor, 1820), 375; Legg, *Three Coronation Orders*, 155; and memorandum by Edward Ratcliffe to Archbishop Lang, 20 July 1936 (*Llp Lang 21*, fo. 19f.). See also Ch. 2, fn. 56.

[56] Reproduced in Kenneth Romney Towndrow, 'Coronation Engravings', *Apollo* (1953), 178–182, here 182. Legg, *Three Coronation Orders*, 155, observes that in the orders of service the General Pardon was omitted from 1727 onwards, and the medals from 1831 onwards.

Benedictus) and the Gloria; in addition, there was the lengthy Litany which until the seventeenth century included also the seven Penitential Psalms.[57] After communion, the monarch returns to the throne again before retiring into St Edward's Chapel, behind the High Altar, to be robed for the 'Recess', the procession out of the Abbey. Instrumental music accompanying the Recess is reported only from 1838 onwards, but may certainly also be assumed for the earlier coronations.

After the service, there used to be another procession back to Westminster Hall, where a coronation banquet took place. No details are known for the music of this procession, but the choir may have walked in it again, as is reported for 1626. Occasionally some details of the music during the banquet survive. Since 1831 there have been carriage processions to and from the Abbey to the monarch's palace, accompanied by music of the military bands walking in the procession or stationed along the route.

Fanfares have probably always been a prominent feature at coronations. Up to the 1838 coronation they were played by trumpets and accompanied by 'the drums', or timpani, as shown on contemporary engravings and corroborated by written sources. The musicians came from the civilian Corps of State Trumpeters that was disbanded by the Duke of Wellington as an economy measure in the mid-nineteenth century.[58] Since the 1902 coronation the trumpeters have come from Kneller Hall.[59] No music survives for coronation fanfares or indeed other fanfares before the eighteenth century and modern reconstructions normally refer to J. Hyde's *Preceptor* from 1798, the first printed account of such music.[60] However, the pieces included here are not strictly 'fanfares': the music (pp. 10–18) is headed 'Trumpet Duty', and some pieces have titles such as 'Stable Call', 'Boots & Saddles', and 'To Horse', which indicates that these are mere

---

[57] Macleane, 84.

[58] Arthur Grimwade, 'The Plate Catalogue', in Claude Blair (ed.), *The Crown Jewels: The History of the Coronation Regalia in the Jewel House of the Tower of London*, 2 vols. (London: Stationery Office, 1998), vol. II: The Catalogues, 385–501; 'The State Trumpets' on pp. 491–6, here 491. See also Eric Halfpenny, 'William Shaw's "Harmonic Trumpet"', *GSJ* 13 (July 1960), 7–13, here App. II, 12f.

[59] F. G. E[dwards], 'The Coronation of Edward the Seventh and Queen Alexandra in the Collegiate Church of St. Peter in Westminster, August 9, 1902', *MT* 43 (1902), 577–86, here 584; 'The Coronation Music and Musicians', *MT* 78 (June 1937), 497–501, here 498. For the Kneller Hall fanfare trumpets see Lilla Margaret Fox, *Instruments of Processional Music* (London: Lutterworth Press, 1967), 60.

[60] *A New and Compleat Preceptor for the Trumpet and Bugle Horn, with the Whole of the Cavalry Duty [. . .] To which is added a Selection of Airs, Marches and Quick Steps for Three Trumpets, Composed and Compiled by J. Hyde* (London: Printed and to be had of the Author, n.d.); '1798', according to Crispian Steele-Perkins, in booklet text to *Coronation of the First Elizabeth*, 7.

trumpet signals for the cavalry. Edward Tarr has pointed out that 'fanfares were distinct from military signals in usage and character'.[61] According to Caldwell Titcomb fanfares were set for several parts, built on a major triad and 'always played three times'.[62] The drums seem to have fallen into disuse after the nineteenth century and were used only in certain fanfares. Gordon Jacob, himself a composer at the 1953 coronation, observed that 'fanfares played on great ceremonial occasions are written for trumpets, usually in four parts, and three trombones, this seven-fold combination being reduplicated and multiplied to any extent'.[63]

Music at the coronation: its role

The lack of information on the music at coronations prior to 1902 could be taken to imply that little importance was attached to the individual pieces performed. At the time of the 1953 coronation, Robert Scarlett remarked sarcastically:[64]

Music has always played some part in every Coronation [. . .] and yet the official records have ignored it so much that the casual reader might be forgiven for believing the ceremony to have been monotoned.

In 1838 William Cooke Taylor commented on the 1727 coronation that 'George II and Queen Caroline were crowned [. . .] with the usual solemnities, but nothing occurred to give any variety or interest to the scene.'[65] This striking neglect of George Frideric Handel's grand coronation anthems, written for and first performed at this occasion, might simply be the personal ignorance of one particular writer. However, it is a good example of the general neglect of the music in such reports. In fact, it had been only from the eighteenth century onwards that there was a slowly growing wider interest in the coronation music, at least in the anthems. This was certainly linked to the fact that from then on they became 'available' to a wider audience, since they were performed in public rehearsals, and repeated at concerts after the coronation, as well as published. Referring to the fact that coronation anthems were

---

[61] Edward Tarr, 'Fanfare', *NG* 8, 543–4, here 543. Cf. below, p. 179.

[62] Caldwell Titcomb, 'Baroque Court and Military Trumpets and Kettledrums: Technique and Music', *GSJ* 9 (1956), 56–81, here 71.

[63] Gordon Jacob, *The Composer and His Art* (Oxford University Press, 1955), 71.

[64] Robert Dalley Scarlett, 'Coronation Music and Its Problems', *The Canon – Australian Journal of Music* 6 (March 1953), 308–11, here 308.

[65] William Cooke Taylor, *Chapters on Coronations: Comprising Their Origin, Nature and History* (London: John W. Parker, 1838), 185.

normally not repeated at other services, it has been observed that they did not become 'repertory pieces'.[66] One reason for this might be that many of these pieces were too special and demanding, too large and requiring too many musicians for use in a 'normal' service.

In 1902, on the occasion of the coronation of Edward VII and Queen Alexandra, Sir Frederick Bridge, who was responsible for the music at the service, explained that it

> was not to prolong the ceremony, and was only to be performed when something was going on. That is the old custom of the Coronation; the King does not come to sit in his crown and listen to a lot of music, though composers abroad seem to think that he does.[67]

It is not known to which 'composers abroad' Bridge referred; however, it appears that these composers were, at least to some extent, right in their assumption. Most of the music indeed accompanied the rituals and, as will be seen, some pieces matched the ceremonial proceedings very well. Nevertheless, occasionally the music was far too long to cover just the respective ceremonies, 'when something was going on'. Anthems such as Purcell's 'Praise the Lord, O Jerusalem', performed after the Crowning in 1689, or Handel's 'My heart is inditing', performed after the Queen's Coronation in 1727, were both heard when not much else was going on. These pieces would, at about seven and ten minutes in length, necessarily have turned into 'a lot of music'.

The situation changed probably only in 1902. Similar to Bridge, Douglas Macleane reported of a 'new idea', and he explained that

> linking [that is 'restricting'] Coronation music to processional and ceremonial movements has profoundly modified the choice of compositions to be performed, which must be of a certain brevity.[68]

Nevertheless, this new scheme was not followed rigidly. First of all, the liturgical pieces generally grew very much in length, becoming 'a lot of music'. Secondly, there were still exceptions. The Crowning was followed by the singing of the *Confortare* during which the monarch simply remained in St Edward's Chair, 'sitting in his/her crown' and holding the Sceptre and the Rod with the Dove: in 1953 for about one and a half minutes. Moreover, at

---

[66] Eric van Tassel, 'A Purcell Coronation Anthem?', *MT* 120 (1979), 114.

[67] This is part of the discussion to Shedlock's paper on Coronation Music. See Shedlock, 159. The same 'instructions' are related in Bridge's *A Westminster Pilgrim. Being a Record of Service in Church, Cathedral, and Abbey; College, University, and Concert-Room, with a Few Notes on Sport* (London: Novello, [1918]), 179.

[68] Macleane, 218.

the 1911, 1937 and 1953 coronations the Homage was followed by an extended fanfare of the trumpets and organ of about two minutes in length, during which nothing else 'was going on'. From 1902 onwards the Gloria, which had been used as a processional at previous coronations, was performed in an elaborate setting during which the monarch was simply 'sitting in his/her crown' and listened to 'a lot of music'. At such moments, the scene in Westminster Abbey must have appeared like a *tableau vivant*: all actions paused, while the grandest music of the time enhanced the overall effect. These pauses may have provided time to marvel at and reflect on the ceremonies. The impression that such a scene may have left is well expressed in Edward VIII's description of his father's coronation in 1911, and his prominent reference to the music is noteworthy:[69]

In that gorgeous, glittering assemblage, watching the stately measures of the prelates and the Great Officers of State in their robes of scarlet trimmed with ermine and gold, listening to the fanfares of trumpets, the rich tones of the organ and the voices of the choir, I became aware as never before of the true majesty and solemnity of kingship.

In 1936 Archbishop Cosmo Lang stated that he 'must try to effect certain abridgements in non-vital matters such as for example the length of some of the Music'.[70] At the same time, however, Lang himself acknowledged that the music was in fact a vital matter of such ceremony when, at a meeting with the king, he suggested a 'shortening of the music which I thought could be simple and majestic without being elaborate'.[71]

Strong observes that the music 'became a hugely significant part of the Coronation in the twentieth century'.[72] As the two aforementioned examples of Purcell's and Handel's anthems indicate, music seems to have been a significant part long before that. With all its ceremonies, the coronation service had always been of enormous length. In 1626, according to a note by one of the bishops, the coronation service of Charles I and his queen took more than five hours.[73] In 1838, at the coronation of Queen Victoria, Sir George Smart, the musician in charge, noted that the service took three hours and 48 minutes 'from the 1st to the last Note of the Music'.[74] In the twentieth century, although the service had been shortened

---

[69] [Edward] Duke of Windsor, *The Crown and the People 1902–1953* (London: Cassell, 1953), 25.

[70] Lang to Dean of Westminster, 21 July 1936 (*Llp Lang 21*, fo. 21f.).

[71] Typed note, 21 July 1936 (*Llp Lang 21*, fo. 24).   [72] Strong, 467.

[73] *Cjc MS L 12*, p. 47: 'King Charles, was Come into Westminster Church before Ten of ye Clocke: And Came forth about a quarter past three.'

[74] London, Westminster Abbey (*Lwa*) Library, 4.c.9, p. 67.

in certain parts, it was still of considerable length. As one commentator observed in 1902: 'The music took an hour and a half to run through, and this gives an idea of the enormous length of the whole ceremony.'[75] Indeed, the coronation service of George V and Queen Mary in 1911 'occupied nearly three hours'; and the coronation of Elizabeth II in 1953, even though it did not include the crowning of a consort, was not much shorter.[76] In such a lengthy service the music provided some variety, while at the same time reinforcing the structure of the ceremonies. After all, music had a much higher status in the days before radio and recordings: it was something very special, of rare occurrence; and music as lavish as at the coronation service may easily be interpreted as a status symbol.[77] The general significance and appreciation of an abundant musical programme at the great occasions of state becomes apparent when looking at the thanksgiving services during Queen Anne's and George I's reigns in the early eighteenth century.[78] Not only was there each time an elaborate orchestral setting of the Te Deum and Jubilate but also at least one lengthy anthem. Music as grand and elaborate as at coronations was a rare thing, even for royalty, and the lavish performance conditions would always have been exceptional.

Moreover, the music at these great ceremonies of state could fulfil one other important purpose. For the 1953 coronation William McKie, the director of music, informed Archbishop Fisher that Handel's 'Zadok the Priest' 'Can't be shortened: c 7 Min. / Gives a welcome pause with Q kneeling.'[79] Notwithstanding the fact that seven minutes is a very generous estimate for the length of this anthem, it is noteworthy that McKie suggests the music as 'a welcome pause': at such a lengthy ceremony the music could provide a moment of contemplation and time to reassemble concentration and strength for those taking part – an aspect that certainly also applies to previous centuries. In the end, 'Zadok the Priest' indeed provided a pause: the queen listened to much of it sitting quietly in her Chair of Estate; her

---

[75] 'The Rehearsals for the Coronation ['By our Representative in the Abbey Choir']', *MH* (1902), 202–3, here 203.

[76] 'The Coronation of King George the Fifth and Queen Mary in Westminster Abbey, June 22, 1911', *MT* 52 (1911), 433–7, here 433. For 1953 see *The Coronation Service of Her Majesty Queen Elizabeth II, 2 June 1953*. 2 discs, CD 7243 5 66582 2 6, digitally remastered (EMI, 1997), first published by EMI on a 3-LP set: ALP 1056–8. The total running time on the two CDs is 158 minutes.

[77] Cf. Ch. 7, fn. 140

[78] For the lists of the music see Donald Burrows, *Handel and the English Chapel Royal*, Oxford Studies in British Church Music [5] (Oxford: Clarendon Press, 2005), 598–603.

[79] McKie to Fisher, 29 October 1952 (*Llp Fisher 123*, fos. 170–73, here fo. 171). Cf. below, fn. 102.

robing began only during the anthem's third part, at the end of which she went to take seat in St Edward's Chair. One of her maids of honour acknowledged the supportive qualities of the music:[80]

I suppose for the first time I was aware of the power of music. It just carried you through.

Finally, it is worth pointing out that the audience or congregation at the coronations up to the twentieth ceremony played a much more active part in the ceremony. The reports about the services show that much of the music was not listened to in silence, as in a concert. For all the coronations up to the twentieth century it may be assumed that the spectators in Westminster Abbey 'participated' actively with occasional shouting and clapping. In 1661, the diarist Samuel Pepys complained in a probably exaggerated way that he could not hear much of the music due to the noise during the Homage, and in 1821 *The Observer* reported that the procession up the nave at the beginning of the service was accompanied by the people's cheering.[81] Similarly, at the coronation of Queen Victoria, the Duke of Wellington, Earl Grey and Lord Melbourne 'were cheered as they went up [to the throne] to do homage'.[82] At such moments the music was indeed almost relegated to background music, but nevertheless with an important purpose: it enhanced the atmosphere of the moment and gave it more dignity. Altogether this produced a curious mixture of all sorts of rejoicing, as Lady Wilhelmina Stanhope, later Duchess of Cleveland, recorded for the coronation of Queen Victoria, where she was one of the trainbearers. She recalled that after her crowning there was a

burst of applause in the Abbey [...] and in the midst of the cheering Handel's magnificent anthem, 'The Queen shall rejoice!' thundered in.[83]

For the next coronation, that of Edward VII in 1902, the congregation still burst out in spontaneous cheering during the procession of the king and

---

[80] Baroness Willoughby de Eresby, quoted in James Wilkinson, *The Queen's Coronation: The Inside Story* (London: Scala Publishers, 2011), 43.

[81] Samuel Pepys, *The Diary of Samuel Pepys: a New and Complete Transcription*, ed. by Robert Latham and William Matthews. Vol. II: 1661, paperback edn (Berkeley: Harper Collins, reissued 2000) [hereafter 'Pepys'], 84. (For this see also Ch. 2, fn. 131.) Supplement to *The Observer*, 16 July 1821, [4]: '[...] upon the entrance of the King into the aisle, [...] the loud anthem, blended with the applauding shouts of the spectators, echoed to the very roof of the Abbey.' For the people's spontaneous participation see also Ch. 6, fn. 133.

[82] 'Diadem', *Crowns and Coronation Ceremonies and the Enthronement of King Edward VII.*, illustrated by Percy Reynolds and John Rowlands (London: Illustrated Publications Company, [1901 or 1902]), 11.

[83] 'A Personal Account by the Duchess of Cleveland', quoted in John Hammerton (ed.), *The Story of the Coronation* (London: Amalgamated Press, [1937]), 140–2, here 142.

queen out of the Abbey after the service.[84] It was probably only during the twentieth century that the spectators in the Abbey adopted a more passive role as quiet listeners. By 1953 their only participation apart from singing in a hymn and the National Anthem were a few acclamations stipulated in the order of service.

Tradition

It has been observed that 'all coronations follow broadly the same pattern but all have their individual *Leitmotif*.[85] The use of this musical term to describe the variations between the different coronations is appropriate, as it is in the music that some of the main differences between the separate events can be observed. It is striking to compare the photographs of the twentieth century coronations with, for instance, the engravings of James II's coronation in 1685. Allowing for the changes in hairstyle and fashion, there is hardly any difference between these pictures; the overall appearance of the scene in the Abbey, down to the ceremonial robes, is essentially the same. However, while most of the arrangements of the service changed but little over the centuries, there was considerable development in the coronation music.

The music at British royal ceremonies and especially at coronations is often described as 'traditional', with the implication of deliberate repeats of earlier music. However, the term must be used with care. There was certainly some tradition as to the texts that were used, but William Boyce's proposal in 1761 to replace even 'Zadok the Priest' with an anthem to another text suggests that traditions were weak and by no means unchangeable.[86] Describing the situation in 1727, one modern writer refers to 'the mythological status' of the coronation music, or music that had 'become a myth', with the composers 'Blow and Purcell at the forefront of its English heroes'.[87] From a modern point of view this judgment is convincing, since the coronation music of these composers is surrounded by a certain myth and awe. However, it is not known that, as early as 1727, any piece of coronation music had a special fame or that Blow's or Purcell's coronation music had any special status. In fact, most of their contributions had simply fallen into oblivion soon after their first

---

[84] E[dwards], 'Coronation of Edward the Seventh', 582.

[85] Philip Ziegler, *Crown and People* (London: Collins, 1978), 47.

[86] For details see below, Ch. 6, fn. 39.

[87] Sabine Henze-Döhring, 'Händels Coronation Anthems', *Händel-Jahrbuch* 49 (2003), 105–13, here 113: '[. . .] die zum Mythos gewordene Coronation Music der englischen Heroen mit Blow und Purcell in vorderster Front.'

performance. Notwithstanding William Child's 'O Lord, grant the King a long life', which may have been performed during the procession from Westminster Hall to the Abbey at all coronations between 1661 and 1821, there were probably few repeats. Henry Lawes's 'Zadok the Priest' from 1661, and perhaps also Blow's 'Behold, O God' from 1689 appear to have been the only anthems that were repeated at more than one coronation before 1727. The 'tradition' of keeping Lawes's setting especially could be interpreted as a means of creating a sense of continuity: all monarchs after the Restoration heard the same anthem during the central act of the ceremony, their anointing. This 'tradition', however, was not acknowledged and was broken with Handel's spectacular new setting in 1727.

Significant changes were introduced at the 1902 coronation. For the first time there is evidence for a comprehensive programme, an overarching idea for all the music of the service: the programme of music should be representative 'of the best English church composers' of the previous centuries.[88] The music at coronations had probably always represented music from different epochs; even if the anthems were mostly new compositions, at least some of the liturgical pieces seem to have been earlier settings. Nevertheless, it was for the first time in 1902 that such a 'historical consciousness' was clearly articulated and that the music was intentionally credited with such an illustrative role.

It is tempting to link this new idea to the concept of 'invented traditions' that Cannadine has suggested for royal ceremonies of the period.[89] From a musical point of view the decisive stimulus for this innovation may have been the growing self-awareness and appreciation in the context of the English Musical Renaissance.[90] The new scheme placed the modern-day composers in a direct line with the great names of the past. For the 1937 and the 1953 coronations Cannadine notes the 'recently established tradition that each great royal occasion was also to be a festival of contemporary British music'.[91] Most of the coronations since 1603 could be described in the same way, however: most of them included much contemporary music by Britain's leading musicians of the day, and with their extraordinarily lavish character each of them was 'a festival of contemporary British music'. In fact, the important difference at the twentieth-century coronations was that they markedly combined contemporary and earlier music; an event as

---

[88] Macleane, 195. For details see Ch. 8.

[89] David Cannadine, 'The Context, Performance and Meaning of Ritual: The British Monarchy and the "Invention of Tradition", *c.* 1820–1977', in Eric Hobsbawm and Terence Ranger (eds.), *The Invention of Tradition* (Cambridge University Press, 1983, repr. 2002), 101–64.

[90] For a general overview see Meirion Hughes and Robert Stradling, *The English Musical Renaissance, 1840–1940: Constructing a National Music*, 2nd edn (Manchester University Press, 2001).

[91] Cannadine, 'Context', 144.

grand as a coronation served as a magnificent showcase for the glories not only of Britain's musical present but also of its great heritage.

John M. Golby and A. William Purdue have generally argued that the concept of 'invented traditions' in regard to the presentation of the monarchy may be overstated.[92] They observed that 'the differences between George III's coronation and that of Elizabeth II are considerable but the differences pale beside the salient similarities'. Referring to the research of William Kuhn, who stressed the importance of continuity and precedent, Andrzej Olechnowicz has pointed out that a more appropriate term for the developments between the 1870s and 1914 would be 'renovation of tradition'; furthermore, he has observed that different types of royal ceremonies provoked different types of 'inventions'.[93] Indeed, as will be seen, for coronations, one could argue that there have always been instances of 'invented traditions', even though the ceremony as a whole was always 'traditional'.[94] At the 1902 coronation there were probably as many 'breaks with tradition' as there were 'invented' or 'renovated' traditions. Nevertheless, at that coronation there was certainly an especially strong emphasis on making the ceremony *appear* 'traditional' and this 're-establishment' of traditions coincided with the emerging scholarship on such royal rituals.[95] The impression that the music and its performance were hallowed by centuries of tradition was deliberately enhanced: the Chapel Royal boys wore their 'scarlet and gold Court uniforms of the time of Charles II'.[96] This appears to have been the first time that it was worn at a coronation: at earlier coronations the Chapel boys were always reported to have worn surplices and scarlet copes. Also, while there had been female singers at the 1838 coronation, in 1902 the choir consisted again exclusively of men.[97] This scheme was followed until 1953, when the only female singers were nineteen

---

[92] John M. Golby and A. William Purdue, *Kings and Queens of Empire. British Monarchs 1760–2000*, rev. edn (Stroud: Tempus, 2000), 19.

[93] Andrzej Olechnowicz, 'Historians and the Modern British Monarchy', in Andrzej Olechnowicz (ed.), *The Monarchy and the British Nation, 1780 to the Present* (Cambridge University Press, 2007), 6–44, here 25f. For Kuhn's critique of Cannadine's ideas see William Kuhn, *Democratic Royalism: The Transformation of the British Monarchy, 1861–1914* (Basingstoke: Macmillan, 1996), esp. 1–14 (Introduction).

[94] Cf. Richard Jenkyns, *Westminster Abbey* (London: Profile Books, 2004), 178f., who questions whether the coronation ceremony can serve as an example for invented traditions at all.

[95] See Olechnowicz, 26.

[96] E[dwards], 'The Coronation of Edward the Seventh', 578. See also Ch. 3, fns. 138–9.

[97] 'In the Choir at the Coronation ['By the "Musical Herald" Representative']', *MH* (1902), 264–6, here 264: 'Miss Timothy, the harpist, the only lady in choir or orchestra.'

representatives from the Commonwealth, which at the time caused some resentment by 'English professional women singers'.[98]

Notably however, such a strong preference for traditions did not mean that certain pieces of music were sacrosanct. In 1911, at a time when traditions – real and 'invented' – were much in vogue, the inclusion of Handel's 'Zadok the Priest' was criticized with respect to its position in the ceremony:[99]

The gorgeous and florid splendour of 'Zadok the Priest,' composed by Handel for George II.'s Coronation, is a masterpiece of jubilant sound, but inappropriate to the awful moment of the Anointing, of which, of course, nothing can be seen or heard save by a very few. Such a mystic ceremony is eminently a moment for the solemn, ancient music. But this 'Zadok' has now been sung at six Sacrings [George II to Edward VII].

With the last sentence the author seems to conclude that the only justification for the inclusion of Handel's anthem was that it had already been performed at so many coronations. In respect to other pieces, the same author lamented that overall 'in modern times' the anthems in the coronation service 'have been chosen less [...] by ecclesiastical traditions than according as certain compositions or composers were popular and well known'.[100] In fact, one aspect even more important than tradition was, at least in the twentieth century, that of timing. As already seen, archbishops were always concerned to keep the music short, so as not to prolong the service. Regarding the 1937 coronation, Archbishop Lang later recalled that he had asked Walford Davies, the Master of the King's Music and Ernest Bullock, the Abbey organist, 'to consider in what ways Handel's Zadoc the Priest might be shortened'.[101] Davies had replied to this that

On reflection, I think 'Zadok the Priest' can be made newly impressive by certain reverent abbreviations of old Handel: the full Handelian choral majesty being reserved for the bursts: [music example – God save the King! Long live the King!] and the lesser words being declaimed in almost ecclesiastical recitation style. I wonder whether you agree.[102]

With such a cut the anthem's intriguing opening, today its probably most famous feature, would have been lost. However, the archbishop at first seems to have favoured such a revision of Handel's grand anthem, writing that 'I am glad you think that Handel's music for Zadok etc. can be shortened without spoiling the music', later changing this to 'without

[98] 'Miscellaneous Notes', p. 2, in *Lwa Library, McKie Collection of Material related to the Coronation, 1953*. See also Frank Howes, *The Music of William Walton* (Oxford University Press, 1973), 177.
[99] Macleane, 218.   [100] Ibid., 195.
[101] 'Coronation Service. Music' (*Llp Lang 21*, fos. 92–3, here fo. 92).
[102] Davies to Lang, 22 July 1936 (*Llp Lang 21*, fo. 25f.)

spoiling its effect'.[103] Interestingly, both he and Davies were concerned about the music's 'effect'; it is notable that Davies had offered the changes not only to save time, but indeed to make the piece 'newly impressive'. In the end, Handel's full original setting was preserved not because it was traditional or because its integrity was appreciated, but because the archbishop 'pointed out that probably five minutes would be taken in the ceremonial clothing of the King before the Anointing', and so a cut in the music would not have saved any time.[104]

The 'historical' idea from 1902 determined the approach to the coronation music up to 1953. Altogether, throughout the twentieth century the music remained traditional in so far as it was European 'classical' music, either from previous centuries or newly composed. New forms of music, including any kind of popular music, were not introduced to accompany this ceremony. In fact, it was only in 1997, at the funeral of Diana, Princess of Wales, with Elton John performing his song 'Candle in the Wind', that pop music was included in a royal ceremony. In the occasions since then there has been a clear emphasis on the earlier, 'traditional' scheme of 'classical music'.

Coronation music and propaganda

It was Handel's 'Zadok the Priest' that became much more than just an anthem from the coronation service; William Weber observed:[105]

By the [1784 Handel] Commemoration *Zadok* had become part of the standard repertory in the concert halls as well as in the cathedrals, and had, indeed, emerged as a kind of musical ritual to the house of Hanover.

This observation provokes another approach to the topic of coronation ceremonial and music. Since the coronation of the monarch is one of the supreme events of the nation state it is worth reflecting on the propagandistic qualities of the ceremonies. Referring to the Investiture of Prince Charles as Prince of Wales in 1969 it has been shown that the elaborate celebration of royal ceremonies, with all accompanying advertising, background information, and last but not least merchandising, is an important factor in shaping the public image and appreciation of the monarchy.[106] More recently, Richard Jenkyns has argued that

---

[103] Lang to Davies, 23 July 1936 and 27 July 1936 (*Llp Lang 21*, fos. 27 and 33).

[104] *Llp Lang 21*, fo. 92.

[105] William Weber, *The Rise of Musical Classics in Eighteenth-Century England. A Study in Canon, Ritual, and Ideology*, paperback edn (Oxford: Clarendon Press, 1996), 226.

[106] J. G. Blumler, J. R. Brown, A. J. Ewbank, and T. J. Nossiter, 'Attitudes to the Monarchy: Their Structure and Development during a Ceremonial Occasion', *Political Studies* 19 (1971), 149–71.

Sociologists and historians debate whether such ceremonies are forms of propaganda by which the ruling classes bolster their authority or means by which communities as a whole articulate and reaffirm popular values. Actually, the coronation is intrinsically neither of these things (whatever its effect may be): a coronation is something which is done because it always has been done.[107]

Indeed, the whole ceremony is heavily dictated by precedent and tradition, even though not unchangeable. Nevertheless, it is precisely in the music, that part of the service that shows the most change over the centuries, that one may detect traces of its being used to promote the monarchic system in general, or even a particular monarch.

In the so-called 'Second Recension', which was used between 973 and 1101, the text of an antiphon after the Anointing mentions the 'people of England' that have 'not been forgotten in the sight of the Lord'.[108] No music to this text survives. In any case, from the seventeenth to the nineteenth century, the music at British coronations did not explicitly refer to the country. With the texts mostly taken from the psalms, such a link was difficult to achieve. At the same time, however, texts from the Old Testament, including the psalms, were understood as referring not only to Israel but also to Britain.[109] In Isaac Watts's *Christianised versions of the Psalms for congregational singing* from 1719, the references to 'Israel' are actually replaced by the words 'Great Britain'.[110] Thus, at a coronation, the king mentioned in the Biblical texts could easily be understood to be the king crowned in Westminster Abbey – and in 1689, 1702, and 1838 the Psalm texts were readily changed to be applicable to the present, then female, monarch. However, the references to the sovereign always remained curiously subtle and general. Regarding the coronation music the so-called *Vivat*s, the aforementioned acclamation 'Long live the King/Queen' in Latin, remain to the present day the only pieces of the service to include the name of the king and/or queen to be crowned. Therefore, one could

[107] Jenkyns, 179f.
[108] See Strong, 28f., who refers to several manuscript sources, which he lists in note 21.
[109] Cf. T. C. W. Blanning, *The Culture of Power and the Power of Culture – Old Regime Europe 1660–1789* (Oxford University Press, 2002, paperback edn 2003), 275. For the concept of 'British Israel' in the eighteenth century see Ruth Smith, *Handel's Oratorios and Eighteenth-Century Thought* (Cambridge University Press, 1995, paperback edn 2005), esp. 213–29. See also Pasi Ihalainen, *Protestant Nations Redefined: Changing Perceptions of National Identity in the Rhetoric of the English, Dutch and Swedish Public Churches, 1685–1772* (Leiden: Brill, 2005), esp. ch. 2: 'Israelite Parallels in the Language of Nation'.
[110] See Linda Colley, *Britons. Forging the Nation 1707–1837*, (first publ. Yale University Press, 1992; repr. with a new preface by the author, London: Pimlico, 2003), 30. See also Ruth Smith, 216.

argue that the other music refers merely to the monarch's 'body politic', but not to the actual person of a particular monarch.[111]

In Shakespeare's *Henry V*, the king asks: "And what have kings that privates have not too, Save ceremony, save general ceremony?"[112] This is a reminder that, for royalty, ceremonies have for long been an important means of distinction. Indeed, in the seventeenth and eighteenth centuries several writers acknowledged the idea that ceremonies are helpful to secure a monarch's power and that the display of splendour and pomp should be used to impress 'the people'.[113] In 1761, on the occasion of the coronation of George III and Queen Charlotte, one commentator put it very bluntly and stated that 'all Pomp is instituted for the sake of the Public'.[114] Such a use of pomp and ceremony to impress the populace applied especially to coronations, which took place early on in the reign; they manifested the source of a monarch's power publicly and included the acclamation of the new sovereign by the masses.[115] In 1659, shortly before the Restoration of the monarchy, William Cavendish, Duke of Newcastle, wrote an 'Advice' to Charles II. This echoes the statement of Shakespeare's Henry V and summarizes the seventeenth century understanding:[116]

Seremoney though itt is nothing in itt Self, yett it doth Every thing – for what is a king, more than a subiecte, Butt for seremoney, & order, when that fayles him, hees Ruiened, – therefore your Majestie willbee pleased to keepe itt upp strickly, in your owne, person, & Courte [. . .] when you appeare, to shew your Selfe Gloryously, to your People; Like a God, for the Holly writt sayes, we have Calld you Gods [. . .]

---

[111] For the theory of the king's two bodies see Ernst Hartwig Kantorowicz's seminal study *The King's Two Bodies. A Study in Mediaeval Political Theology* (Princeton University Press, 1957).

[112] Act IV, sc. i.

[113] See Karl Möseneder, 'Das Fest als Darstellung der Harmonie im Staate am Beispiel der Entrée Solennelle Ludwigs XIV. 1660 in Paris', in August Buck et al. (eds.), *Europäische Hofkultur im 16. und 17. Jahrhundert; Vorträge und Referate [. . .] in der Herzog August Bibliothek Wolfenbüttel vom 4. bis 8. September 1979*, 3 vols. (Hamburg: Hauswedell,1981), vol. II, 421–31, here 421. Möseneder refers to writings by Louis XIV of France (*Mémoirs* ed. by Charles Dreyss, Paris 1860, vol. II, 15) and the German theorist Johann Christoph Lünig. See lately also Andreas Lindner, 'Zur Intention musikalischer Inszenierung. Die Determination weltlicher Festkonzeption im Umfeld höfisch-geistlicher Institutionen', *Studien zur Musikwissenschaft* 56 (2010), 127–52, esp. 141f.

[114] [John Gwynn], *Thoughts on the Coronation of his present Majesty King George the Third, or Reasons offered against confining the Procession to the usual Track, pointing out others more commodius and proper* (London: printed by the proprietor, 1761), 3.

[115] See Matthew Charles Kilburn, 'Royalty and Public in Britain: 1714–1789', unpublished DPhil thesis, University of Oxford (1997), 94.

[116] Quoted after Strong, 299. For a modern transcription of the full text, see William Cavendish Newcastle, *Ideology and Politics on the Eve of Restoration: Newcastle's Advice to Charles II*, transcribed and with an introduction by Thomas P. Slaughter (Philadelphia: The American Philosophical Society, 1984), this quotation on p. 44f.

These were general, pan-European ideas of monarchy. Towards the end of the *ancien régime*, at the time of Louis XVI, one former page explained the use of ceremonies very openly:[117]

Ceremonies are the most important support of royal authority. If one takes away the splendor that surrounds him [the king], he will be only an ordinary man in the eyes of the multitude, because the populace respects his sovereignty less for his virtue and rank than for the gold that covers him and the pomp that surrounds him.

Although the political situation of the monarch in France and Britain was quite different, the considerations about ceremony may certainly apply to both countries – perhaps even more so to Britain, where the monarch had much less 'real' power. The employment of elaborate ceremonies to further the standing of the monarchy was still apparent in the twentieth century; the idea of 'invented traditions' has been mentioned above. However, when considering these points, the obvious question must always be who this 'populace' (or 'the people') was that was to be impressed by the ceremonies. For the coronations, before the arrival of mass media, the 'public' can be divided into several groups: first of all there is the general public, who could witness the proceedings outside the Abbey. This 'populace' was to be impressed by the processions to the Abbey before the service and back to the Hall afterwards. When these processions were abolished in 1831, they were replaced by carriage processions; these, however, were developed to be more spectacular than they had originally been planned to be, specifically 'in order that the public may not be disappointed'.[118] Then, in the Abbey, there was again a 'general public': everybody who could afford the tickets could see the procession of the royal party through the church. There is evidence for such admission tickets as early as for the 1603 coronation.[119] For the actual coronation, taking place in the 'Area', the space before the High Altar, and the 'Theatre', the space under the crossing in the Abbey, the public were primarily the nobility and high clergy, as well as foreign ambassadors, who were to be impressed by the splendour surrounding the British monarchs; furthermore there were those who could afford the more expensive tickets for the temporarily erected galleries in the north and south transepts, such as the aforementioned diarist Samuel Pepys in 1661.

---

[117] [Felix de France] Compte de Hezecques, *Souvenir d'un page de Louis XVI.* (Brione: G. Monfort, n.d. repr. Aubonne, 1983), 189. Here quoted after Sergio Bertelli: *The King's Body. Sacred Rituals of Power in Medieval and Early Modern Europe*, transl. by R. Burr Litchfield (Pennsylvania State University Press, 2001), 4, fn. 30.

[118] *GM* (1831), part II, 169.   [119] Strong, 256.

For many spectators in the Abbey, the music was probably the main aspect of the proceedings that they were able to perceive during the long service. One has to remember that up to the late twentieth century, when screens were put up at columns and corners, the majority of people, even many of those around the Area and Theatre, could not see very much of the proceedings; in the words of Pepys: '[the king] passed all the ceremonies of the Coronation – which, to my very great grief I and most in the Abbey could not see'.[120] While the visual accessibility of the ceremony was much determined by the architecture of Westminster Abbey, the music was affected by fewer obstacles. Except if there was too much background noise, as Pepys complained at another place, the music more than anything else was able to reach every corner of the building and could be enjoyed by many more people than could the visual display of the rituals. It also has to be borne in mind that a printed order of service for the congregation is a relatively recent feature and therefore the music at the important stages in the ceremony may have given some structural guidance.

Referring back to the limitations on witnessing the ceremony and observing that 'there was no cheap, pictorial press', Cannadine summarized that 'great royal ceremonies were not so much shared, corporate events as remote, inaccessible group rites, performed for the benefit of the few rather than the edification of the many'.[121] Similarly, Strong comments that through the arrival of radio and television in the twentieth century 'for the first time the Coronation was no longer some occult ceremonial witnessed by a chosen elite, but progressively one which became a shared experience for the nation'.[122] It is significant, however, that in this respect the coronation music has for long been quite exceptional: music was the one part of the ceremony that was more easily 'repeatable' and could thus become a 'shared experience' long before the introduction of electronic mass media. From the eighteenth century onwards at least some of the coronation music was increasingly disseminated in services, public concerts and prints.

Over the centuries the perception of the coronation ceremony changed, which had consequences for its appreciation as the inaugural rite of a new monarch. In 1685, according to the French ambassador, the coronation of James II was still 'regarded in England as a ceremony absolutely necessary for the establishment of the royal authority'.[123] James II's deposition in the

---

[120] Pepys, 83f.   [121] Cannadine, 'Context', 111.   [122] Strong, 431.
[123] Quoted after F.C. Turner, *James II* (London: Eyre and Spottiswoode, 1948), 256.

'Glorious Revolution' of 1688/89 was a decisive moment, and David Sturdy summarized that 'after 1685 the constitutional and social significance of the coronation went into decline'.[124] This decline caused a change in the overall character of the coronation. Paul Kléber Monod pointed out that it became 'more of a confirmation of constitutional propriety than a sacralization'.[125] Indeed, the constitutional aspect became very important. Lois Schwoerer has shown that the coronation of William and Mary in 1689 was used to 'assist legitimating the Revolution' and to show the government's stability; the new political order became very evident: the monarchs were still anointed with holy oil by a bishop, but now under the eyes of the parliamentarians who had brought them on to the throne.[126] 'Constitutional propriety' as the main reason for the coronation became apparent in 1830/1: when William IV succeeded to the throne, there was the possibility that the coronation might be abolished altogether and 'the subject, as a constitutional one, was brought before the House of Lords by the Duke of Wellington'.[127] At the same time, the coronation was openly described as 'in itself a senseless ceremony', since 'it is a legacy of our forefathers, to which no letters of administration ought to be taken out at the present day'.[128] By the mid-twentieth century the coronation had lost all links with the constitution. On the occasion of the 1953 coronation, Harold William Bradfield, Bishop of Bath and Wells pointed out that the coronation is constitutionally irrelevant, since a monarch ascends to the throne at the moment of his or her predecessor's death.[129]

Important and striking as these changes in the understanding and ranking of the coronation are, they had little or no effect on the nature of the ceremony; it remained the greatest of all the events of state and, even though its 'inner' significance may have waned, its 'outer' expression of an elaborate ceremonial incorporated into a church service remained largely unchanged. Although the aspect of 'sacralization' may have declined after the Glorious

---

[124] David Sturdy, '"Continuity" versus "Change": Historians and English Coronations of the Medieval and Early Modern Periods', in János M. Bak (ed.), *Coronations; Medieval and Early Modern Monarchic Ritual* (Berkeley: University of California Press, 1990), 228–45, here 243.

[125] Paul Kléber Monod, *The Power of Kings. Monarchy and Religion in Europe 1589–1715* (Yale University Press, 1999), 311.

[126] Lois G. Schwoerer, 'The Coronation of William and Mary, April 11, 1689', in Lois G. Schwoerer (ed.), *The Revolution of 1688–1689. Changing Perspectives* (Cambridge University Press, 1992), 107–30, here 109.

[127] For a full quotation see below, Ch. 7, fn. 2.

[128] Huish, *Memoirs of George the Fourth*, vol. II, 311.

[129] [Harold William Bradfield] Bishop of Bath and Wells, 'The Significance of the Coronation', in *The Coronation Book of Queen Elizabeth II* (London: Odhams Press, [1953]; repr. London: Bounty Books, 2006), 19–21, here 19: 'The Coronation from a constitutional point of view adds nothing to the Queen which she does not already possess.'

Revolution, one aspect of the coronation that received more emphasis was the stressing of its being an entirely Anglican affair, with no other denomination represented. Indeed, Michael Schaich observed that after 1689 'the inclusion of anti-Catholic declarations and the more prominent role given to the Bible and the Established church in the ceremony emphasized the Protestant nature of the British monarchy'.[130] This post-1689 emphasis on Protestantism, however, did not readily become apparent in the coronation music. Apart from the fact that the liturgical music followed the Book of Common Prayer, there was nothing particularly Protestant in the music before the twentieth century, when the tune of Luther's hymn 'Ein feste Burg', the apogee of Protestant hymns, was included in the music at various points. It was not until 1953 that a congregational hymn, today often considered as a typical feature of a Protestant service, was introduced to the coronation.

After the Glorious Revolution the coronation was also more and more understood as a grand public spectacle and this had an effect on the music, as James Wilkinson summarized:[131]

Coronations down to that of James II in 1685 have been described as 'liturgical', those from William and Mary's in 1689 to Victoria's in 1838 have been called 'performance or concerto style' – more spectacle than religious observance. The coronations since Queen Victoria's have encompassed the best of both types.

It has been shown that under the Hanoverian monarchs the coronation was used as 'a symbol of a united and assertive Great Britain', which was not just confined to London, but celebrated throughout the whole country.[132] Referring to the work of Linda Colley, Weber has pointed out that 'George III was redefining the British monarchy in national terms'.[133] The climax in the development of the coronation music towards that of a grand 'spectacle', a 'national show', was reached with the coronations of George IV and William IV, the first of which Tanner described as 'a magnificent pageant almost completely devoid of religious significance'.[134] Thomas Attwood's two coronation anthems for these occasions are exemplary with their open national allusions. This was no longer church music with

---

[130] Michael Schaich, 'Introduction', in Michael Schaich (ed.) *Monarchy and Religion – The Transformation of Royal Culture in Eighteenth-Century Europe* (Oxford University Press, 2007), 1–40, here 32.

[131] James Wilkinson, *Westminster Abbey. 1000 Years of Music and Pageant* (Leighton Buzzard: Evolution Electronics, 2003), 51. See also ibid., 79. Strong, 180, interprets the coronation as becoming a 'parade and pageant' as early as in the sixteenth century.

[132] Kilburn, 98.   [133] Weber (1996), 224.

[134] Tanner, 19f. See also Leeper, 561: '[in 1821] The religious significance of the ceremony had been so much overlaid that it had become merely an opportunity for pageantry and display.'

an especially festive character for a special service: it was music with a calculated propagandistic impetus; nationalist feelings mixed with religion, deployed to support the monarchical system. Finally, by the time of Queen Victoria, one commentator stated that 'the main purpose of the Coronation was "to amuse and interest"' the people.[135]

The interest in seeing the actual ceremony is reflected in the fact that the coronation was imitated on the theatre stages, for instance as an addition to Shakespeare's plays.[136] One such production in 1823 included the singing of 'the CORONATION ANTHEM', maybe Handel's 'Zadok the Priest'.[137] But this was not altogether a novelty of the nineteenth century: following the coronation in 1761 a mock coronation had been inserted as an epilogue to *Henry VIII* at Covent Garden, and even 'the whole of the Westminster choir' had been employed in this.[138] Queen Victoria's coronation in 1838 hints also at how the selection of music may have been motivated by political motives. Weber observed that during the Reform Crisis choral concerts had 'sprung up' in London, and that in 1834 the crown initiated a festival of Handel's oratorios in Westminster Abbey.[139] Music could bestow respectability and dignity on an institution such as the monarchy: at the 1838 coronation, Handel was represented with no fewer than three anthems and an orchestral piece.

A shift of emphasis came in the twentieth century, when the religious aspect of the coronation service was given more consideration.[140] This became clear not least in the music: the liturgical pieces received more attention and became in all likelihood more elaborate than previously. In one way or another, the coronation became once again a truly meaningful ceremony of state and A.N. Wilson observed poignantly that the 1953 ceremony was 'a splendid piece of religio-patriotic pageantry'.[141] Patriotic

---

[135] See Strong, 401, who cites *The Greville Memoirs 1814–1860*.

[136] See for instance *Lbl MS Add. 33570*: 'The Coronation / in / Shakspea's [*sic*] Play / Henry the Fourth / (2d part) / Performed at the Theatre Royal / Covent Garden 1821 / Composed, Selected, & Arranged by / Henry R. Bishop / Originale'. For the additions to Shakespeare's plays see also Peter Davison, 'Complete with Orb, Sceptre and Crown – the 'Coronation' was repeated 104 Times', *WAC* 42 (Summer 2006), 44–7.

[137] [William Shakespeare] *King Henry IV. (The Second Part,) An Historical Play; Revised by J.P. Kemble, Esq. And printed as it was revived at The Theatre Royal, Covent Garden, On Monday, June the 25th, 1821; with the Representation of the Coronation, as arranged by Mr. Farley* [...] (London: Printed for John Miller, 1821), 67.

[138] Friedrich Kielmansegge, *Diary of a Journey to England in the Years 1761–1762*, transl. by Countess Kielmansegg (London: Longmans, 1902), 192f. See also Strong, 415.

[139] William Weber, *Music and the Middle Class: The Social Structure of Concert Life in London, Paris and Vienna Between 1830 and 1848* (1975; 2nd edn Aldershot: Ashgate, 2004), 118.

[140] See above, fn. 130, and see Ch. 8.

[141] A[ndrew] N[orman] Wilson, *After the Victorians* (London: Hutchinson, 2005), 528.

it was indeed: from the 1902 coronation onwards this impression was enhanced by a self-conscious stressing of Britishness in the coronation music. The coronation music programme became more and more a thoroughly British, indeed English-Anglican affair. It was the performing body that provided the best opportunity for some acknowledgement of the international-imperial dimension of the event. Before the 1937 coronation, Walford Davies wrote to Archbishop Lang about the idea of representatives from other choirs:

The idea seems certain to commend itself nationally, and clearly it would do measureless good if Canada, Australia, and even India, listening to the service broadcast, knew that they were actually listening to music in which singers of their own nation had some personal part.[142]

As this suggestion illustrates, with the twentieth century there also came a heightened awareness of, and also more possibilities to make use of, the propagandistic qualities of the event. Befittingly David Wright has linked the 1902 coronation to the furtherance of the 'Imperial Project', the building and strengthening of the British Empire.[143] It was with the rise of mass media that the general public of the country, the Empire, and virtually the whole world became partakers in the ceremony. In this respect, the coronations of George VI and Queen Elizabeth in 1937 and that of their daughter, Elizabeth II in 1953, stand out as important turning points: the 1937 coronation was the first broadcast live on radio and the 1953 event was the first coronation, indeed the first major royal occasion, broadcast live on television – the State Opening of Parliament, for instance, was not televised until 1958.[144] Elizabeth II's coronation was certainly the one with the biggest audience ever; millions of people in Britain and all over Europe witnessed the ceremony at the very moment it was happening, and, as in 1937, many more were able to watch it in cinemas shortly afterwards.[145] Also, in 1937 and 1953 sound recordings of the coronation were produced

---

[142] Davies to Lang, 29 October 1936 (*Llp Lang 21*, fos. 112–13).

[143] David Wright, 'Sir Frederick Bridge and the Musical Furtherance of the 1902 Imperial Project', in Rachel Cowgill and Julian Rushton (eds.), *Europe, Empire, and Spectacle in Nineteenth-Century British Music* (Aldershot: Ashgate, 2006), 115–29.

[144] For details of this first broadcast see Burton Paulu, *British Broadcasting in Transition* (Minneapolis: University of Minnesota Press, 1961), 90.

[145] Cf. Cannadine, 'Context', 142 and 158f., and Edward Shils and Michael Young, 'The Meaning of the Coronation', *The Sociological Review*, new series, vol. 1 (1953), repr. (Nendeln, Liechtenstein: 1970), 63–81, here 70f.

and became available for everyone to buy.[146] Overall, the music of these coronations became known to a wider audience than any coronation music previously.

Strong summarized that 'all the evidence points to the Coronation already being a musical event long before the arrival of Handel'.[147] Coronations have always been extraordinary events, and accordingly their music was always some of the finest of its time. Overall, the exceptionally lavish music is one of the core features that characterizes the British coronation service and each coronation was indeed a 'musical event' in its own right.[148]

---

[146] *The Coronation of Their Majesties King George VI and Queen Elizabeth, Westminster Abbey, 12 May 1937*, 2 discs, FL 1001–2/FL 1002–2, digitally remastered (New York: Fleur de Lis Recordings, 2010); first published on fifteen 78rpm records (London: The Gramophone Company Limited: 1937; HMV Album No. 281, RG 1–15). For the 1953 coronation see above, fn. 76.

[147] Strong, 343.

[148] For comparative tables of the music at the coronations since 1603 see Appendices C and D.

2 | After Reformation and Restoration: 1603–1661

As observed in the previous chapter, the Reformation had very little effect on the coronation ceremony. From the coronation of James I and his wife in 1603 the crowning of the sovereign followed the rites of the Church of England. However, the medieval order of service was adopted more or less unchanged and stayed in principle the same; in fact, the *Liber Regalis* was used as the basis for this coronation.[1] The important difference was that the order of service was now for the first time 'an English version of that Latin form [the 'fourth recension'] with certain additions'.[2] All subsequent coronations followed the 1603 model in essence.

Although information on the music is still sparse, a few pieces at least can be linked with this and the following coronation, that of Charles I in 1626. It is only from the coronation of Charles II in 1661 onwards that the music is better documented and that more of it survives. While this was the first coronation after the sharp caesura of the Civil War and ensuing Commonwealth, or Interregnum, ceremonially it was a clear display of the continuation of the medieval coronation traditions.

James I and Queen Anne, 1603

James I had been crowned as James VI of Scotland in 1567 in a service that, apart from the omission of the mass, was still very much the same as at the pre-Reformation coronations.[3] Only when his consort, Anne of Denmark, was crowned in 1590 was the service more distinctly Protestant. However, not much is known about the music at these two Scottish coronations. James VI was crowned as James I of England together with his wife by Archbishop John Whitgift on St James's Day, 25 July 1603. The order of service for

---

[1] Strong, 84.

[2] John Edward Courtenay Bodley, *The Coronation of Edward the Seventh. A Chapter of European and Imperial History* (London: Methuen, 1903), 285, fn. 2.

[3] For this and the following see Reginald Maxwell Woolley, *Coronation Rites* (Cambridge University Press, 1915), 138f.

the coronation survives in several manuscripts.[4] In addition, it was printed in 1685, presumably in anticipation of the coronation in that year.[5] The 1603 coronation service was an entirely Anglican ceremony, with most of the texts translated into English; nevertheless some prayers and important passages were still in Latin – for example the Litany. Furthermore, the king's oath was administered in Latin, English, and French, reflecting the English kings' claim to their former territories in France.[6]

Very little is known about the music at this coronation. The customary procession from the Tower to Westminster on the day before the coronation had been abolished owing to the plague in London, and the king had ordered that 'crowds should not gather'.[7] It is not certain if the procession from Westminster Hall to the Abbey before the service took place. According to Giovanni Carlo Scaramelli, the Venetian Ambassador, the king went from Whitehall to Westminster by boat; 'Their Majesties landed and entered the church'.[8] At the same time, Scaramelli points out that access to Westminster from London was strictly forbidden, both by land and by water. Although this would imply that no elaborate procession took place, Scaramelli clearly describes a procession under the heading 'and the Coronation proceeded in the following order'. The only musicians that he mentions for this procession are 'two drums and ten trumpets' and he thus refers probably to the procession from the Hall to the Abbey. Assuming that this procession took place, and that the choir walked in it, Anselm Hughes stated that this was probably the first coronation at which it was accompanied by an anthem to the words 'O Lord, grant the King a long life' from

---

[4] *Llp MS 1075b*, transcr. in John Wickham Legg (ed.), *The Coronation Order of King James I.* (London: F. E. Robinson, 1902). Further copies are *Ob MS Rawlinson B 40*, fo. 4 and *Lbl MS Add. 39139*, fos. 205–14. A short version of the order of service is found in *Lbl MS Add. 6284*, fos. 36–39v. Finally, there is *Lca MS W.Y.*, fo. 146: 'A. Coronacōn of King James', written at the time of the coronation.

[5] *The Ceremonies, Form of Prayer, and Services used in Westminster-Abby at the Coronation of King James the First and Queen Ann his Consort [...] With an Account of the Procession from the Palace to the Abby [...] With the Coronation of Charles the first in Scotland.* (London: Randal Taylor, 1685).

[6] See Legg, *King James*, 13–16; see also Christopher Wordsworth (ed.), *The Manner of the Coronation of King Charles the First of England at Westminster, 2 Feb., 1626* (London: Harrison and Sons, 1892), 113–15.

[7] Bryan Bevan, *Royal Westminster Abbey* (London: Robert Hale, 1976), 114, and Strong, 261. See also Leanda de Lisle, *After Elizabeth – How James, King of Scots Won the Crown of England in 1603* (London: Harper Collins, 2005), 259f., who points to the 'possibility of riots against the new king' as a reason for abolishing the procession.

[8] See *Calendar of State Papers and Manuscripts, relating to English Affairs, Existing in the Archives and Collections of Venice, and in other Libraries of Northern Italy*, vol. X: 1603–1607, ed. by Horatio F. Brown (London: Printed for Her Majesty's Stationery Office, 1900), 74–7, here 75.

Ps. 61.[9] Under the same premises, Janet Leeper suggested that the anthem was Thomas Weelkes's setting of the text.[10] However, this is an elaborate setting for seven parts and considering that the singers would have been widely separated during the procession, the performance of this anthem would have been very difficult. In the end, it seems more likely that Weelkes's anthem was composed for some other topical service.

The sources for the 1603 coronation contain little information on the music during the service. Anthems are mentioned for four key stages:

1. At the king's entrance into the Abbey, during the procession up the nave: 'Behold, O Lord our protector'.[11]
2. After the Recognition: 'Let thy hand be strengthened'; in one source the full text of this anthem, taken from Ps. 89, is followed by the *Gloria Patri*.[12]
3. During the Anointing: *Veni Creator*, Litany, 'Zadok the Priest'.
4. After the Crowning: 'Be strong and of a good courage' (the *Confortare*) and 'The King shall rejoice' (*Deus in virtute*); both in one anthem.

With little information on the music in the primary sources, much of it is open to conjecture. For instance, it has been stated that there was a fanfare on the king's entrance into the church and that the choir walked before the king in the procession towards the High Altar.[13] However, this description appears to be inspired simply by reports from later coronations.

From a ceremonial point of view it is interesting that there should have been music during the actual moment of the putting on of the crown: 'The Archbishop crowneth the King saying [...] In the meane time the Quire singeth the Anthem'.[14] If the anthem indeed accompanied this act, this may have served to heighten the overall effect of the scene. At all following coronations the actual crowning was accompanied only by the archbishop's words; the congregation watched on in awe-inspiring silence, before this was broken by an outburst of acclamations, fanfares and elaborate music.

It has been suggested that the *Confortare*, 'Be strong and of a good courage', may have been sung in Thomas Tomkins's full setting for

[9] Anselm Hughes, 86.

[10] Leeper, 556. This suggestion is followed by Strong, 260. For the music see Thomas Weelkes, *Collected Anthems*, ed. by David Brown, Walter Collins, and Peter Le Huray, *MB* 23 (1966; *r*. 1975), 53.

[11] It is noteworthy that all the sources explicitly refer to the 'king's entrance' only and do not mention the queen. Considering the queen's entrance see de Lisle, 263.

[12] Legg, *King James*, 12: 'Psal. misericordias dej / Glorie bee to the ffather &c.'

[13] De Lisle, 262.   [14] Legg, *King James*, 31; *Lca MS W.Y.*, fo. 156.

seven-part choir.[15] This anthem was posthumously published in the collection *Musica Deo Sacra*, but without reference to the coronation.[16] In the foreword to his edition of Boyce's *Cathedral Music*, Joseph Warren describes the anthem as 'one of the coronation songs'.[17] Tomkins's relationship with the Chapel Royal at the time is not clear; he probably was not formally appointed until the 1620s.[18] Nevertheless, that does not preclude him from having composed for the 1603 coronation. Indeed, he is supposed to have written most of his anthems 'during the first decade or so of the 17th century' and he clearly did work for the Chapel Royal before the 1620s, when he wrote his anthem 'Know ye not' to commemorate the funeral of the Prince of Wales in 1612.[19]

It is noteworthy that Tomkins's *Musica Deo Sacra* includes a setting of 'O Lord, grant the King a long life', which is described as 'the *Coronation-Anthem*' in the table of contents.[20] The anthem is scored for TrAATB choir with an independent organ part. It begins with a short introduction on the organ and a long bass solo and includes also a short verse for treble, alto and bass. Anthony Boden proposed that this anthem was not sung at the service, but that it was 'written specially for national celebration or for local use at Worcester'.[21] Indeed, the anthem would not be very suitable for the procession from Westminster Hall with which this text is normally associated: although the organ part could well be a transcription of original consort parts (for instance for cornetts and sackbuts), the soloist sections would not make for a good effect in a procession. However, the anthem may have been sung at another point in the ceremony. If, as referred to above, the choir did not take part in the procession to the Abbey, this text could have been sung elsewhere, during the actual service. Intriguingly, the aforementioned sources for the service do not name an anthem for the Homage, but there is evidence that elaborate music was performed at this point in the ceremony. Benjamin von Buwinckhausen, the ambassador of the Duke of

---

[15] Anthony Boden, 'The Life and Times of Thomas Tomkins and his Family', in Anthony Boden (ed.), *Thomas Tomkins: The Last Elizabethan* (Aldershot: Ashgate, 2005), 5–194, here 87. See also Denis Stevens, *Thomas Tomkins, 1572–1656* (London: Macmillan, 1957), 82.

[16] Thomas Tomkins, *Musica Deo Sacra & Ecclesiae Anglicanae* (London, 1668).

[17] William Boyce, *Cathedral Music* [. . .] newly edited and carefully collated and revised, with an Appendix to each Volume [. . .] by Joseph Warren, 3 vols. (London: R. Cocks & Co., 1849), vol. I, 40.

[18] For this and the following see John Irving, 'Thomas Tomkins', *NG* 25, 568–75, here 568.

[19] See Morehen, 68f., and *Ob MS Tenb. 1382* fo. 2r: 'Prince henry his funerall Anthem:'.

[20] For a modern edition see Thomas Tomkins, *Musica Deo Sacra* I, transcr. and ed. by Bernard Rose, *EECM* 5 ([1965]), 73–80.

[21] Boden, 87. His argument is that the anthem 'does not appear among the anthems sung at the coronation of James I or Charles I'.

Württemberg, reports that 'the whole time the organs, voices and other music resounded in intervals'.[22] Tomkins's 'O Lord, grant the King a long life' matches this description with its solo and choral sections and instrumental interludes; the 'other music' mentioned could refer to some parts being performed by other instruments than the organ, such as viols.[23] Moreover, the text of this anthem fits very well to the Homage: the verse 'So will we alway sing praise unto thy name, that I may daily perform my vows' just before the final Hallelujah could be interpreted as a direct allusion to the peers' vows during this ceremony.

In accordance with earlier orders of service there was no anthem after the Queen's Coronation.[24] This was thus a rather short, inconspicuous ceremony between the King's Coronation and the taking of Holy Communion. Also, not many details of the liturgical music are known. The order of service includes the 'Nicen Creede' after the Homage, possibly transferred until after the Queen's Coronation.[25] While it is not clear if this was sung or read, it may be assumed that the service included also the Sanctus and the Gloria as stipulated in the Prayer Book, and that these were sung by the choir. As already mentioned the Litany was sung in Latin; according to the order of service it was to be sung by two bishops or 'cantores', presumably with the choir singing the responses.[26] The Te Deum was to be sung while the crowned king went up to the 'stage', the area under the crossing, for his inthronization.[27] It would have accompanied his going to the Chair of Estate 'below the throne', where he 'reposeth himselfe' until after the Te Deum. This implies that the king's actual ascending of the elevated throne, from the Chair of Estate up the steps, was probably not accompanied by music – at least no extra music is reported for this, or indeed any of the following coronations.

Charles I, 1626

Charles I was crowned by Archbishop George Abbot on 2 February 1626 (1625 OS). Strong has pointed out that, while there had been a 'sense of

---

[22] This report is given in English translation in William Brenchley Rye, 'The Coronation of King James I., 1603', *The Antiquary* 22 (1890), 18–23.

[23] Cf. Peter Phillips, *English Sacred Music 1549–1649* (Oxford: Gimell, 1991), 224.

[24] See for instance *Lbl MS Harl. 4848*, fos. 79v–83: 'The maner of Coronations of the Kinges & Queenes / of Englande.', *c.* 1530, here fo. 82.

[25] Legg, *King James*, 40.

[26] *Ob MS Rawlinson B 40*, fo. 8: 'the Litany to be sung by 2 Bishops, vel y duos cantores [followed by Latin text of Litany]'. See also *Lca MS W.Y.*, fo. 151v.

[27] For this and the following Legg, *King James*, 37; and *Lca MS W.Y.*, fo. 157.

urgency' to have an early coronation in 1603, Charles I was crowned almost a whole year after his predecessor's death.[28] There was therefore ample time for the preparations. Nevertheless, this coronation appears to have been very similar to that of 1603. The order of service survives in several manuscript copies, four of which are of special importance:

1) *Cjc MS L 12*: manuscript copy of the order of service used and heavily annotated by William Laud, then Bishop of St David's, who acted as deputy for the Dean of Westminster at the service.[29]

2) *Lbl MS Harl. 5222*: a probably contemporary copy including some details of the music.[30]

3) Old Cheque Book of the Chapel Royal, fos. 71v–72.[31] This is the only such entry until the coronation of George II in 1727 and may well have served as a guideline for the musicians involved, since it includes particularly detailed information on the music.

4) *Cjc MS L 15*: manuscript copy of the order of service that was probably used by the king himself during the service.[32]

It seems that it was intended that Queen Henrietta Maria should be crowned with her husband and the earlier orders of service include the coronation of the queen. In the end, however, the queen was not crowned 'for Reasons easy to be conjectur'd. (ye Eucharist[)]', as Archbishop Sancroft noted in 1685.[33] He probably referred to the fact that Henrietta Maria was a staunch Roman Catholic: it has been observed that she refused to attend the coronation because it was overseen by Bishop Laud.[34]

It has been suggested that it was Tomkins who had 'prime responsibility for providing music' for the coronation, the reason being that he was chief organist of the Chapel Royal following the death of Orlando Gibbons in June 1625.[35] Indeed, Tomkins was paid 25 shillings 'for composing of many

---

[28] Strong, 251f.   [29] Laud's annotations are reproduced in Wordsworth (see fn. 6).

[30] For a transcription see Francis Carolus Eeles, *The English Coronation Service. Its History and Teaching, with the Coronation Services of King Charles I. and of Queen Victoria* (Oxford: Mowbray, 1902).

[31] This is transcribed in Andrew Ashbee and John Harley (eds.), *The Cheque Books of the Chapel Royal*, 2 vols. (Aldershot: Ashgate, 2000), vol. I, 155–8.

[32] This manuscript contains many later annotations by Archbishop Sancroft, which he inserted in preparation for the coronation of James II in 1685. For a transcription see Wordsworth (see fn. 6). See also Ch. 3, fn. 11. A presumably contemporary copy of this is *Cu Mm. I. 51*, fos. 14–16.

[33] *Ob MS Tanner 31*, fos. 89–96, Sancroft's account of the coronations from Edward II until Charles I, here fo. 96.

[34] Erin Griffin, *Henrietta Maria: Piety, Politics and Patronage* (Aldershot: Ashgate, 2008), 40.

[35] Peter James, 'Sacred Music Omitted from *Musica Deo Sacra*', in Anthony Boden (ed.), *Thomas Tomkins: The Last Elizabethan* (Aldershot: Ashgate, 2005), 285–300, here 291.

songes againste the Coronation of Kinge Charles'.[36] Denis Stevens has pointed out that at James I's funeral 'Tomkins, as organist, was assisted by three senior members of the Chapel: William Heather, Nathaniel Giles, who was then Master of the Children, and John Stevens, recorder of songs', and according to Boden these three assisted also in the preparation of the coronation music.[37] However, none of the three is known to have set any of the music for the occasion.[38]

In contrast to 1603, there is now clear evidence that the procession from Westminster Hall to the Abbey took place. One of the sources states that the archbishop and the bishops went to Westminster Hall 'together with the Church and Quire of Westminster'; the text continues in Latin: 'Ea decantes quae in receptione Regum solent decantare.' (= 'Singing those things which they are accustomed to sing during the reception/receiving of kings').[39] Leeper proposed that Tomkins's aforementioned anthem 'O Lord, grant the King' was written for this coronation and sung during the procession.[40] However, as seen above, this anthem would not have been very suitable for singing in procession.

The anthem texts were generally the same as at the previous coronation but there was one important change: the ancient text of the entrance-anthem *Protector noster* ('Behold, O Lord') was replaced by 'Psalm 122. I was glad &c. X / 1. 4. 5. 6.'; Bishop Laud added a marginal note in his copy of the order of service, explaining that 'This Anthem was newlye appointed and made.'[41] The new choice of text began a tradition that has lasted to the present day. According to the order of service, the anthem was sung during the procession of the king and queen towards the quire.[42] It cannot be said who composed it, but it could be that Tomkins's short full anthem 'O pray for the peace of Jerusalem' is a fragment of this piece: this text was part of the anthem and Tomkins's setting is curiously short to stand on its own.[43]

After the Recognition came the anthem *Firmetur manus*, to which Bishop Laud added the marginal note 'Strong is thy hand, &c', probably emphasizing that it was sung in English.[44] No setting can be linked with this piece. Similarly, it is not known what music was used for the *Veni Creator*, which was sung in the English translation beginning 'Come Holy Ghost eternall

---

[36] Quoted after Strong, 260.   [37] Stevens, 46; Boden, 125.   [38] For Giles see Phillips, 254–60.

[39] *Lbl MS Harl. 5222*, fo. 3v.   [40] Leeper, 556.

[41] *Cjc MS L 12*, p. 15. See also *Cjc MS 15*, p. 9 where the text of 'Behold, O Lord our Protectour' is crossed out and that of 'I was glad' entered in full, indicating that this predates the other copy.

[42] *Cjc MS L 12*, p. 15: 'The KING & QUEENE in the mean while passing up with ye Trayne through the Body of ye Church [. . .]'

[43] For an edition see Thomas Tomkins, *Musica Deo Sacra IV*, transcr. and ed. by Bernard Rose, EECM 27 (1982), no. 27/p. 102.

[44] *Cjc MS L 12*, p. 17.

God, proceeding from heaven'.[45] A contemporary diarist reports for the Litany that 'the organs and quire answered to two Bishopps' who sung it 'uppon their knees'.[46] There is no indication that it was still sung in Latin as at the previous coronation. If it was sung in English, the most likely candidate for the setting is probably the well-known one by Thomas Tallis.[47] However, it is noteworthy that there are also two settings by Tomkins who contributed other music to the service.[48]

It has been suggested that Tomkins contributed new settings of 'Zadok the Priest' and 'The King shall rejoice'.[49] The texts of both anthems are found in a manuscript anthem word-book from the Chapel Royal.[50] This lists 'Sadok the Priest' by 'T: Tomkins', but 'The King shall rejoyce' is ascribed to 'Iohn Tomkins', half-brother of Thomas and Gentleman Extraordinary of the Chapel at the time of the coronation.[51] None of the anthems has an annotation referring to the coronation. In the order of service in the Cheque Book, the text 'The King shall rejoice' is unusually included twice: first at the end of the anthem 'Zadok the Priest', during the Anointing, and then at the beginning of the next anthem, after the Crowning.[52] Overall, it seems more likely that only the latter version was sung, as at later coronations. While the music of 'Zadok the Priest' seems to be lost, John Tomkins's 'The King shall rejoice' has survived.[53] Regarding

---

[45] *Lbl MS Harl. 5222*, fo. 8v.

[46] *Ob MS Hearne's diaries 124*, fo. 18. See also Perkins, 179, who quotes almost the same phrase from the eyewitness account by Sir Syminds d'Ewes.

[47] For other sixteenth and early seventeenth century settings see Peter Le Huray, *Music and the Reformation in England, 1549–1660* (first publ. 1967 by Herbert Jenkins/Alden Press, repr. with corrections: Cambridge University Press, 1978), 161f.

[48] *Cambridge Perne Library, Peterhouse (Cp)*, 'Latter Caroline Set' MS 44 [Decani Medius], A6–A6v; the second one in MS 43 [Cantoris Tenor], A4v: 'Common Litany'. See also Boden, 299.

[49] 'Coronation Music of the Past', 26.

[50] *Lbl MS Harl. 6346*. The manuscript is discussed in Wyn K. Ford, 'The Chapel Royal at the Restoration', *The Monthly Musical Record* 90 (1960), 99–106.

[51] *Lbl Harl. MS 6346*, fos. 13v and 15r respectively. Myles Birket Foster lists a setting of 'The King shall rejoice' by Thomas Tomkins as surviving in St Paul's. See *Anthems and Anthem Composers. An Essay upon the Development of the Anthem from the Reformation to the End of the Nineteenth Century* (London: Novello, 1901), 43. However, he may be referring to the setting by John Tomkins (see fn. 53).

[52] See the transcription in Ashbee and Harley, vol. I, 157.

[53] The anthem was recorded by the choir of St Paul's Cathedral under Christopher Dearnley and Barry Rose, see *Music for a Great Cathedral*, CD GMCD 7118 (Guild Music, 1996), track 12. Unfortunately, no source for the music is given; in the booklet (p. 6) the anthem is simply described as 'an unpublished work'. The library at St Paul's holds the ATB-parts only. *Oxford, St John's College (Ojc) MS 181* contains the tenor-part of a setting of the text by 'John Tomkins', and the treble-part survives in *Llp MS 764*, fos. 192–3. According to RISM a setting of the text by John Tomkins survives in a manuscript in the University of California (*US-Bem MS 751 A-B*). This source still needs to be examined.

the ceremonial, the reports are clear that the anthem was now sung after the actual putting on of the crown, not during it, as at the previous coronation.[54]

The Te Deum was sung as at the previous coronation, as a processional while the king went from St Edward's Chair to the 'stage' under the crossing, to wait in his Chair of Estate before being 'lift[ed] up into the Throne'.[55]

This is the first coronation for which the order of service includes an anthem during the Homage: the text of the entrance-anthem, 'Behold, O God' was moved to this ceremony and an annotation in the order of service explained that 'at this hymn begins the mass in the *Liber Regalis*'.[56] It is noteworthy that the 1626 order of service states explicitly that the anthem was sung 'after the homage is done'.[57] The anthem did thus not accompany the peers' actual paying homage as it may have done at the previous coronation. This would match with the observation that, in 1626, during the Homage the trumpets and drums played fanfares after 'each Degree of the Nobility', which would otherwise have clashed with the anthem.[58] The anthem may have been performed only while all the peers approached the throne again individually, as is reported for the following coronations. Indeed, this would have allowed the vows during the Homage to be heard more clearly.

In any case the anthem would have been a grand finale to the coronation part of the service. Boden suggests that Thomas Tomkins's setting of 'Behold, O God' was used, the one surviving as the second part of his verse anthem 'O Lord of Hosts'.[59] If that was the case, it is likely that the original version was much more elaborate than the surviving one, and like the homage anthem at the previous coronation it may have included 'organs, voices and other music' resounding 'in intervals'.[60]

The order of service in the Old Cheque Book lists much of the liturgical music.[61] It states that the archbishop should begin the Nicene Creed and then 'the Quier singeth' it.[62] During the Offertory the choir sang the anthem 'Lett my prayer be sett forth', and afterwards the organ played until the

---

[54] Ashbee and Harley, vol. I, 157: 'When the Crowne is sett upon the Kinges head, & the Arch:B: hath ended ye exhortacion [...]'

[55] *Cjc MS L 12*, p. 34.

[56] *Cjc MS L 12*, p. 37: 'In the Interim ye Quire singeth. / Behold ô God our Defendor [corrected to 'protector'] & looke upon ye Face of thyne Anointed &. / A quo Hymno incipit Missa in Regalis Libro.' Cf. Ch. 1, fn. 55.

[57] See Ashbee and Harley, vol. I, 157.   [58] Macleane, 172.   [59] Boden, 127.

[60] See above, fn. 22.   [61] For this and the following see Ashbee and Harley, vol. I, 157f.

[62] As in the Catholic tradition, in the Anglican Church it is usual that for the Credo and for the Gloria in excelsis the priest reads or sings the first line and the choir continues.

Offertory was ended. The ensuing Sanctus and Gloria ('the holies, & ye Et in terra pax &c. as in ye Comunion book') were scheduled to be 'songe by the Quier, except the ArchB. Will read them', thus allowing for a degree of flexibility in case the ceremony was becoming too long. Finally, 'after ye Comunion is finished', the choir was to sing the anthem 'O hearken thou'. In accordance with the *Liber Regalis*, this anthem should have been sung while the king received the sacraments.[63] However, at the following coronation it was also sung after the communion, while he went back to his throne, and it is possible that this is what the Cheque Book entry refers to. No details about the settings of any of these pieces are known, but at least two of them could have been by Thomas Tomkins: there are two settings of the Nicene Creed and one of the Gloria in his *Musica Deo Sacra*.

It may be assumed that the musicians were positioned in the Abbey in the same manner as at the following coronations, with the two choirs and a body of instrumentalists in three different galleries around the quire and crossing of the Abbey. Bishop Laud's comments give an interesting insight into the problems of the performance. He noted that the Litany 'was sunge att a faldstoole upon ye stage', that is under the crossing, and he continues to explain that this was done 'that ye Quyer [*sic*] might heare & know when to answere'.[64] Thus the two bishops singing the Litany were moved from the altar closer to the choir to facilitate the coordination. Indeed, the size of the Abbey could cause performance problems, as indicated by another of Laud's remarks: the choir did not sing the Gloria in excelsis 'because they could not take ArchBps voice soe farre of', meaning they could not hear his intonation sung at the altar. However, the reason for this mishap could also have been the fact that the order of service in the Old Cheque Book did not clearly enough indicate whether the Gloria should be sung by the choir or read by the archbishop.

This is the only coronation in the period of this study for which the choir is reported to have sung in the procession from Westminster Abbey back to Westminster Hall. According to the entry in the Chapel Royal Cheque Book

the king returned back againe into Westminster hall in the same manner as he went, the Chappell goeinge in their former order & singinge all the waye, till they came to

---

[63] See *Lbl MS Add. 47184*, fos. 4–23: 'A brief out of the Rytes of the coronacion called Liber Regalis', which according to the catalogue refers to the coronation of Charles I. On fo. 19: while the king kneels to receive the sacrament, in the margin: 'An Anthem / Psalm: 5: 2:'; the text would therefore be 'O hearken unto the voice of my calling'.

[64] *Cjc MS L 12*, pp. 23 and 47.

Westminster hall dore, & their they stayed makinge a lane for yᵉ Kinge & all the
lordes to passe betwixt them, & continued singinge till the Kinge was wᵗʰin the
hall: & frō thence they returned back into the church [...]⁶⁵

Notably, only the Chapel Royal took part and sang in this procession. This
could have been, or become, a custom: in 1727 one of the heralds explicitly
noted that the 'Choir of the Church of Westminster' was not to return to the
Hall.⁶⁶ In any case, it cannot be known what the choir sang during the
procession and the king's entry into the Hall; from the above entry, it
appears that the choir itself did not enter the Hall and thus did not sing
during the banquet.

Charles I was crowned King of Scotland in a separate ceremony in
Edinburgh in June 1633. The texts of the music at this ceremony were the
same as those used at the coronation in Westminster Abbey; however, no
details are known of the respective settings.⁶⁷ For his Scottish coronation the
king brought much of the personal with him from London. For instance,
with him travelled Thomas Tomkins's half-brothers Giles and John who
had been appointed joint organists of the Chapel Royal especially for this
journey.⁶⁸ Therefore it is possible that the music performed at this coronation was very much the same as that at the 1626 coronation in Westminster
Abbey. In any case, this would turn out to be the last full-range coronation
in Scotland.

Strong observed that 'by the Coronation of Charles I there was a "genuine
concern" about the rite being well ordered, and more than one source
records that 1626 was an immaculately choreographed event'.⁶⁹ The meticulous preparations went so far as to include 'something unprecedented,
what amounted to a dress rehearsal', when Bishop Laud went to see the king
and they went through the order of service and tried out the regalia. It
seems, however, that this 'genuine concern' about a good performance of
the ceremonies did not include the music. For instance, the Gloria had
obviously not been rehearsed. However, such performance difficulties
occurred throughout the more than three centuries to follow.

---

⁶⁵ Ashbee and Harley, vol. I, 158.

⁶⁶ *Lca MS S.M.L. 65*: 'Heraldo Memoriale / Or Memoirs of the College of Arms / Part the Second /
From May 1727 to September 1765', written by Stephen Martin Leake, p. 9.

⁶⁷ See fn 5. For details on this coronation in general see Lady Christian Mary Hesketh, *Charles I's
Coronation Visit to Scotland in 1633*, publ. as 'Papers of the Royal Stuart Society' 52 (1998), esp.
p. 5f. See also Roger A. Mason, *Scots and Britons: Scottish Political Thought and the Union of
1603* (Cambridge University Press, 1994), 66.

⁶⁸ Boden, 140 and 233.   ⁶⁹ This and the following: Strong, 246f.

Charles II, 1661

Charles II succeeded to the throne when his father, Charles I, was executed on 30 January 1649. He was crowned 'King of Great Britain' on 1 January 1651 in a 'stripped-down Presbyterian Coronation' at Scone Abbey, Scotland.[70] A brief account of the service, together with the full text of the sermon, was published shortly afterwards and received several re-editions up to the mid-eighteenth century.[71] This account does not mention any music, apart from 'the xx. Psalm. being sung' just before the final blessing.[72] Given that this was a Presbyterian ceremony, taking place in a kirk, the lack of music, and indeed any elaborate ceremonial proceedings, is hardly surprising. It is most likely that the mentioned psalm was sung by the congregation to a simple tune.[73]

It is noteworthy that Charles II at Scone swore his coronation oath as 'King of Great Britain', thus creating a union of England and Scotland decades before the formal union of the two kingdoms in 1707.[74] For reasons that still deserve further investigation, after the Restoration of the monarchy the 1651 coronation was 'held good for Scotland only' and therefore Charles II was crowned as King of England in a grand ceremony in Westminster Abbey in 1661.[75] Despite the strengthened position of parliament after the Civil War, the Restoration meant that the monarchy was literally restored – Charles II had the same power as his father Charles I.[76] This continuity became apparent in his coronation which was directly modelled on those from before the 'Commonwealth'. Overall, Charles II's coronation was filled with much symbolism. This began with the choice of day: the original date chosen was 7 February, but in December, as Edward Walker, Garter King of Arms noted, 'for many weighty reasons it was deferred vnto the 23th of Aprill 1661 being St. George's day'.[77] It is not clear what these 'weighty reasons' were. However, by celebrating the coronation on the feast of the

---

[70] Strong, 351.

[71] [Sir James Balfour], *The Forme and Order of the Coronation of Charles the Second, King of Scotland, England, France, and Ireland. As it was acted and done at Scoone, The first day of Ianuary, 1651* (Aberdeen: Imprinted by James Brown, 1651).

[72] Balfour, 24.

[73] For this coronation ceremony see lately Anna Keay, *The Magnificent Monarch* (London: Continuum, 2008), esp. 56–9. Keay states that there was no singing, by which she probably means no choral singing.

[74] Balfour, 19.   [75] Schramm, 101.

[76] Julian Hoppit, *A Land of Liberty? England 1689–1727* (Oxford University Press, 2000; paperback edn 2002), 2.

[77] *Lbl MS Add. 6338*, p. 2/fo. 4v. For details see the next footnote.

patron saint of England it became a celebration not only of the person of the king, but of the English state in general, underlining the leading role of this biggest part of the king's realm. Indeed, three of the following four coronations took place on 23 April.

Sources

The actual order of service for Charles II's coronation does not appear to have survived. However, there are several accounts that allow for a reconstruction of the event. A very detailed account of the ceremonies is found in a manuscript that belonged to the aforementioned Edward Walker, Garter King of Arms, the highest of the heralds and involved in arranging the ceremonial of the coronation.[78] Two similar accounts appeared in print after the event. Elias Ashmole, appointed Windsor Herald in 1660, published *A Brief Narrative of the Solemn Rites and Ceremonies Performed upon the Day of the Coronation* which is, in fact, more detailed than 'brief'. It appears that this work survives in only two copies; and since it begins with page number 167, it may originally have been part of a more comprehensive work.[79] The second account is by the Scottish impresario John Ogilby who published an account of the procession from the Tower of London to Westminster which took place the day before the coronation; to this he added 'A Brief Narrative of His Majestie's Solemn Coronation'.[80] All three accounts, Walker's manuscript, Ashmole, and Ogilby, were published and re-published in later years, probably in anticipation of later coronations.[81]

[78] *Lbl MS Add. 6338*, pp. 2–60/fos. 4–33. This is, at the end, signed 'Heralds Colledge the / 25. of May 1661 / Edward Walker Garter'; hereafter '*Walker-MS*'. For his responsibility at the 1661 coronation see also Keay, 5 ('chief herald').

[79] (n.p., n.d.), seen as *Oxford, Brasenose College UB/S III. 57*, which includes 'MS Notes by the Author and J. Evelyn' (annotation in the cover by an unknown scribe); hereafter 'Ashmole'. For the other copy see Peter Holman, *Four and Twenty Fiddlers. The Violin and the English Court 1540–1690* (Oxford: Clarendon Press, 1993), 400, fn. 43.

[80] John Ogilby, *The Entertainment of his Most Excellent Majestie Charles II* [...] (London: Tho. Roycroft, 1662); hereafter 'Ogilby'. For a facsimile edition with an introduction by Ronald Knowles see: Medieval and Renaissance Texts and Studies, vol. 43 (Birmingham: Medieval and Renaissance Texts and Studies, 1988). For more details on all three accounts see also Matthew Jenkinson, *Culture and Politics at the Court of Charles II, 1660–1685* (Woodbridge: Boydell & Brewer, 2010), esp. 66–9.

[81] Before the coronation of James II: John Ogilby, *The Kings Coronation: Being an Exact Account of the Cavalcade* [...] *Also the Narrative Of his Majesties Coronation* [...] (London: William Morgan, 1685). Before the coronation of George III: Elias Ashmole and Francis Sandford, *The Entire Ceremonies of the Coronations of His Majesty King Charles II* [...] (London: Printed for W. Owen et al., 1761). Before the coronation of George IV: Edward Walker, *A Circumstantial Account of the Preparations for the Coronation of His Majesty King Charles the Second, and minute detail of that splendid Ceremony* [...] (London: T. Baker, 1820).

Furthermore, another detailed description of Charles II's coronation is included in Richard Baker's sumptuous study *A Chronicle of the Kings of England*.[82] With many passages being identical with Ogilby's account, the two may either have copied from each other or relied on the same source. Finally, there are also two private eyewitness reports from the coronation: the great Restoration diarists John Evelyn and Samuel Pepys were both present in the Abbey and recorded interesting, individual insights with, occasionally, valuable details of the music.[83]

According to custom, Charles II was crowned by the Archbishop of Canterbury, William Juxon.[84] The archbishop was ill, however, and did not perform the whole of the service; Baker reports that the archbishop 'retired from the Ceremonis into S. Edward's Chappel, and thence went home' only just before the Offertory, 'leaving the remainder of his Duty to be performed by the Bishop of London [Gilbert Sheldon]'.[85] It would have been one of these two men who had prepared the order of service; indeed, some facts indicate that it might rather have been Sheldon than Juxon.[86] In any case, the order of service seems to have been very similar to those from before the Civil War.

The music

According to precedent, the music of the service was provided by the combined choirs of the Chapel Royal and Westminster Abbey.[87] The Chapel Royal had been disbanded in 1642 due to the Civil War, but with the Restoration it was re-founded, and it became Henry Cooke's task to build up the new choir.[88] Apart from Cooke, an important figure in the

---

[82] Richard Baker, *A Chronicle of the Kings of England, from the time of the Romans Goverment* [sic] *unto the Death of King James* [. . .] *with a Continuation of the Chronicle, in this Fourth Edition, to the Coronation of His Sacred Majesty King Charles the Second* [. . .] (London: Printed by E. Cotes, 1665). The account of the coronation is on pp. 808–21.

[83] *The Diary of John Evelyn*, with an introduction and notes by Austin Dobson, 3 vols. (London: Macmillan, 1906), repr. in 'Great British Diarists' (London: Routlege/Thoemmes, 1996), vol. II: *1647 to 1676*, 165f.; hereafter 'Evelyn'. Pepys (as in Ch. 1, fn. 81), 83–8.

[84] [Edward Cooke], *The History of the Successions of the Kings of England. From Canutus the First Monarch* [. . .] (London, 1682), 51.

[85] Baker, 817. See also Evelyn, 165; Ashmole, 172 and cf. *Walker-MS*, p. 54/fo. 30v.

[86] The archbishop was not in favour with the king; he was 'overshadowed in church affairs by Gilbert Sheldon' and was made a member of the Privy Council only a year after the coronation. See Brian Quintrell, 'William Juxon', *Oxford Dictionary of National Biography online*. (www.oxforddnb.com, accessed 25 August 2011).

[87] For details see below, fn. 160.

[88] Jack A. Westrup, *Purcell*, first published in 1937, with a new foreword by Curtis Price (Oxford University Press, 1995), 11. For the re-establishment of the Chapel see also Ford, *Restoration*.

Chapel was William Child. He had been organist of St George's Chapel, Windsor since about 1632 and was appointed first organist of the Chapel Royal after the Restoration.[89] With the Restoration Christopher Gibbons (son of Orlando) became organist at the Abbey, and Henry Purcell senior was appointed the new Master of the Choristers, but it is not known if these two provided any music for the coronation.[90]

For the procession from Westminster Hall to the Abbey the relevant engraving in Ogilby does not show the choirs; in fact, drummers and trumpeters are the only musicians depicted. Ogilby does, however, mention the choirs in his description of the procession.[91] An account of the next coronation indicates that the anthem sung during the procession was Child's 'O Lord, grant the King a long life', and this is furthermore supported by one later manuscript source in which the piece is described as 'a Pray'r for yᵉ King, Compos'd at yᵉ Restauration'.[92]

The first anthem of the service, the entrance-anthem, is surrounded by several uncertainties. Ogilby reports:[93]

The *King* being entered the *West*-Door of the *Church* (within which a *Fald-stool*, and *Cushions* were laid ready for him to kneel at) was received with an *Anthem*, begun by the whole *Quire*, viz. The first, fourth, fifth, and sixth *Verses* of the 122ᵈ *Psalm*: beginning thus; *I was glad when they said unto me, We will go into the House of the Lord &c.*

Ashmole gives the same text for the anthem, but explains that it was sung only by the Abbey choir:[94]

The *King*, being entered the West-door of the *Abbey-Church*, was received with an *Anthem*, begun by the *Quire* of *Westminster*; who, with the *Dean*, and *Prebends*, had before fallen off from the *Proceeding* a little on the left hand of the middle Isle, and stayed there to attend his coming, where also a *Fald-stool*, and *Cushions* were laid ready for his Majesty to kneel at [. . .] The King, arriving at the *Fald-stool*, kneeled down, and used some short Ejaculations; which being finished, He thence proceeded into, and through the *Quire* [. . .]⁹⁵

89 For biographical details see Frederick Hudson, W. Roy Large, and Ian Spink, 'William Child', in *NG* 5, 607–11.

90 Wilkinson, *Westminster Abbey*, 45 and 63.

91 Engravings between the description of the 'Cavalcade' and the coronation, and 170/2nd (page numbers 170/171 given twice).

92 *Lbl MS Harl. 7338*: the second volume of Thomas Tudway's manuscript collection of services and anthems (1716), fos. 86–86v.

93 Ogilby, 173. The same in Baker, 811, who does not state who sang the anthem.

94 Ashmole, 172f.

95 The underlining is part of the manuscript annotations in the copy used. For this copy see fn. 79.

This latter arrangement was, in fact, going to become the custom at the following coronations. According to Walker the anthem included furthermore the text 'Behold O Lord our Protector &c. / Psalm 84'. However, it is noteworthy that he gives the same text also for the anthem sung during the Homage.[96] It seems unlikely that the text would have been sung twice, and it is more plausible that the anthem consisted of a selection of verses from Ps. 122 alone. Interestingly, none of the reports mentions the doxology at the end of the anthem, which was to become a regular feature in subsequent coronations.

Not only is there uncertainty about the text of the entrance-anthem, but also about when exactly it was sung. As seen above, Ogilby and Ashmole generally state that the king was 'received' with the anthem at the West door, which could mean that it was sung either while he walked up the nave as in later coronations, or just literally while he was 'received into the church', as a 'welcome anthem'. Evelyn's account is quite unclear and ambiguous:[97]

When his Majestie was enter'd, the Dean and Prebendaries brought all the regalia and deliver'd them to severall Noblemen to beare before the King, who met them at the west doore of the Church singing an anthem, to the Quire.

This could mean either that the choir met the king and then started processing while singing an anthem on their way to the quire, or, which is more likely from the wording, that they met the king while singing an anthem and then the procession started.

The idea that the anthem was performed *in situ* as a welcome anthem may be supported by the fact that both Ogilby and Ashmole report that the procession did not start immediately after the king's arrival; instead the king was kneeling on a 'Fald-stool' for some private prayers first. Walker even implies that the procession stopped for the king to do his prayers while it was moving through the nave:[98]

His Ma.^{ty} being entred the West dore of the Church he was received wth this Anthem [...] / And passing up a third part of the length of the middle Isle, there was a Faldstoole and Cushions placed ready by the Officers of the Wardrobe [...]

Such a break in the procession would probably have severely interrupted the performance of a processional anthem. In any case, this is the only

---

[96]   *Walker-MS*, p. 39/fo. 23r and p. 53/fo. 30r.

[97]   Quoted after Arthur Perceval Purey-Cust, *The Crowning of Monarchs* (London: Ibister, 1902), 44. This is the same in the 1996 edition of the diary (p. 165), except that the spelling is modernized and a comma given before 'singing'.

[98]   *Walker-MS*, p. 39/ fo. 23r.

coronation for which the monarch is reported to have knelt in prayer upon entering the church.

The music of 'I was glad' has not been identified. Only three settings of the text from the period are known: by Child, Michael Wise, and William Tucker. However, Wise was only a chorister of the Chapel Royal at the time of the coronation, and Tucker is not known to have contributed music to any bigger service. Child, on the other hand, was organist of the Chapel and is known to have contributed other music to the service; it is therefore possible that he composed the entrance-anthem as well. The chorus ATB-parts of his setting survive in the archives of St George's Chapel, Windsor.[99] The ascription to 'D:ʳ W:ᵐ Childe' implies that this copy dates from after July 1663, when he took his doctorate at Oxford. Long rests at the beginning of the anthem may indicate an instrumental symphony. The text of the fragment consists only of verses 1, 2 and 5 of Ps. 122. There are another 21 free bars before verse 5; they could indicate that verse 4, which is mentioned in the above reports, was sung by one or several soloists. It is possible that the missing verse 6, 'O pray for the peace of Jerusalem', survives in another of Child's anthems to this text.[100] This anthem concludes with the *Gloria Patri* which is slightly unusual for an anthem (there would normally be an Hallelujah), but which is normal for the entrance-anthem at the coronation.[101] However, the two pieces cannot easily be put together: 'I was glad' is in 'E flat major' (notated with two flats only), whereas 'O pray for the peace' is in E minor, ending in major. It is certainly possible that one of them, or even both, were transposed at some point, maybe when they were split up.[102] Possible combinations of the two parts could be: D major and D minor, or F major and D minor – indeed, two other anthems at the coronation service were in F major and one in B flat major. Yet another possibility is that Child composed only part of the anthem to complement Thomas Tomkins's short setting of 'O pray for the Peace of Jerusalem'.[103] This would explain why Child chose the unusual

---

[99] For details of the sources and an edition (partially reconstructed) see Matthias Range, 'Music at British Coronations from James I to Queen Victoria, 1603–1838 – a Study and Edition', 2 vols., unpublished DPhil thesis, University of Oxford (2008), [hereafter 'Range, thesis'], vol. II.

[100] This was printed in Arnold's edition of Boyce's *Cathedral Music* in 1790, vol. I, 74.

[101] See C.G.P. Batchelor, 'William Child: an Examination of the Liturgical Sources, and a Critical and Contextual Study of the Church Music', 3 vols., unpublished Ph.D. thesis, University of Cambridge (1990), vol. II, 657. Batchelor states that only six of Child's psalm text anthems end with the Doxology; they all date from after the Restoration.

[102] Batchelor, vol. II, 667–8, states that it is not known to what extent anthems were transposed to achieve tonal continuity in the service. According to this, 'I was glad' could for instance have been transposed to E flat major to match Child's service in that key.

[103] For this anthem see above, fn. 43.

key of E flat major for his setting: it had to match Tomkins's existing section in that key.[104]

For the anthem after the Recognition the reports name 'Let thy hand be strengthened', with Ashmole and Baker including the full text.[105] It has been proposed that the anthem was sung to a setting by Henry Cooke,[106] but no setting of the text by him is known. Regarding the ceremonial, the anthem covered the preparations for the communion service, when a carpet and cushions were laid out before the altar.

The *Veni Creator* was sung in the same English translation as at the previous coronation. Ogilby and Baker describe that first 'the *King* was led, in like manner, back to His *Chair* of *State*; and immediately the *Bishop* of *London* begun the *Hymn, Come Holy Ghost, eternal God,* &c. the *Quires* singing the rest of it'.[107] As is suggested for the next coronation, the *Veni Creator* may have been chanted.[108] The following Litany was sung by two bishops with the '*Quires* singing the *Responses*', but it is not known to which setting.[109]

There is detailed information on the exact position of the anthem 'Zadok the Priest'. Ogilby states that it was sung – probably in the sense of 'begun to be sung' – between the anointing of the king's hands and of his breasts, shoulders, elbows and head.[110] Thus the anthem clearly was sung at the very heart of the holy rites, during the actual anointing. Evelyn mentions even more music during this ceremony:[111]

[The king was anointed] first in the palms of his hands, when an anthem was sung, and a prayer read [. . .] and lastly, on the crown of the head, with apposite hymns and prayers at each anointing [. . .].

However, it cannot be determined what these 'hymns' could have been – Evelyn might simply refer to the several sections of 'Zadok the Priest'. The anthem was almost certainly sung to the known setting by Henry Lawes. A contemporary anthem word-book, now in the Harleian MSS in the British Library, contains the text with the annotation 'At the Coronation of King Charles ye second Aprill. 23. 1661.'[112] No composer's name is given (as, indeed, for most of the other anthems in this manuscript), but the text is

---

[104] Batchelor, vol. II, 686, points out that 'I was glad' is Child's only known anthem in this key.

[105] Ogilby, 173f.; *Walker-MS*, p. 40/fo. 23v; Ashmole, 173; Baker, 811.

[106] Anselm Hughes, 93.   [107] Ogilby, 176; Baker, 813.

[108] See Ch. 3. See also Peter Le Huray and John Harper, 'Anglican chant', *NG* 1, 672f. For possible music see Ruth M. Wilson, *Anglican Chant and Chanting in England, Scotland, and America 1660 to 1820* (Oxford: Clarendon Press, 1996), 271–8: Appendix A 'English Chant Tunes: Manuscript Sources 1635–1750'.

[109] Ogilby, 176; Baker, 813.   [110] Ogilby, 178. See also Ashmole, 178, and Baker, 813f.

[111] Evelyn, 166.   [112] *Lbl MS Harl. 6346*, p. 44. Cf. Anselm Hughes, 87.

identical with that as set by Lawes except for a repeat of 'God save the King' before the Hallelujah in his setting. Baker gives a differing text for the anthem. Nevertheless, the similarity of the text in the anthem word-book, bearing the clear ascription to the coronation, with the existing setting by Lawes appears to be strong enough evidence that it was this setting that was sung. The fact that Lawes's anthem was composed only after the Restoration and thus probably specially for the coronation of Charles II is supported by another anthem word-book which clearly dates from before the Civil War; according to a cover note written in 1732, it is 'the very book us'd by K: Charles 1st in his publick Devotions'.[113] This book is nearly identical to the Harleian MS, but 'Zadok the Priest' is not included. Ian Cheverton states that both manuscripts were made before the Civil War, but that the Harleian MS 'was re-covered for further use after the Restoration'; and the seventeen texts for anthems by Cooke were clearly 'added at some time after 1660'.[114]

Lawes's setting survives in several sources.[115] These indicate that the anthem in its original form was an orchestral anthem. The anthem is a straightforward homophonic and syllabic setting and its declamatory character is enhanced by strong harmonic progressions and easily approachable rhythms. This complemented readily the king's well-known musical taste and expectations.[116] Apart from playing the opening symphony, the instruments probably doubled the vocal parts and played short 'echoing' interludes. Despite its modest dimensions, Lawes's anthem is a refined, interpretive setting of the text. The first part ends with a half close on the dominant which serves perfectly to illustrate the text ('[. . .] anointed Solomon King'), the tension generated being relieved by the rejoicing of the people. In this way Lawes's setting emphasizes the text, which can be read as drawing a parallel between the Israelites' acclamation of King Solomon and the Recognition during the coronation service in Westminster Abbey. The anthem text thus heightens the impression that the king rules not only by being anointed with holy oil, but also by the approval of the people, expressed in the form of acclamations.

[113] *Ob MS Rawl. Poet. 23.*
[114] Ian Cheverton, 'Captain Henry Cooke (*c.* 1616–72) The Beginnings of a Reappraisal', *Soundings* 9 (1982), 74–86, here 75. See also Ford, 'Restoration', 102, who proposes that the Harleian volume was copied from *Ob MS Rawl. Poet. 23.*
[115] For details of the sources and an edition (partially reconstructed) see Range, thesis, vol. II. For details of this and the following see also Range, 'Instrumental Musick', here 88–90.
[116] Cf. Cheverton, 82.

The reports state that the anthem after the Crowning was sung while the archbishop was reading the *Confortare* (the prayer 'Be strong and of good courage').[117] If that was the case, not much of the prayer would have been heard in the Abbey; this in turn would imply that not all texts necessarily had to be heard, but that it was enough that they were said. As at the previous coronation the anthem was a setting of 'The King shall rejoice'.[118] Parts of a setting of this text by William Child survive in the archives of St George's Chapel, Windsor with the ascription 'An Anthem sung at the Coronation'.[119] This could refer only to the coronations in 1661 and 1685, being the only two at which Child was present and at which this text was sung. However, in 1685 the anthem is reported to have been composed by William Turner and therefore Child's setting must belong to the 1661 coronation. Its text is nearly identical with the surviving 1661 text, with the addition of a final Hallelujah.[120] From the surviving parts, Child's anthem appears to have been a straightforward, short full anthem for four-part choir, with the text mostly set syllabically. As in Lawes's 'Zadok the Priest', the Hallelujah is melodious and in triple time, but it is here remarkably short. Overall, however, it is possible that the surviving material is only a reworked version of an originally more elaborate anthem, possibly with orchestral accompaniment.[121]

From a ceremonial point of view it is furthermore interesting to note at which point the peers and Kings of Arms put on their coronets and the bishops their caps; Ogilby reports that they did so 'upon this', that is upon the reading of the *Confortare* and the singing of the anthem.[122] From this, it is not entirely clear if the coronets and caps were put on at the beginning, during, or at the end of the anthem, but in any case the anthem seems distinctly linked to the overall ceremonial. The exact point of the peers' 'crowning' was going to see some significant changes during the next hundred years.

---

[117] Ogilby, 180: '[…] the *Arch.Bishop* read the *Confortare* [text] / In the mean while, the *Quires* sung this *Anthem* […]' See also Baker, 814.

[118] Ashmole, 181, and Ogilby, 180, give only the first two verses of the text, followed by '&c.'

[119] *Windsor, St George's Chapel* (*WRch*) Men's part-books, vol. I and vol. II, both p. 28, and vol. III, p. 29. For a list of sources and an edition (partially reconstructed) see Range, thesis, vol. II, 1. Kathryn Pierce has transcribed a different setting by Child. See 'The Coronation Music of Charles II', unpublished MA thesis, Bowling Green State University (2007), Appendix, 67f. and 71–8. However, the text of this verse setting does not match with that in the other sources.

[120] Child set 'given', 'shalt prevent' and 'shalt set', instead of 'granted', 'hast prevented' and 'hast set'.

[121] For details see Range, 'Instrumental Musick', 90.

[122] Ogilby, 180. He does not mention the bishops putting on their caps.

In this context it should be mentioned that Henry Cooke's orchestral anthem 'The King shall rejoice' has also been linked with this coronation.[123] Not only is this ascription clearly contradicted by Child's anthem, but Cooke's setting also uses a much longer text than reported for the coronation. In the autograph score the piece is headed 'Song', and the actual writing is slightly different from that in 'Behold, O God', Cooke's other anthem sung at this coronation, which survives in the same volume. This suggests that the two pieces were not written at the same time. Indeed, while the former employs only two instruments in treble clef with a bass, 'Behold, O God', includes also a tenor part in the orchestra. In the end, Cooke's 'The King shall rejoice' could be the 'impressive verse anthem' that he provided for the installation of the Knights of the Garter in St George's Chapel, Windsor in 1661.[124] The jubilant text and setting would certainly match the occasion.

The next piece of music was the Te Deum. Ogilby, Walker, and Baker all state that it was sung *before* the king ascended the throne:[125]

[after the blessing and the kissing of the bishops, and the king having gone to his Chair of State] Then the *King* reposed Himself in the said *Chair*, whilst both the *Quires* sung *Te Deum*. When *Te Deum* was ended, the *King* ascended His *Throne* [. . .]

Contrary to that, Evelyn reports that it was sung as a processional, *while* the king ascended his throne:[126]

His Majesty then ascending again his royal throne, whilst *Te Deum* was singing, all the Peers did their homage [. . .]

A third possibility is that the Te Deum was sung while the king went from St Edward's Chair to the Chair of Estate: this matches with the description of the previous coronations and is also what is reported in detail from 1761 onwards. While details of the Te Deum are not known, Ian Spink proposed that it was sung to Child's setting in F.[127] This is indeed a plausible suggestion: in the aforementioned manuscript in St George's Chapel, Windsor, Child's coronation anthem 'The King shall rejoice' is linked with his service in F.[128]

---

[123] Anselm Hughes, 93. See also Robert Manning, 'The Anthems of Henry Cooke', *Royal College of Music Magazine* 88 (1991), 25–33, here 28. For an edition see Range, thesis, vol. II, 31.

[124] Peter Dennison and Bruce Wood, 'Henry Cooke', *NG* 6, 385–7.

[125] Ogilby, 182; *Walker-MS*, p. 48/fo. 27v; Baker, 816.

[126] Evelyn, 166f. This account could indeed be read as if the Te Deum was sung during the Homage. That, however, is contradicted by the other reports.

[127] Ian Spink, *Restoration Cathedral Music 1660–1714* (Oxford: Clarendon Press, 1995), 375. Anselm Hughes, 93, suggests Child as composer without referring to a specific setting.

[128] According to Keri Dexter the service dates from 1660–63. See *'A good Quire of voices': The Provision of Choral Music at St George's Chapel, Windsor Castle, and Eton College, c. 1640–1733* (Aldershot: Ashgate, 2002), 164.

For the anthem during the Homage the order of service followed the coronation of Charles I and included an anthem to the text 'Behold, O God our Defender'. The anthem's position was probably the same as at the previous coronation. Ogilby reports that the '*Drums* beat, *Trumpets* sounded, and all the *People* shouted' several times during the Homage: first after the Duke of York (the King's brother), then after the viscounts, and finally at the very end.[129] Such fanfares would certainly have disturbed a performance of the anthem at the same time. Ogilby continues that after the third fanfare all the peers 'singly ascended the *Throne*, and touched the *King's Crown*, promising by that Ceremony to be ever ready to support it with all their power', and that 'During the performing of this Solemn Ceremony' the General Pardon was proclaimed and the medals scattered. After this he concludes:

The *King* being thus enthronized, the *Gentlemen* of His *Chapel* began this following Anthem, *Behold, O Lord, our Defender, and look upon the Face of thine Anointed*. At the ending of which *Anthem*, the *Trumpets* sounded, and *Drums* beat again.

This indicates that the anthem was sung *after* rather then *during* the Homage, and this is the same in Ashmole and Walker.[130] In contrast to that, Pepys reports that everything happened simultaneously: according to him the anthem was sung while the peers paid their homage and while at the same time the General Pardon was proclaimed and the medals scattered. Indeed, he distinctly complains that there was 'so great a noise' that he 'could make but little of the Musique; and indeed, it was lost to everybody'.[131] However, comparing his report with the others it seems most likely that Pepys refers to the individual peers ascending the throne, rather than to the representatives of each rank saying the words of homage. Thus, altogether, it is most likely that the anthem was performed during the individual peers' approaching the king and while the General Pardon was proclaimed and the medals scattered.

The anthem was most probably Henry Cooke's 'Behold, O God our Defender', which survives in an autograph score.[132] Its title differs slightly from that in the printed accounts, which is 'Behold, O Lord'.[133] On the other hand, Cooke's anthem follows exactly the text given in the Old Cheque Book of the Chapel Royal for the coronation of Charles I, which might have

---

[129] For this and the following see Ogilby, 183f. See also Baker, 817.
[130] Ashmole, 185, and *Walker-MS*, p. 53/fo. 30r.   [131] Pepys, 84.
[132] See 'Coronation Music of the Past', 26. For a list of sources and an edition see Range, thesis, vol. II.
[133] Ashmole, 186; *Walker-MS*, p. 53/fo. 30r; Ogilby, 184.

served as the source.[134] The anthem is scored for four-part choir and four-part orchestra. It probably includes several verse and full sections in which Cooke himself may have sung a solo at the coronation: Cheverton has pointed out that Cooke often sang the bass solos in the Chapel Royal.[135] The prominent inclusion of verses in this anthem may reflect the popularity of solo singing in the Restoration period.[136] After all, the number of verses in Cooke's setting would seem to complement Pepys's report that the music 'was lost to everybody': the subtle verses would easily have been drowned by the noise of people grasping for the coronation medals. Similarly, the numerous short instrumental ritornellos in the anthem match Baker's statement that 'the Violins, and other Instrumental Musick' answered the choir 'alternately'.[137]

The first entry of the vocal parts in the anthem is especially interesting. The tenor and bass still enter in an *alla breve* bar as in the preceding symphony (bar 25), but the metre changes in the very next bar to triple time. This suggests that there should be no gap between the instrumental symphony and the entry of the singers. Even though the score does not indicate that the instruments should play along with the vocal parts, they may at least have doubled the treble part, as implied by the notation in bar 100: ATB have a breve while the ritornello begins on the fourth beat; the treble part alone has a dotted minim, so as to make a 'full' bar with the two quavers of the ensuing ritornello.[138] The verse sections were accompanied at least by a basso continuo group, as is evident from the partly independent bass line. While the organ may not have played in the symphony of 'Zadok the Priest' it appears to have played in the ritornellos in Cooke's anthem: in bar 82 the last bass note of the chorus section is a dotted minim to which the first crotchet of the ensuing ritornello is tied. This implies that the basso continuo, which probably accompanied the chorus, also played in the ritornellos.[139] More than half of the anthem consists of the jubilant final 'Alleluia' that has both an instrumental and a vocal 'Prelude' (bars 62–125).[140] Such a lavish finale may have been intended to mark the end of the actual coronation part of the service.

[134] See Ashbee and Harley, vol. I, 157.

[135] Cheverton, 77f. His evidence consists of the reports in Samuel Pepys' diary. See also Rebecca Herissone, '*To Fill, Forbear, or Adorne': The Organ Accompaniment of Restoration Sacred Music* (Aldershot: Ashgate, 2006), 111.

[136] Cheverton, 81.   [137] Baker, 817.   [138] Cf. also fn. 163.

[139] Cf. Herissone, 15, who states (referring to Peter Holman) that the strings and the organ did not normally play together.

[140] According to Manning, 32f., 'Behold, O God' is the only one of Cooke's surviving anthems with a final Hallelujah.

For the remainder of the service Ashmole and Baker state that the Nicene Creed and 'the rest of the special *Musick*, for the Solemnity' was 'set by Captain Cook'.[141] None of this music is known to have survived, but the two accounts imply that the Nicene Creed was an elaborate setting, 'sung by the *Gentlemen* of the *Chappel*, with *Verse*, and *Chorus* [...] The *Violins*, and other *Instrumental Musick* [...] alternately playing'.[142] Given the length of the text, this must have been a long piece. The anthem 'Let my prayer come up', the 'Gradual', was sung as a processional while the king 'descended' from his throne to a faldstool near the altar.[143] It has been stated that the text of a setting by Cooke is included in John Clifford's *Divine Services and Anthems* from 1664.[144] However, this collection contains only the text of 'Let my prayers be set forth', which is at the end assigned to 'Mr. Henry Cooke'.[145]

None of the reports mentions the singing of a Sanctus. After the king had taken communion and while he returned to his throne 'the Quire sang this Anthem / Intellige clamorem &c Psal: 5.2.', or 'O hearken unto the voice of my calling'.[146] Again only the words of a setting by Cooke may survive.[147] According to Walker, 'O hearken' was followed by the last prayer and then the singing of 'Gloria Patri &c.' which is most probably a misspelling and refers to the 'Gloria in excelsis'.[148] It would thus appear that the Gloria accompanied merely the king's sitting on his throne.

For the King's procession into St Edward's Chapel, where he would prepare for the Recess, Ashmole and Baker mention 'the *Organs* playing all the while'.[149] However, no music is reported for the actual Recess, the king's procession from the Confessor's Chapel to the West door. The same applies to the return to Westminster Hall, and it may be only assumed that there was some festive instrumental music during these processions.

---

[141] Ashmole, 186; Baker, 817.

[142] Ibid. NB this is not the same text as quoted above, in fn. 136.

[143] Ogilby, 184; Baker, 817 and Ashmole, 186. See also *Lbl MS Stowe 580*, p. 14: the archbishop reads the 'Offertory Intend: / voce &c / While that is singing the King discends [...]'

[144] Dennison and Wood, 387.

[145] John Clifford, *The Divine Services and Anthems usually sung in His Majesties Chappell, and in all Cathedrals and Collegiate Choires in England and Ireland*. 2nd edn with large additions (London: 1664), 380. See also Manning, 33. This text, with the ascription to Cooke, is also found in *Lbl Harl. 6346*, p. 275/ fo. 96. According to Clifford this was a full setting, but according to *Harl. 6346* it included verses.

[146] *Walker-MS*, p. 54/fo. 30v. See also Ogilby, 185; Ashmole, 187f.; and Baker, 818.

[147] See Dennison and Wood, 386f.: 'music lost, text in *Lbl*', but it is not clear to which source they refer. Westrup, 18, mentions 'three anthems' by Cooke for this coronation without naming them.

[148] *Walker-MS*, p. 54/fo. 30v. Ashmole, 188, simply states that 'the Bishop of London went on with the Communion'.

[149] Ashmole, 188; Baker, 818.

The musicians

The performance conditions in 1661 are much better documented than those at the previous coronations. Holman, in referring to Ashmole, states that Cooke's verse anthems

were performed in a polychoral manner, with the main choir in a gallery on the north side of the Abbey, the 'Violins, and other Instrumental Musick' in a gallery next to them, and a small choir of 'twelve Gentlemen, four Children, and one Organist' (who presumably took the verse passages) in a 'Gallery, raised on the South-side of the Upper Quire, peculiarly appointed for them'.[150]

Three different galleries are also confirmed by Walker. Regarding the gallery that Ashmole described as the one with the main choir, on the north side of the Abbey, Walker reports that 'neare the Organ some of the Quier were placed'.[151] This gallery would thus have been over the north quire aisle, the place of the old Abbey organ.[152] The other two galleries, however, would have been near the High Altar; Walker refers to 'the Gent. of the Chappell, who had a Scaffold prepared for them on the Southsyde of the Altar and other Musick placed on a Scaffold opposite to them'.[153] Ogilby reports that 'the *Quire of Westminster*, with the *Gentlemen* and *Children* of the *King's Chapel* [. . .]' were all placed in one gallery on the north side.[154] However, the disposition of the musicians as reconstructed from Walker and Ashmole, with two singers' galleries and one for the orchestra, seems to be more likely, as it is the same as that at the next coronation, in 1685. Indeed, for the anthem 'O hearken unto the voice' Walker, Ogilby, Ashmole, and Baker state that it was sung 'by the upper *Quire*', which may refer to the Chapel Royal gallery near the High Altar.[155]

The arrangement of the musicians in different corners of the church has been likened to the Venetian *cori spezzati* style.[156] Indeed, it has been suggested that it was Cooke who established this technique in England and that he first tried it out at the coronation.[157]Notably, however, English composers of the time did not write polychoral music with effects

---

[150] Holman, *Four and Twenty Fiddlers*, 400. For the original see Ashmole, 172 and 186. The same disposal in Baker, 811 and 817.

[151] *Walker-MS*, p. 33f./fo. 20r and v.

[152] See Wilkinson, *Westminster Abbey*, 68. This old position of the organ also explains the position of most of the musicians' graves and memorials in the aisle north of the quire.

[153] *Walker-MS*, p. 53/fo. 30r.   [154] Ogilby, 172.

[155] *Walker-MS*, p. 54/fo. 30v. See also Ogilby, 185; Ashmole, 187f.; Baker, 818.

[156] Robert King, *Henry Purcell* (London: Thames and Hudson, 1994), 24; see also the following fn.

[157] Dennison and Wood, 386.

of rapid changes as in the Venetian tradition; they merely made use of the effects of placing different parts of the performing body in different locations within the building.[158] In a broader context, this corresponded with the performance practice at services in the Restoration Chapel Royal at Whitehall Palace.[159] After all, this practice may, especially at coronations, have been derived from necessity, as it was not possible to find a place big enough for all the musicians together.

From a practical point of view such a disposition of the musicians in the Abbey would require some practice to coordinate them. This is the earliest coronation for which a rehearsal of the music is confirmed: Cooke received payment for 'Torches and Lights for practiceing the Musicke against his Ma^{ts} Coronacōn'.[160] However, the fact that candlelight was used may imply that the musicians did not practise in the challenging conditions of Westminster Abbey: it would have been very difficult, and expensive, to light the building enough for the musicians to see a conductor, being placed in separate galleries far away from each other.

There are no exact numbers for the musicians at this coronation. The choir consisted probably of about seventy singers. The 'official record drawn up by the King's command' mentions twelve boys and thirty-three Gentlemen for the Chapel Royal, which were complemented by the 'Quire of Westminster'.[161] The Abbey choir could have had a similar size as reported for the next coronation, eight boys and sixteen gentlemen. The relatively small number of trebles in the choirs is striking: twelve and eight trebles against thirty-three and sixteen adult men's voices. From this proportion it may be deduced that either the standard of the trebles' singing must have been significantly higher than it is nowadays, when the number of trebles normally about doubles the number of adult singers, or that in those days one preferred a different balance between the voices.

Ashmole's description of the galleries mentions 'one Organist' as the only instrumentalist in the gallery with the 'small choir'. At least from 1661

---

[158] Phillips, 454, points out that the English 'antiphonal writing [. . .] grew up quite separately from the Venetian *cori spezzati* though it presumably derived from the same practice of antiphonal chant singing'.

[159] See Holman, *Four and Twenty Fiddlers*, 389–93, and 398f. For 'some exceptions to this general rule' see Herissone, 16f.

[160] Andrew Ashbee (ed.), *Records of English Court Music*, 9 vols., (Scolar Press, 1991), vol. V, 109. See also Leeper, 558.

[161] W. J. Passingham, *A History of the Coronation* (London: Sampson Low, Marston, [1937]), 224. A list with the names of the adult members of the Chapel Royal at the time of the coronation was entered into the Chapel's Cheque Book. See Ashbee and Harley, vol. I, 120f. Many of the gentlemen held posts in both choirs and therefore had to engage deputies in the other choir.

onwards it appears that the main Abbey organ, above the choir stalls, was not normally used during coronation services, but that a new, smaller instrument was built in the gallery for the Chapel Royal.[162] The fanfares were played by the State Trumpeters who had their place in yet another, separate gallery on the quire screen:[163]

Over the dore in the entrance of the Quier were the Drumes & Trumpetts in rich Liveryes placed.

The orchestra at this coronation may have consisted of the newly created string band, the '24 viollins', as well as of several wind instruments for which there is evidence to have taken part at same stage of the coronation celebrations.[164] It is not unlikely that wind instruments reinforced the vocal parts of the choir, as was the custom in the Chapel Royal at the time. Moreover, they could also have been added to the strings during the symphonies and ritornellos so as to enrich the sound for the vast space of Westminster Abbey. Considering that the accompaniment by a consort of wind instruments was the more traditional way and that the inclusion of a modern-style string band was a fashionable novelty, it is little surprising that the latter featured more prominently in the reports and that details on the former are sparse.

Despite the lack of precise information, the music of the service in the Abbey is better documented than that of the other festivities of the corona-tion. This coronation would turn out to be the last to include the traditional procession from the Tower to Westminster on the day before the service.[165] It has been stated that Matthew Locke's two five-part suites and the six-part pavan-almand for sackbutts and cornetts were written for this proces-sion.[166] For the Coronation Banquet in Westminster Hall Pepys reports that he 'took a great deal of pleasure [. . .] to hear the Musique of all sorts; but above all, the 24 viollins'.[167] This indicates that instrumental music accompanied the banquet, but the exact pieces cannot be known.

In sum, it seems that almost all the music for Charles II's coronation was newly written – the Litany probably being a rare exception. This seems to clash with the overall ceremonial, which was much the same as at the

[162] For details see Knight, ch. 5.

[163] *Walker-MS*, p. 33f/fo. 20r and v. For the 'Drums and Trumpets' see also Ashmole, 176.

[164] For this and the following see Range, 'Instrumental Musick', esp. 90–2.

[165] For details see Eric Halfpenny, 'The "Entertainment" of Charles II', *ML* 38 (1957), 32–44.

[166] Leeper, 557, and Peter Holman, 'Matthew Locke', *NG* 15, 44–52, here 45. For the music see *Lbl MS Add. 17801*, fos. 63v–65, and *Cambridge, Fitzwilliam Museum MS 734, passim*.

[167] Pepys, 86.

pre-Civil War coronations. Indeed, it has been observed that the heralds at this coronation 'carried out to the letter the king's order for continuity'.[168] Regarding the music, however, there may have been a purely technical, or logistical, reason for composing much new music: it is possible that much of the earlier music had been lost or fallen into oblivion during the Interregnum. The time-honoured texts with their accustomed place in the liturgy were kept according to the *Liber Regalis*, but they were now dressed in new musical settings according to the latest fashion. Thus the conjunction of the old, traditional system of the monarchy with the present time was made 'audible' for those present at the ceremony in progressive and modern music. Furthermore, the music at this coronation service had indeed an extraordinary status: for instance, despite their appearance at the coronation service, strings were not introduced into the regular Chapel Royal services before 1662, more than a year after the coronation.[169] It appears that the coronation was considered as a special occasion and that the music was not necessarily linked to the ordinary performance practice at the Chapel Royal; as Evelyn pointed out, it was 'rare music'.[170] The special character of the 1661 coronation music might also be the reason why almost none of it entered the general repertoire: the only anthem that was more widely circulated seems to have been Lawes's 'Zadok the Priest'. Such exclusivity of the coronation music emphasizes the fact that this was a very special occasion, a grand ceremony for which it was appropriate to have the most extravagant and most modern music possible.

Overall, at the three coronations before and after the Restoration, the medieval tradition was continued in regard to the place of the music in the service and also concerning the texts chosen. Nevertheless, this tradition was thoroughly 'updated': in the seventeenth century, the coronation music readily accepted new styles and innovations in performance practice. With its outstanding elaborateness, the musical programme at these coronations set the tone for the next centuries to come.

---

[168] Keay, 5.

[169] See Cheverton, 84, who also states that Pepys and Evelyn in their diaries 'mention the "first time" of this innovation on different dates three months apart'. For the first appearance of strings in a Chapel Royal service see also Holman, *Four and Twenty Fiddlers*, 395–7.

[170] Evelyn, 166.

3 | Truncation and elaboration: 1685

The medieval coronation traditions had survived the Reformation and Interregnum without drastic changes. However, in 1685 they faced a severe challenge with a significantly abridged service. Incidentally though, this truncation of the coronation service allowed for unprecedented elaboration of its music, furthered by the extraordinary quality of the Chapel Royal personnel at the time. Overall, this is one of the best documented coronations before the twentieth century and one for which most of the music can be reconstructed.

James II and Queen Mary of Modena, 1685

James II succeeded his brother Charles II on 6 February 1685. He and his wife, Mary of Modena, were both devout Roman Catholics and are said to have attended a private, Catholic coronation ceremony in Whitehall Palace on 22 April.[1] However, if this ceremony was performed, then it would have been in secret, not as a great state occasion, and it is not known what music was performed – if any at all. The following day, St George's Day, the king and queen were crowned in Westminster Abbey according to the rites of the Church of England. As at the previous coronation, the choice of day probably had much significance. In 1685, it may have been a deliberate attempt to make the king appear more 'English', as public opinion about a 'Catholic' king was already polarized.[2] At the same time, the great public spectacle of the procession through London before the coronation was

---

[1] For details see Shirley Bury, 'The Coronation from the Restoration of the Monarchy to 1953', in Claude Blair (ed.), *The Crown Jewels*, vol. I: The History, 355–680, here 404–6.

[2] Cf. Patrick Dillon, *The Last Revolution: 1688 and the Creation of the Modern World*, first publ. 2006, paperback edn (London: Pimlico, 2007), 3. For this 'polarization' cf. also Mark Kishlansky, *A Monarchy Transformed: Britain 1603–1714*, first publ. 1996 (London: Penguin, 1997), 265–76. See also the observations by Carolyn Andervont Edie in 'Succession and Monarchy: The Controversy of 1679–1681', *The American Historical Review* 70 (1965), 350–70, esp. 351f.

abolished, not to be re-introduced, in very different form, until the twentieth century.[3]

This coronation is outstandingly well documented: many details of the preparations and the actual proceedings are preserved in a lavishly printed account published by Francis Sandford, Lancaster Herald of Arms, two years after the event:[4]

THE / HISTORY / OF THE / CORONATION / Of the Most High, Most Mighty, and Most / Excellent MONARCH, / JAMES II. / By the Grace of God, KING of / England, Scotland, France and Ireland, / DEFENDER OF THE FAITH, &c. / and of his Royal Consort / QUEEN MARY: / Solemnized in the Collegiate Church of St. PETER in / the City of *WESTMINSTER*, on *Thursday* the 23 of *April*, being / the Festival of St. GEORGE, in the Year of Our Lord 1685. / With an Exact Account of the several PREPARATIONS in Order thereunto, Their / MAJESTIES most Splendid Processions, and Their Royal and / Magnificent FEAST in *WESTMINSTER-HALL*. / The Whole WORK illustrated with SCULPTURES. / By His Majesties Especial Command. / By *FRANCIS SANDFORD* Esq; *Lancaster* Herald of Arms. / *In the Savoy*: Printed by THOMAS NEW COMB, One of His MAJESTIES Printers. 1687.

The format and scale of Sandford's publication suggest that all attention was to be focused on this one account, in contrast to the three different accounts of the previous coronation. It was James II himself who had commissioned this work 'at the very first meeting of the Coronation Committee'.[5] Edmund Bowles has summarized that

printed in limited editions at great expense, these so-called festival books served as court propaganda as well as memorials, testaments to the power, wealth and prestige of the ruling houses of Europe.[6]

Indeed, Sandford's publication is a good example of how the coronation was used for the promotion of a new monarch: this publication, with its detailed descriptions and engravings, created a permanent reflection of the king's magnificence displayed at the coronation. There is evidence that '300 copies

---

[3] Strong, 308f. According to E.W.F. Tomlin, this procession was abolished due to the cost of the Queen's jewels, but no reference for this explanation is given. See 'Charles II to William IV: Magnificence and Muddle, Seventeenth to Nineteenth Century', in John Hammerton (ed.), *The Story of the Coronation* (London: Amalgamated Press, [1937]), 227–34, here 227. See also below, Ch. 7, fn. 9.

[4] In the following 'Sandford'. There is also a handwritten account of the coronation by an unknown scribe (*Lbl MS Add. 6286*); the two may be connected, since they are similar in many ways.

[5] Strong, 312.

[6] Edmund A. Bowles, 'Music in Court Festivals of State: Festival Books as Sources for Performance Practices', *EM* 28 (2000), 421–43, here 421.

of this book were printed which cost £100'.[7] Thus this publication was probably intended only for the elite of the country. They were provided with a constant reminder not only of the 'pomp and circumstance' of the event, but, at the same time, also of the country's sworn loyalty to James II.

The order of service

Although this coronation has been the subject of much research, the origin and development of the order of service have not been studied in detail. The examination of this issue, however, will prove useful as it contextualizes the musical items in the overall ceremony. The order of service was prepared by the Archbishop of Canterbury, William Sancroft, and the surviving manuscripts give an interesting insight into how it evolved. Sancroft's first step was to look at the *Liber regalis* and many previous coronations, including those of Edward II, Henry IV, Henry VIII, James I, and Charles I.[8] Furthermore, he used 'other collections and accounts by Ashmole, Fuller, Prynne, and Heylin', and referred to a transcription by Ashmole of the manuscript that Charles II had used at his coronation in 1661.[9] However, Sancroft's work was based substantially on the order of service for the 1626 coronation of Charles I, which had the advantage that it provided also for the coronation of a queen consort. Sancroft used the copy of the order of service that included annotations by Bishop Laud (*Cjc MS L 12*).[10] In addition, he possessed a second copy, which he believed was 'the very book' Charles I had 'held in his Hand' during the service (*Cjc MS L 15*).[11] In this, the king's copy, Sancroft entered some changes. He then prepared a copy of this manuscript incorporating the alterations and adding some annotations, especially concerning the music (*Cjc MS L 13*).[12] After this

---

[7] Pencil annotation on the front cover of the copy in *Ob G.2.8.Jur*. The annotation refers to 'Rawl. MS. D 807 f. 158 WDMacray' which, however, is (temporarily) lost.

[8] See Wordsworth, xxxvii. Sancroft mentions all his sources in *Ob MS Tanner 31*, fo. 37. See also *Ob MS Tanner 31*, fos. 89–96: Sancroft's account of the coronations from Edward II until Charles I.

[9] Wordsworth, xxxvii (including also more information on the authors named) and 84. See also *Ob MS Tanner 31*, fo. 96: 'For Mʳ Elias Ashmole in his MS great Collectiõ of Coronatiõ-Offices, hath one (wᶜʰ begiñs p. 301r) transscrib'd (as he told me) frõ the very MS wᶜʰ Charles yᵉ 2ᵈ us'd at yᵉ time of his Coronatiõ [...]' It appears that Ashmole's manuscript itself is now lost.

[10] Cf. Wordsworth, xiv, who states that Sancroft, according to his own words, had used 'a form on large folio paper in the King's Paper Office' for the Queen's Coronation.

[11] *Cjc MS L 15*, annotation on the front page.

[12] *Cjc MS L 13*: 'Order of Coronation of King Charles I, in the handwriting of Archbishop Sancroft.' Inside the cover: 'This Book is an original, in Archbp: Sancroft's own hand, containing several Forms of Prayer, most very scarce, & hard to be met with. With some Observations by the ArchBp: (a great Ritualist) pretty curious.'

revision work in the order of service for Charles I, Sancroft started preparing his own order of service for the forthcoming coronation. The probable first draft of this survives in the Tanner Manuscripts in the Bodleian Library, Oxford.[13] Sancroft wrote his text only on the recto sides of the pages, so as to allow enough room for later changes or additions. After some more revision work on details, Sancroft made a copy of the order of service in the Tanner MS, similar in size and appearance, including all his changes to the text; this was richly bound and was probably the copy that he used during the service (*Cjc MS L 14*).[14]

The most notable feature of this coronation is that it did not include a communion service. James II and Queen Mary, both being Catholic, were not willing to receive communion according to the Anglican rite. The king, 'with expresse command', asked 'to leave out the Communion Service' and also demanded 'to abridge (as much as conveniently might be) the extreme length of the rest' of the service.[15] Since this was the first coronation of a king and a queen for over eighty years – the last queen consort to be crowned had been Anne of Denmark in 1603 – there may indeed have been concerns about the service's 'extreme length', even without the communion service.

In any case, it appears that the archbishop was not easily willing 'to leave out the Communion Service', and his uncertainty about its omission is well reflected in the order of service in the Tanner MS. Sancroft had begun to enter the communion service after the Queen's Coronation.[16] In the end, however, he included an anthem instead, after which he wrote: 'But there being no Cōmunion; here follow THE FINAL PRAIERS.' Despite the circumstances, Sancroft still included the communion service after the Final Prayers and the Recess, heading it 'When there is to be a

---

[13] *Ob MS Tanner 31*, fos. 75–81v: 'The Coronation of the Queen', followed by the Communion Service; fos. 97–103 and 104–12: 'The Coronation-Office'. (The three are bound in separate booklets.)

[14] *Cjc MS L 14*: 'The Forme of the Coronation Service'; a note reads: 'This Book is an Originall, in Arch Bp: Sancroft's own hand, the same that he made use of at the Coronation of KING JAMES the 2nd & the Queen his Consort.' The note was written by Thomas Baker (1656–1740), a nonjuring Church of England clergyman, antiquarian, and fellow of St John's College, Cambridge. The manuscript includes the signatures of the bishops who officiated with Sancroft. See also Wordsworth, xxx.

[15] *Ob MS Tanner 31*, fo. 31 (transcr. App. B1a).

[16] *Ob MS Tanner 31*, fo. 77: '[the Queen] reposing herself there till ye Anthem is Ended; & then, Imediately the ArchBp should beg imediately begin / THE COMMUNION. v. p. . . . ...'.

COMMUNION'; in addition, perhaps simply for reasons of comparison, he also included 'The Cõmuniõ. as it stood in Ch. I.'ˢ Book'.[17] In his final order of service (*Cjc MS L 14*) Sancroft continued to make provision for the communion service, stating that 'yᵉ Archbishop should immediately begin' with it after the Queen's Coronation. The use of the word 'should' might indicate Sancroft's concern about omitting the communion service. However, in the end, he omitted it and noted after the Queen's Coronation and Inthronization: 'But there being no Cõmunion; / THE FINAL PRAYERS.'[18] Nevertheless, it appears that Sancroft was still very reluctant to abandon the traditional incorporation of the communion service: for he still included, after the Final Prayers and before the Recess, 'The communion service as it stood in King Charles Iˢᵗˢ time.'[19] The archbishop may have done this to have a last-minute chance to reverse the omission, which would indeed have been possible, since other necessities had also been planned for. F.C. Turner observed that

It appears that the original intention was that James and Mary should both take the Communion, for provision was made for a silk towel each 'to be held before them at the Communion'.[20]

In addition to leaving all options open, Archbishop Sancroft may have intended to provide a 'complete' order of service for future coronations. After all, at one point Sancroft had considered having the order of service printed.[21] Indeed, the king signed a warrant to print it,[22] but there this no evidence that this actually occurred. This would have been the earliest printed order of service for a coronation, and it seems that the idea was not put into practice until 1727.

The ultimate decision about cutting the communion service was probably reached only two days before the coronation: the aforementioned king's 'express command' to omit it dates from 'the 21ᵗʰ [*sic*] day of Aprill 1685'.[23] Notably, this document also states that the king had inspected Sancroft's order of service and had given his approval. Since a copy of the king's instructions is entered at the end of *MS L 14*, it was probably this order of service of which he had approved.[24]

---

[17] *Ob MS Tanner 31*, fo. 80f. [18] *Cjc MS L 14*, fo. 50. [19] *Cjc MS L 14*, fo. 51.
[20] Turner, 257, fn. 1.
[21] *Ob MS Tanner 31*, fo. 37: 'Qu. of printĝ yᵉ Anthems; & yᵉ whole Office. instead of MS. Copies.' [this is crossed out].
[22] See *Ob MS Tanner 31*, fo. 59 (transcr. App. B1b). [23] See fn. 15. [24] *Cjc MS L 14*, fo. 58v.

For better comparison, the different sources for the order of service and their relationships are given in Table 3.1 in chronological order (OS = order of service):

Table 3.1 The development of the order of service for the 1685 coronation.

1) *Cjc MS L 12*
   (OS Charles I and Queen Maria Henrietta, with corrections by Laud)
2) *Cjc MS L15*
   (OS Charles I and his Queen, king's own copy, with changes by Sancroft)
3) *Cjc MS L 13*
   (copy of *MS L 15* by Sancroft, incorporating his changes)
4) *Ob MS Tanner 31*
   (OS James II and Queen Mary by Sancroft, with many changes)
5) *Cjc MS L 14*
   (copy of Tanner MS, incorporating the changes, including some new ones)
6) *Lbl Add. MS 6286*
   (manuscript account of the coronation including drawings, possibly produced in preparation of the next item)
7) Sandford, 1687: printed account of the 1685 coronation
   (following the OS as in *Cjc MS L 14*)

Sancroft has been harshly criticized for his 'revolutionary vandalism' of the traditional order of service.[25] Such criticism, however, underestimates the importance of the king's command to exclude the communion, to which Sancroft had to react – willingly or not. In any case, the 1685 coronation was very important for the history of the coronation service. Strong has observed that it was the previous coronation, in 1661, which 'became the template for every one which followed it in terms of the physical arrangements and also of what was worn or the artefacts needed'.[26] Nevertheless, in terms of the ceremonial it was the 1685 coronation that was used as a 'guideline' for a long time, even though the order of service was unusual in being deprived of the communion service.[27] Referring to the meticulous preparations and the 'august and splendid Manner' in which this coronation was performed, one early writer went so far as to state that it 'was questionless design'd for the Model of all future Coronations'.[28] One of the main reasons why this coronation could become a 'model' was certainly Sandford's printed

---

[25] Perkins, 88f.   [26] Strong, 311.   [27] See below, Ch. 6, fn. 140.
[28] *A Complete Account of the Ceremonies observed in the Coronation of the Kings and Queens of England*, 4th edn (London: Printed for J. Roberts and D. Browne, 1727), 5.

account with its detailed descriptions and illustrations. This publication was the first of its kind, and remained unsurpassed for more than 130 years.

The Music

Archbishop Sancroft's manuscripts and Sandford's printed account provide an unprecedented amount of detail concerning the music of the coronation service. They include the full texts of the anthems and Sandford furthermore lists the names of the composers and whether the anthems were 'full' or 'verse anthems'.

While the archbishop's material does not cover the procession from Westminster Hall to the Abbey, Sandford provides a meticulous account of this. He reports that the choirs of the Chapel Royal and of Westminster Abbey sang 'this known* ANTHEM' and gives the full text of 'O Lord, grant the King a long life'; in the margin he adds that it was '*Composed here-tofore by Dr. *Child*'.[29] The fact that Sandford refers to it as a 'known' anthem and that he uses the word 'heretofore' indicate that this was not a new composition, but an older setting. As already seen, Child's setting of the words is in one later source described as 'Compos'd at ye Restauration'.[30] Sandford mentions instrumentalists walking with the choirs: Edmond Flower and Theophilus Fittz 'playing on a *Sackbut*', and Henry Gregory 'playing on a *Double Courtal*'.[31] Since they walked between the gentlemen of the two choirs it is very likely that they played during the anthem. Eric Halfpenny states that their purpose was 'obviously to keep the choir in pitch during the singing in procession'.[32] He supports the interpretation that the group shown in the respective engraving in Sandford consists of 'a cornett and "two large trumpets"', and not the instruments named in the text. Indeed, although 'the cornett-sackbut group is, however, what we should expect to see at this period, supporting voices', he observes that the two larger instruments 'are decidedly not sackbuts' and may have been 'slide or "flat" trumpets'.[33]

---

[29] Sandford, 80. See also *Lca MS L 19*: Coronation of James II, pp. 1–48, on p. 18 (only the title of the anthem, but not Child's name).

[30] See Ch. 2, fn. 92.   [31] Sandford, 70.

[32] Eric Halfpenny, 'Musicians at James II's Coronation', *ML* 32 (1951), 103–14, here 109. Cf. the practice at the 1661 Garter ceremony in Windsor. See Holman, *Four and Twenty Fiddlers*, 401–3.

[33] Halfpenny, 'Musicians', 109–11. He refers to Lyndesay G. Langwill, *The Bassoon and Double Bassoon* (Hinrichsen, 1948). For the identification of the instruments in the engraving and especially for the flat trumpet see also Trevor Herbert, 'The Sackbut in England in the 17th and 18th Centuries', *EM* 18 (1990), 609–16, here 611f., and James Arthur Brownlow, *The Last Trumpet: a History of the English Slide Trumpet* (Stuyvesant, NY: Pendragon Press, 1996), 8–13.

According to Sandford, the choirs sang the anthem 'all the way from the *Hall* to the *Church*', and the procession would have taken the choir about fifteen minutes.[34] Given this length of the procession, it is conceivable that, in addition to accompanying the choir, the instruments played for some time on their own, to make the music long enough for the procession: alternating of the singing of the choir with instrumental music is confirmed for later coronations.[35] Also, as indicated by the engravings in Sandford, the State Trumpeters and Drums may have sounded at some stage during the procession.

In a list with queries about the necessary preparations, Archbishop Sancroft included the line 'Tallis's TE DEUM to be sung in ye processiō to ye Church'.[36] It is not clear if he thought of the Te Deum to be sung in addition to the anthem or instead of it. This note is remarkable, since it is the only instance of the archbishop's giving a composer's name for the coronation music. In any case, this 'query' is crossed out, and Sandford does not mention this piece in his account of the procession. The Te Deum is also part of the service, and its inclusion in the procession would have been very unusual.

The Entrance-Anthem: 'I was glad'

Sandford provides a detailed account of the beginning of the service. From that it is clear that the entrance-anthem was sung by the choir walking in the procession before the king and queen. Sandford describes the scene as follows:[37]

By the time the KING and QUEEN being entred the *Church*, were received by the *Dean* and *Prebendaries*, who, with the *Choir* of *Westminster*, proceeding a little before THEIR MAJESTIES, Sung the full * Anthem following [text of 'I was glad'].

It has been shown that the anthem was most likely the now well-known five-part setting of 'I was glad' discovered by Bruce Wood in 1977.[38] The

---

[34] The processional route is shown in one of Sandford's engravings, and the time can be deduced from the text: the beginning of the procession left the Hall at 'about Twelve of the Clock' (p. 65) and reached the Abbey 'at about a quarter past Twelve of the Clock' (p. 81).

[35] See a report from the coronation of George IV in Ch. 6, fn. 121.

[36] *Ob MS Tanner 31*, fo. 37.

[37] Sandford, 82. Correspondingly, one of Sancroft's queries during his preparations had been: 'In w^t place must ye Qre of Westm~r fall into ye processiō w^{t}hin ye Church'. See *Ob MS Tanner 31*, fo. 38v.

[38] Bruce Wood, 'A Coronation Anthem. Lost and Found', *MT* 118 (1977), 466–8. For details of this and the following see also Matthias Range, 'The 1685 Coronation Anthem *I was glad*', *EM* 36 (2008), 397–408.

piece is a full setting, and thus matches Sandford's description. Furthermore, the structure of this anthem also supports its having been written for the coronation, as will be seen in the following discussion. Since Sandford with the asterisk explains that the anthem was 'Composed by Mr. *Hen. Purcel*' this setting has been ascribed to Purcell; however, there is no other reason to question the ascription to John Blow in the only source of the music.

The performance of the entrance-anthem

According to Sandford's report the choir sang the entrance-anthem only during the procession from the West door up to the quire screen; he reports that 'the *Anthem* being ended, the *Children* and *Choir* of *Westminster* turned to the *Left-Hand*, to the back-side of the *Choir*, and went up into their *Gallery* by the *Great Organ*'.[39] The local conditions in the Abbey at the coronation are shown in a 'Ground-Plot' included in Sandford (see Illustration 3.1). While the Abbey choir went to their gallery, the procession of the royal couple continued; Sandford reports that, when they 'Entred the *Choir*', the king and queen were greeted by the '*Kings Scholars* of *Westminster-School*' who sang the *Vivats*, which will be considered in detail later.

The complete full setting of 'I was glad' would have been too long to be sung during the short distance from the West door to the quire entrance. At the same time, one would expect some music to have accompanied the end of the procession, after the *Vivats*. Altogether it seems possible that the anthem was split into two parts, with the *Vivats* in the centre. Wood observes that the opening of the anthem with its 'simple chordal textures and the swinging triple-time rhythm' is 'perfectly suited to processional performance'.[40] When walking in a stately, ceremonial manner, it may be expected that the steps of those processing correlate with the rhythm of the accompanying music, and as the beginning of the anthem is in triple time, going one step per bar would seem appropriate here.[41] As in 1626, it is known that the king and queen had some sort of 'rehearsal' before the coronation, and it is possible that they were also informed about the processional music.[42] The length of the choir's procession up the nave

---

[39] This and the following: Sandford, 83.   [40] Wood, 'Coronation Anthem', 468.

[41] Cf. Martin Neary's report about the preparations for the initial procession at the funeral of Diana, Princess of Wales in Westminster Abbey in 1997. See 'Timing is Crucial as the Music Takes Shape', *WAC* 3, no. 8 (Winter 1997/98), 6–10, here 9.

[42] *Ob MS Tanner 31*, fo. 83: 'The Dean of Westm^r is to p^Esent y^e K. & Q. wth y^e Form of y^t pt of y^e Ceremonie, wch is to be pformd in y^e Church: & to be wth y^e K. & Q. cert. Daies before y^e time p^Efixt, to instruct them in y^e Manner of y^e Solemnity [. . .]' Cf. above, Ch. 2, fn. 69.

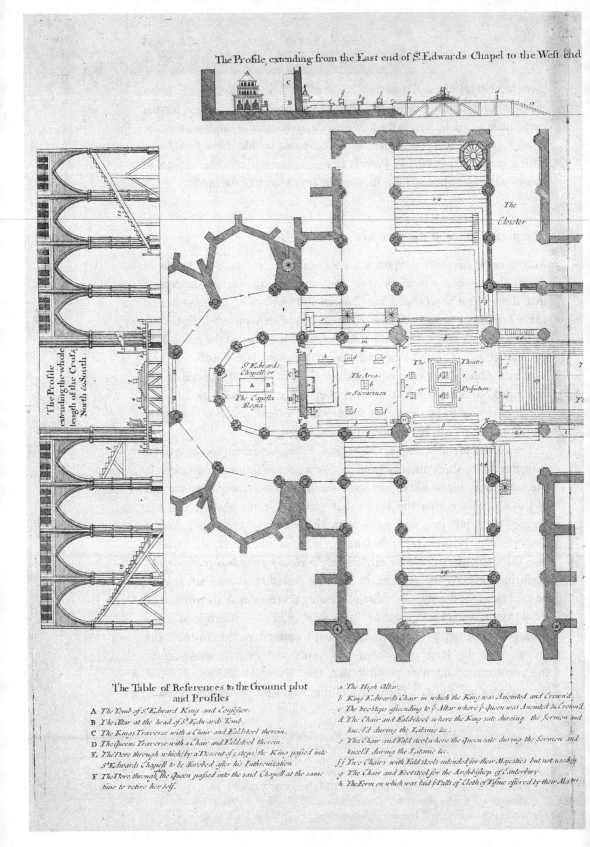

The Profile, extending from the East end of St Edwards Chapel to the West end

The Profile extending the whole length of the Crofs, North & South.

The Cloister

St Edwards Chapell or The Capella Regia

The Area or Sacrarium

The Theatre Pulpitum

The Table of References to the Ground plot and Profiles

A *The Tomb of St Edward King and Confessor.*
B *The Altar at the head of St Edwards Tomb.*
C *The Kings Traverse with a Chair and Faldstool therein.*
D *The Queens Traverse with a Chair and Faldstool therein.*
E *The Dore through which (by a Descent of 3 steps) the Kings passed into St Edwards Chapell to be disrobed after his Inthronization.*
F *The Dore through which the Queen passed into the said Chapell at the same time to retire her self.*

a *The High Altar.*
b *King Edwards Chair in which the King was Anointed and Crown'd.*
c *The two Steps ascending to ye Altar where ye Queen was Anointed & Crown'd.*
d *The Chair and Faldstool where the King sate during the Sermon and kneel'd during the Litanie &c.*
e *The Chair and Faldstool where the Queen sate during the Sermon and kneel'd during the Litanie &c.*
ff *Two Chairs with Fald stools intended for their Majesties but not used.*
g *The Chair and Footstool for the Arch-bishop of Canterbury.*
h *The Form on which was laid ye Palls of Cloth of Tissue offered by their Maties*

3.1 'Ground-Plot' and side elevation of Westminster Abbey for the 1685 coronation, engraving in Sandford [split over two pages]. © Dean and Chapter of Westminster.

t end of the Choir

The GROUND-PLOT of
The COLLEGIATE CHURCH of
St PETER in WESTMINSTER.
With two Profiles relating thereunto,
Shewing the Position and Erection of the Theatre,
Sacrary, Altars, Thrones, Traverses, Chairs, Pulpit.
Forms, Benches, Seats and Galleries,
on the day of their Majesties Coronation,
Seil! 23 Apr:1685.

A Scale of Feet.

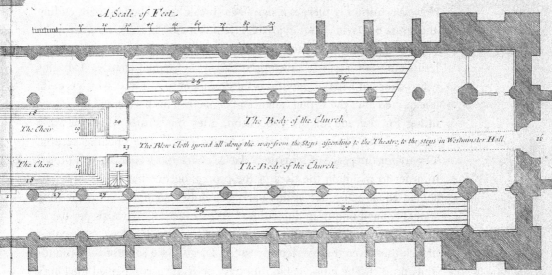

The Choir

The Body of the Church.

The Blew Cloth spread all along the way from the Steps ascending to the Theatre, to the steps in Westminster Hall

The Choir

The Body of the Church.

1. The Place where the Prebonds of Westminster stood.
2. The Bench on which sate the Dukes of Normandie and Aquitain, and the Great Officers.
3. Two Benches on which sate the Bishops.
m. A Large Box in which sate Prince George and the Princess Anne of Donmark and some other persons of the Chiefest quality.
n. A little Organ for the Kings Choir.
o. The Gallery in which sate the Kings Choir of Vocall Musick.
p. A Large Gallery in which sate Ambassadors, Forcign Minifters and Strangers of quality.
q. Another large Gallery in which sate the Master and Kings Choir of Instrumental Musick.
r. Two steps of ascent from the Area to the Theatre.

1. The Kings Throne being an ascent of 5 Steps above the Theatre.
2. The Queens Throne adioyning thereto being an ascent of 3 steps.
3. The Chair of state in which the King was inthroned.
4. The Chair of state in which the Queen was inthroned.
5. The Chair and Faldstool where the King first kneeled and sate and where he stood during the Recognition.
6. The Chair and Faldstool where the Queen first kneeled and sate.
7. The Desk at which the Litanie was sung.
8. The Benches where the Peers sate.
9. The Benches where of Peeresses sate.

10. Seats railed in, on the Inside of the 4 great Pillars for the Kings Heralds and Pursuivants at Arms.
11. The Pulpit.
12. Galleries or Seats in the South Cross for Spectators.
13. A Gallery for § Princess Anne of D. Maids & Serv.ts and over it another Gallery.
14. A Gallery where sate severall of the Nobility of Scotland and Ireland others of the best quality and over it another Gallery for the QueenDowagers Servants.
15. Galleries or seats in the North Cross for Spectators.
16. The Rail where the Serieants at Arms stood, both within and without.
17. The 12 steps ascending from the Choir to the Theatre.
18. The Benches or seats on each side, and west end of the Choir, where sate the six Clerks, Kings Chaplains, Aldermen, Masters in Chancery, Serieant at Law,
18. Esquires of the body, Gentlemen of the Privy Chamber, and Iudges.
19.19. The stairs whereby the former part of the Proceeding descended into the Choir, in order to their return to Westm.r Hall.
20. A Gallery for § Queens Maids and Servants.
21. The Gallery in which the Choir of Westm.r sate.
22. The Great Organ and Organ Loft in which sate severall spectators.
23. The dore at the entrance into the Choir.
24.24. The Gallery over the Choir dore for the Serieants Trumpeter and the other Trumpets and Kettle Drums
25.25. Galleries for Spectators in the North and South Iles of the Church
26. The great West dore of the Church.
27. The Gallery where § Kings Scholars of Westminster sate in number 40.

would have been little more than thirty metres. Firstly, they would not have begun the procession immediately at the West door, since the Dean, Prebendaries and choir who 'received' the royal couple, being lined up, would be about the length of the first one and a half bays. Secondly, so as to turn left in a dignified way, the choir probably left the procession in the last bay before the quire screen. The remaining distance can comfortably be walked in about fifty-six steps; and this correlates with the number of bars after which there is a clear break in the anthem. Nothing is marked in the manuscript at this point, except that bar 57 begins on a new system. However, musically there is a significant break here. The first part, ending 'the house of David', is set in joyful, bright G major, in triple time through-out. In contrast to that, the second part, from 'O pray for the peace of Jerusalem' onwards, is characterised by key and tempo changes. It begins with a chord of E major, serving as the dominant to A minor, which is quite unexpected after the strong cadence in G major. This part would have been fitting for the end of the procession, after the *Vivats* when the king 'ascended the Theatre' and walked to his seat.[43] The opening section, 'O pray for the peace of Jerusalem', has six bars and is marked 'alla breve': in order to maintain the pace of the procession one bar in the first part should equal half a bar in this part, or a dotted semibreve in triple time should equal a minim in duple time.[44] When walking two steps per bar in duple time (one for each minim) this would make twelve steps. As a matter of fact, there were twelve steps up to the Theatre (see Sandford's 'Ground-Plot', no. 17). The music could thus have perfectly accompanied the king's slow ascending of the steps, with the change in time highlighting the invitation to pray. The following section 'Peace be within thy walls', has twenty-three bars in triple time – with twenty-three steps the king could easily walk from the end of the steps, passing his throne, to his Chair of Estate (Sandford's 'Ground-Plot', no. 5). Once he had arrived at his chair, the choir would have begun the *Gloria Patri* and the king and queen 'made an humble Adoration [. . .] and used some Private Devotions' before taking seat in their Chairs of Estate.[45]

This idea of the anthem's performance is also supported by Wood's observation that the use of extended counterpoint is reserved for the end of the piece (for the text 'As it was in the beginning'). As he concludes, by then 'the choir would have come to a halt after processing the length of the

---

[43] Sandford, 83.
[44] NB In contrast to modern editions, the manuscript notes a three-minim bar, not three crotchets.
[45] Sandford, 83.

nave'; it 'would be safely arrived in its gallery and able to watch a conductor' which would have facilitated 'the coordination of more complex textures'.[46] Indeed, the Abbey choir would have had enough time to reach its gallery while the scholars of Westminster sang their *Vivats*.

Incidentally, such a tripartite scheme for the entrance-anthem (first part of anthem – *Vivats* – second part of anthem) corresponds with C.H.H. Parry's setting of 'I was glad' composed for the coronation of Edward VII and Queen Alexandra in 1902. Parry reported in detail how the entrance-anthem was expected to be performed:[47]

Sir J.B. [John (Frederick) Bridge] told me that the Westminster Choir are to begin the so called Anthem at the West door & march up singing in front of the King. That when the King arrives at the entrance of the Choir the music is to stop, & time is to be given for the Westminster boys in the Triforium to shout out three times, 'Vivat Regina Alexandra, Vivat Rex Edwardus!' And that the Music is to be resumed after they have done. It being suggested that the Choir should take up the Vivats followed by the two last verses 'O pray for the peace' etcet while the King passes up the Choir. I have thought out the general scheme on these lines, but before going further I should be glad to have Sir F. Bridge's instructions confirmed.

F.G. Edwards described Parry's anthem as being 'laid out upon lines conditioned by the ceremony'.[48] It appears that the 1685 setting of 'I was glad' may equally have been composed to match the ceremonial proceedings. Apart from the 1685 setting there are three others written for coronations before 1902 by the composers Francis Pigott (Queen Anne, 1702), William Boyce (George III and Queen Charlotte, 1761), and Thomas Attwood (Queen Victoria, 1838). It is striking that they all have a clear break before the section beginning 'O pray for the peace of Jerusalem', usually a fermata on 'David' and/or a clear change of harmonies. One may wonder if it was not a tradition to schedule the *Vivats* for performance within the entrance-anthem – even if they may in the end have been performed differently.[49] The reason why such a 'tradition', if it existed, was not referred to by Parry

---

[46] Wood, 'Coronation Anthem', 468, and Wood, Booklet notes to *Coronation Music for James II*, Archiv Produktion CD-447 155–2 (Hamburg: Polydor International, 1987), 4.

[47] *Lwa WAM 58362*: Parry to Canon Robinson at the Abbey, 12 May 1902. This letter was first discussed by Charles Knighton, 'Random *Vivats* threaten Coronation chaos', *WAC* 3, no. 9 (Summer 1998), 20–2, here 21. Cf. also the letter in which Sir Frederick Bridge asked Parry to compose the anthem (*Lcm MS 7281*, transcr. App. B1c).

[48] F.G. Edwards, Foreword to *The Form and Order of the Service* [...] *in the Coronation of Their Majesties King Edward VII. and Queen Alexandra* [...] *With the Music to be sung*, ed. by Sir Frederick Bridge (London: Novello, 1902), iii. For a short account of the origins of Parry's composition, and in particular the inclusion of the *Vivats*, see Shedlock, 157–9.

[49] Cf. Knighton, 20–2.

or others in 1902 may simply be that it had by then been forgotten: after all, the last coronation before that had been in 1838 – over sixty years ago. Sir Frederick Bridge, the Director of Music in 1902, stated that the king and queen were to be greeted with the singing of Ps. 122 and that 'yet it seemed that traditionally also they were simultaneously to be greeted with stentorian shouts from the Westminster scholars of [the *Vivats*]'.[50] This indicates that there was at least some awareness of such a custom.

The *Vivats*

Sandford provides detailed information about the performance of the entrance-anthem. He points out: 'And it is to be Noted, That when the QUEEN Entred the *Choir*' – when she passed through the quire screen – she was 'Entertained [. . .] with this short Prayer or Salutation, *VIVAT REGINA MARIA*', sung by the '*Kings Scholars* of *Westminster-School*, in Number Forty, all in *Surplices*, being placed in a *Gallery* adjoining to the *Great Organ-Loft*'.[51] It has to be remembered that the king and queen did not walk next to each other, but she preceded him with her attendants.[52] The scholars continued singing until the king entered the quire, 'whom they entertained in like manner with this Prayer or Salutation, *VIVAT JACOBUS REX*', and they sang this until 'His MAJESTY ascended the *Theatre*.'

This coronation is believed to be the earliest at which the King's/Queen's Scholars of Westminster exercised the privilege of being the first to greet the new king and queen at the beginning of the service, their *Vivat*s being 'the last relic of Latin in the service' and 'the last survival of the spontaneous recognition of the Sovereign by the people of England'.[53] M.F. Johnstone observed that this was the first coronation at which the Westminster scholars were present.[54] Indeed, it has been suggested that James II had

---

[50] Bridge, *Westminster Pilgrim*, 182f., where he also claims 'a little credit for having suggested the arrangement'.

[51] Sandford, 83.

[52] See the respective engravings of the procession in Sandford. Their reproduction in Strong, 310f. is the wrong way round.

[53] John Dudley Carleton, *Westminster School – A History*, 2nd rev. edn (London: Rupert Hart-Davis, 1965), 109. See also Wilkinson, 56. For the earlier, medieval *Vivat*s see Andrew Hughes, 'Antiphons'. According to John Cannon and Ralph Griffiths the *Vivat*s were introduced at the coronation of Charles I in 1626; see *The Oxford Illustrated History of the British Monarchy*, reissue of the 1st rev. paperback edn 1998 (Oxford University Press, 2000), 118. However, the evidence for that statement is not clear.

[54] M.F. Johnstone, *Coronation of a King, or, The Ceremonies, Pageants and Chronicles of Coronations of All Ages* (London: Chapman and Hall, 1902), 118.

been 'so doubtful of his subjects' loyalty that he ordered the schoolboys to be present and acclaim him in case there should be any lack of cheering'.[55] If this was the case, then one could interpret this newly introduced form of the *Vivats* as an early example of an 'invented tradition', with their Latin text attempting to appear like a pre-Reformation, time-honoured custom. It is not known if at earlier coronations any such *Vivats* were sung for queen consorts, or just for the sovereign. If the queen consort's *Vivats* were introduced only in 1685, this would have meant quite an acknowledgement of Mary of Modena's role within the service, and indeed maybe in James II's reign. In any case, as Shirley Bury observed, the *Vivats* in 1685 'set a precedent which has been followed ever since'.[56]

It is noteworthy that Sandford states the *Vivats* were 'sung', not merely shouted. There is, however, no report of exactly how they were 'sung', and no setting of the words as given by Sandford is known. Since the *Vivats* were sung by the 'Scholars of Westminster', who were certainly not trained to the high standard of the choir, they were most probably sung to an easy tune, in unison. In medieval *Vivat*-chants the text is different ('Vivat Rex in aeternum'),[57] and these probably would have been forgotten by 1685. Another possible tune could be the 'F G A B♭ A' motif that features in several Tudor compositions, most notably in Thomas Ashwell's mass *God save King Harry*.[58] However, the text of the *Vivats* is too long for just five notes and the tune used would probably have been a longer piece: the distance from the screen to the steps ascending to the Theatre equals about thirty steps, which would be the equivalent of about thirty bars of music. In the search for the tune used for the *Vivats* in 1685 it is tempting to imagine that they could have been sung to an early version of 'God save the King/Queen'.[59]

With respect to the uncertain authorship of the anthem, Robert Manning states that 'whoever wrote this work was adding something quite unique to the repertory of Restoration church music'.[60] Indeed, in its above suggested

---

[55] *The Coronation of King George VI and Queen Elizabeth* (London: Odhams Press, [1937]), 52. Similarly, referring to the *Vivats* Fletcher, *British Court*, 93, states that 'James II granted to the King's Scholars the privilege of the Service of Acclamation'.

[56] Bury, 412.   [57] See Andrew Hughes, 'Antiphons', esp. 155.

[58] On this see Nick Sandon, 'F G A B-Flat A: Thoughts on a Tudor Motif', *EM* 12 (1984), 56–63. See also John Caldwell, *The Oxford History of English Music*. Vol. I: *From the Beginning to c.1715* (Oxford University Press: 1991), 240f.

[59] For details and a hypothetical example see Range, '1685 Coronation Anthem', 401f.

[60] Robert Manning, Review of Bruce Wood (ed.), *A Purcell Anthology: 12 Anthems* (Oxford: University Press, 1995), in *ML* 77 (May 1996), 313.

original form and performance, 'I was glad' would have been one of the most impressive compositions of any coronation service.

Music during the service

The Recognition was followed by acclamations and a fanfare. Intriguingly, a fanfare at this stage is not reported for the earlier coronations and could have been another innovation in 1685. With a Roman Catholic king on the throne, the Recognition in 1685 had gained a heightened importance and it is possible that the acclamation of the new ruler was meant to be reinforced and increased by the added element of a fanfare. Also, this is the first fanfare mentioned by Sandford in the 1685 coronation. While no music of any of the fanfares survives, it is known that this fanfare, for instance, was played by the trumpets and timpani.[61] During the ensuing anthem the archbishop was to go the altar where he 'revesteth himself with a Cope'.[62] This would have been in preparation for the communion; but since this was cut it is not clear if the archbishop eventually vested himself and what the anthem accompanied.

For this anthem Archbishop Sancroft had initially followed the order of service for the coronation of Charles I which scheduled the text of 'Let thy hand be strengthened', based on Ps. 89, verses 14 and 15 in the Prayer Book, as well as 'Ps. 89. Misericordia Dei. v. 1–6. Gl~ia P~ri'.[63] However, in the margin of his copy Sancroft added 'This may be omitted for want of time', possibly in response to the king's aforementioned demand that the service should be kept as short as possible. In the end, Sancroft did not include the psalm, but only the anthem, to which he added 'Allelujah' at the end.[64] Sandford reports that 'a Full* *Anthem* was sung by the *Choirs*, [...] * Composed by Dr. *John Blow*, *Master* of the *Children* of His *Majesties Chapel*; and *Organist* to the *King*'.[65] A full setting of the text in Blow's autograph score survives in a manuscript at the Barber Institute in Birmingham; it precedes Blow's anthem 'Behold, O God our Defender' – which has the same text as given for an anthem to come later in the service.[66] The anthems bear the inscription 'Anthem ye 2nd' and 'Anthem ye 5th'

---

[61] Sandford, 84: 'the *Trumpets* Sounded, and *Drums* Beat'.   [62] *Ob MS Tanner 31*, fo. 98.
[63] *Cjc MS L 13*, fo. 7.   [64] *Ob MS Tanner 31*, fo. 98.   [65] Sandford, 85.
[66] *Bu MS 5001*, p.268/fo.142r and p. 270/fo.143r respectively. Both anthems are also found in an eighteenth-century copy in *Lcm MS 1069*, fo. 6 ('Behold, O God') and fo. 9 ('Let thy hand'). For a modern edition and a list of sources see John Blow, *Coronation Anthems and Anthems with Strings*, ed. by Anthony Lewis and Watkins Shaw, *MB 7* (1953; 2nd rev. edn 1969). An additional source is *Lbl Add. MS 33289*, fo. 137 ('Behold, O God') and fo. 138v ('Let thy hand').

respectively, which tallies with the numbering of anthems to these texts in Sandford. There can be no doubt that these two are Blow's anthems for this coronation. 'Let thy hand be strengthened' is a short, simple homophonic setting for four-part choir in jaunty triple time. Blow takes the very short text as an opportunity to repeat important passages, notably the first line. The final 'Allelujah' takes nearly half the length of the whole anthem, thus underlining the festive character.

The next musical item in the service was the Litany. At the previous coronations this had been sung after the sermon, and during the anointing ceremony, between the *Veni Creator* and the anthem 'Zadok the Priest'. However, Archbishop Sancroft moved it to a position before the sermon, which thus separated the Litany and the Anointing.[67] A 'Litany Desk' was placed between the two most eastern pillars of the crossing: as in 1626 this was probably installed in order to make the cantor better audible.[68] Sandford reports that the Responses to the Litany were sung by 'the *Choirs*'. Surprisingly, he does not mention any further details, as he does for the other music. He may have interpreted the Litany as being a purely liturgical piece and therefore thought the details not to be as important as for the other pieces. Also, it is possible that it was obvious to which setting it was sung, and there was therefore no need for further details. As for the previous coronation, it is most likely that it was sung in the setting by Tallis.

The *Veni Creator* was, for the first time at a coronation, sung to the translation by John Cosin beginning 'Come, Holy Ghost, our souls inspire'.[69] This is the shorter of the two English versions of the *Veni Creator* included in the 1662 Prayer Book. According to Sandford it was sung as a 'Full Anthem', 'Composed or set by Mr. *William Turner*, Gentleman of His Majesties Chapel-Royal'.[70] No setting of the text by Turner is known, and Don Oscar Franklin proposed that 'Turner's music may well have been a four-part chant setting', pointing out that Sandford for all the other anthems 'simply says "composed by"'.[71] There are several chants by Turner, many of which are included in the Oxford, Christ Church manuscript *Mus. 49*.[72] Sandford uses the same wording as for the *Veni Creator* later, when he describes the Te Deum:[73]

---

[67] See Sandford, 86f. This change was made late: in *Ob MS Tanner 31*, fo. 101, the Litany is still between the *Veni Creator* and 'Zadok the Priest'.
[68] See Illustration 3.1, no. 7; and Ch. 2, fn. 64.
[69] Cf. Ch. 2, fns. 45 and 107. See also Bradley, 88.   [70] Sandford, 89.
[71] Don Oscar Franklin, 'The Anthems of William Turner (1651–1740): an Historical and Analytical Study', unpublished Ph.D. thesis, Stanford University (1967), 23.
[72] See Ruth Wilson, esp. 71–4.   [73] Sandford, 96.

This done, the CHOIRS began to sing, *Te Deum Laudamus, &* [in the margin:] Set or Composed by Dr. *William Child.*

In the end, it is possible that Sandford did not distinguish between a chant, which is certainly plausible to have been used for the *Veni Creator,* and a simple homophonic setting, which could have been used for the Te Deum.

For the anthem 'Zadok the Priest' during the Anointing, Archbishop Sancroft followed the text as in the orders of service from the coronation of Charles I.[74] This is also the same text as given by Baker for the coronation of Charles II, and as found in a printed account of Charles I's Scottish coronation of 1633, which was published in 1685.[75] However, in his final order of service Archbishop Sancroft elaborated on the phrase 'for ever' after 'God save the King' and extended it to read 'Long life ye K~g. May ye K~g live for Ever.'[76] This longer version of the text is also found in Sandford's account and notably Sandford does not give a reference for this anthem text, as he does for the other anthems.[77] With the additional words at the end of the anthem, the archbishop had created a threefold acclamation that is not found in the Biblical source of the text. The origins of this extension remain obscure; the additions might be entirely by Sancroft, maybe included to heighten the effect of the anthem as a direct acclamation of the king in Westminster Abbey, not merely of the Biblical king.

Sandford states that the anthem was 'Composed by Mr *Henry Laws*', and it is generally accepted that this refers to his surviving full setting of the text associated with the previous coronation.[78] However, it must be noted that, as in the previous coronation, the text in Lawes's setting differs considerably from the text in the reports and from that in the orders of service.[79] Because of the differing text, Wood at one point suggested that Lawes's anthem was sung in 'a modified version of the full setting'.[80] There is no evidence that a 'modified version' ever existed and discrepancies between the actual anthems and the texts given by Sandford are not unusual. A repeat of Lawes's setting from 1661 might have had a symbolic meaning at this

---

[74] *Ob MS Tanner 31*, fo. 103. Cf. *Cjc MSS L 12*, p. 26; *L 13*, fo. 9v; and *L 15*, p. 33.

[75] See Baker, 813. For the 1685 printed account see *The Ceremonies, Form of Prayer, and Services used in Westminster-Abby at the Coronation of King James the First and Queen Ann his Consort.* [. . .] *With an Account of the Procession from the Palace to the Abby* [. . .] *With the Coronation of Charles the first in Scotland.* (London: Randal Taylor, 1685), 18.

[76] *Cjc MS L 14*, fo. 34.   [77] Sandford, 91.

[78] Sandford, 91. And see for example Wood, *James II*, 4.

[79] For a comparative table of the different texts see App. A2a.

[80] Bruce Wood, 'John Blow's Anthems with Orchestra', 5 vols., unpublished Ph.D. thesis, University of Cambridge (1977), [in the following 'Wood, thesis'], vol. V, 5.

stage in the ceremony, since it helps in stressing the idea of continuity. The spiritually most significant part of the ceremony would have been accompanied by the same music as at the previous coronation, thus musically/symbolically linking the king with his predecessor. Spink states that 'Zadok the Priest' was performed 'with winds doubling the voices', and this matches with the observations in the previous chapter.[81]

The Anointing ended with 'Behold O God our Defender', the first of two newly introduced anthems in this service. According to the *Liber Regalis*, this text ('Protector noster') was sung as the introit to the mass.[82] As seen above, it had been sung as the entrance-anthem at the beginning of the service at the coronation of James I in 1603; and at the two intermediate coronations, 1626 and 1661, the text had been taken for the anthem during the Homage, which thus became the introit to the rest of the communion service. Archbishop Sancroft had not included an anthem after the Anointing when he entered his revisions in the order of service of Charles I.[83] In his own copy of this order of service, he noted 'Music. a verse.' in the margin, next to the text 'a shallow coife is putt upõ yᵉ K.ˢ Head' after the actual anointing; and later, while the king is vested in his robes for the delivery of the regalia, Sancroft wrote 'Music' in the margin.[84] It is not clear to what these annotations refer. A complete anthem after the Anointing, while the holy oil is drying, is included for the first time in the Tanner MS order of service. The actual text of the anthem, nevertheless, appears to have been an afterthought. The main text (on fo. 104) reads merely 'in yᵉ mean time yˢ short Anthem is to be sung', without giving a text. Sancroft entered the anthem text later on the reverse side of the preceding folio (fo. 103v), its place in the main text being made clear by a '♯'-sign. Sancroft's choice of this anthem for this part of the ceremony was a thoughtful one and shows the archbishop's attention to detail. In his early drafts for the order of service, he appears to have scheduled 'Behold, O God' as the text for the entrance-anthem.[85] However, the text, which refers to 'the Lord's anointed' in the first verse, is much better suited for an anthem after the Anointing than for the entrance-anthem, when the monarch is not yet 'anointed'.

Sandford describes the anthem as a 'short *Anthem*' and 'Composed by Dr. *John Blow*'.[86] This refers most probably to Blow's five-part TrTrATB setting of 'Behold, O God, our Defender', which, as seen above, survives in an autograph score, together with his anthem 'Let thy hand be

---

[81] Ian Spink, *Henry Lawes* (Oxford University Press, 2000), 131. [82] See Legg, *King James*, lix.
[83] *Cjc MS L 15*, p. 33f. [84] *Cjc MS L 13*, fo. 10v.
[85] See *Cjc MS L 15*, p. 9; *Cjc MS L 13*, fo. 6; and *Ob MS Tanner 31*, fo. 97. [86] Sandford, 92.

strengthened'. With only forty-nine bars, which take about two minutes to perform, Blow's setting matches Sandford's description of a 'short' piece perfectly.[87] It is noteworthy that Blow set 'O God', not 'O Lord', as given in Sandford. He thus used the text as originally written by Archbishop Sancroft in the Tanner MS, where the word was changed only as an afterthought.[88] This may indicate that Blow, and maybe all the composers involved, were given the texts to set to music on the basis of the order of service in the Tanner MS.

The Crowning was followed by an anthem based on Ps. 21, beginning 'The King shall rejoice'. Sancroft gives interesting details about the choice of text.[89] He states that after the Crowning 'ye ArchB~p reads ye Confortare', which is followed by the full and underlined text of 'Be strong and of [later added: 'a'] good Courage'. A marginal note to this reads:

~~to be sung. K.J.~~ / The L^d prosper ye Worke of thy Hands upon thee; the L^d ps̲p̲ [prosper] thy Handy work / [the following passage is crossed out altogether:] This of old was no p̲^{t} of ye Exhortŏn; but sung by ye Quire E.2. And after (I suppose) ye 21 Ps. came instead of it.

Thus Sancroft explains that the *Confortare* had by tradition not been part of the archbishop's blessing, the 'Exhortation', but was sung by the choir. In accordance with the rest of the manuscript, 'E.2.' probably refers to Edward II. That would mean that Sancroft assumed that since the coronation of Edward II the *Confortare* had been replaced by Ps. 21. At the same time, he crossed out the reference that the *Confortare* was sung at James I's coronation in 1603 ('to be sung K.J.').[90] The archbishop again paid close attention to detail and appears to have questioned that the anthem should be sung 'during' the reading of the *Confortare* as reported for the previous coronation; his uncertainty is implied by the several changes in the text:

~~Then After this / In ye main while~~ Then ye Quire singeth y^e ~~Anthem~~, Deus in Virtute. ~~Psalm. XXI. 1, 2, 3.~~

In his printed account, Sandford describes that, after the king had been crowned, the 'Choirs' sang the '*Full Anthem* (*Deus in Virtute, &c.*)', a setting of 'The King shall rejoice', 'Composed by Mr. *William Turner* aforementioned'.[91] Turner's setting is lost, but it has been proposed that his anthem 'The Queen shall rejoice' for the coronation of Queen Anne in 1702 was based

---

[87] See Simon Preston's recording with the Choir of Westminster Abbey: *Coronation Music for James II*, Archiv Produktion CD-447 155–2 (Hamburg: Polydor International, 1987), track 7.

[88] *Ob MS Tanner 31*, fo. 103v.   [89] For this and the following see *Ob MS Tanner 31*, fo. 107.

[90] For this reference cf. Wordsworth, xxxviii.   [91] Sandford, 94.

on his 1685 setting.[92] There are notable differences in the texts of these two anthems: for the coronation of James II, both Archbishop Sancroft's manuscript order of service and Sandford's printed account give the first three verses of Ps. 21.[93] 'The Queen shall rejoice', on the other hand, uses verses 1, 3, 5, and 6 of the Psalm. Nevertheless, it is certainly possible that Turner in 1702 reused older material when he wrote his anthem.[94]

It is notable that the king's 'Investiture per Annulum, & Baculum' – the delivery of the Ring and the Rod with the Dove – took place only after the Crowning, and not before, as was to become the custom in subsequent coronations.[95] This suggests that the single moment of the Crowning was not the concentrated climax of the service, but that the investiture ceremonial as a whole was important. Indeed, as Fletcher observed:[96]

The crown is not even by tradition the most important of the emblems with which the Monarch is invested. That distinction our ancestors would have granted to the sceptre, the most ancient symbol of power.

In 1685 the anthem was an integral part of the Crowning: 'While the *Anthem* was singing', the king delivered the orb to the Dean of Westminster and went to the altar to offer his sword which was immediately 'redeemed' by the Earl of Oxford.[97] Furthermore, it was notably not the single moment of the king's crowning that determined when all the peers put on their coronets, but probably the duration of the anthem. In the Tanner MS order of service Sancroft had noted: 'As soon as yᵉ King is crownd, yᵉ Peers put on yʳ Coronets; & so yᵉ provincial Kings of Arms. W.A.'[98] However, it seems as though this instruction is crossed out. Sandford's account of the ceremony strongly implies that the coronets were put on only after the anthem:[99]

The *Anthem* being *sung*, all the PEERS (*viz.* the *Dukes, Marquiss, Earls, Viscounts* and *Barons*) put on their CORONETS.

---

[92] Spink, *Restoration Cathedral Music*, 142. For an edition see Range, thesis, vol. II.

[93] *Ob MS Tanner 31*, fo. 108 and Sandford, 94.

[94] Andrew Gant used the 1702 setting in his recording of the coronation music. See *Music at the Coronation of James II, 1685*, Choir of the Chapel Royal and The Musicians Extra-Ordinary, SIGCD094 (Signum, 2006), track 8. Simon Preston, in his recording (see fn. 87), includes Turner's orchestral setting of 'The King shall rejoice' for the 1697 St Cecilia's Day celebrations. However, in the booklet notes (p. 4) Bruce Wood explains that there is no claim that the piece is similar to the lost anthem.

[95] Sandford, 95.   [96] Fletcher, *British Court*, 80.

[97] For this and the following see Sandford, 94.   [98] *Ob MS Tanner*, fo. 108.

[99] Sandford, 94. See also Bury, 419, who describes this order of events as 'a strange innovation which has not endured'.

With the peers waiting until after the anthem to put on their coronets, the music would have been of decisive structural importance for the ceremonial at one of the key moments in the service.

The king's procession from St Edward's Chair to his throne was accompanied by the Te Deum. Sandford states that it was sung to a setting by Child, without any further details, but his explanation that it was 'Set or Composed' might hint at a simple homophonic setting.[100] It is likely that it was the same setting that may also have been sung at the previous coronation, the one in F.

Next in the service came the Homage. At the two previous coronations the text for the Homage anthem had been 'Behold, O God'. However, in *MS L 13* Sancroft suggested 'or Ps. 89.19–29' as an alternative.[101] The choice of another text for the anthem during the Homage allowed him to take the text of 'Behold, O God' for the newly introduced anthem after the Anointing. Indeed, it was only in his order of service in the Tanner MS that Sancroft introduced both a new text for the anthem during the Homage and the text of the anthem after the Anointing.[102] The text for the Homage anthem begins with verse 20 of Ps. 89: 'God spake sometime in visions.' It is not clear on which grounds Sandford chose the new text: it refers generally to King David, the Lord's anointed and Divine protection. Nevertheless, it could be that Sancroft intended a concrete reference to James II. Verse 26 reads 'I will set his Domination also in the Sea: And his Right Hand in the Flouds.' The choice of this verse could be an allusion to the fact that James, when Duke of York, had been 'noted for his excellent performance as the Lord Admiral of England', and had achieved some fame in the Anglo-Dutch war in the 1670s.[103] Strong goes so far as to suggest that 'James II saw his accession as a progression from a naval to a regal crown.'[104]

Sandford explains that the anthem was 'Composed by Dr. Blow', and Blow's autograph score survives.[105] Blow set the text as in the Tanner MS order of service, this time including the archbishop's later changes.[106] The anthem is written on a grand scale: being scored for eight-part choir

---

[100] Sandford, 96. Cf. also above, fn. 71.   [101] *Cjc MS L 13*, fo. 13v.

[102] *Ob MS Tanner 31*, fos. 104 and 111.   [103] Edie, 351.   [104] Strong, 341.

[105] *Ob MS Tenb. 1008*. For a modern edition and list of sources see John Blow, *Coronation Anthems and Anthems with Strings*, ed. by Anthony Lewis and Watkins Shaw, *MB 7* (1953; 2nd rev. edn 1969).

[106] For this text see App. A2b.

(TrTrAATBBB) and four-part orchestra, Blow does not write for a double choir, but rather uses the number of parts for sophisticated counterpoint within the full texture.[107]

The archbishop's orders of service scheduled the anthem to be sung while the peers did their homage and while the medals were 'scattered'.[108] Sandford lists seventeen 'Lords Spiritual' (the two archbishops, fourteen bishops and the Dean of Westminster), and ninety-seven 'Lord's Temporal' (the secular peers) who paid homage to the king. Not all of the 'Lords Temporal' presented their vows to the king directly, but instead there were representatives from each rank of peerage, who did this in turn, either alone or in a pair: a duke, a marquess, two earls, two viscounts, and two barons (whom Sandford in his list simply calls 'Lords'). After that, all the peers ascended the steps to the throne individually and touched the king's crown and several of them also kissed the king's cheeks. Sandford reports that 'In the mean time the Gentlemen of the Chapel Royal, with the Instrumental Musick, and the Choir of Westminster, sang and played together this* Verse-Anthem, as a solemn Conclusion of the KINGS part of the CORONATION.'[109] As at the previous coronations, it seems likely that the anthem was performed only after the 'Lords Spiritual' and the representatives of the 'Lords Temporal' had paid their homage – and while the remaining peers came to the throne individually.

The Homage marked the end of the king's part of the coronation service; it ended with a fanfare of trumpets and drums and another acclamation of the people shouting 'God save the King'.[110]

The Coronation of the Queen

The ceremonies of the king's coronation were followed immediately by the coronation of the queen. In the Tanner MS the pages which include the Queen's Coronation are, and probably always have been, bound separately. At the same time, Sancroft had, in this manuscript, initially included 'The Communion' following right after the King's Coronation, and later crossed it out.[111] Both facts could indicate that, at some point, the Queen's Coronation was intended to be omitted, perhaps following the example of

---

[107] The lavish choral scoring in this coronation anthem is a rare but not singular occurrence in Blow's oeuvre: for instance, he uses a TrTrAATTBB choir in 'God is our Hope and Strength'.

[108] *Ob MS Tanner 31*, fo. 111 and *Cjc MS L 14*, fo. 46.

[109] For this and the following see Sandford, 97–9.   [110] Sandford, 100.

[111] *Ob MS Tanner 31*, fo. 112.

Queen Henrietta Maria, wife of Charles I, who was not crowned because she was a Catholic.

The orders of service for previous coronations of a queen consort, from 1603 and 1625, had not included any music. At the 1685 coronation, however, Sancroft introduced an anthem to be sung after the queen's crowning, while she walked in procession to her throne, next to that of the king (fig. 1 and 2 in Sandford's 'Ground-Plot'; see Illustration 3.1). It has been suggested that it was the exclusion of the communion that caused Sancroft to make provision for two more anthems as a replacement: the one after the King's Anointing and the other after the Queen's Coronation.[112] However, it is possible that Sancroft had added these anthems even before the communion was ultimately omitted from the service: he included music after the King's Anointing as early as in *MS L 13*, and the queen's anthem is first found in the order of service in the Tanner MS. This is also the first order of service to bring into question the inclusion of the communion. Strikingly, the final order of service in *MS L 14* includes both, the two anthems and the order for the celebration of communion.

In the Tanner MS order of service, Sancroft entered the full text of the queen's anthem; this text was not changed in later versions and is the same as in Sandford.[113] Since there was no precedent for an anthem at this place, the text was probably entirely Archbishop Sancroft's own choice. In stark contrast to all the other coronation anthems, for which the texts are taken from one psalm or book of the Bible, for this anthem Sancroft chose texts from different parts of the Bible: he chose a selection of verses from Ps. 45, beginning with verse 1 'My heart is inditing'; to these he added a verse from Ps. 147 and one from Isaiah 49.[114] Sancroft took care to choose passages that refer directly to a queen; in particular the verse from Isaiah ('Kings shall be thy nursing fathers and their queens thy nursing mothers') stands out, as it is the only part of the text not taken from the psalms. Even though it was not an unusual feature that anthem texts were selected from two or more psalms,[115] the inclusion of other books and the resulting mixture of Biblical texts was rather uncommon.

In his printed account, Sandford reports that the anthem was a '*Verse-Anthem*, performed by the whole *Consort* of *Voices* and *Instruments*' and composed by Henry Purcell.[116] Purcell's anthem 'My heart is enditing' (Z30) survives in an autograph score, where it bears the ascription 'one of the Anthems Sung at yᵉ Coronation of King James the 2.ᵈ'.[117] In this anthem,

---

[112] Franklin, 22.   [113] Sandford, 102.   [114] For the full text see App. A5b, and Illustration 3.5.
[115] See Morehen, 66.   [116] Sandford, 101.
[117] *Lbl. R.M. 20.h.8.*, fos. 53v–66v. For a modern edition see *PS* 17: Sacred Music, part III (1996), 78. NB Purcell wrote 'enditing'.

Purcell wrote on the same grand scale as Blow in 'God spake sometime in visions', employing an eight-part choir (this time scored for TrTrTrATBBB) and four-part orchestra. Wood points out that the combination of clefs in these two anthems is 'unique, at least in English music'.[118] This shared 'uniqueness' might indicate a close cooperation of the two masters. At the same time it is another indication of the coronation music being different from the normal practice in the Chapel Royal. The orchestral accompaniment of 'My heart is enditing' may originally not have been intended by the archbishop, as no such detail is found in any of his orders of service.[119] Thus the inclusion of the orchestra could have been Purcell's idea. The text of the queen's anthem is the longest of the whole service in any case, and the inclusion of orchestral symphonies makes it even longer. The extraordinary length can be explained by examining afresh the structure of the anthem. It is probable that, similar to the entrance-anthem, the queen's anthem was 'laid out upon lines conditioned by the ceremony'.[120] The graphical arrangement of the text in the archbishop's orders of service suggests that he thought of the anthem being in three distinct sections: the passages beginning with 'Hearken, O daughter' and 'Praise the Lord' are clearly singled out.[121] In Sandford's printed account the text is structured in exactly the same way, which supports the idea that the archbishop's graphical arrangement was intended and meaningful (see Illustration 3.2).

ANTHEM IX.

Pſalm 45. Verſ. 1. *My Heart is Inditing of a good Matter ; I ſpeak of the Things which I have made unto the King.* Verſ. 10. *At His Right Hand ſhall ſtand the Queen,* Verſ. 14. *all Glorious within, Her Clothing is of wrought Gold.* Verſ. 15. *She ſhall be brought unto the King in Rayment of Needle-work ; the Virgins that follow Her ſhall bear Her Company.* Verſ. 16. *With Joy and Gladneſs ſhall they be brought, and ſhall enter into the Kings Palace.*

Verſ. 11. *Hearken, O Daughter, and conſider, incline Thine Ear, forget alſo Thine own People, and Thy Fathers Houſe.* Verſ. 17. *In ſtead of Thy Fathers, thou ſhalt have Children, whom Thou mayſt make Princes in all Lands.*

Pſalm 147. Verſ. 12. *Praiſe the Lord, O Jeruſalem : Praiſe Thy God, O Sion.* Iſaiah 49. Verſ. 23. *For Kings ſhall be Thy Nurſing Fathers, and Their Queens Thy Nurſing Mothers.* AMEN. ALLELUIA.

3.2. Text of the anthem after the Queen's Coronation, Sandford, p. 102 (detail). © Dean and Chapter of Westminster.

---

[118] Wood, *James II*, 132.

[119] Cf. below, fn. 142: Sancroft's clear instructions for the Homage anthem.

[120] See above, fn. 48.   [121] See *Ob MS Tanner 31*, fo. 77.

As a matter of fact, Purcell's setting follows this structure and has indeed three distinct sections, the first two beginning with a 'symphony' and the third being singled out by a short ritornello at the end of the preceding section. After all, such a tripartite structure of the anthem corresponds with Sandford's report of the ceremonial proceedings:[122]

As soon as this *Anthem* began, the QUEEN arose from Her *Faldstool*; and, being supported by the Two *Bishops*, and Her Train born, and attended as before, went up to the *Theatre*; and as She approached towards the KING, bowed Her Self reverently to *His* MAJESTY sitting upon His Throne; and so was Conducted to Her Own THRONE on the Left Hand of the KING, where *She* reposed Her Self till the *Anthem* was ended.

The queen's procession to her throne is unlikely to have taken longer than the opening symphony and the first part of the anthem. Since the queen was processing to the music, the change from binary to triple time in the symphony should probably be in proportion, similar to the afore-discussed time changes in 'I was glad'. In the first part of the anthem the inclusion of the text 'At his right hand did stand the queen' is slightly confusing, since the queen was actually going to sit on the king's left hand side. Nevertheless, the verse 'She shall be brought unto the king' recalls her procession to her throne vividly.

Once the queen was enthroned, the choir would have sung the second part, 'Hearken, O daughter'. The text for this part was chosen carefully: verses 11 and 17 ask her to 'forget also thine own people, and thy fathers house'; instead of her 'fathers' she shall have 'children [...] whom thou mayst make princes in all lands'. This might well be an allusion to the queen's foreign, Italian background: she is subtly reminded to 'forsake her homeland and devote herself to her husband's dynasty'.[123] With the explicit reference to her 'own people' this text might at the same time also be a challenge to her Catholicism, since she is now becoming the queen of a Protestant nation. If such a reading of the text was intended it is ironic that the symphony of Purcell's anthem has been described as 'something of a

---

[122] Sandford, 102.

[123] This was first suggested by Eric van Tassel, 'Music for the Church', in Michael Burden (ed.), *The Purcell Companion* (London: Faber, 1995), 101–99, 187f. See lately also Sandra Jean Sullivan, 'Representations of Mary of Modena, Duchess, Queen Consort and Exile: Images and Texts', 2 vols., unpublished Ph.D. thesis, University College, London (2008), vol. I, 249.

landmark', with Purcell 'moving towards the methods of Italian composers nearer his own generation'.[124]

The third section is especially noteworthy: Sancroft (who chose the text) or Purcell (who set it to music) may have seen the potential for a grand finale to the crowning rites which lies within the text. The verse from Isaiah was very appropriate for the ending of the whole of the coronation service since it includes a reference to both king and queen. Musically there is a distinct break before this third section, and the anthem assumes a more representational, stately character. Purcell scored this section for the full forces, writing in a more majestic style. Indeed, the abrupt change from minor to major key, and the homophonic entry of all the voices, together with the instruments, evokes the impression that a new anthem begins at this point.[125] In order to enhance the congregation's perception of the king and queen's splendour, their combined Inthronization was accompanied by some of the most elaborate music of the service. The scene is captured in one of the lavish engravings in Sandford (see Illustration 3.3). Indeed, at the actual ceremony, this would have been a perfect example of the idea of the *tableau vivant* ('living picture'); the royal couple merely sitting in state on their thrones, listening to the music while the ceremonial paused. The onlookers could indulge in this majestic scene until Purcell's anthem was ended.

In his list of queries, the archbishop wrote 'Why no Shouts with <u>GOD SAVE THE QUEEN</u> Drums, & Trumpets after ye Qu.'^s Antheme'.[126] The answer does not survive, but Sandford does not report of acclamations or a fanfare, and nothing is mentioned for any subsequent coronation until 1831: according to one source 'a loud shout of "God save the Queen" resounded through the Abbey' after the Inthronization of Queen Adelaide, consort to William IV.[127] This, however, appears to have been a spontaneous acclamation rather than part of the scheduled ceremonial. Thus it was probably the Hallelujahs at the end of Purcell's anthem that concluded the whole of the 1685 coronation service.

Apart from the anthems, the *Veni Creator* and the Te Deum, Sandford gives little information on the other music of the service. He mentions the

---

[124] Martin Adams, *Henry Purcell: the Origins and Development of his Musical Style* (Cambridge University Press, 1995), 43. Adams, 182f., also provides a more detailed analysis of how Purcell's setting highlights the text of this second section.

[125] Cf. the recording by the Choir of New College under Edward Higginbottom, where this part of the anthem is listed as a separate track. See *Coronation Anthems*, CD 470 226–2 (Decca 2002), tracks 14 and 15.

[126] *Ob MS Tanner 31*, fo. 37.   [127] *MLAI* 18 (1831), 188.

2.3 Ink engraving of James II and Queen Mary, an engraving in Sandford © Dean and Chapter of Westminster

usual organ music for the procession of the king and queen into St Edward's Chapel, where they prepared for the Recess.[128] However, generally no details are known of the instrumental music at the service. Similarly, no details are known of the music at the other ceremonies of the coronation day. Although Sandford includes a very detailed description of the banquet in Westminster Hall, he does not give any information on the music played. Nevertheless, a violin band is seen in a gallery in the Hall in the corresponding engraving, which indicates that, as in 1661, instrumental music was played during the banquet. Also, in the engraving 'The Manner of the Champions Performing the Ceremony of the Challenge' the State Trumpeters and Timpani can be seen in a gallery over the main entrance, while two trumpeters walk in the Champion's procession. These musicians probably contributed fanfares and/or ceremonial music at various stages during the banquet.

Overall, the amount of music by different composers at this coronation is noteworthy: Blow, Purcell, Turner, Child, and Lawes. This variety is especially striking as there is no evidence that they followed an overall programme or 'scheme' that linked their pieces.

Musicians and Performance

As already seen in the discussion of the entrance-anthem, Sandford is an invaluable source also for the performance of the music. The choir consisted of the combined choirs of the Chapel Royal and Westminster Abbey, and Sandford lists all the singers by name.[129] According to this, there was a total of twenty boys and forty-eight Gentlemen: the Choir of the Abbey had eight boys and sixteen Gentlemen, and the Chapel Royal twelve boys and thirty-two Gentlemen. Jeremy Noble argued that, at least in the bass group, the ordering in Sandford does not reflect the respective voices of the gentlemen, but that the names were ordered according to importance in the Chapel.[130] However, it is notable that Purcell, who composed a grand orchestral anthem, is not listed at a prominent place among the basses: he is the fifth out of sixteen.

While there is no evidence that any musician had overall responsibility for the organization of the music, it appears that its performance was

---

[128] Sandford, 103.

[129] Ibid., 69f. See also *Lbl MS Add. 39864*, fo. 49 (transcr. App. B1d, with a short comparison of the other sources). Since this list does not mention as many deputies as Sandford, it was probably prepared before the service and does not reflect the actual singers at the coronation.

[130] Jeremy Noble, 'Purcell and the Chapel Royal', in Imogen Holst (ed.), *Henry Purcell, 1659–1695, Essays on his Music* (London: Oxford University Press, 1959), 52–66, here 62.

led solely by Blow. According to Sandford, Blow received 'Five Yards of fine Scarlet Cloth for his Mantle as Composer', and in the procession from Westminster Hall to the Abbey Blow's place amongst the basses was 'suppl. by *Fra. Forcer*'.[131] A manuscript list of the musicians confirms that Forcer took Blow's place also during the service in the Abbey: 'D.[r] John Blow supplied by Mr Francis Forcer being engaged in beating time to both the Quires (by y[e] little organ)'; and another annotation reads that Forcer 'supplyed his [Blow's] place in the Church also as Organist'.[132] Thus it appears that he sang for Blow during the procession, and, once in the Abbey, played the organ. This would probably have been the afore-mentioned 'little organ', which was situated in the gallery provided for the Chapel Royal.[133] Purcell received payment for 'providing and setting up' this organ, and 'for the removing the same'.[134] Jack Westrup sug-gested that it was Purcell's 'duty to play at the coronation service', the reason being that he was the organist of the Abbey.[135] However, there is no evidence that the actual Abbey organ was used and no payment for a second organist is recorded; it is therefore possible that Forcer was the sole organist. Generally, no special attires or deputies are mentioned for Purcell, Turner and Child, who also composed music for the service.[136] In fact, as already mentioned, Sandford lists Purcell as walking among the basses during the procession from the Hall to the Abbey, whereas Blow employed a deputy singer and was free to conduct.[137] All this implies that Blow was the only conductor, which in turn would mean that he also conducted the music written by the other composers.

It is an interesting side note that all the singers were dressed in surplices. According to Sandford, the boys of the Chapel Royal were also wearing '*Surplices*, with *Mantles* over them of Scarlet Cloth'.[138] David Baldwin has shown that the boys received special state uniforms as early as September 1661, which they have worn at state occasions until the present day.[139]

[131] Sandford, 71.   [132] *Lbl MS Harl. 6815*, fo. 186.

[133] See also Stanley Webb, 'The Westminster Abbey Organs', *MT* 124 (1983), 637–41, here 637; and Franklin B. Zimmermann, *Henry Purcell, 1659–1695: his Life and Times*, 2nd, rev. edn (Philadelphia: University of Pennsylvania Press, 1983), 125.

[134] See Ashbee, vol. V, 273.   [135] Westrup, 54.

[136] At the previous coronation scarlet cloth was provided for the attire of '4 composers of musick 5 yards each'. See Ashbee, vol. I, 17.

[137] Sandford, 71.

[138] Ibid., 69. See also the engraving of the procession, which depicts them wearing cassocks with surplices, and the mantles over these.

[139] David Baldwin, *The Chapel Royal – Ancient and Modern* (London: Duckworth, 1990), 191 and 325.

Nevertheless, it appears that they continued to wear surplices for at least some services.[140]

Sandford does not provide any details about the orchestra, but the number of instrumentalists is confirmed by other sources. 'Habits' were ordered for '36 musicians who are to attend at the Coronation'.[141] Archbishop Sancroft, in the order of service, had stipulated the Homage anthem to be performed 'wth Instrumental Musick of all sorts'.[142] By comparison of the available documentary and pictorial sources it may be suggested that, as in 1661, the orchestra may have included both a full string band and also several wind instruments.[143]

As already mentioned the positioning of the musicians within Westminster Abbey is also very well documented by Sandford. The engravings of the King's Crowning shows all the musicians in their respective galleries and the included ground plan of the Abbey helps to clarify any uncertainties that may arise from the engravings (see Illustrations 3.1 and 3.4).[144] Overall, the arrangement was similar to the previous coronation: the Chapel Royal choir can be seen in a gallery on the left, the South side of the altar, the instrumentalists are in a gallery on the opposite side, and the choir of the Abbey is beyond the crossing, in a gallery also on the right (North) side. Furthermore, the State Trumpeters are positioned in a gallery over the quire entrance. They may have been as many as sixteen trumpets and four drums and kettle-drums in addition to the Drum-Major and Sergeant-Trumpeter.[145]

It is not known how the musicians in their different galleries were coordinated: only one conductor is depicted, leaning forward from the gallery of the Chapel Royal with a long conducting stick in his hand. As Jocelyn Perkins remarked with appropriate puzzlement: 'How in the world they managed to keep together in rendering the lengthy musical programme passes one's comprehension.'[146] At the twentieth-century coronations, for instance, sub-conductors were employed who relayed the beat to the different groups of musicians.[147] It cannot be determined if there were any in

---

[140] Cf. also 'The Sacred Choire', frontispiece engraving in John Weldon, *Divine Harmony, Six Select Anthems* [. . .] (London: Walsh, [1716]). This depicts a service in the Chapel Royal at the time. See also Ch. 1, fn. 96.

[141] See Ashbee, vol. VIII, 261.   [142] *Ob MS Tanner 31*, fo. 111; and *Cjc MS L 13*, fo. 46.

[143] For details see Range, 'Instrumental Musick', 92–8.

[144] Some musicians can also be seen in the engravings of the interior of the Abbey before the service and of the Inthronization of the king and queen.

[145] Sandford, 81 and 105.   [146] Perkins, 23.   [147] See Ch. 8.

A Perspective of WESTMINSTER-ABBY from the High-Altar to the Weſt end, ſhewing the manner of HIS Majeſtie's CROWNING.

W. Sherwin, Sculp.

3.4. The Crowning of James II, engraving in Sandford. © Dean and Chapter of Westminster. The Chapel Royal choir can be seen on the far left, with – presumably – John Blow leaning forward with his conducting stick. The instrumentalists are in a gallery on the opposite side, and the Abbey choir is beyond the crossing, in a gallery on the North side of the quire (right).

1685, but no payment for any is recorded. The conductor in Sandford's engraving therefore is most likely to be John Blow, who presumably conducted all the music of the service. It is possible that this is an actual portrait of him, as there was an order by the king that the figures should be portraits of 'such Persons in the Proceeding'.[148] The coordination of the music at this coronation is even more astonishing, as no rehearsal is documented. The arrangement must have worked out in some way, however, for otherwise it would certainly not have been repeated at succeeding coronations.

The music at the coronation of Charles II in 1661 had been impressive, but the music in 1685 seems to have been even more outstanding. Even though the service was heavily truncated by the omission of Holy Communion, the overall ceremonial was as elaborate as could be. It may have been intended that a royal couple whose religion differed from the majority of their subjects, and from that of the archbishop who crowned them, should have a coronation the splendour of which surpassed everything seen – and heard – before. The sheer display of power and wealth in this impressive ceremony would have reflected and supported their royal authority.

With the two newly introduced anthems, the music formed an even greater, or at least more prominent part of the service. As mentioned above, it is possible that musicians such as Blow and Purcell, who certainly must have felt that the future for the Chapel Royal was looking increasingly precarious, took the opportunity provided by the archbishop and tried to mollify the king's radical position towards this Protestant institution by offering him their most splendid compositions. Overall, the music greatly contributed to enhancing the sumptuous effect of this coronation. The principle of divine right and the power of the monarch were made evident to the people by the display of earthly pomp, at least a glimpse of which was captured for posterity in Sandford's lavish account and in the surviving music.

---

[148] See Strong, 313.

The reign of James II ended after a little more than three years with the 'Glorious Revolution' in 1688. James II's leaving the country was interpreted as a 'flight' and thus an abdication.[1] This meant that there was technically no actual 'revolution' and the previous regime was not condemned per se, but instead the events were interpreted as a lawful succession. Due to the cuts introduced in 1685, the 1689 coronation saw significant revisions in the order of service, and it was this order that became the model for all the following ones up to the nineteenth century.

William III and Mary II, 1689

James II's newly born, Catholic son was not officially acknowledged and therefore the king's eldest daughter, Princess Mary, remained as his successor. However, this succession depended on the military power of Mary's husband, William of Orange. As William would not accept being a mere 'prince consort' and, at the same time, Mary refused to be queen alone, this caused a special arrangement: both were proclaimed joint monarchs on 13 February 1689.[2] Four weeks later, on 16 March, the coronation was proclaimed to take place on 11 April.[3] The choice of date already pointed out that this coronation was going to be somewhat unusual, as the 11 April 'contrary to custom, was neither a feast-day nor a Sunday'.[4]

Historically it was unique to have a king and a queen regnant at the same time (as opposed to a king and a queen consort). Since the queen theoretically had the same status as the king, this presented a significant ceremonial challenge for their joint coronation. The order of service needed to be adjusted considerably as their coronations were not separated: both were anointed, invested, and crowned immediately one after the other. Nevertheless, the ceremonial left some room for distinction, and

---

[1] For a fuller discussion of this and the following see Hoppit, 3 and 15–23. Cf. also Strong, 313.
[2] It has been pointed out that a precedent was found in Mary I and Philip of Spain. See Cannon and Griffiths, 427.
[3] For details see Schwoerer, 108f.   [4] Tomlin, 229.

it has been observed that 'subtle gestures were devised to indicate that [Mary II] was not her husband's equal'.[5] For instance, the queen came second to her husband in all the ceremonies and was anointed only on her hands. At the same time, the new regime may have felt a need to defend its legitimacy – and this was done by 'self-consciously' fashioning the coronation 'to look traditional'.[6] Liturgically, the most important change from the previous coronation was the reintroduction of the communion. However, this was clearly not simply a return to the time-honoured form of the service. After the event the queen herself much regretted the inclusion of 'receiving the Sacrament', pointing out that it was included in the service only 'because it had been left out by my father'; overall she complained that 'there was so much pomp and vanity in all the ceremony that left little time for devotion'.[7] The communion service at this coronation was very much a political statement in openly displaying the monarchs' adherence to the Church of England.[8] This dedication to Protestantism was manifested in the same year by the Bill of Rights, which forbade all Roman Catholics, or anyone married to a Roman Catholic, to succeed to the throne.[9]

The order of service

The Archbishop of Canterbury, William Sancroft, refused to crown the new monarchs, since he felt that he still owed loyalty to James II.[10] In the end, the service was conducted by Henry Compton, the Bishop of London. For his preparations, Compton could use Sandford's printed account of the previous coronation; in addition, he was in contact with Archbishop Sancroft and asked him for the sources he had used to prepare his order of service in 1685 – it is not known whether Sancroft replied.[11]

The 1689 order of service is well preserved in two manuscript copies.[12] These generally appear to present a slightly 'idealized' form: they mention the 'Archbishop', although he was not present at the coronation. An account of

---

[5] Schwoerer, 117.   [6] Ibid., 107.

[7] Mary II, *Memoirs of Mary, Queen of England (1689–1693), together with her letters and those of Kings James II and William III to the Electress, Sophia of Hanover*, ed. R. Doebner (Leipzig: Veit, 1886), 12.

[8] Cf. also Ch. 1, fn. 7.   [9] Cannon and Griffiths, 431.

[10] For the opposition to William and Mary among the British nobility and clerics see Kishlansky, 282.

[11] Compton to Sancroft, undated (*Ob MS Tanner 27*, fo. 8).

[12] *Llp MS 1077* and *Lca MS L 19*, pp. 53–117. The latter is transcribed in Legg, *Three Coronation Orders*.

the coronation was published by order of the Earl Marshal, but it does not include any details of the music.[13] Wood mentions a fragment of an illustrated description of the service, which was 'perhaps another sumptuous volume like those by Francis Sandford' and which 'in all likelihood' gave the composers' names.[14] This work, however, is similar to many other contemporary prints that were mainly concerned with details of the procession from Westminster Hall to the Abbey. The surviving part of the description of the service is very short and superficial and it is unlikely that it formed part of a publication of Sandford's dimensions. A manuscript in the British Library, which is likely to have been planned as a detailed account of the music, unfortunately survives only as an outline; it gives the titles of the anthems with much space beneath, as if to enter the full texts or other details later.[15]

In addition to reintroducing the communion, Compton made some other considerable changes to Sancroft's order of service: for instance, he newly introduced the custom of presenting the sovereign with a copy of the Bible. Ceremonially, however, one of the most significant changes was probably that Compton placed the Crowning after the investiture with the other insignia – at previous coronations the Sceptre had been the last item. This change enhanced the perception of the Crowning as the ceremonial climax of the service.[16] As Fletcher worded it, this alteration 'gave justification to the whole ceremony being called the coronation'.[17] Indeed, the emphasis was furthermore heightened by a change regarding the 'crownings' of the peers; in contrast to the previous coronation when they had put on their coronets at the end of the anthem, they now put them on during the anthem. The order of service stipulated:

As soon as the King and Queen are Crown'd; while the Anthem is singing, the Peers and Peeresses put on their Coronets; and so also the Kings of Arms.[18]

If this is what happened there would have been a return to the order of 1661. However, the aforementioned printed account of the coronation seems to indicate that the peers and peeresses put on their coronets even before the anthem began:[19]

---

[13] *An Exact Account of the Ceremonial at the Coronation of Their Most Excellent Majesties King William and Queen Mary* [...] (London, 1689).

[14] Wood, thesis, vol. V, 7, fn. 30. He refers to *Ob Wood 276A* (105).

[15] *Lbl MS Harl. 6815*, fo. 168: 'The Anthems &c. at ye Coronation of King William & Queen Mary 11. Apr. 1689'.

[16] Perkins, 89, points out that with this change Compton went back to Archbishop Egbert's order from before the Norman conquest.

[17] Fletcher, *British Court*, 85. Cf. also Ch. 1, fn. 52.

[18] *Llp MS 1077*, p. 30 and Legg, *Three Coronation Orders*, 27.

[19] *Exact Account of the Ceremonial*, 3.

[after the King and Queen were crowned] at sight whereof all the People shouted, the Drums Beat and the Trumpets Sounded, and the great Guns at the Tower, and in St. *James*'s Park. &c. were discharged, and all the Peers and Peeresses put on their Coronets.

In any case, it is noteworthy that this coronation is the earliest for which the peeresses, too, are mentioned to have put on their coronets. Indeed, for the 1553 coronation of Mary I, for instance, it is known that, in contrast to the peers, they wore their coronets on their heads from the outset.[20] For the 1685 coronation Sandford mentions only the peers putting on their coronets after the King's Crowning; it can be deduced only from the included engravings that the peeresses put on their coronets at some point between the King's Crowning and the Queen's Inthronization.[21]

The Music

For the procession from Westminster Hall to the Abbey two sources stipulate an anthem to the text 'O Lord, grant the King a long life'.[22] Although this is the traditional text for this anthem, its precise wording is surprising: this time there was both a king and a queen in her own right, and the text of the final anthem in the service was changed accordingly. Thus the text of the processional anthem could have been changed to 'O Lord, grant the King and Queen a long life'. No setting with this text survives, and an adaption of Child's setting, used at the previous coronations, would have been problematic. However, Child was still present at this coronation, being now the most senior Gentleman of the Chapel, which increases the possibility that his setting was used.[23] The 'textual problem' could have been solved by singing the anthem alternately with the words 'king' and 'queen'.

It is not possible to say to which setting the entrance-anthem 'I was glad', was sung. It has been assumed that it was again sung in the five-part full setting associated with the previous coronation; however, the anthem text in the order of service is slightly different from that of 1685.[24] As in 1661, the reports are contradictory as to who sang the anthem. According to one

---

[20] Strong, 207.
[21] Sandford, 94. Bury, 421, states that the peeresses in 1685 put on their coronets as soon as the queen was crowned, but the evidence for this is not clear.
[22] *Lca MS L 19*, p. 88. and *MS Ceremonials 14*: Manuscript papers relating to the coronation.
[23] Cf. Leeper, 557, who states that Child 'acted as a sort of bridge between the old music and the new'.
[24] Bruce Wood, Booklet notes to *Music for Queen Mary*, CDSK 66243 (Sony: 1995), 5. For a comparative table of the texts see App. A3a.

source it was again sung by 'the Choire and Prebends of Westminster'.[25] One of the surviving orders of service, on the other hand, scheduled it to be sung by the combined choirs of the Chapel and the Abbey.[26]

The Recognition was again followed by a trumpet fanfare. From this coronation onwards, as in 1661, the following anthem covered the preparations for the reintroduced communion, the archbishop and bishops vesting themselves and a carpet and cushions being laid out before the altar.[27] For this anthem in 1689 Compton introduced a new text which is not found at any other coronation: 'Blessed art thou, O land'.[28] These words may be rather general in meaning, but in the 1689 context have an obvious political purport: the anthem's text may be read as pointing out how blessed 'the Nation' (Britain) is, having turned again to the 'true religion' (Protestantism). William's claim to the throne is justified, and he is mentioned as the 'son of Nobles'; the queen, however, is not mentioned in this anthem, in contrast to those that came later in the service. There is no evidence for any setting of this text and it cannot be determined if it was actually sung at the coronation.

Compton did not move the Litany back to its traditional place between the *Veni Creator* and 'Zadok the Priest', but retained it where Sancroft had placed it in 1685: it was sung after the Recognition, before the Anointing and notably before the communion service proper began.[29] With the restoration of the communion service, Compton also reintroduced the Nicene Creed, which had been omitted in 1685.[30] However, there was again a change in position: at the earlier coronations it had been sung in the second part of the service, after the Homage, but Compton moved it before the Sermon, Oath, and Anointing. It is not clear what caused this change in position; however, one may wonder if it was done to ensure that the monarchs had publicly declared their faith before being anointed and crowned. According to the order of service both Litany and Creed were sung by the choir, but it cannot be established to which settings.

[25]　See 'Ceremonial of the Coronation of King William and Queen Mary', Appendix viii in Legg, *Three Coronation Orders*, 91–111, here 99. Legg refers to *Lbl Add. MS. 6338* 'a collection of heraldic papers [...] certainly drawn up by one of the officers of arms on duty.'

[26]　*Lca MS L 19*, p. 89: 'The Children and Gentlemen of the Chapel Royal and the choir of Westminster fell off from the Proceeding at the Entrance into the Church, and there staid on the left hand of the middle Ile till their Majesties were Entred, and then went before them and sung the following Anthem.'

[27]　*Llp MS 1077*, pp. 4f. and Legg, *Three Coronation Orders*, 16.

[28]　Ibid. Anthem text transcribed in App. A3b.

[29]　*Exact Account of the Ceremonial*, 3: 'Then the Litany was Sung by the Bishops of *St. Asaph* and *Bangor*, which ended, the Communion Service began.' See also Macleane, 84.

[30]　*Llp MS 1077*, p. 10; Legg, *Three Coronation Orders*, 17f.

Similarly, it is not known to which settings the *Veni Creator* and 'Zadok the Priest' were sung. The first may have been the lost setting, presumably a chant, by Turner from the previous coronation. The text of 'Zadok the Priest' differs considerably from that given in Sandford for 1685 and also from that used in Lawes's setting.[31] It has been proposed that the anthem could have been composed by Nicholas Staggins.[32] Indeed, Staggins was paid 'for fair writing and pricking of compositions for the Coronation Day'.[33] However, he did not hold a composing appointment at the Chapel Royal and no church music by him is known. He was the Master of the King's Musick and the payment could refer to music for the banquet in Westminster Hall. After all, since there is no strong evidence for a new composition of 'Zadok the Priest', it may be assumed that Lawes's 1661 setting was repeated.

After the Anointing followed the anthem 'Behold, O God, our Defender' which had been one of Sancroft's innovations at the previous coronation, perhaps because of the omitted communion. If the latter had been the reason, it is curious that the anthem was not cut in 1689, when the communion service was restored and the service was once again longer in duration.[34] Compton scheduled that the Investiture should begin during the singing of this anthem, with the Delivery of the Spurs.[35] This might indicate that he kept the anthem to enrich the lengthy ceremony of the king's and queen's joint investiture. Compton made considerable changes to the text.[36] The revised text mentions the king explicitly but does not mention the queen; however, Compton changed the words from 'David his Anointed' to the gender-neutral 'thine Anointed'.

The anthem was set by John Blow and survives in an autograph score together with his anthem 'The Lord God is a Sun and a Shield', which was sung later in the service.[37] It has been observed that 'there is no specific reference to the coronation on the manuscript of Blow's setting, but it is the only contemporary setting of these identical words' and moreover that the

---

[31] See App. A3c and cf. App. A1.   [32] Anselm Hughes, 98.

[33] Ashbee, vol. II, 46: 'Warrant to pay £59. 2s. 6d. to Dr. Nicholas Staggins, master of His Majesty's musick, for fair writing and pricking of compositions for the Coronation Day and the Queen's Birthday [...]'

[34] Cf. Bruce Wood, Introduction to John Blow, *Anthems IV – Anthems with Instruments*, ed. by B. Wood, *MB* 79 (2002), xxix: 'The coronation of William and Mary [...] shared [*recte* 'showed'?] some curtailment of the unprecedented elaboration, including two new anthems, which Archbishop Sancroft had introduced in 1685 in order to gloss over the fact that the Catholic James II was not taking the customary Communion.'

[35] *Llp MS 1077*, p. 21 and Legg, *Three Coronation Orders*, 22.

[36] For the different versions of the text see App. A4a.

[37] *Lcm MS 1097*. For details and a modern edition, see Blow, *Coronation Anthems*, in *MB* 7.

opening is the same as in his anthem to the text from the previous coronation.[38] In contrast to this 1685 anthem, in 1689 Blow reduced the scoring to
a four-part choir and changed the earlier setting accordingly. However,
overall the statement that Blow 'reworked' his five-part setting is mislead-
ing.[39] As described above, the text had been changed substantially after the
first verse – and so was Blow's setting: the music after the first verse does not
have any resemblance to that in the 1685 setting; these are two separate
anthems. Thus the four-part setting is not a 'later version' or a 'reworking';
rather it begins with a 'self-borrowing'.

For the anthem after the joint Crowning of the king and queen Compton
introduced a new anthem text beginning 'Praise the Lord, O Jerusalem'. The
text of the first two verses had been sung at the previous coronation, at the
end of the queen's anthem, 'My heart is enditing'. As argued above, they
may then have been understood almost as a separate anthem to mark the
end of both the king's and the queen's coronation. Such an interpretation
might explain why the text was chosen in 1689 to be sung after the joint
Crowning. Compton added two more verses and an Hallelujah to complete
the anthem.[40] In the anthem's second verse, with the kings as 'nursing
fathers' and the queens as 'nursing mothers', the direct reference to
William and Mary was made clear by a significant textual change: in both
the original Hebrew text and in the King James version of the Bible, 'queens'
is preceded by the possessive pronoun 'their'; Compton, however, omitted
this word, thus removing the implication of 'queens' as 'queen consorts' in
the original text, and underlining Mary's status as joint sovereign. The
appropriateness of Compton's choice of text was acknowledged by a later
Archbishop of Canterbury; in 1761 Thomas Secker remarked:[41]

In the 6th Anthem ['Praise the Lord, O Jerusalem'], the Words, For Kings shall be
thy nursing Fathers, & Queens thy nursing Mothers, were peculiarly proper at the
Revolution, when they were first used, because the King & Queen were both
Sovereigns, & both were crowned together.

It has been shown that the setting used in 1689 was almost certainly
Purcell's orchestral anthem (Z46) to the text.[42] The order of service had,
at this place, stipulated a 'short Anthem', which does not easily match

---

[38] Lewis (in *MB 7*), xv.   [39] See for example Wood, Introduction to *MB 79*, xxix.
[40] For the full text see App. A3d. (Compton took the Psalm texts from the Prayer Book.)
[41] *Llp MS 1130*, (38).
[42] This had already been proposed by Anselm Hughes, 81, and a conclusive argument was provided later
by Maurice Bevan, 'A Purcell Coronation Anthem?', *MT* 119 (1978), 938. See also the two responses
to Bevan by Robert Manning in *MT* 120 (1979), 1 and 22, and by Eric van Tassel in *MT* 120 (1979),
114. The only source for the anthem is *Lbl R.M. 20.h.8.*, fos. 75–81. For an edition see *PS* 17, 146.

Purcell's elaborate composition.[43] Moreover, it is interesting that at this coronation the anthem after the Crowning was an orchestral anthem. At previous coronations, elaborate orchestral anthems were sung during the Anointing, the Homage and, in 1685, after the Queen's Coronation. Since this time there was only one, joint, Crowning, one could argue that the anthem after the King's Crowning was combined with the queen's elaborate anthem. Purcell's 'Praise the Lord, O Jerusalem' does not begin in the jubilant manner that might be expected given the text; the opening is of a sombre and serious character in D minor which makes the entry of the choir peculiarly imposing, stately and dignified.[44] For the verse 'For kings shall be thy nursing fathers and queens thy nursing mothers' the manuscript explicitly states 'voices only'.[45] Although this probably still implies the inclusion of the basso continuo it could have been intended to enhance the understanding of this specific text with its direct reference to both kings and queens. At the beginning of the anthem's final third the music changes abruptly to a more straightforward jubilant tone: the key changes to bright D major, in which it remains for the rest of the anthem. With such striking contrasts Purcell's anthem must have produced a splendid effect at the ceremonial climax of the service.[46]

No details are known for the Te Deum, sung before the joint Inthronization of the king and queen. Since Child was present at the coronation, it could be that his setting as in 1685 was repeated. Equally, Blow's setting in D major could have been used: he was a prominent musician at the coronation and parts of his D major service could have been sung later in the service.[47]

As at previous coronations, an elaborate anthem was performed 'while the Peers are doing their Homage, and ye Pardon is reading'.[48] It is striking that this anthem is now called the 'Final Anthem' in the order of service.[49] At the previous coronation Sandford had described it as 'a solemn *Conclusion* of the KINGS part of the CORONATION.'[50] However, in 1689, the remainder of the communion service was still to follow. By naming the anthem the 'Final Anthem', the communion was, via terminology, degraded to a mere appendix of the crowning spectacle. This is astonishing for two reasons: firstly, in liturgical terms, the communion is the most solemn part of the service, and,

---

[43] *Llp MS 1077*, p. 30. Cf. Wood, thesis, vol. V, 8: '[. . .] It is amusing to note that Compton's draft of the service hopefully prescribed a "short Anthem" at this point.'

[44] Cf. Spink, *Restoration Cathedral Music*, 164: 'One wonders, though, why he [Purcell] chose the minor key in view of the words and the occasion.'

[45] *Lbl R.M. 20.h.8.*, fo. 76.   [46] For details see also Range, 'Instrumental Musick', 99f.

[47] See below, fn. 58.   [48] *Lbl MS Harl. 6815*, fo. 169.

[49] *Llp MS 1077*, p. 42; *MS L 19* in Legg, *Three Coronation Orders*, 31.   [50] Sandford, 99.

secondly, as already mentioned, the reintroduction of the communion into the coronation service was of great significance in 1689.

The Homage anthem was 'The Lord God is a Sun and a Shield'. The beginning of its text (Ps. 84, verse 11 in the King James Bible) had been part of the anthem 'Behold, O God our defender' at the 1685 coronation (then in the Prayer Book version as verse 12: 'The Lord God is a Light and Defence'). However, in 1689, Compton gave this verse the prominent role of opening the Homage anthem. This was a thoughtful innovation: during the Homage, the peers of the realm swore allegiance to their new king and queen; at the same time, the music prominently reminded them that God himself was the royal couple's 'Sun', their guidance, and their 'Shield', their defender and protector. Bearing in mind the controversy surrounding the accession of the new monarchs, this allusion was of great importance.

The orders of service indicate four different sections or movements for this anthem, described as 'Chorus', 'Vers', 'Partes', and 'Chorus'.[51] Similar details are not given for any other anthem. An anthem by Blow to the same text and following this scheme survives in autograph score.[52] It is set for four-part TrATB choir and ATB soloists; the accompaniment is a four-part orchestra, but in the choral sections only one instrumental line, in violin clef, is given on top of the vocal parts, and in the verse sections only the continuo line is given. The implication is that the other parts were extracted from the score.

At this coronation the Homage was paid to both king and queen; nevertheless, at about eight minutes in length, Blow's anthem is approximately one third shorter than its 1685 counterpart. The shorter duration might suggest that fewer peers paid homage. Many of them may have followed the example of Archbishop Sancroft and other abstaining clergymen, who still felt they owed allegiance to James II and later became known as 'non-jurors'.

It has been remarked that Blow's 'The Lord God is a Sun and a Shield' is more modest than his 'God spake sometime in visions' from the previous coronation.[53] While this point will be discussed later, it may here be observed that Blow's 1689 anthem has some remarkable features: there is no independent overture, as would have been usual for an orchestral anthem. Instead, Blow writes only a short orchestral introduction to the opening chorus, thus anticipating the development of the orchestral anthem in the eighteenth century. The verse 'For the king and queen trust in the Lord' is of special interest. It is the prime example of a procedure common

[51] *Llp MS 1077*, p. 43; *MS L 19* in Legg, *Three Coronation Orders*, 31. See also App. A4b.

[52] *Lcm MS 1097*. For details see Wood's modern edition in *MB 79* (2002). See also Range, 'Instrumental Musick', 98.

[53] See, for example, Wood, Introduction to *MB 79*, xxiii.

up to the nineteenth century: the aforementioned adaptation of the Biblical texts to the present reign. As long as the monarch was a king any Biblical texts which mention kings might easily – and yet in a subtle way – be understood as referring to both the kings of Israel and the present king. However, when the monarch was a queen, or a king and queen reigning together as in 1689, the text could not easily be understood as referring to her or them. By changing the anthem texts, the Holy Scriptures were related to contemporary Britain more directly: the ideological parallel between the Biblical rulers and the monarchs crowned in Westminster Abbey could not have been pointed out more strikingly.

There are some earlier examples of a similar direct reference to the monarch in an anthem, for instance Orlando Gibbons's 'Grant, Holy Trinity' or Byrd's 'O Lord, make thy servant Elizabeth our Queen'.[54] The anthem word-book *Ob MS Rawl. Poet. 23* includes several anthem texts with explicit reference to Britain or to certain monarchs: (p. 42) 'Praise yee the strength of Britaines hope' by 'William Childe', which mentions 'Charles his Anointed' in the second verse; (p. 147) 'O Lord make Thy Servant CHARLES our Gratious King to rejoice in thy Strength' by 'W.m Cranfoord'; (p. 164) 'Preserve, most mighty Lord [corr. to God] this blessed BRITAINE land' by 'Dr. Bull', which includes the verse 'Lord, bow Thine eare and ever heare, our King, Queen, Prince, Amen.'; (p. 170) an anthem by 'Bird' including the text: 'Behold (O God) with thy all-prospering ey the happy state of this our blessed King [. . .] and ever bleße with true foelicitie our Soverain Lord King CHARLES of Britanie.' However, all these anthem texts are not strictly Biblical and the adaptation of a text from the Scripture appears to have been introduced only at the 1689 coronation. Such a procedure is even more surprising given William III's Calvinism: the Protestants' strict adherence to the Scripture would not condone such a change for plainly political purposes. However, in the event, there appears not to have been any objection; at least none is recorded.

The passage 'Some trust in chariots' is musically interesting as Blow set it in a polychoral manner: at one point the solo ATB group alternates with the four-part choir, which recalls the *cori spezzati* technique mentioned in relation to the previous coronations. The final chorus, 'Blessed be the Lord', leads into 'Amen, Alleluja', which brings the anthem to a stately conclusion employing the full forces.

---

[54] *Lbl MS Add. 65477*: manuscript copy by V. Novello with the ascription 'for the King's Day / (the "Full" Parts only)': 'Grant, Holy Trinity, that thy servant Charles our King may evermore rejoice in thee [. . .]' The anthem by Byrd was subsequently changed according to each reign. See for example *Lbl MS Harl. 6346*, fo. 2r./p. 13: 'O Lord make thy servant Charles our King', and similarly *Oxford, Christ Church (Och) Mus. 1221*, p. 310: 'O Lord, make thy servant Our soveraigne Lord King Charles'.

Given the importance of the reintroduction of the communion at this coronation, it is surprising that only few details are known of the liturgical music. Notably, the choir sang the Offertory anthem 'Let your light so shine'.[55] The setting cannot be established but it is noteworthy that this text should have been sung. It had probably not been sung at earlier coronations, and although its inclusion followed the order for the communion service according to the 1662 Book of Common Prayer, it is there scheduled only to be read. After this the choir sang 'Let my prayer come up', in a presumably new setting by Blow, a short and simple composition for four parts which is included in the same manuscript as his other anthems for this coronation.[56] This accompanied the royal couple's descending from their thrones and going to the altar. Both of these anthems were probably performed with organ accompaniment, as is confirmed for the latter: 'Then the Organ plays, and the Quire singeth [. . .]'

The order of service scheduled the choir to sing the Sanctus and Gloria, the latter of which to accompany the king and queen's 'return to their Throne'.[57] These also could have been settings by Blow, perhaps from his services in D or in G.[58] This was probably the first time that the Gloria at a coronation service was scheduled to accompany this procession and it was kept in this place in all subsequent orders of service up to the nineteenth century. Similar to the reports of the 1661 coronation, the order of service makes provision for 'the Organs playing all the while' during the procession of the king and queen from their thrones into St Edward's Chapel.[59]

Musicians and performance

It is commonly stated that the music at the coronation of William III and Mary II was less grand than that at the previous coronation.[60] However, firstly, it seems that not much earlier music was re-used: at least four anthems

[55] For this and the following *Llp MS 1077*, pp. 44f., and Legg, *Three Coronation Orders*, 32.

[56] *Lcm MS 1097*. For details and an edition see *MB 7*. An additional source to those given by Lewis is *Lbl MS Add. 33292*, fo. 110v.

[57] *Llp MS 1077*, p. 49; Legg, *Three Coronation Orders*, 33f.

[58] The D major service contains a Sanctus and Gloria in Excelsis. For an edition see Musical Appendix no. 18, *The Choir, and Musical Record* 1 (November, 1863), 197–202. The service in G includes three settings of the Creed and two each of the Sanctus and Gloria. For details see Bruce Wood, 'John Blow', *NG* 3, 718–27, here 722f.

[59] *Llp MS 1077*, p. 51; Legg, *Three Coronation Orders*, 35.

[60] See, for instance, Wood who calls it 'less elaborate' (Introduction to *MB 79*, xxix) and a 'less lavish affair' (booklet notes to *Coronation Anthems*, CD 470 226-2 (Decca, 2002) [p. 1]). Spink, *Restoration Cathedral Music*, 164, describes the whole service as 'a more modest affair than the previous one'.

are known to have been newly written for the occasion, two of them orchestral anthems. Secondly, the performing forces were still considerable. No numbers are known for the Abbey choir, but they are well documented for the Chapel Royal. The number of boys appears to have been the same as in 1685: in a warrant from March 1688/89 coronation liveries for the 'master of the children and twelve children of the Chapel' were ordered.[61] The number of Gentlemen was smaller than in 1685.[62] While there had been thirty-two Gentlemen in 1685, for 1689 a list in the Chapel Royal Old Cheque Book gives the names of only twelve Gentlemen plus Child, Blow and Purcell as three organists. The smaller number of Gentlemen has been described as 'an economy clearly reflected in the reduced vocal scoring of several of the anthems written for the occasion'.[63] However, the slightly smaller number of adult singers cannot have been the reason for the reduction in treble parts from two to one, as at the beginning of Blow's 'Behold, O God'. A reduction in parts does not automatically imply less grandeur in any case. A 'decline' in the performing standard of the coronation music was not noted at the time; in fact, reports about this coronation stress that it was 'performed [...] much in the manner the former was'.[64] Furthermore, a drastic decline in standard is unlikely: with Blow, Purcell and Turner, the Chapel had still the same personnel as in 1685, and regular services had continued for James II's daughter, Princess Anne (later Queen Anne), a staunch Anglican.

In addition, it appears that the orchestra at this coronation was, if anything, slightly bigger than that in 1685 (when there were thirty-six musicians). In a warrant dated 22 March 1688/89 the provision of 'scarlet mantles for the master of the musick and 38 Musicians that are to attend at their Majesties' coronation' was ordered; and shortly after that a 'Lyst of the Musick who are to attend at theire Maties Coronation' provided the names of thirty-seven musicians who would all have been instrumentalists.[65] As in 1685 the order of service stipulated the Homage anthem to be performed 'with Instrumental Musick of all sorts'.[66] Again, it may be suggested that the orchestra accompanying the choir included both string and wind instruments.[67] As at previous coronations, a new organ was built in the gallery used

---

[61] Ashbee, vol. II, 23f.

[62] See the respective entries in the Old Cheque Book, transcribed in Ashbee and Harley, vol. II, 135f. and 140; cf. Sandford, 69.

[63] Wood, thesis, vol. V, 7.

[64] See Narcissus Luttrell, *A Brief Historical Relation of State Affairs from September 1678 to April 1714*, 6 vols. (Oxford University Press, 1857), vol. II, 520.

[65] Ashbee, vol. II, 23 and 25.   [66] *Llp MS 1077*, p. 42. Cf. also Ch. 2, fn. 142.

[67] For details see Range, 'Instrumental Musick', 98–100.

by the Chapel Royal.[68] Holman suggests that the Abbey organ supported the main choir while 'a portable instrument' played in the verse passages.[69] If this was the case, it would be the earliest use of the Abbey organ at a coronation.

Style

In reference to William III's austere tastes, Blow's anthem 'The Lord God is a Sun and a Shield' has been described as 'probably long and elaborate enough for the new king'.[70] However, the reason for what superficially seems like a 'simplification' of the music may have had more significance; the musicians responsible may have realized that the 1685 music was altogether too elaborate for its purpose. It is conceivable that Blow's straightforward setting of 'The Lord God is a Sun and a Shield' was more impressive, and was easier to perform, in a packed Westminster Abbey than his highly complicated 'God spake sometime in visions' from the previous coronation. The sophistication of the latter could probably not easily be discerned in the surroundings of the vast packed building, with the Lords paying their homage at the same time and people grabbing for the coronation medals that were scattered – one need but recall Pepys's comment about the anthem during the Homage in 1661.[71] At coronations, the music helped to enhance the representation of the monarchy, and for this purpose it had to appeal to the audience at the ceremony very directly. While the 1685 coronation was still a ceremony for the upper echelons of society, in which the music could be considered as mainly intended for the worship of God, this had changed by 1689. The service itself had become more of a 'spectacle', with a clearly growing public interest in it.[72]

There were other signs that pointed out the new priorities at this coronation. The 'Bill of Rights' had won Parliament more power at the expense of that of the Crown, and the House of Commons was present at a coronation for the first time.[73] A special gallery was erected for them in the North transept, facing the thrones.[74] Thus in 1689 the representatives of

[68] Webb, 637. [69] Holman, *Four and Twenty Fiddlers*, 401.

[70] Wood, thesis, vol. V, 8. See also Wood, Introduction to *MB* 79, xxix, where he describes the anthem as 'a far more modest affair than its 1685 counterpart ['God spake sometime in visions']'.

[71] See Ch. 2, fn. 131. [72] Strong, 323. Cf. also Queen Mary's own comments (see fn. 7).

[73] Arthur Penrhyn Stanley, *Historical Memorials of Westminster Abbey*. 5th edn, with the author's final revisions (London: John Murray, 1882), 79.

[74] Strong, 323, and Schwoerer, 117, whose evidence consists of contemporary reports and an order to Christoper Wren for the building work. Some writers state that the gallery was behind the altar, above St Edward's Chapel. See Stanley, 79 and Purey-Cust, 41. However, the gallery for the House of Commons over the altar is first reported for the coronation of William IV.

the Commons must have had some of the best places from which to see and hear the ceremonies. Indeed, their presence had a considerable effect on the ceremonial. Unlike their predecessors, William and Mary were not crowned in the Sacrarium, before the High Altar, but under the crossing. According to a contemporary report, for their crowning

Their Majesties were conducted to Their Regal Chairs placed on the Theatre (near the East side thereof) that they might be more Conspicuous to the Members of the House of Commons, (who, with their Speaker, were Seated in the North Cross) [. . .][75]

The coronation of William III and Mary II marked a caesura in the history of the coronation service. Without doubt, ceremonially it was the coronation of James II and his queen in 1685 that had a great impact on those that followed; although it was different from the 'norm' in that it did not include the communion, it was considered as a model for some time.[76] This impact was probably mainly due to its accessibility in Sandford's lavish and detailed publication. Nevertheless, it was the order of service from 1689 that became the direct model for the following coronations.[77]

Queen Anne, 1702

The joint monarchy after the Glorious Revolution lasted for little more than five years. Following the death of Mary II in 1694, her husband continued to reign alone. William III died on 8 March 1702 and was succeeded by his sister-in-law, Princess Anne, the younger daughter of James II.

The order of service for Queen Anne's coronation on 23 April was compiled by the Archbishop of Canterbury, Thomas Tenison, and is preserved in a manuscript in the Library of Lambeth Palace.[78] Tenison closely followed the order of service from the previous coronation; even in their physical appearance the two manuscripts are very similar. Henry Compton,

---

[75] *Exact Account of the Ceremonial*, 3.

[76] Cf. *LG*, no. 3800, 9–13 April 1702: 'Advertisements. The History of the Coronation of King James the Second [. . .] which will chiefly be followed at the Coronation of Her present Majesty Queen Anne [. . .]' See also Ch. 3, fn. 28.

[77] Legg, *Three Coronation Orders*, xxx.

[78] *Llp MS 1078*: 'A / FORMULARY / of that part of the / SOLEMNITY / which is performd in ye Church / at the / CORONATION / of her Majestie / QUEEN ANNE / at / WESTMINSTER / 23. Apr. 1702.' A nearly exact copy of this is *Lbl MS Harl. 6336*, fos. 16–21. Indeed, a warrant was written for 'four Manuscript Books of the Church Service & Ceremony of the Coronation, One for the Queen, One for the Prince, One for the Arch Bishop of Canterbury & One for the Dean of Wesm:^r to be richly bound [. . .]' See *London, National Archives, formerly Public Record Office (Lna) LC 2/15*, 'N. 34'.

who had compiled the earlier order of service, was still in place as Bishop of London (and thus also Dean of the Chapel Royal) and Tenison could easily have asked him for advice. A further valuable source for Queen Anne's coronation is *Lbl MS Harl. 6118*, a shortened copy of the order of service, 'which appears to have belonged to some herald or officer concerned in arranging the whole affair'.[79]

In contrast to the previous two coronation services, this time there was only one act of crowning: Queen Anne's husband, Prince George of Denmark, was not crowned and did not play any significant role in the service as a whole.[80] According to E.W.F. Tomlin this caused much disapproval at the time, but he also points out that the prince was allowed to pay homage with the peers and sat at the queen's table during the Coronation Banquet.[81] Even though the fact that there was only one crowning should have meant a shorter service than at the previous two coronations, the total length was still considerable. The ceremonies would presumably have started around midday (as reported in 1685), but the queen was not crowned until four in the afternoon, leaving much of the service still to take place.[82]

For the anthem during the procession from Westminster Hall to the Abbey, the text of the traditional 'O Lord, grant the King a long life' would again have been changed appropriately. Anthems with the text 'O Lord, grant the Queen a long life' exist by William Croft, James Hawkins, and Henry Aldrich.[83] While these are sometimes suggested as coronation anthems, none of them is a likely candidate. Croft's anthem includes extensive verse sections – even one verse for eight parts – and therefore is not very suitable to be sung by a full choir in an outdoor procession; Hawkins and Aldrich were not linked with the Chapel Royal. There is also a setting of the words by John Church, Gentleman of the Chapel Royal at the time of the coronation and later Master of the Children of Westminster Abbey (1704–40).[84] Anselm

---

[79] J.R. Planché, *Regal Records: Or, A Chronicle of the Coronations of the Queens Regnant of England* (London: Chapman and Hall, 1838), 97.

[80] For a detailed study of the prince's general role see Charles Beem, '"I am her majesty's subject": Prince George of Denmark and the transformation of the English male consort', *Canadian Journal of History* 39 (2004), 457–87, for the coronation esp. 478.

[81] Tomlin, 229.   [82] See *LG*, no. 3804, 23 April to 27 April 1702. Cf. Ch. 3, fn. 34.

[83] *Ob MS Tenb. 788*, no. 8 (Croft); *Lbl MS Harl. 7341*, p. 198 (Hawkins); *Lbl MS Add. 17840*, fo. 35 (Aldrich).

[84] *Lbl MS Harl. 7341*, p. 547: 'O Lord grant ye Queen a long life / Psalm ye 61. ver: 6. 7. Psal: 8. v: 9. Psal: 132. v: 9. / A Full Anthem / Compos'd by Mr John Church, one of ye Gentlemen of ye Chappel Royall; Master of ye Boys, & one of the choir of St Peters Westminster'.

Hughes states that it is 'highly probable' that this setting was sung at the coronation.[85] From its structure, Church's anthem would indeed have been perfectly suitable for the occasion, being a full anthem with only short verses for the three lower parts. In these verses, Church combines the text with that of another traditional coronation anthem, 'Behold, O God our defender'. The opening bars and text ('O Lord, grant the Queen') are used like a refrain to give the anthem a firm structure. The act of repeating these significant words gives them special emphasis, and could have been a means to ensure that more people in the crowd could hear them. At some places an independent bass line indicates an obligatory accompaniment. As at previous coronations, the anthem would have been accompanied by instruments, and the surviving organ version could be an arrangement for later performances in the Chapel Royal. However, being mostly in sombre E minor this anthem seems less suited for so joyful an occasion as the coronation procession, and it is in fact not clear why Hughes declared it 'highly probable' that this piece was sung. Thus, after all, it seems that the most plausible candidate for the anthem during the procession is an adaptation and repeat of Child's earlier setting; the fact that Child's piece was performed in Queen Anne's reign is confirmed by several sources with the altered text.[86]

For the queen's entrance into the Abbey the order of service stipulates the choir 'going before her to sing' the anthem 'I was glad'.[87] This was most likely the straightforward, four-part full anthem by Francis Pigott who was organist of the Chapel from 1697 until his death in 1704.[88] As shown in detail for the 1685 coronation, the anthem could have been scheduled to be sung in two distinct parts, divided by the *Vivat*s. The first part of the anthem (up to bar 36) would equal sixty-three steps: two in each 4/4 bar and one in each 3/2 bar. This is about the distance from the West door to the screen – Queen Anne, not in best health (see below), would probably have made smaller steps than James II in 1685 (about fifty-six bars/steps). As in the 1685 setting, the harmonic progressions are far more 'daring' in the second

---

[85] Anselm Hughes, 88. Spink, *Restoration Cathedral Music*, 295, suggests that the anthem was written for Queen Anne's accession. For the music see Range, thesis, vol. II.

[86] See the entries in Richard Andrewes, Anne Osborne, and Lydia Smallwood, *A Catalogue of Ascribed Music in pre-1800 Music MSS Deposited in British Libraries*, compiled between 1965 and 1969, prepared for microfilming by Richard Andrewes in 1981 [microfilm]. See also Range, thesis, vol. I, 104.

[87] *Llp MS 1078*, p. 1f.

[88] For details see Matthias Range, 'Francis Pigott's "I was glad" and its Performance at Three Coronations', *Music in Eighteenth Century Britain* 19 (2008), 47–57. For a transcription and a full list of sources see Range, thesis, vol. II.

part, beginning at 'O pray for the peace of Jerusalem' (bar 37).[89] The use of extended polyphony is also confined to this second part, and the Gloria Patri is very elaborate, accounting for forty-three of the anthem's total hundred-and-one bars. Having arrived in its gallery the choir would have been able to concentrate on the conductor; also it could have been supported by instrumental accompaniment. As at the previous coronation, it is possible that the whole anthem was sung by the combined choirs of the Abbey and the Chapel, as is suggested by one source.[90]

After the Recognition came the anthem 'The Queen shall rejoice', the text being an adaptation of Ps. 21. In earlier coronations, this text had been sung after the Crowning. However, at the previous coronation, it had been replaced by 'Praise the Lord, O Jerusalem' and was not sung at all; in 1702, Archbishop Tenison kept this change, but also reintroduced the text of Ps. 21, using it for the anthem after the Recognition. 'The Queen shall rejoice' was composed by William Turner. The main source is Thomas Tudway's collection of anthems, where it is described as 'ye 2^d Anthem Sung at y^e / Coronation Solemnity / of her Majesty Queen Ann'.[91] The anthem is scored for four-part choir (the treble line is divided for three bars only), probably accompanied by the organ or instruments doubling the vocal parts. It is a straightforward full setting and Turner set the text in a lively and joyful manner. It has been proposed that in this 1702 setting Turner 'merely adapted the words of the earlier piece', referring to 'The King shall rejoice' which he is known to have written for the 1685 coronation.[92] Since that setting is lost, this claim is difficult to substantiate; the differences in the texts are significant and would have required major revisions. However, the opening of the anthem and the final Hallelujah are similar in style to the 1685 coronation anthems by Blow and anthems by Purcell, suggesting that Turner may indeed have used some earlier material.

As in 1689, the next musical items were the Litany, the Nicene Creed and the *Veni Creator*.[93] No details about the settings are known, but for the latter two the order of service states that the archbishop was to begin them and the choir sing them. The text for 'Zadok the Priest' in the order of service is the same as in 1689, and thus again differs from that in Lawes's setting from

[89] NB especially the change from F major to B major from b. 50 to b. 51.

[90] *Lbl MS Harl. 6118*, fo. 10v: 'The Children of the Chapel, the Choir of Westm.^{r}, and the Gent. of the Chapel, when the Anthem is ended, doe not enter the Choir, but fall off, and repair to the Galleries above the North side the Choir, except such as have another Gallery near the High Altar, and go no more in the Proceeding.' See also Planché, 97.

[91] *Lbl. MS Harl. 7341* (Tudway Collection, vol. V, 1718), p. 147. For a new transcription and list of sources see Range, thesis, vol. II.

[92] Spink, *Restoration Cathedral Music*, 142.   [93] *Llp MS 1078*, pp. 8f. and 18.

1661. Nevertheless, without evidence for any other setting of the text, one may assume that Lawes's anthem was again repeated.

After the Anointing came 'Behold O God our Defender', following the precedent established in 1685 and 1689. However, Archbishop Tenison shortened the text, so that it now consisted only of two psalm verses with a final Hallelujah; furthermore, 'King' was changed to 'Queen', making the reference obvious.[94] Since Blow's four-part setting to the text from the previous coronation is, at two minutes, already very short, it is possible that he simply discarded the textual changes and repeated his anthem as it stands.

As already mentioned, for the anthem after the Crowning Tenison retained the text of 'Praise the Lord, O Jerusalem'. A new setting of this was contributed by Jeremiah Clarke, a fact that is somewhat unusual: Clarke was not composer or organist of the Chapel and was only a 'Gentleman-extraordinary' at the time of the coronation. However, the link of the anthem with the coronation is clearly secured by the sources, the most important of which is *Ob MS Tenb. 1232*, a volume with odes and anthems mostly by Clarke.[95] Whereas the music is written by a copyist, the table of contents and several annotations are in the hand of William Croft, Clarke's Chapel colleague and later Master of the Children and Composer of the Chapel.[96] Clarke's 'Praise the Lord, O Jerusalem' is headed by the copyist 'Anthem / For ye Coronation of Queen Anne' and there is no comment by Croft.[97] The anthem survives in many eighteenth-century manuscript copies and furthermore William Boyce published it in the second volume of his *Cathedral Music* in 1768. All this indicates that Clarke's anthem must have been both a popular and well-known part of the eighteenth-century repertoire. Indeed, Charles Burney described it enthusiastically as 'extremely natural and agreeable, and as modern and graceful as the gravity of the choral service, will, with propriety, allow'.[98]

Clarke's setting is stylistically similar to those by Pigott and Turner, displaying a preference for a homophonic and melodious style. Also, they all follow the tradition of the Restoration anthem in that each new line of text is stressed by new musical material; in this way they are divided into different sections rather than independent movements.[99] While in all the

---

[94] *Llp MS 1078*, p. 24 (transcr. App. A4a).

[95] For a list of sources and new transcription see Range, thesis, vol. II.

[96] For biographical details on Croft see below.   [97] fos. 16–17b.

[98] Charles Burney, *A General History of Music: from the earliest ages to the present periode: To which is prefixed, A Dissertation on the Music of the Ancients*, 4 vols. (London: Printed for the author, 1789), vol. III, 597.

[99] Cf. Thomas F. Taylor, 'The Life and Works of Jeremiah Clarke (*c.* 1673–1707)', unpublished Ph.D. thesis, Northwestern University (1967), 19f.

manuscript sources the anthem is scored for four-part choir only, Boyce, in his edition, added a figured bass line. At the coronation the anthem would certainly have been performed with at least organ accompaniment.

Clarke's setting of the second verse, 'For Kings shall be thy nursing fathers and Queens thy nursing mothers' deserves special attention. This passage, from the Book of Isaiah (49:23), would already have been very familiar to the coronation congregation, since it was on this text that John Sharp, the Archbishop of York, had preached the sermon earlier in the service.[100] In the two previous coronations this verse had self-evidently been appropriate since it refers to both kings and queens. For Queen Anne's coronation the text posed a problem, as there was no king. In the previous coronation there had already been a slight textual change to reflect Queen Mary's status as joint sovereign, namely the omission of the word 'their' before 'Queens'. In his sermon, the Archbishop of York had used the original version of the text, speaking of 'Kings [...] and their Queens'.[101] However, when it came to the text of the anthem, Archbishop Tenison quite rightly took the version from the previous coronation and omitted the word 'their'. Robert Bucholz argued that this text generally was chosen to uphold Queen Anne's image as the 'common mother' of her subjects – in contrast to Elizabeth I's image of a '"Virgin Queen" who was 'wedded to her first love, the people of England'.[102] In fact, Archbishop Sharp in his sermon made a strong point about the queen being her subjects' 'nursing mother'.[103]

Clarke found an original solution for the setting of this verse (see Example 4.1). He made it clear that his anthem was for the coronation of a queen alone. The first half of the text (concerning 'Kings') is presented only fleetingly in the lower voices, but in the second half the word 'Queens' attracts special attention by being sung on a long top 'f' in the treble part; in addition to that, the lower voices join in with staggered entries (ATB, bars 19–21), so that the words 'and Queens' are heard four times before the

[100] John Sharp, *A Sermon preach'd at the Coronation of Queen Anne* [...] (London: printed and sold by H. Hills, 1708).

[101] At the beginning Sharp diplomatically avoided the issue by generally speaking about 'Christian Princes' (p. 4) and later he observed that '*Queens* are joyn'd as equal sharers with *Kings*, in making up the Blessing which is here promis'd To God's People.' (p. 11).

[102] R[obert] O. Bucholz, *The Augustan Court: Queen Anne and the Decline of Court Culture* (Stanford University Press, 1993), 206.

[103] See esp. p. 15: 'But always bear in Mind what Returns of Duty, and Gratitude, and Filial Obedience, this Consideration of the Queen's being a Nursing-Mother to her People doth call for from us, and all other her Subjects.' For a study of Queen Anne's public image see Edward Gregg, *Queen Anne* (first publ. 1980 by Routledge and Kegan Paul, new edn Yale University Press, 2001), chapter 5/ pp. 130–50: '"Thy nursing Mother" – The Role of the Monarch, 1702–14'.

Example 4.1. Setting of Isaiah 49:23 in J. Clarke, 'Praise the Lord, O Jerusalem' (1702), (extract).

trebles sing the whole phrase 'and Queens thy nursing mothers'; the repeat of the section with the staggered entries heightens the effect all the more.

It is interesting to compare Clarke's setting with both Purcell's 'My heart is enditing' from 1685 and Purcell's 'Praise the Lord, O Jerusalem' from the 1689 coronation (see Example 4.2). While both of these works include the verse from Isaiah, the earlier one was written for a queen consort, the latter one for the joint sovereign Queen Mary II. It appears that Clarke was not the first composer to take the opportunity of a textual interpretation of this verse in his music. One might already see some special emphasis on 'Queens' in Purcell's second setting; it is Clarke, however, who makes the importance of this word in his anthem unmistakably clear.[104]

Much of Clarke's anthem is in full style, and reduced scoring would probably apply only to the polyphonic passages: in *Tenb. 1021* the final Hallelujah is headed 'Chorus', which would imply that the immediately preceding passage was a verse. By generally adopting a simple, more homophonic approach, Clarke manages to give his anthem a combination of brevity and grave dignity most appropriate for the occasion. In addition, with its brevity it also follows more exactly the demands of the order of service that 'ye Choir singeth this short Anthem'.[105]

From a ceremonial point of view it is noteworthy that this was the first coronation at which the order of service instructed that 'As soon as the QUEEN is crowned, the Peers, &c. put on their Coronets and Caps.'[106] The anthem, which had still been mentioned in the 1689 order of service, was removed from this rubric. Thus it would have been solely the moment of the queen's crowning that determined the peers' putting on their coronets and the anthem, sung only after this, no longer had a structural role at the Crowning. During the queen's procession to the throne for her inthronization the choir sang the Te Deum, the identity of which cannot be established.[107]

As in 1689, the order of service scheduled the 'Final Anthem' for the Homage, to be performed 'while the General Pardon is proclaim'd'.[108] The anthem was probably again performed during the individual peers' approaching the throne. Celia Fiennes, who was present in the Abbey, reports about the Homage that 'all this while anthems are sung and the Medals are cast'.[109] Her use of the plural form 'anthems' might simply refer

---

[104] For possible references to Purcell's anthem 'O God, thou art my God' (Z35) see Range, thesis, vol. I, 108 and 111.

[105] *Llp MS 1078*, p. 34.   [106] *Llp MS 1078*, p. 35.   [107] *Llp MS 1078*, p. 40f.

[108] *Llp MS 1078*, p. 46, and *Lbl MS Harl. 6118*, p. 37/fo. 19 .

[109] Celia Fiennes, *The Journeys of Celia Fiennes*, with an introduction by John Hillaby (London: Macdonald, 1983), 343.

Example 4.2. Settings of Isaiah 49:23 in H. Purcell, 'My heart is enditing' 1685 Z30, and 'Praise the Lord, O Jerusalem' (1689) Z46, both taken from *PS* 17 (extracts).

Example 4.2. (cont.)

to the separate sections of one anthem rather than to several independent works. The text of the Homage anthem was again a selection of verses from Pss. 84, 20, and 21 – 'The Lord God is a Sun and a Shield'. However, the text from 1689 was shortened considerably.[110] The reason for the shortening of the text has been seen in the fact that some of the verses – like the phrase 'no good thing will he withhold from them that walk uprightly' – might have been embarrassing for the queen.[111] The queen was in poor health and she had 'the Conveniency to be carried in a low open Chair all the Way' during the coronation procession.[112] Indeed, even on contemporary playing cards the queen was depicted being carried in a sedan-chair, under a canopy.[113] Fiennes confirms that the queen was able to walk unaided, at least during the service in the Abbey.[114] Nevertheless, her walking was probably still not exactly 'upright', thus rendering the phrase inappropriate. Another reason proposed for the shortening of the text is the queen's gender: the verse beginning 'Some trust in chariots' had been 'presumably rejected as being too martial for a queen'.[115] However, notably the 'chariots' and 'horses' refer to 'the others', the heathens; the contrasting 'We' refers to the people of God, which at the coronation could be understood as the British. This verse would hence be rather the opposite of 'martial' – calling for the trust in God, not in chariots and horses.

The surviving sources provide no information on the composer of the anthem. As for the previous coronations, the order of service states that it should be performed 'with Instrumental Musick of all sorts'.[116] It has been suggested that Blow reworked his 1689 orchestral setting of 'The Lord God is a Sun and a Shield'.[117] The evidence for Blow as composer is the programme for a concert in London, organised by Cavendish Weedon

---

[110] See App. A4b.

[111] See Bruce Wood, 'Cavendish Weedon: Impresario Extraordinary', *The Consort* 33 (1977), 222–4, here 223f., and Burrows, *Handel and the English Chapel Royal*, 38.

[112] Abel Boyer, *The History of the Life and Reign of Queen Anne digested into Annals*, vols. I–XI for 1702–1712 (London, 1703–1713), vol. I, 25. For the same see *The Life and Reign of Her late excellent Majesty Queen Anne* [...] (London, 1738), 45. See also Luttrell, vol. V, 162.

[113] See James Sutherland, *Background for Queen Anne* (London: Methuen, 1939), illustration between pp. 54 and 55.

[114] Fiennes, 341: 'Thus to the Quire doore she came, then leaveing the cannopy (the chaire she left at the Abby doore) she is conducted to the Alter [...]'

[115] Wood, 'Cavendish Weedon', 223.   [116] *Llp MS 1078*, p. 46.

[117] Wood, 'Cavendish Weedon', 223f. This suggestion was followed by, for instance, Donald Burrows, 'Theology, Politics and Instruments in Church: Musicians and Monarchs in London, 1660–1760', *Göttinger Händel-Beiträge* 5 (Kassel: Bärenreiter, 1993), 145–60, here 155, and Burrows, *Handel and the English Chapel Royal*, 38.

and performed shortly after the coronation.[118] This programme includes the shortened version of the text with the heading 'Compos'd by Dr. *Blow, And Sung in / WESTMINSTER-ABBY, / AT / Her Majesty's Coronation*'.[119] A comparison of the 1689 and 1702 texts with the music makes it clear that a reworking of Blow's 1689 anthem would not have been easy: the shortening of the text affects only parts of sections, which complicates matters. For instance, the entire second half of the opening chorus text was among the passages cut, but Blow could not simply have cut it in his 1689 setting, since the first section is very short and would not easily make a chorus in its own right. Alternatively, he would have had to repeat the initial text in the second part of the chorus which in turn would certainly have been too much repetition for a movement of such length. Also, it would be rather difficult to change the central chorus 'For the King and Queen trust in the Lord' to the shorter 'for the Queen trusteth in the Lord'. Blow would have had to write at least this passage anew. After all, Blow would have had to compose a new anthem or rework the older setting considerably. An annotation on the copy of Weedon's programme in the Bodleian Library, Oxford reads next to the year '29. Apr.' and the concert was first advertised in the *Post Boy* on 30 April.[120] This was less than a week after the coronation, suggesting that the printed programme was prepared before the ceremony and is not necessarily a reliable source regarding either the coronation or the concert. In fact, none of the descriptive texts included in the programme refers directly to the pieces performed, but merely to sacred music in general. On the other hand, when preparing the concert programme, the shortened anthem text could have been provided only by Blow himself, since the order of service was not accessible to the public. Moreover, Weedon clearly refers to 'new Anthems composed by Dr. Blow'. However, it is possible that the changes to the text were simply ignored and that Blow repeated his older anthem as it stood in 1689 – the music contradicting the text in the order of service would not be unusual.[121] In any case, it is remarkable that Blow's anthem

---

[118] *The Oration, Anthems and Poems, Spoken and Sung at the Performance of Divine Musick, at Stationers-Hall, for the Month of May, 1702*. Undertaken by Cavendish Weedon, Esq. (London: Printed for Henry Playford, 1702). For general details about Weedon's concerts see Alexander H. Shapiro, '"Drama of an Infinitely Superior Nature": Handel's Early English Oratorios and the Religious Sublime', *ML* 74 (May, 1993), 215–45, here 220f.

[119] The only difference in the text is a clearer punctuation and 'mercies' instead of 'mercy' in the third verse; in the same verse the text is changed to 'his hand shall find out all Her Enemies'.

[120] *Ob Gough Lond. 42 (1)*; Wood, 'Cavendish Weedon', p. 224, fn. 14.

[121] Wood, 'Cavendish Weedon', 224, states that the final concert programme 'discreetly glossed over its [the anthem's] earlier origins'.

was scheduled to be performed at a public concert: this is not known of any earlier coronation music. Therefore this was probably the first anthem to become known to a wider public than just the 'coronation congregation'.

As in the previous coronations little can be said about the remaining liturgical music of the communion service. The order of service again scheduled the choir to sing the Sanctus and Gloria, and before that the anthems 'Let your light so shine' and 'Let my prayer come up'. It may be assumed that at least the latter was again sung in Blow's setting from 1689.

The performance

According to a note in the College of Arms the choirs were positioned within the Abbey in the same manner as in 1685.[122] From a document relating to the preparation of the next coronation, it can be deduced that Sir Christopher Wren was responsible for building the 'theatre', thrones and scaffolds, or galleries, in the Abbey.[123] Fiennes reports that the Litany and the prayers were 'sung and repeated by two Bishops, with a small organ'.[124] This refers presumably to a specially built small instrument in the musicians' gallery south of the altar as in previous coronations.

The number of singers is known from several sources. Scarlet cloth was provided for seventeen Laymen, ten Children, an Organ Blower and an Organ Builder of the Chapel Royal.[125] On the other hand, a 'List of the Officers, Gentlemen & Children of her Majesty's Chapel Royal at Whitehall who attended at the Coronation' also mentions the 'Ten Children of ye Chappel', but gives the names of twenty-three Gentlemen and in addition lists Blow (who would have been the Composer, first Organist, and Master of the Children), Pigott (named as organist) and a 'Mr of the Children' as well as a number of other officers.[126] To the Chapel Royal must be added the Abbey choir, which might still have had a size similar to that in 1685, when it had eight boys and sixteen Gentlemen.[127] That leaves a total number of probably eighteen boys and about forty adult singers. In comparison, a total of twenty boys and forty-eight adult singers are reported for the coronation in 1685. The slightly smaller number of singers might reflect the gradual

[122] *Lca MS L 19*, pp. 119–38, here p. 128.   [123] *Lna PC 1/14/76.*   [124] Fiennes, 342.

[125] *Lna LC 2/15*, 'Lord Chamberlaine Books': 'Coronation of Her Maj.ᵗʸ Queen Anne April 1702.', no. 19.

[126] See Ashbee, vol. II, 71f.

[127] A list from 1709 gives the names of eleven Gentlemen without specifying the number of the boys. See *Lwa WAM 33741*.

decline of the Chapel Royal and the scant musical interest of the previous king. Nevertheless, similarly to the previous coronations the orchestra consisted of thirty-six instrumentalists, probably including both a string band and wind instruments.[128] Altogether, there was the considerable number of nearly one hundred musicians: about fifty-eight singers and thirty-six instrumentalists, which does not yet include the thirteen State Trumpeters and three Drummers who played the fanfares.[129] This was certainly the biggest performing body of the time.

There is evidence that elaborate new music was also heard during the Banquet in Westminster Hall after the service. Peter Holman proposed a suite by John Eccles as having been played, since it is described as 'made for the Queen's Coronation' in a contemporary source.[130] Eccles had been Master of the Queen's Musick and it would therefore have been appropriate for him to contribute music to the occasion. His suite is intriguing for two other reasons: firstly, it was published after the event and was thus the first coronation music to have been made available to the public.[131] Indeed, similarly to Blow's anthem from this coronation Eccles's music was afterwards also performed in public concerts.[132] Secondly, Holman observes that the writing in the individual movements of Eccles's suite might refer to the Scottish, English, and Irish style, representing the 'different musical idioms of Queen Anne's kingdoms'.[133] Such possible musical references to Britain have not been detected in any of the earlier coronation music. Regarding the performance of Eccles's suite Holman states that it 'clearly needs a trumpet in some of the movements', and he realizes that in his recording of the piece.[134] If a trumpet was included in the music during the banquet, that might support the idea that a trumpet also played with the orchestra in the Abbey.[135]

---

[128] For details see Range, 'Instrumental Musick', 101.

[129] For these see *Lna LC 2/ 15*: 'Lord Chamberlaine Books': 'Coronation of Her Maj.^ty Queen Anne April 1702.', warrants no. 2 and 3.

[130] Peter Holman, Booklet notes to *Sound the Trumpet, Henry Purcell and his Followers*, The English *Orpheus* 35, CDA66817 (Hyperion, 1996), 5. For the source of the music see the next footnote. See also Curtis A. Price, *Music in the Restoration Theatre. With a Catalogue of Instrumental Music in the Plays 1665–1713* (UMI Research Press, 1979), 240.

[131] See William C. Smith, *A Bibliography of the Musical Works Published by John Walsh during the Years 1695–1720* (London: Oxford University Press, 1948). Eccles's suite was 'included in *Harmonia Anglicana* (Fourth Collection, No III; BM. b. 29. a)', which was advertised in *PM*, 6–9 June 1702.

[132] Kathryn Lowerre, *Music and Musicians on the London Stage, 1695–1705* (Farnham: Ashgate, 2009), 269 and 305f.

[133] Holman, Booklet, 5f.   [134] See fn. 130.   [135] Cf. fn. 67.

It is noteworthy that at least three important anthems were newly written for this coronation, the ones by Pigott, Turner and Clarke. To these may possibly be added a new setting of 'The Lord God is a Sun and a Shield'. The number of new compositions might be indicative of the relief that the austere days of the Calvinist William III were over and of the hope for a revival of the former status of the Chapel and music at court. At the same time, the lavish musical programme accompanying the 1702 coronation supports Bucholz' suggestion that Queen Anne made extensive use of the 'Theatre of Power'.[136] Furthermore, with Blow's and Eccles's contributions afterwards being performed in public concerts and Eccles's suite being published, this appears to be the first coronation at which a concrete public dissemination of the music took place. The coronation music thus enters the eighteenth century in which it will leave the restraints of the actual ceremony and become more independent and public than ever before.

George I, 1714

Queen Anne's death on 1 August 1714 meant the end of the Stuart line. A Catholic succession had been forbidden by the Act of Settlement of 1702 and the closest Protestant heir to the throne was the Elector of Hanover, who succeeded as George I. It is an often neglected fact that the succession of the Elector of Hanover had already been foreseen for more than twenty years.[137] However, his accession incited an attempt by the Catholic Stuarts to regain the throne, culminating in the Rebellion at Preston in 1715 where James Stuart, the 'Old Pretender' ('James III' for his supporters) was defeated. These circumstances make it easily understandable that the new king's installation was accomplished within a short period of time. On 23 August, one day before the late queen's funeral, the Privy Council appointed a committee to settle the manner of the coronation, and on 1 September the Archbishop of Canterbury, Thomas Tenison, was asked to prepare the order of service.[138] Since the new king had separated from his wife, there was again only one crowning, and Tenison could simply adapt

---

[136] Bucholz, *Augustan Court*, 289.

[137] In a letter to the Electress Sophie of Hanover from April 1689, William III mentions that her son is likely to become King of England one day. See Mary II, *Memoirs of Mary*, 72f.

[138] For this and the following see *Lna PC 2/85*: 'Council Register 1. Aug. 1714–25 Feb. 1716/7', pp. 28 and 61–90.

his 1702 order of service.[139] His order of service was approved by the Council on 8 September and a proclamation on 1 October announced the coronation to take place on 20 October. It has been argued that the coronation was 'so overshadowed by the excitement of George's landing in England and drive through London' that the public interest in it was small.[140] Matthew Kilburn called it a 'hurried affair', concluding that the 'Lords Justices were more concerned with their efforts to ensure an untroubled ceremony, following the precedent established in 1689, than with innovation'.[141] Indeed, even though this was the first coronation of a monarch of 'Great Britain', the union of the two kingdoms of England and Scotland having been established only in 1707, this fact was not reflected in the overall ceremonies: the only changes were the presence of the Scottish peers and the inclusion of a special phrase in the coronation oath; also, the figure of Britannia was shown on the coronation medal.[142] The ceremonial proceedings, however, remained unchanged. Indeed, for the next coronation, in 1727, it was explicitly noted that 'the Attendance of Lyon and the High Constable of Scotland had never been before'.[143] With the absence of Lord Lion King of Arms, the highest of the heralds of Scotland, it is implied that the organization of the ceremonial aspects of the 1714 coronation was still exclusively an affair of the English College of Arms. Indeed, it has been observed that after 1603, there was 'no attempt [...] to repeat the explicit British references' included at the coronation of James I.[144] The reason for this may again have been the pressure of time: a full, ceremonial, acknowledgement of the union of the two kingdoms would probably have required much preparation; and in the interest of national security it was probably thought best to have the king crowned as soon as possible 'in case of popular doubts as to his right to reign and to forestall any attempt to replace him with James III'.[145]

---

[139] *Llp MS 1078.* It was presumably from this manuscript that the other copies were made: *Lwa WAM Library, CA 53* and *Lbl MS Harl. 6117. Lwa WAM 56760,* '1714 / An Account of ye Alterations in ye Formulatory at ye Coronation of King George', is very similar to the Lambeth MS.

[140] Philip Lindsay, *Crowned King of England. The Coronation of King George VI in History and Tradition* (London: Ivor Nicholson & Watson, 1937), 230.

[141] Kilburn, 79. He stresses the role of the Prince of Wales in the service; this, however, did not affect the liturgical side.

[142] Kilburn, 92; Strong, 359.   [143] *Lca MS S.M.L. 65,* vol. II, fo. 11.

[144] Keith M. Brown, 'The Vanishing Emperor: British Kingship and its Decline, 1603–1707', in Roger A. Mason (ed.), *Scots and Britons. Scottish Political Thought and the Union of 1603* (Cambridge University Press, 1994), 58–90, here 65.

[145] Kilburn, 92f. See also Monod, 311.

The music

Little is known about the music at this coronation. Altogether there were only ten weeks to prepare the service after Queen Anne's death; and unlike that of William III in 1702, Queen Anne's funeral on 24 August 1714 was a more elaborate affair.[146] The musician primarily responsible for both the funeral and the ensuing coronation was William Croft. Since Blow's death in October 1708, Croft had held the posts of Organist, Master of the Children and Composer of the Chapel Royal as well that of organist of Westminster Abbey; and he kept these posts until his death in 1727.[147] He thus combined the most important church music positions in the country and was indeed 'the most eminent musician in the land' until 'Handel's rise to fame'.[148] Curiously, the official records provide little information on Croft's participation in the coronation, merely noting that he was paid £18 for 'pricking and fair writing of Musick for Voices and Instruments'.[149] This payment is especially intriguing since only a few months later, when Croft provided a new anthem and the canticles for a thanksgiving service at St Paul's, he was paid the larger sum of £24.[150] However, it is conceivable that the £18 was not the only payment that Croft received for the coronation music, the remainder coming from another purse.

Given the pressure of time it is possible that much of the coronation music in 1714 was the same as in 1702. The newspapers reported many details about the festivities but little about the service in the Abbey. Regarding the music, the most detailed information is that 'the Te Deum and other Hymns and Anthems were Sung by the Gentlemen of his Majesty's Chappel and the Choir of Westminster'.[151] A contemporary printed account published in Dublin contradicts the other material in several respects.[152] The anthem texts partly differ from those in the order of service: for instance, the anthem

---

[146] Cf. Paul S. Fritz, 'From "Public" to "Private": The Royal Funeral in England, 1500–1830', in Joachim Whaley (ed.), *Mirrors of Mortality – Studies in the Social History of Death* (London: Europa Publications, 1981), 61–79; here 61. Fritz shows that, although Queen Anne's funeral was designated as a 'private funeral', it still included an elaborate ceremonial.

[147] For biographical details see Watkins Shaw and Graydon Beeks, 'William Croft', *NG* 6, 713–16.

[148] Cedric Lee, Foreword to William Croft, *'With Noise of Cannon', from the Ode, for bass, two violins and continuo* ([Richmond]: Green Man Press, [2005]), 2.

[149] For this and the following see Burrows, *Handel and the English Chapel Royal*, 600. 'Pricking' is an old expression for the writing down of (polyphonic) music. Before the Reformation 'pricksong' was a synonym for polyphonic music, and thus the opposite of 'plainsong' (*cantus planus*).

[150] *Lna LC 5/156*, p. 134. See Burrows, *Handel and the English Chapel Royal*, 600.

[151] *DC*, 21 October 1714.

[152] For this and the following see *The Whole Ceremony of the Coronation of His Most Sacred Majesty King George* [...] *By Order of W. Hawkins Esq; Ulster King of Arms of all Ireland* (Dublin: J. Carson, 1715), 17, 23, and 27.

after the Recognition is 'Let thy hand be strengthened' ('The King shall rejoice' in the order of service), but at the same time, the anthem after the Crowning is 'Praise the Lord, O Jerusalem' in both sources. Thus the selection of anthems in this report is a mixture of the 1685 and the 1689/1702 coronations. For the anthem at the Homage it gives '*Psalm* 20. v. 9. *psalm* 22. v. 18', which does not correspond with any known anthem. The reliability of this report is doubtful – at least as to the music. It may have been prepared before the coronation, mainly following Sandford as the easiest accessible source, which becomes clear in many details of the wording and the texts given.

The procession from Westminster Hall to the Abbey was presumably accompanied by the customary 'O Lord, grant the King a long life'. John Bumpus suggested that Croft composed his anthem to the text for this coronation, and G.A. Thewlis supported this ascription with the argument that the anthem was printed in Croft's *Musica Sacra*, which is dedicated to the king.[153] However, while the first volume of *Musica Sacra* is indeed dedicated to the king, the anthem is found in the second volume and this is dedicated to the Prince of Wales. In any case, first of all, this anthem must have been written earlier, in the reign of Queen Anne, since there are versions with 'Queen' instead of 'King'.[154] Secondly, with its verse sections its suitability for an outdoor procession is doubtful. In the end, the most plausible possibility appears to be a repeat of Child's setting of the text.

Regarding the entrance-anthem, the alto part of a setting of 'I was glad' by Croft survives in the Chapel Royal part-books.[155] This, however, was clearly a verse setting, and it concludes with an Hallelujah, not with the Gloria Patri. It is therefore more likely that Pigott's setting from 1702 was repeated. After the Recognition, Tenison kept the anthem as in 1702, with the text adjusted, and 'The King shall rejoice' could have been sung in Turner's setting from the previous coronation. The fact that his anthem was revised for use at the time of George I is clear from the treble part in *Lbl MS Eg. 3767* where the text is changed accordingly.[156]

The anthem after the Crowning may again have been endowed with more structural importance. According to an order of service in the College of

[153] John S. Bumpus, *A History of English Cathedral Music, 1549–1889*, 2 vols. (London: T. Werner Laurie, 1908), vol. I, 204. G.A. Thewlis, 'Coronation of George I', *MT* 78 (1937), 310–11, here 310.

[154] For instance, *Ob MS Tenb. 788*, no. 8/fo. 98 and *Och MS 1230*, p. 109.

[155] *Lbl. RM. 27. a. 1*, p. 39/fo. 22, attributed to Croft in the index. It is listed under Croft in Walter Coward's manuscript catalogue of the Chapel Royal's music of 1917, which probably refers to the same manuscript. This is still kept in the Chapel Royal, St James's Palace.

[156] For further details see the commentary in Range, thesis, vol. II, 47.

Arms the peers put on their coronets only after the anthem.[157] This would have meant a return to what was done at the 1685 coronation, rather than in 1689 or 1702. This may have meant that at least the peers listened to the anthem more carefully, so as to be prepared for the putting on of the coronets. The text was again 'Praise the Lord, O Jerusalem', but if Clarke's 1702 setting was repeated this would be quite ironic. As mentioned above, Clarke seems to have tailored his setting distinctly to a queen's coronation, and his stressing of the word 'Queens' must have seemed slightly inappropriate at a coronation of a king only, who lived in separation from his wife.

It was Croft who contributed the most elaborate composition to the coronation: the orchestral anthem 'The Lord is a Sun and a Shield' that was performed during the Homage.[158] The two earliest surviving manuscript sources of the anthem state merely that it was performed at the coronation but in two later copies it is described as having been written for this occasion.[159] It has been suggested that Croft had been 'ordered' ('angeordnet') to compose this anthem by the Sub-Dean of the Chapel Royal.[160] However, the evidence for this is not clear and it cannot be determined who was responsible for Croft's composing the anthem.

Although Croft set the text as in the order of service, there is one striking change: the omission of the word 'God' after 'Lord' in the first line and thus in the anthem's title. This change is derived neither from the King James Bible, from which the rest of the text is taken, nor from the Prayer Book. Nevertheless, in a list of the anthems for the 1689 coronation, the title of the anthem is already given in the version used by Croft.[161] This shorter form is also found in the aforementioned copy of the order of service from 1702 which seems to have belonged to 'some herald or officer concerned in arranging the whole affair'.[162] One of these could have been Croft's source for the text.

'The Lord is a Sun and a Shield' is Croft's earliest surviving orchestral anthem and it furthermore deserves the credit of being the first coronation anthem for which trumpet parts survive.[163] The architecture of the anthem is

---

[157] *Lca MS Ceremonials 18*, item 90: 'The King being Crowned, and the Anthem Sung, all the Peers put on their Caps and Coronets.'

[158] For a discussion of the sources and a transcription see Range, thesis, vol. II.

[159] *Lbl RM. 24.g.2 (1)*, fo. 2r: 'Perform'd att yᵉ King's Coronation, 1714', the same in *Lbl MS Add. 31405*, fo. 118. In *Lbl MS Add. 17843*, fo. 123, at the end 'Compos'd by D:ʳ Croft / for the Coronation of his Majesty King George 1.ˢᵗ', and similar in *Ob MS Mus. d. 27*, no. 5/p. 100, at the end.

[160] Hans Joachim Marx, *Händel und seine Zeitgenossen. Eine Biographische Enzyklopädie*, published as 'Händel-Handbuch', ed. Hans Joachim Marx, vol. I, two parts (Laaber: Laaber-Verlag, 2008), 345.

[161] *Lbl MS Harl. 6815*, fo. 169.   [162] *Lbl MS Harl. 6118*, fo. 19; and Planché, 97.

[163] For details see Range, thesis, vol. I, 125f. and Range, 'Instrumental Musick', 101f.

symmetrical and well balanced: it is divided into five distinct movements, following the disposition of the text in the order of service. Three four-part choruses in D major are interspersed with two verses for ATB, the first in D minor, the second in B minor, which were probably sung by the full ATB parts, as the writing is more choral than soloistic. Croft follows the example of Blow's setting of the text from 1689 in beginning the anthem with just a few bars of instrumental introduction to the opening chorus.

A few analytical considerations will suffice to show that Croft's anthem was probably tailored specifically to the coronation of George I. In the central chorus ('For the King trusteth in the Lord') Croft followed the graphical arrangement in the order of service more closely than Blow: in Blow's anthem this section is the continuation of the previous verse and is set for ATB only, but Croft wrote a movement in its own right, for the full choir with orchestral accompaniment. Croft gives this text more importance, and the king's trust in God literally becomes the centre of the anthem. Moreover, he sets it as a loose double fugue: the second theme, on the text 'through the mercy of the Most High', is at the same time the counter-subject to the first theme on the text 'For the King trusteth in the Lord'. This display of solid craftsmanship and the steadiness of the counterpoint underline the idea of trust and timelessness of the prayer. An unusual feature is the end of this movement, where the instruments hold the final chord longer than the singers. This could perhaps symbolize the becoming silent of the 'enemies' mentioned in the text. In the final movement ('Blessed be the Lord') Croft's treatment of the text 'for ever' is remarkable: strong chords in the chorus interrupt a repeating quaver figure in the instruments. The rests between the chords further enhance this dramatic effect and this example has been suggested as a probable model for Handel's famous 'For ever, for ever, Hallelujah' passages.[164] Curiously, the anthem does not end with an Hallelujah as given in the text, but only with two simple 'Amen' chords at the end.

Overall, Croft's anthem seems to convey an important message. The symbolism of the Homage had assumed an acute significance after the 'Glorious Revolution': the leading noblemen of the country paid homage to the new political circumstances and reaffirmed the status quo. In 1714, with the accession of a king from a new dynastic line, such a public display of loyalty and support to the monarch was more than necessary; after all there were still the Pretender's strong claims to the throne. The newly significant act of the Homage was accompanied by new and especially festive music which would help underline the significance of the ceremony.

---

[164] Adrian Carpenter, 'William Croft's Church Music', *MT* 112 (1971), 275–7, here 276.

As for the liturgical music, it could all have been sung to settings by Croft or by John Weldon, the second Composer of the Chapel.[165] Spink mentions the anthem 'Blessed is thy people' by the Lincoln composer George Holmes as having been composed for the coronation, but he refers to a local celebration at Lincoln.[166] This in turn illustrates that nationwide ceremonies with especially composed music took place to celebrate the event.

Performance

The performance conditions at this coronation were probably the same as at previous coronations, with the musicians positioned in three different galleries around the crossing. This is indicated by the instructions for the choir after singing the entrance-anthem.[167] A list for the required benching in the Abbey mentions a 'Singing Mens Gallery next the South East Corner' which was to hold twenty-four people.[168] From the context this probably refers to the south east corner of the crossing and thus probably to the place of the Chapel Royal gallery, on the south side of the High Altar. A 'Musick Gallery over the Quire Door' was specifically mentioned as part of the temporary galleries that were again built by Wren.[169] This, however, probably simply refers to the customary gallery for the State Trumpeters and Timpani at this place. The building of such a special gallery over the 'Quire Door' would have been necessary as the old quire screen did not have a full-length gallery on the top, but was divided into two parts in the middle.[170] Regarding the orchestral accompaniment, it is again possible that the orchestra included more instruments than the strings and trumpets indicated in Croft's anthem, for instance oboes and bassoons.[171]

---

[165] A Te Deum, Responses to the Commandments, and setting of the Nicene Creed, all in A major, by Croft survive in *Ob MS Mus. c. 14*. A Te Deum in D major by Weldon is found in *Lcm MS 2043* and Margaret Laurie lists a Communion Service in E flat major, see 'John Weldon', *NG* 17, 265–6, here 266.

[166] Spink, *Restoration Cathedral Music*, 286, and private correspondence.

[167] *Lca MS Ceremonials 18*, item 90. The text is the same as in *Lbl MS Harl. 6118*, fo. 10v, quoted in full in fn. 90.

[168] *Lca Coronations. Queen Anne. George I.*, no. 46: 'Oct.ʳ 11ᵗʰ. 1714. / An Accoᵗ. of the Number of Feet running of Benching and Persons Seated (at 18. Inches each) in the Choir and North and South Crosses of Westminster Abbey'.

[169] *Lca MS Ceremonials 18*, item 34: 'Oct. 1714/ Draught of the Lord Marshals Order to Sʳ Chr. Wren to set up the Galleries in Westm.ʳ Abbey against the Kings Coronation'.

[170] See John Dart, *Westmonasterium or the History and Antiquities of the Abbey Church of St. Peters Westminster* [. . .], 2 vols. (London 1723), vol. I, engravings between pp. 66 and 71: 'The Inside Prospect of the Church [. . .]'

[171] For details see Range, 'Instrumental Musick', 101–3.

At the coronation of the first monarch of the House of Hanover one might have expected an even grander spectacle than usual so that the new king could impress his nobility and subjects. It seems, however, that all effort was simply concentrated on an early coronation to confirm the new king's standing. This may have seemed to be a good solution at the time. In retrospect, however, one may wonder if it was not a lost opportunity. A more splendid public spectacle at George I's coronation might have facilitated the establishment of the new dynasty in Britain.

Overall, the revisions of the order of service after the Glorious Revolution affected the coronation service considerably. With the reintroduction of the communion it was again much longer and at least theoretically placed emphasis on the religious aspect of the ceremony. This, however, was not necessarily reflected in the coronation music, which followed a rather different development and placed more and more emphasis on the perform-ance of the specially composed anthems. The music thus appears to have followed the general trend of the coronation becoming more and more of a mere ceremonial spectacle devoid of spiritual significance.

5 | The 'concert coronations' I: 1727

As noted in the introduction, the coronations from that of William III and Mary II onwards have been described as being in 'performance or concert style'.[1] This description applies particularly well to the three coronations of 1727, 1761 and 1821: in these the music had an especially prominent role and became a characterizing feature of the service.

George II and Queen Caroline, 1727

The coronation of George II and Queen Caroline has received much attention from scholars as it was for this occasion that Handel composed his four Coronation Anthems. Nevertheless, while Handel's anthems are well preserved, the full details of the music of the service are difficult to reconstruct. The present study provides a re-examination of the sources and suggests a different order of performance for the anthems than is commonly assumed; also there are new insights regarding the remainder of the music of the service and in respect to the performing body.

The order of service

George I died on his way to Hanover, on 11 June 1727. As early as 24 June, London newspapers reported that the coronation of the new king and queen was 'fixed for October next'.[2] The Privy Council formed a committee 'to consider of the preparations necessary to be made for the Coronation', and William Wake, the Archbishop of Canterbury, was asked to 'inspect' the order of service 'and present the same to this Committee'.[3] Wake's earliest report on the subject is found in a letter of 20 August.[4] He informed the Privy Council that he could not think of a better form for the order of service than that which his predecessor Tenison had used at the two previous

---

[1] Wilkinson, *Westminster Abbey*, 51 and 79. [2] *BJ* and *LJ*, 24 June 1727.
[3] Minutes of the Privy Council, entries of 2 and 8 August 1727 (*Lna PC 2/90*).
[4] *Lna PC 1/15/6* (transcr. App. B2a).

coronations. This praise could have been based on his memories of the 1714 coronation, which Wake attended, presumably in his capacity as Bishop of Lincoln.[5] The only problem with Tenison's order of service was the missing part of the Queen's Coronation and Wake explained that he would take this from Sancroft's 1685 order of service for James II and Queen Mary. Wake prepared a draft order of service and presented it to the Privy Council on 5 September, when it was discussed and some changes demanded.[6] The archbishop later noted that, since 'no book could be got of the late Kings Coronation', the Privy Council had 'order'd' him to make his draft order of service generally similar to that of 1685.[7] Wake presented his revised version to the Council and it was agreed upon on 8 September.[8] It does not seem to have survived. However, ten days later, Wake reported to the Privy Council that he 'had lately obtained' a copy of the order of service for George I and he was asked to change his version to make it 'agreable thereto', with the addition of the Queen's Coronation.[9] Wake's final order of service survives in his manuscript copy where he noted on the title page 'This book is now made exactly agreeable to that of King Georges Coronation'.[10] This order of service was approved by the king on 20 September.[11] On the same day the coronation was postponed from 4 to 11 October due to a forecast spring tide which might have flooded Westminster Hall.[12] The archbishop was asked to print off a hundred copies of the order of service, '50 [. . .] for the use of the Lords of His Majestys most Honourable Privy Council and the other 50 for the Service of those who are to officiate in the Abby'.[13] This is the earliest coronation for which a printed order of service survives and Leake later recalled that 1727 was 'the first Instance of printed those Ceremonials [*sic*]'.[14]

None of the anthem texts in Wake's order tallies exactly with those of Handel's anthems. Handel's texts are very much identical with those found in a second order of service, written down in the New Cheque Book of the

[5] See *Llp MS 1770*: Diary of Archbishop Wake, March 1705–25 January 1725, fo. 150.

[6] *Lna PC 2/90*, p. 82.

[7] *Llp Cod. Misc. 1079A*: order of service for the coronation of George II and Queen Caroline (1727), handwritten by Archbishop Wake, annotation on title page (transcr.App. B2b).

[8] *Lna PC 2/90*, p. 84.   [9] *Lna PC 2/90*, p. 88 (transcr. App. B2c).

[10] *Llp Cod. Misc. 1079A*; pp. 5–33 are in a professional writer's hand, the remainder by Wake.

[11] Letter dated Kensington Palace, 20 September 1727, included in *Llp Cod. Misc. 1079A*. See also *Lna PC 2/90*, p. 114f.

[12] *Lna PC 2/90*, p. 112. The postponement had been proposed two days earlier (see p. 88).

[13] *Lna PC 2/90*, p. 114f.

[14] *The Form and Order of the Service that is to be Performed, and of the Ceremonies that are to be Observed, in the Coronation of Their Majesties, King George II, and Queen Caroline in the Abbey Church of S. Peter, Westminster, On Wednesday the 11th day of October 1727* (London: John Baskett, 1727); hereafter OS (1727). *Lca MS S.M.L. 65*, vol. II, p. 292.

Chapel Royal: 'The Order of Performing the Several Anthems at the Coronation of their Majesties King George the Second, & Q: Carolina'.[15] There is no evidence as to who compiled this order, but the scribe has been identified as Jonathan Smith, Clerk of the Cheque from 1720 until 1752.[16] The entry bears no date, but the fact that it is written in the present and future tenses throughout suggests that it was produced before the coronation.[17] The two orders of service differ considerably: the printed order is a full order of service including all necessary texts; the Cheque Book version, on the other hand, presents the service merely in draft form. As indicated in its heading, its prime function was probably to indicate what music was required in the service and when. Indeed, otherwise it would not be easy to understand why this order should have been entered in the Cheque Book in the first place.[18] Except for 'My heart is inditing', the anthem texts in the Cheque Book are identical with those in Sandford's account of the 1685 coronation. The fact that Sandford was the source for this order of service is furthermore supported by the peculiarity that the Cheque Book gives few details about the communion service, which had been omitted in 1685. Given that Handel used the texts as entered in the Cheque Book, it is very likely that this was his general guide for the order of service. However, the text of 'The King shall rejoice' is slightly different in his setting which may indicate that this order of service was written before he began the composition and that, in the process of writing, he still made some changes. Not only the texts but also the order of the anthems are different in the Cheque Book and in the printed order of service. Only two of them are in the same position in both orders: 'Zadok the Priest' during the Anointing and 'My heart is inditing' after the Queen's Coronation. 'The King shall rejoice' is in different positions in both orders, and 'Let thy hand be strengthened' is not included in the printed order at all.

According to precedent, the musician in charge of the coronation music should have been the Composer of the Chapel Royal. Croft, who held this position, had died on 14 August and was succeeded by Maurice Greene on 4 September.[19] Greene's appointment is somewhat surprising as he had no

---

[15] The original is preserved at HM Chapel Royal, St James's Palace, London. For a transcription see Ashbee and Harley, vol. I, 281–5. For a facsimile of the first two pages see Burrows, *Handel and the English Chapel Royal*, 260f.

[16] Ashbee and Harley, vol. I, 281, fn. 85.

[17] The only exception is the annotation to the Te Deum, see below.

[18] For other suggested explanations see Burrows, *Handel and the English Chapel Royal*, 259–62.

[19] Greene is first mentioned as Croft's successor in London newspapers as early as at the end of August, see *PB*, 29–31 August 1727. For the idea that Croft would have been in charge of the music see also Lieselotte Bense, 'Händels Anthems für die Krönung Georgs II. und seiner

previous connection with the Chapel; a more obvious choice for the post would have been John Weldon, who had been second Organist and additional Composer since 1708.[20] In any case, in the end, Greene did not write any music for the coronation and Handel is the only composer known to have contributed his works. Since Handel was not the regular composer of the Chapel Royal, his contribution implies some special circumstances.[21] Indeed, a direct intervention by the king is confirmed in a remark, possibly written by George III, in a copy of John Mainwaring's Handel biography from the royal collection of books:[22]

that wretched little crooked ill natured insigni[fi]cant writer Player and musician the late D.ʳ Green Organist and composer to King George II. who forbad his composing the Anthems at his Coronation Oct. 22.ᵈ 1727. and ordered that G. F. Hendel should not only have that great honour but except the I.ˢᵗ choose his own words. He had but four Weeks for doing this wonderful work which seems scarcely credible as to the first it is perhaps the most perfect if possible of all His superb Compositions.

No other records concerning Handel's appointment are known. The first notice of Handel as the composer of the coronation music appears to date from 9 September.[23] He would thus have been appointed at about the same time or shortly after Greene took over the official post at the Chapel. Handel did not receive any official payment for the coronation;[24] but he may well have been paid from the King's Privy Purse or other sources for which no records survive.

The annotation in Mainwaring is also significant in that it confirms that Handel should 'choose his own words' for all but 'the I.ˢᵗ' anthem. It is not

Gemahlin Königin Caroline in der Westminster-Abtei am 11. Oktober 1727', *Händel-Jahrbuch* 49 (2003), 307–26, here 309.

[20] For Weldon see Laurie in *NG* 27, 265–6. For details of Greene's appointment see H. Diack Johnstone, 'The Life and Work of Maurice Greene', 2 vols., unpublished DPhil thesis, University of Oxford (1967), vol. I, 126–8 and 186–8. Johnstone suggests that Handel may have had ambitions to obtain the place. For this cf. also Burrows, *Handel and the English Chapel Royal*, 254.

[21] See Burrows, *Handel and the English Chapel Royal*, 251–5.

[22] See William C. Smith, 'George III, Handel, and Mainwaring', *MT* 65 (1924), 789–95, here 790. The original was destroyed during World War II, but photographs survive, and Smith includes one of this passage. Baldwin, 220, has remarked that the handwriting is 'remarkably similar to that of George III'.

[23] The *Norwich Mercury* reported on 16 September that Handel had been appointed 'to compose the Anthem at the Coronation'. This report is dated 'September 9' and the delay in publishing it may be explained by the fact that it was not a London newspaper. Otto Erich Deutsch assumes that this note had 'certainly' been published in London earlier, but observes that 'no newspaper with it has been traced'. See *Handel – A Documentary Biography* (London: Adam and Charles Black, 1955), 213.

[24] Peggy E. Daub, 'Music at the Court of George II (r. 1727–1760)', unpublished Ph.D. thesis, Cornell University (1985), 111.

clear to which anthem this refers. On the one hand, the first anthem of the service ('I was glad') was not set by Handel. On the other hand, the description 'the most perfect [...] of all His superb Compositions' seems too enthusiastic to refer to 'Let thy hand be strengthened', which is the first anthem set by Handel if he followed the Cheque Book order of service. This remark could refer to 'Zadok the Priest', which is the first anthem in Handel's autograph score.[25] Another possibility is that it refers to 'The King shall rejoice' which, as will be seen, may have been the first of Handel's anthems performed, or to be performed, in the service. The fact that Handel was completely free regarding the choice of texts for the other anthems is also supported by an anecdote recorded by Burney:[26]

At the coronation of his late majesty, George the Second, in 1727, HANDEL had the words sent to him by the bishops, for the anthems; at which he murmured, and took offence, as he thought it implied his ignorance of the Holy Scriptures: 'I have read my Bible very well, and shall chuse for myself.'

Burney's anecdote, however, might be somewhat overstated. William Herrmann has shown that Handel is unlikely to have chosen the texts of his anthems for himself since they do not agree with the King James Version, the Book of Common Prayer or 'any other existing translation'.[27] Donald Burrows observed that 'Handel's "chusing" seems to have been influenced by the coronation liturgy from 1685.'[28] Indeed, as seen above, Handel mostly used the texts as given in Sandford and the Cheque Book. He changed only a few details, but made no major decisions: his texts are still taken from the same places in the Scriptures, only the selection of verses and some wording varies. Burney does not explain why exactly Handel 'took offence' when he was sent the texts. It is questionable whether he was offended because he wanted to choose the texts entirely for himself; after all, it was normal for an eighteenth-century composer to be assigned the texts to be set. Another reason for Handel's irritation could have been that he had already begun setting other words when the second,

---

[25] Donald Burrows and Martha J. Ronish, *A Catalogue of Handel's Musical Autographs* (Oxford: Clarendon Press, 1994), 212. It is not known when the heading 'Anthem I' was added and when the anthem became the first piece in the score.

[26] Charles Burney, 'Sketch of the Life of Handel', in *An account of the musical performances in Westminster-Abbey, and the Pantheon [...] In commemoration of Handel.* (London: Printed for the Benefit of the Musical Fund, 1785), 1–56, here 34.

[27] William Herrmann, Introduction to George Frideric Handel, *Coronation Anthem No. 1 (Zadok the Priest)*, ed. and with keyboard reduction by William Herrmann (New York: Schirmer, [1969]), iv.

[28] Donald Burrows, *Handel*. The Master Musicians. (first publ. 1994; paperback edn Oxford University Press, 1996), 160.

revised set of texts was sent.[29] According to the aforementioned annotation in Mainwaring, Handel had only 'four Weeks' for the composition of the anthems. This may refer to the period from 9 September to 6 October: the first being the day of the earliest newspaper notice of him and the second being the date of the first public rehearsal in the Abbey.[30] Notably, 9 September was also one day after the Privy Council had agreed on Wake's first version of the order of service. As seen above, the archbishop had been asked to model it on Sancroft's order for the 1685 coronation; the anthems would therefore have been the same as in the Cheque Book order.

In addition to the two orders of service, there are two contemporary printed accounts of the coronation.[31] The first was published in Dublin and is very similar to the printed order of service; it mentions only three of the anthems set by Handel (omitting 'Let thy hand be strengthened').[32] Friedrich Chrysander explained that such descriptions were published in advance and that they describe only what was normally to be expected at such an occasion.[33] The second report was published in Hanover after the coronation and is written in German throughout.[34] It does not mention any anthems for the 1727 coronation, but the titles of the four anthems as set by Handel are included in the general description of the coronation service. They appear in the same order as in the Cheque Book, which hints at Sandford as the source for this account.

The most detailed report of the actual coronation service appears to be a copy of the printed order of service used by Wake and into which he entered 'notes of w^t was done or omitted at that Coronation'.[35] Almost no other report from those present at the ceremony is known. Table 5.1 shows the references to the music in the two orders of service, together with Wake's annotations.

It has been proposed that Wake's annotations stem from at least two stages: some written before the service (such as the annotation that the Litany should be read) and some afterwards (his observations of what

[29] Cf. Donald Burrows, 'Handel and the 1727 Coronation', *MT* 118 (1977), 469–73, here 469.

[30] Daub, 110. Cf. Burrows, '1727 Coronation', 469, fn. 9.

[31] These have previously been discussed by Friedrich Chrysander, *G. F. Händel*, vol. II (Leipzig: Breitkopf und Härtel, 1860), 170ff. See also Deutsch, 214.

[32] *The Ceremonial of the Coronation of His most Sacred Majesty King George II. and of His Royal Consort Queen Caroline* [. . .] *By Order of William Hawkins Esq; Ulster King of Arms of all Ireland.* (Dublin: Printed by and for S. Powell, 1727).

[33] Chrysander, *G. F. Händel*, 172.

[34] *Vollständige Beschreibung der Ceremonien, welche sowohl bei den Englischen Crönungen überhaupt vorgehen, Besonders aber bey dem Höchst=beglückten Crönungs=Fest Ihro Königl. Königl. Maj. Maj.* [sic] *Georgii des II. und Wilhelminae Carolinae* [. . .] (Hanover: Nicolaus Förster und Sohn, 1728).

[35] *Llp Cod. Misc. 1079B*, title page. This was first described in detail by Winton Dean in his sleeve notes to Handel, *Coronation Anthems*, Argo ZRG 5369 (1963).

Table 5.1 The music in the two orders of service for the 1727 coronation, together with Archbishop Wake's manuscript annotations.

Ceremony	Printed Order of Service with Archbishop Wake's annotations (W:), *Llp Cod. Misc. 1079B*	Order of Service in the New Cheque Book of the Chapel Royal, incl. some annotations (=>)
Procession from Westminster Hall to the Abbey	not included	'O Lord, grant the King a long life' (text as in Sandford) => 'Full Anthem'
Entrance into the Abbey	'I was glad' (text as in 1689) => W: 'This was omitted and no Anthem at all Sung: in the Coronation of K. G2. by the Negligence of the Choir of Westm.'	'I was glad' (text as in Sandford, but in Verse 5 'Seat' instead of 'Throne' and no *Gloria Patri* at the end.) => 'Full Anthem'
Recognition	'ANTHEM II': 'The King shall rejoice' (text as in 1714) => W: 'The Anthems [*sic*, the 's' is crossed out] in Confusion: All irregular in the Music. (Coron. G. 2.)'	'Let thy hand be strenghned' [*sic*] (text as in Sandford) => 'verse Anthem'
Litany	'Then followeth the Litanie to be sung [W: ^or read], by two Bishops [...].' => W: To shorten the Service let this be Read: So it was G. 2. –'	'The Litany to be read'
Anointing	'ANTHEM III': 'Come, Holy Ghost' => W: 'This Hymn by the mistake of the Music not sung; but the next Anthem instead of it.'	'Come Holy Ghost', full text entered => 'This Chanted for Shortness Sake.'
	'ANTHEM IV': 'Zadok the Priest'	'Zadock the Priest' (text as in Sandford) => 'Verse Anthem'
	'ANTHEM V': 'Behold, O God our Defender'	'Behold, O Lord, our Defender' (text as in Sandford) => 'This Chanted'
Crowning	'ANTHEM VI': 'Praise the Lord, O Jerusalem'	'The King shall rejoice' (text as in Sandford, but verse 2 and the first word of verse 3 cut) => 'Verse Anthem'
Te Deum	'ANTHEM VII': 'We praise Thee, O God'	'Te Deum of Gibbon's was Sung.'
Inthronization	W: 'Anthem. vij. / Let thy hand be strengthed [*sic*], and thy right hand be Exalted. / Let Justice and Judgment be the preparation of thy seat, let Mercy & Truth Go before thy face. Psal: 89. 14.15'	no music mentioned for this ceremony

Table 5.1 (cont.)

Ceremony	Printed Order of Service with Archbishop Wake's annotations (W:), *Llp Cod. Misc. 1079B*	Order of Service in the New Cheque Book of the Chapel Royal, incl. some annotations (=>)
Homage	[*During* Homage] – 'ANTHEM VIII': 'The Lord is a Sun and a Shield'	[*After* Homage] – 'God spake sometimes in Visions' (text as in Sandford, but without 'Allelujah') => 'This Chanted'
Queen's Coronation	'ANTHEM X': 'My heart is enditing' (apart from 'enditing', text as in Sandford)	'My heart is inditing' (text probably own compilation)
Second Part of the Communion Service	*'Then the Organ plays, and the Choir singeth:* / ANTHEM X' ('Let my prayer come up into thy presence') *'The Choir sings* Therefore with Angels [. . .] *Then shall be sung,* Glory be to God on high'	'Nicene Creed to be Read.' 'During yᵉ Offertory the Organ plays, till the Alms are done Collecting. Sanctus &c. sung in Musick. The Gloria in Excellis [*sic*] sung in Musick.'

happened).[36] Furthermore, Wake seems to have entered at least some of his annotations with improvements for future such events in mind. For instance, his annotation to the 'Investiture *per Annulum* / & *Baculum*', reads: 'Instead of the form then used, I found among Abp Sancrofts papers this following, wᶜʰ seems much better but his Matⁱᵉ would have nothing changed'; and even though nothing was changed at this coronation, Wake inserted the text of a long prayer that he thought more suitable.[37] It may have been this mixture of observations and suggestions for future coronations that caused Wake to refer explicitly to George II in some of the observations. Overall, it appears that he was a meticulous writer with scrupulous attention to detail.

The order of performance

One of the main questions surrounding the music at this coronation is the order of performance of Handel's anthems. In the catalogue of his works, they are listed in the order 'Zadok the Priest', 'Let thy hand be strengthened', 'The King shall rejoice', and 'My heart is inditing'.[38] This ordering follows

---

[36] Burrows, *Handel and the English Chapel Royal*, 262.   [37] *Llp Cod. Misc. 1079B*, p. 45.
[38] HWV 258–61 in *HHB*, vol. II, 719–25.

that in the autograph score, which resulted only from a later binding.[39] Two important early copies of the music follow the order as in the Cheque Book, and most modern writers assume that the anthems were performed in that order.[40] However, it seems more likely that Archbishop Wake's official, printed order of service was followed. Shedlock concluded that, at the service, nothing would have happened 'that was not printed in the Official Book'.[41] Similarly, Sabine Henze-Döhring remarked: 'In the end it seems inconceivable that the regulation of liturgy and ceremonial should have been left to a composer.'[42] Winton Dean accepted Wake's order of the anthems when he first described the archbishop's annotated copy of the order of service.[43] Nevertheless, in support of the Cheque Book order, the reliability of Wake's annotations has been questioned. It has been argued that the archbishop had been 'evidently puzzled, if not shocked' by Handel's '"individual" handling' of the order of service, by his not following the printed version; the archbishop's annotations have therefore been interpreted as a critique of the composer.[44] However, there is no evidence for Wake's being offended and it is not clear whether such a reaction would have influenced his annotations. For instance, it is notable that his harsh remark about the entrance-anthem ('I was glad') criticizes the 'Negligence of the Choir of Westm.'". But Handel was not involved with the choir of Westminster; he was solely connected with the Chapel Royal, and therefore this remark would not have applied to him at all. On the contrary, the explicit reference to the Abbey choir clears Handel of the responsibility for this mishap. In the end, one cannot deny the importance of Wake's remarks for the evidence they provide regarding the music's performance at the coronation. As Walter and Margret Eisen conclude, the Cheque Book entry

---

[39] Clifford Bartlett (ed.), Preface to *George Frideric Handel, Four Coronation Anthems*, full score (Oxford University Press, 1990), vii. See also Burrows and Ronish, 212.

[40] *Cambridge, Fitzwilliam Museum, Department of Manuscripts and Printed Books, Barrett-Lennard-Collection*, vol. 30 ('in the handwriting of his [Handel's] amanuensis John Christopher Smith'), and *Manchester, Central Library, Henry Watson Music Library, Newman Flower Collection*, vol. 49 ('written by one of the Smith copyists'). See the editorial notes by Damian Cranmer (ed.), *George Frideric Handel, Zadok the Priest – Coronation Anthem*, miniature score (London: Eulenburg, 1980), p. xii. For another manuscript copy following this order see *London, Gerald Coke Handel Collection (Lch) MS 674*, formerly in the possession of the Earl of Shaftesbury, from *c.* 1740.

[41] Shedlock, 157.

[42] Henze-Döhring, 106 ('Schließlich scheint es undenkbar, dass die Festlegung von Liturgie und Zeremoniell einem Komponisten anvertraut worden war.').

[43] See Dean, Sleeve notes. This was followed by Christopher Dearnley, *English Church Music 1650–1750 in Chapel, Cathedral and Parish Church* (London: Barrie & Jenkins, 1970), 255; and H. C. Robbins Landon, *Handel and His World* (London: Weidenfeld and Nicolson, 1984), 122.

[44] Henze-Döhring, 107 ('[. . .] nachweislich irritierte, wenn nicht empörte'). See also ibid., 113.

'shows the planned procedure, whereas Wake's annotations describe the actual course of events'.[45]

Handel's anthems

'Let thy hand be strengthened'

At least since the *Liber Regalis* an anthem on the text 'The King shall rejoice' had followed the Crowning. However, since 1689 'Praise the Lord, O Jerusalem' had been sung after the Crowning, and 'The King/Queen shall rejoice' had been used at the Recognition in 1702 and 1714. Wake kept both anthems in these places, presumably because he had been told to model his order of service on that of George I. In the Cheque Book order, which follows Sandford, the anthem after the Recognition is 'Let thy hand be strengthened'.

In his annotated copy of the order of service Wake inserted the full text of 'Let thy hand be strengthened' after the prayer of the Inthronization, before the Homage.[46] Burrows argued that the archbishop inserted the anthem at this place because Handel had already composed it and because this was 'where it least disturbed his [Wake's] numbering of the anthems' and caused 'as little disturbance to his overall plan as possible'.[47] This explanation is supported by the fact that Wake entered the whole text of Handel's anthem and amended the numbering of the others: he headed it 'Anthem. vij.' and deleted 'Anthem VII' over the Te Deum.

A change of the anthem after the Recognition, on learning about Handel's setting, might have seemed difficult for the archbishop – after all, according to Wake's own statement 'his Mat[ie] would have nothing changed' when he proposed to replace one of the prayers after the order of service had been approved.[48] Hence it would not be surprising if the archbishop did not dare to change the anthems in his order of service so as to match Handel's settings, but found it 'safer' simply to add one more. The anthem performed at the Recognition would therefore most probably have been 'The King shall rejoice'. Furthermore, if 'The King shall rejoice' was the first of Handel's

---

[45] *HHB*, vol. IV, 154: '[Der Eintrag im New Cheque Book der Chapel Royal] spiegelt [...] den geplanten Verlauf wider, während Wake's Eintragungen den tatsächlichen Hergang schildern'.

[46] *Llp Cod. Misc. 1079B*, p. 59.

[47] Burrows, '1727 Coronation', 471, and Burrows, *Handel and the English Chapel Royal*, 262.

[48] See above, fn. 37.

anthems heard at the coronation, this would match with the aforeseen enthusiastic description of 'the I.st' anthem in the annotation in Mainwaring.

Wake remarked about the anthem at the Recognition: 'The Anthems [*sic*, the 's' is crossed out] in Confusion: All irregular in the Music. (Coron. G. 2.)'.[49] Without further explanation, it has been proposed that the organist of Westminster Abbey, John Robinson, may have contributed to this 'confusion'.[50] Burrows, on the other hand, explains the remark with the existence of the two different orders of service: while some of the musicians followed the printed order (with 'The King shall rejoice') others followed the order from the Cheque Book (which has 'Let thy hand be strengthened' at this position).[51] Altogether, Burrows' explanation seems convincing, as it might also account for the deleted 's' in Wake's annotation: the archbishop might have realized that the musicians began to perform two anthems at the same time. It is ironic that the printing of the order of service, which had been done 'in order to the preventing any Mistakes or Confusions that may otherwise happen', in the end might have been responsible for some considerable confusion.[52] However, for the anthems later in the service, all musicians seem to have followed the same order of service, since no other 'confusion' is reported.

'Let thy hand be strengthened' is the only one of Handel's four anthems that does not incorporate trumpets and timpani. The absence of these instruments has been explained by the fact that the respective musicians had to be elsewhere in the Abbey and could not play in the orchestra: this is based on the assumption that Handel had followed the Cheque Book and composed the anthem for the Recognition, which was to be followed by 'the sounding of the Trumpets and the beating of drums'.[53] The fanfares were played by the State Trumpeters and Timpani from the gallery at the West end of the quire; the 'Instrumental Musick' which accompanied the anthems, on the other hand, was placed at the opposite end.[54] The explanation that the trumpets could have had to join both performance bodies alternately is supported by a report from the coronation of Queen Victoria; at that coronation musicians were, indeed, going from one gallery to another several times during the service, playing in the fanfares from a

---

[49] *Llp Cod. Misc. 1079B*, p. 5. The annotation is written next to the anthem text.

[50] Webb, 638. Webb explains that Robinson was 'something of a showman'.

[51] Burrows, '1727 Coronation', 471.

[52] *Lna PC 1/15/6*: Preparations for the Coronation, Part iii, p. 2.

[53] Burrows, '1727 Coronation', 471. Similarly in the printed *OS* (1727), 4: 'Then the Trumpets sound. And after that, the Choir sing this Anthem:'

[54] For the positioning of the musicians in the Abbey see the discussion below.

special gallery as well as their part in the orchestra.[55] However, an anthem preceded by fanfares also occurs after the Crowning, but the anthem which Handel probably intended for this place ('The King shall rejoice') incorporates trumpets and timpani from the first movement on.[56] Moreover, even if the trumpeters and timpani player in 1727 had to be away to play in the fanfares, they should have had time to be back for the anthem's last movement, a jubilant Hallelujah.

There is another explanation for the absence of the trumpets and timpani in 'Let thy hand be strengthened': as suggested by Henze-Döhring, Handel may have wished to 'save' these 'regal instruments' to be able to use them at a later point to greater effect.[57] Since he is likely to have composed the anthems following the Cheque Book order, Handel would have thought of 'Let thy hand be strengthened' as the first of his anthems, to be sung after the Recognition. It would then have been only in 'Zadok the Priest' that the congregation in the Abbey heard the choir, orchestra, and trumpets and timpani performing together for the first time during the service. Such a calculated use of the orchestration would undoubtedly have made a grand effect, which could have been intended by Handel for the spiritual climax of the ceremony, the consecration of the new king with holy oil – the Anointing.[58]

The effect would have been heightened by the fact that with these anthems Handel may have been the first composer to use trumpets together with timpani in English church music.[59] Also, his coronation anthems are the first to include three independent trumpet parts. 'Let thy hand' not only does not include trumpets and timpani, its style is generally 'less showy' than that of the other anthems. Whereas these have a predominantly homophonic texture, 'Let thy hand' is characterized by imitative entries at the beginning of the first two movements and in the final Hallelujah. Especially the long reflective middle section 'Let justice and judgment' in E minor is in striking contrast to the almost exclusively jubilant tone of the other anthems.

---

[55] See Ch. 7, fns. 144–5.

[56] There is only a short prayer between the fanfare and the anthem. See *OS* (1727), 49f.

[57] Henze-Döhring, 110f.

[58] For this and the following cf. Henze-Döhring, 110f., who summarizes that 'the effect of *Zadok the Priest* cannot have been anything other than astonishing/shocking ['frappierend']'.

[59] See Burrows, *Handel and the English Chapel Royal*, 265, 273 and 486. See also Gerald Hendrie, preface to Georg Friedrich Händel, *Te Deum zur Feier des Friedens von Utrecht, HWV 278 und Jubilate zur Feier des Friedens von Utrecht, HWV 279, HHA*, series III, vol. 3 (Kassel: Bärenreiter, 1998), vii–xvii, here xvii.

'Zadok the Priest'

For the Anointing Wake reports a grave mishap in the proceedings. According to custom, the archbishop should have begun the *Veni Creator* by singing the first line, after which the choir should have 'sung it out'. However, Wake noted: 'This Hymn by the mistake of the Music not sung; but the next Anthem instead of it.'[60] This would mean that the musicians did not take up the hymn, but began with 'Zadok the Priest' instead. This would have been a strange sight, leaving the archbishop at the altar with his call for the Holy Ghost all alone and it is therefore likely that the anthem was begun before the archbishop had had a chance to intone the hymn.[61] The order in the Cheque Book gives the full text for 'Come, Holy Ghost' with the remark 'This Chanted for Shortness Sake'. This is another indication that this order was written during the preparations for the service and does not reflect what actually happened.

The mistake in omitting the *Veni Creator* may also have ruined Handel's own calculations for 'Zadok the Priest': from later coronations it is known that with the anthem the disrobing of the monarch began, in preparation for the anointing. It is possible that Handel had designed his anthem to match the ceremonial proceedings minutely: the unusually long orchestral introduction may have been meant to cover the changing of the robes, while the stately choir entry to the words 'Zadok the Priest and Nathan the Prophet anointed Solomon King' could then very appropriately have accompanied the actual anointing, to be followed by the jubilant acclamations in the anthem's third section. In any case, the ceremonial lapse was probably realized by only a few people – those familiar with the order of service. The lengthy instrumental prelude to Handel's anthem creates a notable calm pause in the otherwise loud and showy proceedings and by the time of the grand entry of the choir any listener (apart from Archbishop Wake) would probably have forgotten that the *Veni Creator* should have come instead.

The text of 'Zadok the Priest' in the printed order follows that from the coronations since 1689. Handel set the text as found in the Cheque Book, which is the same as in Sandford, except that 'Amen, Alleluia' are added at the end. The Cheque Book describes the anthem as a 'Verse Anthem', but Handel set it as a full anthem with orchestra, which supports the theory that he took this order merely as a guide. He was probably the first to replace

---

[60] *Llp Cod. Misc. 1079B*, p. 34. Whereas in the printed order the *Veni Creator* is headed 'Anthem III', Wake uses the more common term of 'Hymn'.

[61] Lindsay, 233, states that 'Owing to a quarrel with dean and chapter, the *Veni Creator* was omitted by accident.' Unfortunately, no further details are provided.

Lawes's setting from the first coronation after the Restoration. If, as argued above, this had been performed at coronations until 1714, then Handel would certainly have known it. Indeed, Handel follows Lawes in some crucial structural points. Both composers divide the anthem into the same three parts: the first part describes Solomon's anointing, the second part the rejoicing of the people, and the third part is the acclamation of the king including an Hallelujah. Furthermore, Handel like Lawes uses half closes to generate accents stressing the text. The first is after the first line of the text (on 'King') and is relieved in the description of 'and all the people rejoiced', (Lawes: 'and joyfully approaching [...]'); the second is at the end of the middle section on 'and said' (Lawes: 'and cried') which leads into the section beginning with 'God save the King'. Owing to the loss of the orchestral parts of Lawes's anthem, the extent of its influence on Handel cannot be fully assessed; the similarities in the surviving material, however, suggest that Handel used it as a model at least in some respects.

It was probably Handel's idea to combine the threefold acclamation of the people, 'God save the King! Long live the King! May the King live for ever!', in one movement with the final 'Hallelujah, Amen'. In the final order of service a similar threefold acclamation follows after the Homage when

the Trumpets sound, and all the People shout, crying out, God save King GEORGE the Second. / Long live King GEORGE. / May the King live for ever.[62]

The recurrence of the text creates a link between the anthem during the Anointing and the Homage of the Peers. This supports the impression that the scene from the Old Testament as reported in 'Zadok the Priest' is transferred to Britain in 1727: the acclamation in the anthem can be understood to refer to both the Biblical King Solomon and to George II.[63] Indeed, ten years after its first performance, Handel's 'Zadok the Priest' was widely known simply as the anthem 'God save the King', the text which is so dominant in its final section.[64] Handel presents the threefold acclamation in strong, self-confident chords, using the full forces, and the Hallelujah is also set in a clear, homophonic way. In striking contrast, the word 'Amen' is used for sophisticated polyphonic writing. The 'stuttering' of this word in

---

[62] *Llp Cod. Misc. 1079A* , p. 43, and *OS* (1727), 63. There is nothing like that in the Cheque Book, where the text of the anthem during the Homage is immediately followed by the Coronation of the Queen.

[63] Cf. above, p. 24.

[64] Friedrich Chrysander, 'Henry Carey und der Ursprung des Königsgesanges God save the King', *Jahrbücher für musikalische Wissenschaft*, vol. I (Leipzig: Breitkopf und Härtel, 1863), 287–407, here 291–3.

some parts while others sing long melismas of semi-quavers (the first time being in bars 69–72) gives it further emphasis and might represent the people's being awestruck and literally speechless by the impression of the ceremony.[65] Incidentally, Handel was probably the first to introduce this technique of dividing a word by pauses so prominently into English church music.[66]

'The King shall rejoice'

For the anthem after the Crowning, Wake had retained the text of 'Praise the Lord, O Jerusalem' as in the previous three coronations. Its verse 'For kings shall be thy nursing fathers, and queens thy nursing mothers' occurs also later in the service, in the queen's anthem 'My heart is inditing'. It is unusual to have the same text in two different anthems in one service, and one wonders if this repeat may have escaped the archbishop's otherwise meticulous attention.[67] On the other hand, the recurrence could have been specifically intended – ultimately, both are anthems following a Crowning, and the repeat of the text could have been intended to point out the unity of the king and queen.

The Cheque Book order follows Sandford and gives the text of 'The King shall rejoice', with slight changes.[68] It is therefore possible that Handel's anthem to the text was originally intended for this moment in the service. However, whereas the Cheque Book declares it as a 'Verse Anthem', Handel's setting is full throughout. Furthermore, he altered the text slightly by replacing the second verse of the psalm by words from the fifth ('Glory and worship hast thou laid upon him') and omitting 'for' at the beginning of the third verse. The idea of including this verse could have come from Turner's setting of this anthem, which Handel most probably knew as it was still sung in the Chapel Royal during George I's reign.

Wake did not write any remark to the anthem after the Crowning in his order of service, which suggests that everything went according to the printed text. In any event, as previously argued, Handel's 'The King shall

---

[65] For this idea see Chrysander, 'Henry Carey', 290.

[66] Gregory Barnett calls this the 'Amen *topos*', explaining that it goes back to Handel's second setting of the *Laudate* from 1707 (HWV 237). See 'Handel's Borrowings and the disputed *Gloria*', *EM* (Feb. 2006), 75–92; the term is first mentioned and explained on p. 77. Landon, 124f., shows that Handel had used this technique in *Nisi Dominus* from 1707 (HWV 238), which generally served as a source for 'Zadok the Priest'. Furthermore, Handel used this technique also in the last movement of his Birthday Ode for Queen Anne, 'Eternal Source of Love Divine' (HWV 74) from 1713/14.

[67] Cf. Ch. 6, fn. 44.   [68] For a comparative table of the texts see App. A5a.

rejoice' had probably been sung at the Recognition and would then not have been repeated after the Crowning. Upon receiving the final, printed order of service, Handel could easily still have scheduled Clarke's 'Praise the Lord, O Jerusalem'.

Following the two previous coronations the order of service instructed that 'As soon as the King is crowned, the Peers, &c. put on their Coronets and Caps'.[69] From this coronation onwards up to 1953 the anthem was performed only after the peers had put on their coronets and had acclaimed their monarch; the music had thus ultimately lost an important structural role in the ceremonial.

'My heart is inditing'

For the Queen's Coronation Wake followed Sancroft's order of service and included the anthem 'My heart is enditing' [sic] as in 1685. The Cheque Book includes the same anthem, but with a considerably revised text: several verses are cut and some new passages are added.[70] Intriguingly, verse 10 is now included in full. In 1685, the beginning of this verse ('Kings' daughters [...]') had been omitted, perhaps in consideration that James II's wife, Mary of Modena, was not a king's, but a duke's daughter. Whoever compiled the text in 1727 apparently did not worry about such details (Queen Caroline was the daughter of John Frederick, Margrave of Brandenburg-Ansbach).

Handel followed the text as in the Cheque Book almost exactly. Conceptually, this anthem is somewhat different from the others. The opening chorus includes verse passages which, although still sung by several singers per part,[71] create a more intimate character compared to the other anthems. The trumpets and timpani appear only near the end of the opening chorus, thus possibly scheduled to highlight the moment when the queen's procession from her crowning to the throne had arrived and when she was enthroned next to her husband. In the second movement, on the text 'Kings' daughters were among thy honourable women', the music charmingly illustrates the text: whereas the word 'Kings' is given a long, 'stately' note at the beginning of the theme, the 'daughters' are represented by a characteristic dotted-quaver-semiquaver figure (presumably with a trill, as written in the instrumental parts at the beginning of the movement). The whole phrase is 'echoed' by the instruments (bars 110–11),

---

[69] OS (1727), 50.   [70] For a comparative table of the texts see App. A5b.
[71] Burrows, *Handel and the English Chapel Royal*, 270.

enhancing the effect. As the beginning of the previous movement, this movement might have been sung as a verse with several voices per part, indicated by the singers' names in the autograph score.[72]

There occurs an intriguing linguistic problem in the text of the next movement. The beginning of the second half of the tenth verse of the psalm ('Upon thy right hand did stand the Queen in vesture of gold') is followed by the newly inserted text from verse 12 ('and the King shall have pleasure in thy beauty'). The new combination of the two verses, however, is rather confusing and does not work grammatically: the word 'thy' in verse ten referred in the psalm to God, meaning that the queen stood on God's right hand. In the 1685 anthem text Sancroft had changed 'upon *thy* right hand' to 'at *his* right hand', to make clear that he meant the verse to refer to the king, upon whose right hand the queen stands. In the text from verse 12, on the other hand, 'thy' refers to the queen, not to God.[73] Handel sets these two verses in a very pictorial way, in a movement in slow triple time without trumpets and timpani. His setting makes the textual problem easily ignored. After an orchestral introduction the first verse is presented by treble and first alto, accompanied by the oboes and echoed by the strings; this is answered by a repeat of the text in the lower voices (A1, A2, T and B), with continuo only. The complete forces of this movement are not employed until the text reaches the words 'and the King shall have pleasure' (b. 189) and the full entry may well have been intended to characterize the king's majesty. The word 'pleasure' is emphasized by tripping, dotted quavers which had already been heard in the orchestral introduction. After the word 'pleasure' has been repeated for several bars, the listener is unlikely to notice the fact that the word 'thy' should grammatically refer to God or the king, and can easily understand it to refer to the queen, and that it is in her beauty that the king shall have pleasure. It is important that only the beginning of verse 12 was chosen for the text. In the Prayer Book the verse ends: '[. . .] thy beauty: for he [the King] is thy [the Queen's] Lord God, and worship thou him'. Thus, the original text in the end makes clear that 'King' refers to the Heavenly King, to the 'Lord God'. The shortened anthem text, however, could perfectly well refer to George II and Queen Caroline.[74]

The text of the last chorus is solely the verse 'Kings shall be thy nursing fathers and Queens thy nursing mothers' from Isaiah 49:23. Handel follows

---

[72] See Burrows and Ronish, 213.

[73] In the psalm this verse follows the verse 'Hearken, O daughter'.

[74] Ruth Smith points out that it was not usual at the time to select non-consecutive psalm verses. For this and for a general discussion of the adaptation of Biblical texts see *Handel's Oratorios*, 94–103.

the 1689 version of the text in omitting the word 'their' before queens. This implies that he did not simply copy the text for this anthem from that given in Sandford for Purcell's anthem in 1685, but in such details did indeed 'chuse for [him]self'.[75] As in the preceding verses, there is some textual ambiguity here: in the original psalm context, the word 'thy' referred to Sion, and in the earlier anthem context this was made clear by the preceding verse ('Praise the Lord, O Jerusalem [. . .]'). In Handel's anthem, however, this verse is cut. Therefore, in the new context, 'thy' is not obviously linked to any word and could refer either to the king or queen just crowned, or even to God himself, whose nursing fathers and mothers should be kings and queens.

In the same way as Clarke in 'Praise the Lord, O Jerusalem', Handel creates a musical contrast between the 'Kings' and 'Queens'. 'Kings shall be thy nursing fathers' is presented in strong staccato chords in the full choir, with vivid scales in the orchestra. The first 'Kings' is singled out by a repeat after a short instrumental passage, which gives it more martial fervour. When the text comes to 'and Queens thy nursing mothers' (b. 273) the character of the music changes considerably: the text is sung only in the upper voices, first by treble and alto, later joined by the tenor, and the music's significant features are reverential appoggiaturas and many rests, which give the whole setting a thinner effect (even visually). However, the two texts of 'Kings' and 'Queens' are not juxtaposed sharply – on the contrary, they are combined throughout and alternate quickly with each other. Before the movement's 'coda' (beginning in b. 300) the word 'Kings' is heard four times in strong chords – with the following delayed entries of the trebles and the lower voices altogether six times. Harmonically, this stressing of the word is dressed in a strong cadence (B major – E minor – A major – D major) with the entry of the trumpets on the fourth 'Kings'. Since this is the only one of Handel's four anthems that does not have a final 'Hallelujah, Amen' chorus, it is the line 'and Queens thy nursing mothers' in the full forces in the final adagio bars that brings the movement, the anthem, and indeed presumably all of Handel's choral contribution to the service to a triumphant close. As seen above, in 1685 Purcell may have used the ending of his anthem as a finale for the whole service. Handel seems to have followed this idea and marked the end of the coronation part of the service with this chorus.[76]

[75] Cf. above, fn. 26.

[76] Cf. Burrows, *Handel and the English Chapel Royal*, 270: 'Even though this was the anthem associated with the Queen's coronation, he [Handel] seems to have been principally concerned with making a good finale [. . .]'

Henze-Döhring proposes a 'strategy' of Handel's that was based on a 'characterizing, descriptive/meaningful setting' ('charakterisierenden, zeichenhaften Vertonung').[77] She interprets that he had set the anthems for the king in a 'heroic, theatrical way' ('heroischem theatralen Duktus'), using the trumpets and timpani as the most obvious 'instrumental regalia' ('instrumentalen Herrschaftsinsignien'). The queen's anthem, on the other hand, he had set in a 'lyrical, songlike way' ('lyrisch, liedhaften Duktus'), except for the last movement. At the same time, this anthem – being as 'jubilant and extrovert' as the others – has been interpreted as reflecting the queen's 'lively influence [...] in court life and indeed in consequent political activity'.[78] Similarly, it has been argued that the ceremonies surrounding Queen Caroline's coronation had celebrated her status almost like that of a 'joint monarch'.[79] However, the order of service clearly followed that of 1685, not, for instance, that of 1689 which had included the coronation of a king and a queen regnant. In 1727, Queen Caroline is celebrated as the king's consort only. Handel illustrates that perfectly well in the second movement of his anthem: the queen stands at the king's right hand and he shall have pleasure in her beauty. In referring to both the king and the queen equally, the anthem naturally requires the same 'jubilant and extrovert' music as the king's anthems. If anything, the 1727 text and Handel's setting give the king a more prominent place in this anthem than he had had in 1685.

Based on the observation of the role of the trumpets, and assuming that Handel followed the order in the Cheque Book, Henze-Döhring identifies an overall plan for his Coronation Anthems. She calls them a 'comprehensive setting that transcends its division into separate "numbers" and reveals a dramaturgical intent that cannot be missed'.[80] Indeed, the claimed 'dramaturgical intent' complements the liturgical order and makes for a good effect. Consequently, at a performance of all four anthems they should be performed in the order in which Handel may have intended them to be heard: 'Let thy hand be strengthened', 'Zadok the Priest', 'The King shall rejoice', and 'My heart is inditing'.

---

[77] For this and the following see Henze-Döhring, 112.

[78] Burrows, *Handel and the English Chapel Royal*, 270.

[79] Andrew Hanham, 'Caroline of Brandenburg-Ansbach and the "anglicisation" of the House of Hanover', in Clarissa Campbell Orr (ed.), *Queenship in Europe 1660–1815. The Role of the Consort* (Cambridge University Press, 2004), 276–99, here 292.

[80] Henze-Döhring, 110 ('Betrachtet man nun Händels vier Coronation Anthems in ihrer Faktur und Abfolge, so zeichnet sich eine – wenn man so will – "nummern"-übergreifende Vertonung ab mit nicht zu übersehendem dramaturgischen Kalkül.').

Other music

Handel's pupil Christopher Smith was paid 'Thirty Pounds Ten Shillings for Copying the Anthems composed by Mr. Handel for His Majesty's Coronation'.[81] However, there is no warrant for copying anyone else's music. No music by Greene and Weldon, the official Chapel Royal composers at the time, can be linked with the service, although both were at least present and contributed to the performance.[82] The fanfares of the day may have been similar to the 'Grand Trumpeter March' which J.A. Kappey describes as a 'fanfare in the ancient style', and which appears to date from 'the period around 1725'.[83] For the anthem during the procession from Westminster Hall to the Abbey the Cheque Book gives the text of 'O Lord, grant the King a long life' as found in Sandford for 1685 and this makes it likely that Child's setting was sung. The performance of the anthem in the procession may at this coronation have been particularly difficult. Leake reports about the lack of space on the specially built processional route:[84]

And it should be remembered that the Floor of the Stage, upon which the proceeding went to the Abbey being about two feet and one half from the ground, was too narrow, So that those who according to the Order of Council should have gone four a breast, could not, and it was with difficulty the Heralds passed on either side to Marshal the Procession.

This means that the singers, too, could have walked with at best three in a row, not four as in Sandford's depictions from 1685 and as reported for the next coronation.[85] This arrangement would have further stretched out the choir and increased the difficulties of the performance. César de Saussure reported that the choir was 'followed by a band of musicians with hautboys, fifes, bassoons, bugles, and other instruments'.[86] This appears to be the first

---

[81] *Lna LC 5/18*, p. 15. Transcribed in Burrows, *Handel and the English Chapel Royal*, 610.

[82] Burrows, *Handel and the English Chapel Royal*, 274.

[83] Jacob Adam Kappey, *Military Music. A History of Wind-Instrumental Bands* (London: Boosey, [1894]), 50–3, here 52; for the date see Titcomb, 79. For a reproduction, together with another fanfare, see Range, thesis, vol. II.

[84] *Lca MS S.M.L.* 65, p. 12.

[85] Handwritten annotations by one of the heralds in *The Form of the Proceeding to the Royal Coronation of their most Excellent Majesties King George III. and Queen Charlotte* [. . .] (London: Printed with William Bowyer, 1761), 5. See *Lca Coronation of George III 1761*, vol. III.

[86] César de Saussure, *A Foreign View of England in the Reigns of George I. and George II. The Letters of Monsieur César de Saussure to his Family*, transl. and ed. Madame van Muyden (London: Murray, 1902), 243.

time that a full band is reported for this procession and it would most probably have accompanied the choir and performed music alternately.[87]

The anthem at the entrance of the king and queen into the Abbey is in both orders of service 'I was glad'. As with the anthems set by Handel, the printed order follows the text of the previous coronations and the Cheque Book follows Sandford. When conductor Robert King reconstructed the musical programme of the service, he proposed that the anthem was sung in the five-part full setting associated with the 1685 coronation.[88] This idea appears to stem from the assumption that this setting had been sung at every coronation since 1685. However, it seems altogether more likely that Pigott's more recent setting from 1702 would have been scheduled for 1727. In any event, as already mentioned, according to Wake the anthem was 'omitted and no Anthem at all Sung [. . .] by the Negligence of the Choir of Westm.".[89] The explanation for this omission could be that it was simply not physically possible for the Abbey choir to perform the anthem in the nave. That this could have been the case is indicated by a source related to the next coronation: William Boyce, the musician responsible for the music in 1761, wrote to the archbishop reminding him that 'a proper Space may be reserved in the Isles, for the Choir to perform the First anthem'.[90] If the situation was similar in 1727 and the choir had no 'proper Space' to wait for the royal party's arrival, they would have had to go to their gallery instead; Wake would then have interpreted their not waiting as 'Negligence'. Finally, it is also possible that the singing of the entrance-anthem was omitted seemingly by the choir's 'negligence', but in fact rather because of a general confusion at the beginning of the service. James Risk refers to a report of the ceremony by Leake, according to which there was 'an odd contretemps in the Abbey':[91]

The Royal Procession was already in motion with the King about to make his entrance when, 'The Judges refused to take the places assigned to them, because the Knights of the Bath were to sit above them, though the Order in Council had done it with a Salve Jure to their rights; It was done they said by Anstis [Garter King of Arms] in favour of his darling Order; but when I urged the Order in Council to

---

[87] Cf. Ch. 6, fn. 122.   [88] *The Coronation of King George II*, CDA 67286 (Hyperion 2001).
[89] *Llp Cod. Misc 1079B*, p. 2.   [90] *Llp MS 1130*, vol. I, (40). For a full transcription see App. B3a.
[91] James C. Risk, *The History of The Order of the Bath and Its Insignia* (London: Spink and Son, 1972), 20. Risk refers to 'Leake, SML. Vol. III, pp. 12, 13 ['Leake, Stephen Martin. A Manuscript by Leake preserved in the College of Arms']'. This does not match with any of the shelfmarks in the College, and it may be a misprint. A similar situation is described in two other accounts by Leake: *Lca MS S.M.L. 65* ('Heraldo Memoriale', vol. II), p. 8f., and *Lca MS S.M.L. 44* ('Heraldic Annals', vol. I), p. 26.

them, and that whilst they were disputing his Majesty and all the Procession were stopt, they sat down grumbling.'

If there was indeed so much confusion as to stop the royal procession, it would be easily understandable that the choir's singing of the entrance-anthem could have been missed out.

As seen above, the *Veni Creator* should have been 'Chanted for Shortness Sake' according to the Cheque Book. The remark 'Chanted' appears here for the first time in this order of service and the reason of 'Shortness' may probably also account for the following such annotations. Wake had claimed that 'the whole may be setled in one Hours time' and this has been interpreted to mean that he wanted to cut down the service to one hour in length.[92] However, that would have been a very short coronation service and Wake may have referred to his hoping that the Privy Council could agree on the order of service 'in one Hours time'. After all, it is worth remembering that Wake had restored the lengthy recital of the Decalogue which had been omitted at the previous coronation.[93] In his annotated order of service the archbishop had suggested a shortening of the music only for the Litany ('To shorten the Service let this be read'), but he did not suggest any chanting. If the Cheque Book order had been followed in the service, this coronation would probably have included more chanting than any other before or afterwards. However, the exact meaning of the word 'chanting' is worth reconsidering. On the one hand, it could simply refer to harmonized chant tunes.[94] But on the other hand, the verb 'to chant' was at one point also a synonym for 'to sing', in the sense of both a simple homophonic setting, or even of a complex choral setting such as Handel's 'Zadok the Priest' or his Hallelujah Chorus.[95] If chanting was intended to save time the word would

---

[92] Letter to the Privy Council of 20 August 1727 (*Lna PC1/15/6*; transcr. App. B2a), and Bense, 317.

[93] Norman Sykes, *William Wake, Archbishop of Canterbury 1657–1737*, 2 vols. (Cambridge University Press, 1957), vol. II, 186.

[94] For a repertory of chant tunes at the time, especially in the Chapel Royal and at Westminster Abbey see Ruth Wilson, 271ff. See also *Lbl MS Add. 17784*, fo. 177v.

[95] Cf. the entry in the OED. For 'Zadok the Priest' see *Ceremonial of the Coronation of His Most Sacred Majesty King George the Fourth* [...] (West-Minster: Printed by John Whitaker, 1823), 19: 'While the Anthem "Zadok the Priest was chaunted" his MAJESTY was disrobed [...]' For the Hallelujah Chorus see *Ceremonial to be observed at the Baptism of His Royal Highness The Prince of Wales, in the Royal Chapel of St. George* [...] *on Tuesday, January the 25th, 1842* (Westminster: Francis Watts [1842]), 3: at the end of the service: 'The Hallelujah Chorus will then be chaunted by the full Choir.' See also below, Ch. 6, fn. 175. More research on the etymology and usage of the word would be necessary to determine its possible meaning(s) in 1727.

probably have referred to chanting in the modern sense or to a straightforward homophonic setting.

For the anthem after the Anointing, both orders of service stipulate 'Behold, O God'. While the printed order gives the shortened text as it appeared at the two previous coronations, the Cheque Book follows Sandford's text from the 1685 coronation. The annotation in the margin reads 'This Chanted', which might here imply a short full anthem. Robert King, in his reconstruction of the service, used Blow's four-part setting of the text from 1689, explaining that 'this shorter version seems to be the one more likely to have been on the Abbey music shelves'.[96] Given that it was probably this setting that was sung at the two previous coronations, it is likely that it was also sung in 1727.

The Te Deum, sung during the king's procession to his throne, is the only piece for which details about the composer are given in any of the sources for this coronation. The Cheque Book states that before the Homage 'Te Deum of Gibbons's was Sung'.[97] This probably refers to Orlando Gibbons, rather than to his brother Edward or his second son Christopher, all of whom were composers and connected with the Chapel Royal in one way or another.[98] No Te Deum settings by the latter two are known whereas there are two English Te Deum settings by Orlando.[99] It may be assumed that the 'Te Deum of Gibbons's' was a piece that was well known and popular in the Chapel Royal and/or in Westminster Abbey, or even a favourite of Handel's. Otherwise the compiler of the Cheque Book order, who followed Sandford for the rest of the music, would certainly have followed Sandford at this point, too, and proposed a Te Deum by Child.

Herrmann observed that Handel had 'composed one anthem for each of the major divisions of the service'.[100] That is true except for the Homage, which traditionally gave opportunity for the most elaborate music in the service. Handel's not composing an anthem for this ceremony could have been due to a misunderstanding. The Cheque Book follows Sandford and gives the text of 'God spake sometimes [sic] in visions', as set by Blow in 1685 – but there is again a note in the margin which reads 'This Chanted'. The chanting of the anthem during the Homage would be very surprising for two reasons: firstly, at the previous coronation services this ceremony had included a very elaborate

[96] Robert King, Booklet notes to *The Coronation of King George II*, 11.

[97] As seen above this is the only instance that the text of this order is in the past tense.

[98] Cf. the respective articles in *NG* 9: Christopher D.S. Field on 'Christopher Gibbons', 830–2; and John Harper and Peter Le Huray on 'Orlando Gibbons', 832–6. Edward Gibbons does not have a separate article.

[99] King in his reconstruction offers the one from Gibbons's Second Service.   [100] Herrmann, v.

anthem, to be performed 'with instrumental musick of all sorts' and a reduction to a mere chant or a simple homophonic setting would have been a great break with established practice. Secondly, the necessity of saving time in this anthem is not easily explained: the ceremony of the Homage takes as much time as the peers need to pay homage to the king; and at this coronation they numbered '128 English and 21 Scotch' peers.[101] The shortening of the musical contribution would not have helped to 'shorten the service'. The reason for this annotation could have been a misunderstanding: all the previous orders of service had in a general way stated that the anthem was to be performed *during* the ceremony, but the Cheque Book explicitly states that it should be sung only *after* the Homage.[102] The scribe could have referred to the fact that the anthem should commence only after the vows of the peers, during the individual peers' ascending the throne. When Handel chose which anthems to compose anew, he probably selected those which gave him the best opportunity to write some grand music – and in the Cheque Book order, which he presumably used, the Homage anthem would not have seemed to fall into this category. However, such a misunderstanding would have been rectified at the latest when Handel received the printed order of service. It is unlikely that a musician of his calibre would then have rejected the opportunity to perform elaborate music during one of the most splendid ceremonies of the coronation in favour of a simple chant. Thus it is plausible that Handel, in the end, followed the printed order of service and performed an 'Anthem, with Instrumental Musick of all sorts'.[103] This order includes the full text of 'The Lord is a Sun and a Shield', identical with that at the previous two coronations and as set by Croft. It is therefore possible that Handel repeated Croft's settings for which the Chapel may easily still have had the music.

As for the previous coronations very little is known about the liturgical music. Wake followed his predecessors and left the Nicene Creed at its place before the Anointing; in his manuscript draft he scheduled that, as customary, he would begin it and that the choir 'Singeth it', but in the printed version this explicit instruction was omitted.[104] The explanatory text reads only '*The Nicene Creed, by the Archbishop, the King and Queen with the People standing, as before*', and this seems to be linked to the explanatory text of the preceding Gospel: '*To be read by another Bishop, the King and Queen with the People standing.*' Thus it is possible that Wake, in the printed order of service, had intended the Creed to be read, at best with the congregation

[101] *Lca MS S.M.L. 65*, p. 9.

[102] Cheque Book, 105/Ashbee and Harley, vol. I, 283: 'After the Lords have done Homage to the King, and after the scattering the Coronation Medals, the following Anthem is Sung.'

[103] OS (1727), 62.   [104] *Llp Cod. Misc. 1079A*, p. 13; OS (1727), 26.

joining in after the first line. This would match with the order of service in the Cheque Book, which states explicitly that the Nicene Creed was simply 'to be Read'. Intriguingly, this order has the Creed in the same place as the pre-1685 orders of service, namely in the second part of the service, after the Homage. In this particular point, the scribe could have followed the order of service for Charles I's coronation, entered in the Old Cheque Book.[105] Thus Sandford was probably not the only source for this order of service.

For the royal couple's procession from the thrones to the altar to receive communion the printed order of service includes the usual phrase 'Then the Organ plays, and the Choir singeth', followed by the text of 'Let my prayer come up'.[106] The Cheque Book does not mention this anthem, but it mentions that the organ should play during the offertory until all the alms are collected, which implies improvised organ music to match the duration of the ceremony.

Both orders of service make provision for a Sanctus and Gloria, with the Cheque Book stating that they were both to be 'sung in Musick', meaning in polyphonic settings. As at the preceding coronations, the Gloria accompanied the royal couple's procession from the altar back to their thrones after the taking of communion.[107] For their procession from the thrones into St Edward's Chapel, the printed order of service mentions the customary organ music: 'and so they proceed in State into the Chapel, the Organs all the while playing'.[108] Again this could have been partly improvised music to achieve a close ceremonial match.

Henze-Döhring, who concludes that no other elaborate music than Handel's anthems was performed during the service, states – with self-confessed exaggeration – that the whole ceremony had thus been turned into a 'Handel concert'.[109] This justly acknowledges the prominent role of Handel's music, although it is worth remembering that his four anthems would still have been followed by several pieces of liturgical music as part of the Communion Service. There are no reports about the instrumental music of the service. In his reconstruction, King uses the overture of Handel's *Occasional Oratorio* as a 'Grand Instrumental Procession' to cover the procession of the clergy and the Chapel Royal before the service.[110] While the oratorio dates from only 1746, Handel may of course have provided some similar music for the coronation.

---

[105] See Ch. 2, fn. 31.   [106] *OS* (1727), 70f.   [107] Ibid., 83.   [108] Ibid., 86.
[109] Henze-Döhring, 110: '[...] die Mutation der traditionellen Krönungsmusik zu einem – überspitzt formuliert – Händelkonzert [...]'
[110] King, Booklet notes, 9.

It has been proposed that Croft had composed his last anthem, 'Give the King thy judgments' for the coronation. As Burrows has shown, however, this is unlikely.[111] The text has never appeared in a source for a coronation before or afterwards. Anselm Hughes, following an idea by Thewlis, suggested that Croft's anthem was sung instead of 'Let my prayer come up'.[112] However, there is no evidence for that claim. Burrows explains that the piece, as a normal verse anthem for singers and organ, was probably intended only as a 'topical offering' for a regular Sunday morning service at the Chapel Royal.[113] Indeed, the fact that Croft's anthem was performed at some time is indicated by the singers' names and corrections in the autograph score.

Again there are but few details for the music during the coronation banquet. A warrant from 22 August required the Surveyor General 'to Erect a Box in Westminster Hall for the Kings Private Musick'.[114] However, no details of the music performed survive, and it could be only speculated if Handel contributed to this.

The 1727 coronation service seems to have been the first in which all the important anthems were genuine orchestral anthems. The reason for such an innovation is not clear: it might have been Handel's conviction that orchestral anthems are more suitable for such representative pieces. Also, considering his German background, anthems without orchestral accompaniment must have seemed a waste of the forces available to him: all German cantatas normally included a variety of instruments. Indeed, Handel composed hardly any church music without instrumental accompaniment.[115] Considering the history of the English orchestral anthem, Handel's Coronation Anthems are especially noteworthy: notwithstanding the soloistic sections in 'My heart is inditing' they are the earliest more complex 'full anthems' with independent orchestral accompaniment, all earlier orchestral anthems having included verse sections.[116] Furthermore, it is noteworthy that the Coronation Anthems are almost Handel's only examples of this new 'genre'; all his later anthems – from the wedding

---

[111] Burrows, '1727 Coronation', 469, where he also refers to the earlier literature, and Burrows, *Handel and the English Chapel Royal*, 174. See also Shaw and Beeks, 715, and lately Marx, 346. The autograph score in *Lbl MS Add. 17861* is dated 'July y.ᵉ 13.ᵗʰ / 1727'.

[112] Anselm Hughes, 95, n. 17. The idea that the anthem could have been intended for the coronation was probably first suggested by F. G. E[dwards], 'Dr. William Croft (1678–1727)', *MT* 41 (1900), 577–85, here 583.

[113] Burrows, *Handel and the English Chapel Royal*, 174, fn. 33.

[114] *Lca Coronation of George III 1761*, vol. III, copies of the minutes of the Privy Council from 1727, [p. 7].

[115] See the two versions of 'As pants the hart', HWV 251a and 251d.

[116] Lawes's 'Zadok the Priest' and Child's 'I was glad', which appear to have been orchestral full anthems, were very straightforward short settings.

anthems for the royal children to the 1749 Peace Anthem – include movements for soloists. And even the grand Dettingen Te Deum had the choruses interspersed with solo sections. The Funeral Anthem for Queen Caroline from 1737 comes closest to the structure of the Coronation Anthems, consisting mainly of full choruses.[117] It thus appears that Handel reserved the full orchestral style for only the grandest of occasions. It was not before the 1760s, with Boyce's anthems for the funeral of George II and the coronation of George III and Queen Charlotte, that the orchestral full style returned to the great occasions of state.

Performance

The 1727 coronation set new standards not only in the compositional style of the music, but also regarding its performance; Boyce later called it the 'first grand Musical Performance in the Abbey'.[118] The number of musicians was probably bigger than at any previous coronation. On the first page of the autograph score of 'The King shall rejoice', Handel entered the names and numbers of altogether 47 singers:[119]

C.[anto] 12 / H[ughes] et 6 [Alto 1] / Fr.[eeman] et 6 [Alto 2] / Church et 6 [tenor] / W[heely] et 6 [Bass 1] / Gates. et 6 [Bass 2]

It has already been pointed out that Handel had to cope with the loss of five of the ten Chapel Royal boys because their voices had broken.[120] Nevertheless, the usual 'Scarlet cloth' was provided for '20 Laymen' and '10 Children'.[121] Thus there should have been ten boys again by the time of the coronation. To these thirty singers the Abbey choir must be added, so that the total number of forty-seven seems possible, although one might then expect the number of trebles noted by Handel to be higher.[122] Indeed, it has been argued that the 'list' of the performers on the score is unlikely to be complete.[123] Also, it may, after all, not refer to the coronation: F.G. Edwards suggested that the numbers refer to 'a subsequent concert performance'.[124] Burrows has pointed out that 'Handel named only singers

---

[117] No. 3 'When the ear heard her' and no. 10 'They shall receive' could have been performed either by soloists or chorally. See Burrows, *Handel and the English Chapel Royal*, 398 and 492.

[118] *Lna LC 2/32*. For a full quotation see Ch. 6, fn. 94.

[119] See Burrows, *Handel and the English Chapel Royal*, 275 (facsimile on p. 278).

[120] Bartlett, vii.   [121] *Lna LC 5/159*, p. 92.

[122] Regarding the Gentlemen, those with positions in both choirs would have engaged a deputy for their place. See Burrows, *Handel and the English Chapel Royal*, 275.

[123] Deutsch, 214; Burrows, *Handel and the English Chapel Royal*, 275, states that these numbers 'are obviously rounded figures'.

[124] F. G. E[dwards], 'Handel's Coronation Anthems', *MT* 43 (1902), 153–5, here 154.

from the Chapel Royal as the section leaders'.[125] This, too, might be an indication for a later concert performance: one at which the Chapel Royal was the leading choir.

Several newspapers reported that 'Italian voices', or Italian opera singers, sang at the coronation service.[126] Burrows has shown that, according to the records of the Lord Chamberlain's department, there may have been fourteen 'additional singers', and about the participation of opera singers he remarks:[127]

Perhaps the castrati Senesino and Baldi sang with the altos, Boschi and Palmerini with the basses: it seems rather less likely that the voices of Faustina and Cuzzoni were mixed with the trebles.

Nevertheless, if the choir had a shortage of trebles, there would probably not have been any other choice than filling up their line with sopranos. It has been argued that 'soloists of the Italian opera [. . .] would hardly have agreed to sing as choristers'.[128] However, beside the fact that there are at least some soloistic sections in the Coronation Anthems, one has to appreciate that a coronation is an important event at which to sing, certainly an enhancement for any singer's reputation. One other source must be mentioned, which has been given in support of 'Italian voices' at the coronation: a leaf with the beginning of the treble/soprano chorus part of 'My heart is inditing' with phonetic English text, probably for Italian singers.[129] However, Burrows has shown that the watermark allows dating the leaf to the 1730s and it thus probably belongs to a later concert performance.[130]

The number of instrumentalists is confirmed by several sources. Scarlet cloth for new liveries was provided for the Master of the Musick and thirty-three musicians.[131] To these must be added the two players of the lute and bass viol from the Chapel establishment.[132] Furthermore, the number probably does not include the trumpeters and timpani player in the

[125] Burrows, *Handel and the English Chapel Royal*, 279.
[126] For a full quotation see below, fn. 148.
[127] Burrows, '1727 Coronation', 473, and *Handel and the English Chapel Royal*, 275.
[128] *HHB*, vol. IV, 154.
[129] *US-NYp JOD 72–75*. Quoted in Jonathan Keates, *Handel. The Man and His Music* (London: Gollancz, 1985), 134.
[130] Donald Burrows, 'Handel's 1738 *Oratorio*: A Benefit Pasticcio', in Klaus Hortschansky and Konstanze Musketa (eds.), *Georg Friedrich Händel – ein Lebensinhalt, Gedenkschrift für Bernd Baselt (1934– 1993)* (Halle an der Saale: Bärenreiter, 1995), 11–38, here 23.
[131] *Lna LC 5/159*, p. 91. Only twenty-four of these musicians were present at the banquet in Westminster Hall after the service. See ibid., 136f. 'A List of Servants above Stairs Appointed to be in the Hall to attend at His Majesty's Coronation who are intitled to Medals', which mentions one 'Master of the Musick' and twenty-four 'Musitians'.
[132] Burrows, '1727 Coronation', 473. Peter Holman suggests that the 'bass viol' was actually a violoncello – details of this idea will be found in a forthcoming book.

orchestra who may have come from the State Trumpeters, at least four musicians more. On top of these, fifty-seven additional instrumentalists are confirmed by a warrant, 'Certified by M.ʳ Handal [*sic*]'.[133] This would make a total of about a hundred instrumentalists alone (34+2+4+57). One newspaper report mentioned an astonishing number of instrumentalists:[134]

Yesterday there was a Rehearsal of the Coronation Anthem in Westminster-Abbey, set to Musick by the famous Mr. Hendall: There being 40 Voices, and about 160 Violins, Trumpets, Hautboys, Kettle-Drums, and Bass's proportionable; besides the Organ, which was erected behind the Altar: And both the Musick and Performers, were the Admiration of all the Audience.

However, Burrows has shown that the number of 160 is unlikely to be correct.[135] Landon proposed that the number '160' could refer to the combined number of singers and orchestral players.[136] Indeed, the heralds' records also seem to have calculated for a total number of 185 musicians. A 'Memorandum for Ld Marshall, what will be contain'd in Westmʳ Abby.' lists 'One Box next ᵉy Theatre' on the 'Northside ᵉy Choir'; and the next entry reads:[137]

In ᵉy [*sic*] two Arches joyning, westward for ᵉy Church Musick – 65. / Seats over ᵉy Alter, and in the side Arches, is for vocall & Instrumental Musick – 120.

Whatever the exact total number was, the arrangements seem to have followed the eighteenth-century custom of engaging 'a huge orchestra, and [. . .] a much smaller choir'.[138] It should be born in mind that many instruments in those days were less powerful than their modern equivalents and moreover, the sound may have been balanced out by the spatial arrangement: it is possible that the choir was placed in front of the orchestra, as is known for the Handel Commemoration concerts in 1784 and for the 1821 coronation.[139] In any case, the fact that it was Handel who 'certified' the bill for the fifty-seven additional instrumentalists confirms that he was not only the composer of some of the coronation music, but that he was furthermore also responsible for the overall performance during the service.[140]

[133] *Lna LC 5/18*, p. 16 (transcr. App. B2d). See also Burrows, '1727 Coronation', 473.
[134] *Norwich Gazette*, 14 October 1727. Quoted in Deutsch, 215.
[135] Burrows, *Handel and the English Chapel Royal*, 274.   [136] Landon, 130.
[137] *Lca Coronation of James II and William and Mary* [also up to George II], fo. 133r.: 'Memorandum for Ld Marshall, what will be contain'd in Westmʳ Abby.' [1727 coronation], here nos. 18 and 19.
[138] Landon,127.   [139] For details see Ch. 6.
[140] This is also confirmed by César de Saussure's report, see fn. 86. It was probably not a matter of fact that a composer always conducted his own works. Cf. John Fussel Harrison, 'The Secular Works of William Croft', unpublished Ph.D. thesis, Bryn Mawr College, Pennsylvania (1976),

Although the musicians seem again to have been placed in several galleries, their positions in the Abbey were probably different from those at previous coronations, when there had been three different galleries. For 1727 it is reported that

the Children and Gentlemen of his Majesties Chapel Royal, go to their Galleries on each side of the *Area*, the Vocal and Instrumental Musick before the Organ over the Altar.[141]

The fact that the report refers specifically to the 'Organ over the Altar' lends it extra credibility: a music gallery at this place is not reported for any earlier coronation and the writer could thus not simply have based his account on an earlier source. Indeed, it is known that a new organ was built by Christopher Shrider and installed 'above' and 'behind' the altar.[142] In addition, a note by Boyce from the next coronation confirms that in 1727 there was a 'Gallery appointed for the Music' at the east end of the quire, over and behind the High Altar, on top of St Edward's Chapel.[143] The material from the next coronation also supports the report that the Chapel Royal was placed in galleries 'on each side of the *Area*', that is in galleries on the sides of the space in front of the altar. Although the musicians were now probably closer together than at any previous coronation, their coordination would still not have been easy. According to Boyce, Handel afterwards complained about the difficult performance conditions. Intriguingly, he may have calculated with them and tailored his anthems accordingly: in a rather unusual way 'Let thy hand be strengthened' and 'My heart is inditing' both begin with a simple chord. This could easily have been given by one or two players (organ and basso continuo), so as to cue in the other musicians who could perhaps not easily see the conductor.

An order by the Earl Marshal concerning the building of scaffolds in the Abbey mentions the 'Musick Gallery over the Choir Doore'.[144] This, however, probably refers to the gallery for the State Trumpeters and Timpani which had their traditional place here, and not to members of Handel's choir and orchestra. The timpani used in Handel's orchestra could have

---

51. Harrison states that before 1727 Croft was 'undoubtedly responsible for the performance of the works of Handel.' See also the considerations about Blow in 1685 in Ch. 3.

[141] *The Ceremonial of the Coronation [...] George II*, 19.   [142] Webb, 638. See also fn. 134.

[143] *Lna LC 2/32* (transc. App. B3b). For details see Ch. 6. It is probably this arrangement that is referred to in the above-mentioned memorandum (see fn. 137).

[144] *Lwa WAM 51181*: 'The Earl Marshall's Order for Scaffolding in yᵉ Abbey.', dated 30 August 1727.

been the 'large military drums from the Tower' which Handel frequently hired for his oratorio performances in later years.[145]

Handel continued what had probably been started by Blow in 1702: the popularization of the coronation music. This coronation is the earliest for which there is evidence for public rehearsals of the music. The musicians and singers were paid for 'two Rehearsals and P[er]forming the Anthems at his Majesty's Coronation'.[146] From the detailed coverage in newspapers it can be deduced that these rehearsals took place on 6 and 9 October.[147] There might also have been some sort of a public rehearsal before these two; on 4 October *Parker's Penny Post* reported:[148]

Mr Hendle has composed the Musick for the Abbey at the Coronation, and the Italian Voices, with above a Hundred of the best Musicians will perform; and the whole is allowed by those Judges in Musick who have already heard it, to exceed any Thing heretofore of the same Kind: It will be rehearsed this Week, but the time will be kept private, lest the Crowd of People should be an Obstruction to the Performers.

A public rehearsal or a performance before a limited invited audience would have been the only opportunity for 'those Judges in Musick' to have heard the music.[149] But not only did Handel present the coronation music in public rehearsals before the service, he also repeated his anthems in services afterwards.[150] In addition, Handel made extensive use of the anthems in

---

[145] Cf. Burrows, *Handel*, 293–4, 333 and 359. There is evidence that the timpani came from the army. See *LJ*, no. 427, Saturday, 7 October 1727: 'The Kettle-Drums and Trumpets of the four Troops of Life-Guard being to be employed in the Procession, and in the Abbey and Westminster Hall, on the Day of their Majesties Coronation [. . .]'

[146] *Lna LC 5/18*, p. 15, transcr. in Burrows, *Handel and the English Chapel Royal*, 610. See also *Lca Coronation of George III 1761*, vol. I, pp. 217–33: 'Observations on the proceedings at the Coronation of King George the third and Queen Charlotte', here 222: 'Note_ Sir Septimus Robins on Black Rod observed as did several others [. . .] that at the preceeding Coronation they remembered two rehearsals before the Coronation [. . .]'

[147] Burrows, *Handel and the English Chapel Royal*, 258f.

[148] Quoted in Deutsch, 214. According to Deutsch the same notice was printed on 6 October in *Norris's Taunton Journal* and again, in a slightly varied form, in the *Norwich Gazette* of 7 October, in a report from London of 5 October. In addition to these, the report had also appeared identical or with similar wording in *FP*, no. 5409, 30 September–3 October 1727; *PM*, no. 75101, 30 September–3 October 1727; *SJEP*, no. 1933, 30 September–3 October 1727; and later in *CJ*, no. 66, Saturday, 7 October 1727.

[149] See also Burrows, *Handel and the English Chapel Royal*, 258, and H. Diack Johnstone, 'Coronation Rehearsal', *MT* 118 (1977), 725, according to whom the two rehearsals of 6 and 9 October 'were not the only rehearsals, though they were almost certainly the only public ones'.

[150] For instance, three of the anthems were performed in different services in Oxford on Act Sunday, 8 July 1733. See *Oxford Musical Festival, May 5th–12th, 1935: Handel, Bach, Born 1685* (Oxford, 1935), 9.

later works and thus made the music well known, even if perhaps not under its original title. Moreover, Handel's were the first coronation anthems to appear in print, being constantly available through several editions from 1742 onwards and thus more easily accessible than any coronation music before.[151]

Winton Dean called Handel's Coronation Anthems 'side-shows' in his oeuvre.[152] However, it is notable that they contain only a small number of borrowings from earlier music.[153] This may indicate that Handel himself accredited his Coronation Anthems with a special status and Alfred Mann concluded that 'the style of the *Coronation Anthems* became of lasting importance for Handel's choral oeuvre'.[154] Indeed they appear to have been of great importance to further the composer's fame. When advertising his 1732 performance of *Esther*, in which he included substantial parts of the anthems, Handel claimed explicitly that the music would be 'disposed after the Manner of the Coronation Service'.[155] His reference to the coronation indicates that the music must by then already have been famous, at least by way of reputation. It was through such distinct incorporation in later works that the coronation anthems had a clear, direct influence on Handel's compositions for years after 1727. Thus overall they were much more than mere 'sideshows': they were essential to Handel's fame and success, influenced his other compositions, and are the prime examples of his grand ceremonial style. Indeed, Ruth Smith appropriately described them as 'the *Pomp and Circumstance* of their day'.[156]

With his four anthems Handel set new standards for the composition and the performance of the coronation music. In particular with his anthem for the Anointing, Handel set a milestone in the history of British music: 'Zadok the Priest' has been performed at every coronation since 1727.

[151] See *HHB* vol. II, 725 (for a full list of the borrowings) and 723 (for editions).

[152] Winton Dean, 'Handel and the Theatre', in Richard G. King (ed.), *Handel Studies: A Gedenkschrift for Howard Serwer* (Hilsdale, NY: Pendragon, 2009), 244–6, here 244.

[153] For details see *HHB*, vol. II, 725. See also Burrows, *Handel and the English Chapel Royal*, esp. 267, fn. 46, and Damian Cranmer, 'Handel Borrowings', *MT* 122 (1981), 524.

[154] Alfred Mann, 'Our Handel Image', in Richard G. King (ed.), *Handel Studies: A Gedenkschrift for Howard Serwer* (Hilsdale, NY: Pendragon, 2009), 189–94, here 191.

[155] *London Daily Journal*, 19 April 1732 (quoted after *HHB* vol. II, 725).   [156] Ruth Smith, 94.

6 | The 'concert coronations' II: 1761 & 1821

While the 1727 coronation service has been described as a 'Händelkonzert', the 1761 coronation would deserve even more to be described as a 'Boyce concert', and the 1821 coronation, following contemporary terminology, as a 'concert of ancient music'.[1] Indeed, the term 'concert' is a poignant description: by 1761 the ability to hear the music had become a clear incentive to buy tickets for the service:[2]

> For Seeing the CORONATION. SEATS are to Lett in Westminster Abbey, from the West Door to the Choir [. . .] It is not necessary to expatiate on the Preference these Places will have from every other to lett, as being within the Abbey, and secure from the Inclemency of the Weather, the great and certain Opportunity of View, and of hearing all the Music, &.

George III and Queen Charlotte, 1761

George III acceded to the throne on 25 October 1760. The political instability that had followed the Glorious Revolution in 1688 was clearly over and, since the Young Pretender's defeat in 1745, the Hanoverian dynasty was firmly established. Thus the king's coronation did not have to follow his accession as urgently as in the past and took place nearly a year later, on 22 September 1761.[3] George III was married to Charlotte of Mecklenburg-Strelitz one week before the coronation, and therefore

> after the king's nuptials, another proclamation was published, to give notice, that it was his majesty's intention, her majesty should be crowned at the same time and place.[4]

The music at this coronation is better documented than that for any other such event before the twentieth century. Much material on its origins and

---

[1] See Ch. 5, fn. 109, and cf. Ch. 1, fn. 131.
[2] *PL* 17 September 1761 (and again on 19 September). [3] See Bodley, 220.
[4] *The Annual Register, or a View of the History, Politics, and Literature for the Year 1761. The Sixth Edition* (London: printed for J. Donsley, 1796), 217.

performance survives in the collection of William Secker, the Archbishop of Canterbury.[5] In addition, a comprehensive collection of material related to the ceremonial and practical arrangements at this coronation is preserved in the College of Arms.[6]

Following the example of his predecessors Archbishop Secker undertook some research into the orders of service of previous coronations.[7] In addition, he met with Stephen Martin Leake, Garter King of Arms, to settle 'some particulars of the Church Ceremonial'.[8] Eventually, Secker based his order of service very much on that of 1727. In fact, he entered his revisions into a printed copy from then, noting: 'This is the Copy, revised by me, & presented to the Committee of Council: & the Impression [printed version], used at the Coronation, was made from it.'[9] While in 1727 only 100 copies were printed, there were now 200 copies produced; these were, however, solely 'for the use of the Privy Council and the rest for the Service of those who are to Officiate in the Abby'.[10] Two copies were given to the composer of the music.[11]

The music 1: the anthems

The full responsibility for the music at this coronation lay with William Boyce. Boyce had been one of the two Composers of the Chapel Royal since May 1736, and Master of the King's Musick since December 1755; he appears to have been the first to combine these two positions. There is no hint as to how much – if at all – William Nares, the other Composer of the Chapel Royal, was involved in the coronation music except for his playing the organ.[12] Boyce composed eight anthems for the service, the scores of which are preserved in two volumes in the Bodleian Library, Oxford.[13] The collection contains also some corresponding part-books, which are

[5] *Llp MS 1130*, vol. I. All references to this manuscript refer to volume I and most of them are transcribed in App. B3a.

[6] *Lca Coronation of George III 1761*, 3 vols. This was compiled by Henry Hill, Windsor Herald since 1760.

[7] See the letters to the archbishop in *Llp MS 1130* (51), (54) and (55).

[8] *Lca MS S.M.L. 65*, p. 292.

[9] *Llp Cod. Misc. 1082* and *The Form and Order of the Service* [...] *Coronation of Their Majesties, King George III and Queen Charlotte* [...] (London: Mark Baskett and Robert Baskett, 1761); hereafter *OS* (1761).

[10] Minutes of the Privy Council, 20 August 1761 (*Lna PC 1/3025*). See also *Lca MS S.M.L. 65*, p. 292.

[11] *Llp MS 1130* (79). See also fn. 14.   [12] See below, fn. 81.   [13] *Ob MSS. Mus. c. 11* and *c. 12*.

presumably those used at the coronation.[14] It has been observed that there is 'conflicting evidence' as to whether all eight of Boyce's anthems were performed at the coronation service.[15] Indeed, one newspaper reported that Boyce had composed 'the Music of the five Anthems' and this curiously matches with the surviving part-books which contain only five of Boyce's anthems.[16] However, as will be seen, there is little reason to doubt that all eight of Boyce's anthems in the score-books were performed at the ceremony.

The surviving sources document a close cooperation between Boyce and Secker, who paid close attention to the details of the coronation music. It cannot be determined when the two first discussed the matter of the music, let alone when Boyce started his work. The fact that Boyce composed almost all of the anthems for the service anew was probably not a deliberate decision. It appears that, originally, Secker stipulated only a few new anthems; he noted:[17]

Anthems. Orderd to be new set. / 36. Zadock the priest / 50. For Kings shall be / Brevity desired / Anthem I. p. 2. & Anthem 8 p. 62 are from the new version.

The page numbers refer to the printed order of service, according to which the anthems 'to be new set' would have been 'Zadok the Priest' and 'Praise the Lord, O Jerusalem', which includes the line 'For Kings shall be'. It is not clear if 'Anthem I' ('I was glad') and 'Anthem 8' ('The Lord is a Sun and a Shield') were also to be set anew and what Secker meant by 'new version' – he probably referred to the translation used. Secker later recalled that Boyce had told him 'that he was orderd by the Committee of Council to set all the Anthems anew'; however, 'On Examination' the archbishop 'found there was no such order, but he [Boyce] had mistaken the Ld Chamberlains Directions'.[18] The 'Ld Chamberlains Directions' to Boyce are not known. In any case, due to this misunderstanding this coronation is the only one for which almost all of the music was written by the same composer.

---

[14] *Ob MSS. Mus. Sch. d. 268–97* (vocal parts), *Mus. Sch. c. 116a, 116b, 116c* (instrumental parts). One of the composer's copies of the order of service may survive in *Ob Vet. A5 d. 1569*, as this is wrapped in the same paper as the part-books. For a transcription of Boyce's anthems, with short introductory comments, see Billy Wayne Summers, 'The Coronation Anthems of William Boyce (1761): A Performing Edition', unpublished DMA thesis, University of North Carolina at Greensboro (2001).

[15] John Robert Van Nice, 'The Larger Sacred Choral Works of William Boyce (1710–1779): A Study and Edition of Selected Compositions for Choir and Orchestra', 3 vols., unpublished Ph.D. thesis, Iowa State University (1956), 80f.

[16] *PL*, 25 September 1761.   [17] *Llp MS 1130* (72).   [18] *Llp MS 1130* (81).

The anthem 'O Lord, grant the King a long life' during the procession from Westminster Hall to the Abbey may again have been sung in the setting by Child. Boyce could have understood his order to compose 'all the Anthems anew' to refer to the service only. Regarding the entrance-anthem Secker reminded Boyce that it

> must not be omitted: for it will enliven the Procession, and the Service will not be the longer for it. The fuller it is, and the more exactly it takes up the Time of the Kings walking through the Church, the better.[19]

Secker appears to refer to Archbishop Wake's annotation from the previous coronation, according to which the anthem had been omitted 'by the Negligence of the Choir of Westm.'.[20] In his account of the 1761 coronation, Richard Thomson states that the anthem was sung in a setting by Purcell.[21] However, a setting of 'I was glad' by Boyce in the score-books bears the ascription 'First Anthem / On the Queen's Entrance in the West door of the Abbey'.[22] Thomson, writing sixty years after the event, probably took his information from Sandford's report of the 1685 coronation. The fact that Boyce's setting is not contained in the part-books may be easily explained by the custom that the entrance-anthem was sung by the Abbey choir alone. Generally, the surviving part-books are probably incomplete: the vocal parts consist of three each for the first and second treble, four for the first alto, only one for the second alto, three for the first tenor, five for the second tenor, six for the first bass, and five for the second bass. It is possible that the part-books used by the Abbey choir are altogether missing, accounting for some of the imbalance in the surviving parts.

According to the printed order of service, the anthem was to be sung at the entrance of both the king and queen.[23] This description is probably a generalization as the king was the last to enter the Abbey, the queen walking before him in the procession.[24] Boyce's annotation indicates that the anthem started as soon as the queen entered, without waiting for the king: altogether, it appears that there was no break in the procession from Westminster Hall, but that it continued directly into the church. Boyce was concerned about the practicalities of the procession and planned it meticulously: on 17 August he requested from the archbishop 'that a proper

---

[19] *Llp MS 1130* (38).　　[20] *Llp Cod. Misc. 1079B*, p. 2.

[21] Richard Thomson, *A Faithful Account of the Processions and Ceremonies observed in the Coronation of the Kings and Queens of England: exemplified in that of their late Most Sacred Majesties King George the Third, and Queen Charlotte* [...] (London: Printed for John Major, 1820), 48f. Anselm Hughes, 95, probably follows this source.

[22] *Ob MS Mus. c. 11*, fo. 2.　　[23] *OS* (1761), 2.　　[24] *Annual Register* (1761), 222.

Space may be reserved in the Isles, for the Choir to perform the First anthem', that is some space for them to wait for the arrival of the royal procession.[25] Boyce explained that 'the Scaffolding to be errected within the Abbey, will be a great hindrance to the performers appointed for this particular occasion'. Indeed, Leake recalled that the space left for the procession was in danger of becoming too narrow:[26]

The Dean and Prebends on their part, having let out the body of the Abby to workmen to Erect Scaffolds, they had already Erected some on the N° side, by which it appeared they intended to leave no more than 18 feet for the procession to pass, and to build 3 stories right up on either side. This being complaind of [. . .] it was left to Mr Garter to ascertain the Breadth which he fixed at 24 feet.

There is no date for this entry, but the next one is dated 20 August. It is thus plausible that with the phrase 'This being complaind of' Leake could refer to Boyce's letter of 17 August.

In the same way as Blow's setting from 1685 and Pigott's from 1702, Boyce's 'I was glad' could have been performed in two parts, incorporating the *Vivat*s of the King's Scholars in the middle: a fermata in bar 34, on the word 'David', indicates the end of the 'first part'. One eyewitness reported that at the king's entrance 'the Kettle Drums, & fifes sounded a March, ye Orgins [*sic*] play'd, & there was all sorts of musick, join'd, which was a grand Sound'.[27] This vague description could refer to a fanfare preceding the anthem. Overall, Boyce followed the archbishop's demand that the anthem should match the time of the procession exactly: it is set in a straightforward way without much elaboration. The Gloria Patri especially, probably sung when the royal couple had arrived at their seats, is surprisingly short. However, Boyce's effort for a close match of music and ceremonial was not necessarily rewarded. According to Leake there was some confusion at the end of the procession: the king was first seated next to the queen, on the South side of the altar, whereas he should have gone to the chair in front of the throne; this error was put right by Garter King of Arms.[28] The resulting 'extra' time, while the king was relocated, may have been covered by improvised organ music.

For the anthem after the Recognition, Secker retained 'The King shall rejoice'. Boyce followed the grand ceremonial style established by Handel and wrote a full anthem with orchestral accompaniment. Incidentally, in 1741

[25] *Llp MS 1130* (40). See also Ch. 5, fn. 90.   [26] *Lca MS S.M.L. 65*, p. 291.
[27] Mark Milbank to his parents, 23 September 1761. Quoted in Owen Hedley, *Queen Charlotte* (London: John Murray, 1975), 52.
[28] *Lca MS S.M.L. 65*, p. 301f. See also Ch. 1, fn. 30.

Secker himself had indicated a preference for the full style over soloistic singing for 'psalms and spiritual songs' and Ruth Smith pointed out that the words of Secker's description 'chime with contemporary descriptions of Handel's oratorio choruses'.[29] Boyce also uses a similar scoring to Handel in his coronation anthems: six-part choir (TrTrAATB) and an orchestra of three trumpets, timpani, two oboes, three violins, viola, and basso continuo. In the opening chorus, he reuses substantial material of the chorus to the same text from his anthem for the king's wedding.[30] Considering that this had taken place only about two weeks previously, those present at both occasions may easily have noticed this 'self-borrowing'. It is not known if it was intended, but Boyce thus created a neat musical link between the two ceremonies, calling to mind an old analogy: the interpretation of the coronation as 'the marriage of the monarch to the people'.[31]

Thomson stated that the *Veni Creator*, 'Come, Holy Ghost', was 'composed by Turner'.[32] However, as with 'I was glad', he may again have referred to Sandford's account of the 1685 coronation rather than to the 1761 ceremony itself; a setting of the text by Boyce is included in the score-books, headed 'Anthem / To be sung Soft, Throughout the whole'.[33] The part-books do not contain any setting of this text, but the answer to this discrepancy may be deduced from the music list which is entered in some of them:[34]

First Anthem
Second Anthem
The Litany
Commandments and Creed
Third Anthem (by part of the Choir only)

---

[29] Ruth Smith, 83. For Secker's quotation see Norman Sykes, *Church and State in England in the XVIIIth Century* (Cambridge University Press, 1934), 241.

[30] For details see Matthias Range, 'William Boyce's Anthem for the Wedding of King George III', *MT* 147 (Summer 2006), 59–66, here 63.

[31] William Le Hardy, *The Coronation Book. The History and Meaning of the Ceremonies at the Crowning*, rev. edn (London: Staples Press, 1953), 35. See also the Lord Keeper's speech in Parliament on 6 February 1626: 'His Majesty having, at His Royal Coronation, lately solemnized the Sacred Rites of that Blessed Marriage between Him and His People [. . .]' For this, see *Journal of the House of Lords*. Volume III: 1620–1628 (1802), 492–4, reproduced on www.british-history. ac.uk/report.asp?compid=30469&strquery=coronation (Date accessed: 29 August 2011). In 1603, a copy of the order of service had explicitly stated that the coronation ring be put on the 'wedding finger'; see *Lca MS W.Y.*, fo. 156. In 1761, the printed order of service (45) stated merely that the ring was to be put 'on the Fourth Finger of his Majesty's Right Hand'.

[32] Thomson, 55.   [33] *Ob MS Mus. c. 11*, fo. 28.

[34] *MS Mus. Sch. d. 275*, 'First Contratenor' and *286*, 'Second Tenor'. In others the list is entered and later crossed out.

Fourth Anthem
Fifth Anthem
Sixth Anthem
Seventh Anthem
Eighth Anthem
Ninth Anthem

According to the printed order of service, the 'Third Anthem' was 'Come, Holy Ghost'.[35] The annotation that it was sung 'by part of the Choir only' may explain why the music is not found in the surviving part-books: as with 'I was glad', they may have belonged to that section of the choir that did not sing in the *Veni Creator*.

'Zadok the Priest' was probably the only piece of music at this service not composed by Boyce. It is ironic that this had initially been one of the few anthems 'Orderd to be new set'.[36] In a note to the archbishop, which appears to date from an early stage and could indeed be a response to Secker's order of new anthems, Boyce explained that 'The Anthem Zadock the Priest cannot be more properly set than it has already been by M.ʳ Handel.'[37] It was probably this or a similar remark to which John Hawkins referred when he famously wrote that Boyce 'declined composing an anthem on occasion of his present Majesty's coronation, to the words "*Zadok* the priest, &." alledging that it would be presumption in him to attempt it after Mr. *Handel*'.[38] Hawkins continues that Boyce's 'excuse was accepted and he made one to other words, which was performed'. Indeed, Secker reports that Boyce had proposed to set a different text, taken 'from, Sam. XVI. 13 & other places'.[39] However, this anthem was probably never composed. For Boyce's 'excuse' was not accepted; Secker informed him that 'His Majesty hath signified his Pleasure, that the 4th Anthem, Zadok the Priest &c should be performed as it was set for the last Coronation.'[40] Boyce obligingly replied, confirming that he would perform Handel's anthem and he also sent the full text of this.[41] Secker may have asked for the text so that he could change it accordingly in the order of service. It is noteworthy that neither Boyce nor

---

[35] In the music of the other part-books, the anthem referred to as 'Third Anthem' is 'The Lord is a Sun and a Shield'. However, these inscriptions were added later and appear to refer to its being the third orchestral anthem ('The King shall rejoice' and 'Praise the Lord, O Jerusalem' are referred to as 'first' and 'second').

[36] See above, fn. 17.   [37] *Llp MS 1130* (66).

[38] 'Memoirs of Dr William Boyce, written by J.H.' (vii: 'supposed to be John Hawkins'), in William Boyce (ed.), *Cathedral Music* (London: J.A. Novello, 1849), i–vii, here vii.

[39] *Llp MS 1130 (81)*, [p. 4].   [40] *Llp MS 1130* (38). See also *Llp MS 1130* (81), [p. 4].

[41] *Llp MS 1130* (40).

the archbishop refer to the fact that 'Zadok the Priest' is the traditional text for the anthem before the Anointing: this alone should have been reason enough not to change it. Indeed, one may wonder if the king's concern about 'Zadok the Priest' was not mainly related to the traditional text rather than specifically to Handel's setting. Weber has pointed out that 'there is little evidence that the King had much special interest in Handel prior to the [1784 Handel] Commemoration [...] Even though the King attended chapel regularly, he did not encourage it to offer the music of Handel.'[42]

The next anthem was 'Behold, O God our Defender', after the Anointing. Boyce's setting appears to be the first to follow the shortened text as stipulated in the orders of service since 1702. Boyce wrote a short full anthem for four-part choir with continuo. However, despite its modest dimensions the piece is an intriguing gem among all coronation anthems: Boyce deploys antiphonal writing between the Decani and Cantoris choirs, thus making effective use of the acoustics in Westminster Abbey. Overall, the anthem is reminiscent of the polychoral writing in the seventeenth-century anthems.

Secker followed the previous orders of service and retained the text 'Praise the Lord, O Jerusalem' for the anthem after the Crowning. Whereas Boyce had originally intended that it should 'be sung with Voices alone accompanied with the Organ', it was the archbishop who proposed that it 'should be accompanied with the other Instruments, as well as the Organ', because 'it follows immediately the Principal Act of the Day, setting on the Crown'.[43] It is an interesting side-note that the archbishop himself seems to consider the Crowning to be more important than the Anointing. In the end, Boyce provided an elaborate orchestral anthem, making use of the full forces. Secker gave the anthem texts detailed consideration and realised a discrepancy in the texts from 1727: he observed that the verse from Isaiah 23 ('For Kings shall be thy nursing Fathers [...]') appears in the text of both the anthem after the Crowning and in the anthem after the Queen's Coronation.[44] He argued that this verse is more appropriate for the queen's anthem, at the same time criticizing the fact that the text would be repeated. Therefore, he changed the text in 'Praise the Lord, O Jerusalem', and replaced the Isaiah 23 verse with 'Behold, a King shall reign in Righteousness: & Princes shall rule in Judgment. Is. XXXII.1'.[45] However, it is not evident why Secker did not also change the verse 'Praise the Lord, O Jerusalem', which still appears in both anthems.

---

[42] Weber, *Musical Classics*, 233f. See also Alec Hyatt King, 'The Royal Taste', *MT* 118 (1977), 461–3, here 462.

[43] *Llp MS 1130* (66) and (38).   [44] For this and the following *Llp MS 1130* (38) and (81), [p. 3].

[45] *Llp Cod. Misc. 1082*, p. 50.

As in previous coronations, the Te Deum covered the king's procession from St Edward's Chair to his inthronization. According to one detailed report the king first 'seated himself in a chair of state below the throne', and ascended the throne 'when the Te Deum was ended', thus possibly in silence.[46] Neither the score-books nor the part-books contain the Te Deum. John Bumpus stated that Boyce composed his Te Deum in A for this coronation.[47] This ascription may be based on sources for the next coronation which confirm that the Te Deum in 1761 was Boyce's full setting in A.[48] Furthermore, a list of the *ANTHEMS To be Sung at the CORONATION of Their Majesties* [. . .] *All composed for this Occasion by Dr. Boyce* includes the Te Deum as 'Anthem VII'.[49] However, according to the list of Boyce's works by Robert Bruce, the full setting in A dates from as early as 1750.[50] It is possible that Boyce did not consider the Te Deum as an 'anthem', but as a piece of liturgical music. That could explain why he did not write a new setting and reused an earlier one; after all, he thought he had been asked to compose only 'all the anthems anew'. Regarding its performance Boyce stated that the Te Deum was 'to be sung with Voices alone accompanied with the Organ'.[51] Nevertheless, one of the cello parts includes the annotation 'The Te Deum, should come after this / look at ye End for it', which might indicate that at least some of the cellos played in it.[52]

For the Homage, Boyce wrote a new setting of 'The Lord is a Sun and a Shield', an elaborate orchestral anthem for the full forces. He followed Croft's 1714 setting of the text in several aspects: the trumpets are used only in the outer movements and Boyce deploys a similarly strong declamatory style in the opening chorus. However, the middle section 'For the King trusteth in the Lord', an elaborate, contrapuntally designed movement in Croft, is in Boyce's setting a short full section of only seven bars – increasing the clarity of the text while at the same time complying with the general wish for brevity.[53]

---

[46] *The Scots magazine* (1761), 503.   [47] Bumpus, vol. I, 272.   [48] See below, fn. 174.

[49] *ANTHEMS To be Sung at the CORONATION of Their Majesties King George III. And Queen Charlotte, in the Abbey Church of St. Peter, Westminster, on Tuesday the 22d September, 1761. All composed for this Occasion by Dr. Boyce, Composer to his Majesty, and Master of the King's Band, except the Fourth, which was composed by the late Mr. Handel* (London: Printed by T. Gardner, opposite St. Clement's Church in the Strand, 1761). The fact that this was published before the coronation is known from the respective newspaper advertisements: *LEPC*, 18–21 September 1761; *PA*, 21 September 1761; *WEP*, 22–24 September 1761.

[50] Ian Bartlett and Bruce Wood, 'William Boyce', *NG* 4, 155–62, here 159.

[51] *Llp MS 1130* (66).

[52] *Ob MS Mus. Sch. c. 116a*, (75). In the cello part in (93) it reads 'Te Deum Tacet'.

[53] See above, fns. 17 and 19; see also below, fn. 72.

Following the precedents of 1685 and 1727 the Queen's Coronation was followed by an anthem to the text 'My heart is inditing'. In his new setting Boyce followed the order of service and thus used the longer version of the text from 1685 as set by Purcell. Like his predecessor, Boyce divided the anthem into three distinct parts. The first part is written for full six-part choir (TrTrAATB), but it begins with a verse for solo tenor and later includes a section for two trebles and another verse for the tenor. Thus Boyce follows both Purcell and Handel, who also used verses in this one coronation anthem to evoke a more intimate tone in contrast to the other full anthems. The second part ('Hearken, O daughter') contains subtle writing, the solo tenor being accompanied by the strings only. In the third part (beginning with 'Praise the Lord, O Jerusalem'), Boyce again follows both his predecessors and takes the opportunity to use the end of the anthem as a grand finale to the coronation part of the service: it is lavishly scored for double TrATB choir and the full orchestra. The verse from Isaiah ('Kings shall be thy nursing fathers') receives special attention: it is here that Boyce deploys the trumpets and timpani for the first time in this anthem. This underlines that this section is the climax of the anthem, and indeed of all of Boyce's orchestral anthems for the service. The text being the same as in 1685, it includes the word 'their' before 'queens', stressing that they are 'queen consorts'. Nevertheless, Boyce does not make this distinction in the music: he uses the same musical theme for both the kings and queens, which gives them – at least musically – an equal status. This section leads directly into the final 'Amen, Hallelujah', the close link further marking this part as the climax of the anthem.

The music 2: liturgical music

Little is known about the liturgical music of the service. While none is contained in the score-books, the tables of contents in some of the part-books list 'The Litany' and 'Commandments and Creed'.[54] Indeed, according to some sources the Litany, just read at the previous coronation, was again sung by two bishops and the choir.[55] As at the previous coronations, this could again have been Tallis's setting which Boyce himself had edited in the first volume of his *Cathedral Music* in 1760.[56]

---

[54] See for instance *Ob MS Mus. Sch. d. 275*.

[55] *Annual Register* (1761), 225. See also *PL* 25, September, 1761.

[56] William Boyce (ed.), *Cathedral Music: Being a Collection in Score of the Most Valuable and Useful Compositions for that Service by the Several English Masters, Of the last Two Hundred Years* [...] 3 vols. (London: printed for the editor, 1760–73), vol. I, 1–2 and 16–19. For this see also Cole, 141f.

For the offertory, which accompanied the royal couple's procession to the altar for the taking of communion, the choir sang 'Let my prayer come up'.[57] Boyce's newly composed setting survives in the score-books with the other anthems. Following Blow's example from 1689, Boyce wrote a very short and simple homophonic piece, with the instruction 'To be sung soft', as an appropriate introduction to this solemn part of the service.[58]

It was only one day before the coronation that Boyce asked the archbishop if the choir should sing the 'Responses to the Ten Commandments' and the 'Response after naming the Gospel, viz: Glory be to God on high'.[59] In the printed order of service these Responses are not marked to be sung; in fact, the Response after the naming of the Gospel is not included in the order of service at all.[60] It is not found in the 1662 version of the Book of Common Prayer, but in that from 1549, and Spink comments that it was 'frequently sung' after 1662.[61] It may thus also have been sung at coronations. However, the usual text is 'Glory be to thee, O Lord', whereas Boyce cites the beginning of the 'Gloria in excelsis', presumably simply confusing the two texts. Regarding the Responses to the Commandments Archbishop Secker recorded that they were 'sung to the Organ'.[62] This is the first coronation for which these responses are reported to have been sung, which raises the question whether they had not been sung at previous coronations also. Indeed, it has been pointed out that they generally 'continued to be chanted or sung in harmony by custom rather than rubric' after the Restoration and up into the nineteenth century.[63] These too may have been sung to music by Boyce: an A Major setting of the Sanctus and 'Kyrie' (that is the Responses to the Commandments) by him survives in the part-books of the Chapel Royal.[64] Both were entered in 1814 with the ascription 'Given by the late D.ʳ Boyce to J.S. Smith and by him for the use of the Chapel Royal only', which might indicate a special status of these pieces. The fact that they correspond in key with Boyce's Te Deum might support the view that these Responses and Sanctus could have been used at the coronation. According to Secker the Nicene Creed was also sung with organ accompaniment.[65] While it cannot be established to which setting this was sung, the fact that it was sung

[57] *OS* (1761), 70f. and *Annual Register* (1761), 227.   [58] *Ob MS Mus. c. 12*, fo. 45.

[59] *Llp MS 1130* (65).   [60] For the Responses see *OS* (1761), 21.

[61] Spink *Restoration Cathedral Music*, 7. See also Ruth Wilson, 152.

[62] *Llp MS 1130* (81), [p. 13].   [63] Ruth Wilson, 152.

[64] *Lbl R.M. 27 g 1–4*. They were later printed, together with the *Te Deum* and a *Jubilate*. See William Boyce, *Services and Anthems, with a separate accompaniment for the organ or piano forte by Vincent Novello*, 4 vols. (London: Novello, 1846–49), vol. III, 1–15. For a new transcription see Range, thesis, vol. II.

[65] *Llp MS 1130* (81), [p. 13].

at all is notable, as this long text had probably been simply read at the previous coronation and was to be read at the following coronations.

Two of the treble part-books contain music under the heading 'Sanctus'; but this belongs in fact to the final chorus of a Gloria.[66] Judging from this surviving part, the Gloria was in D minor, ending on an A major chord, thus matching the other probable pieces. It is yet to be determined whether the fragment belongs to an already known Gloria, or if it is indeed part of a setting otherwise lost. As at previous coronations the Gloria was to accompany the royal couple's return to their thrones, after receiving the sacrament at the altar.[67] It is interesting that, according to the surviving music, this processional piece should have included a verse for three voices instead of being a full-style piece throughout.

Apart from Boyce's anthems and Handel's 'Zadok the Priest', the part-books contain also two movements from *Messiah*, and some of them include parts of three secular cantatas.[68] However, these latter pieces were most probably not part of the coronation music and may have been inserted in the part-books for later concert performances. Indeed, similarly to Handel, Boyce repeated his coronation anthems in concerts: two of them were performed at the Three Choirs Festival in September 1764 and it has been observed that one of them 'was heard at three different festivals of the Three Choirs gatherings, the last in the year following his [Boyce's] death in 1779'.[69]

It is intriguing that the anthem texts were published separately before the coronation. Together with the quotation seen at the beginning of the chapter, this indicates that the coronation music had gained its own inherent attractiveness for the public.[70] The actual music of Boyce's anthems, however, would probably not have been accessible beyond its performance at the coronation and at the concerts. A letter to the editor of the *Monthly Magazine* in 1799, anonymously signed 'Y', includes a list of Boyce's works 'pointing out those in which his taste and learning is particularly displayed'.[71] The 'Eight Coronation Anthems' appear under the heading 'Already published'; however, no such editions are known and this list may refer merely to the published texts, not the music.

---

[66] *Ob MSS Mus. Sch. d. 272* and *273*, fo. 9v. For details and a reproduction see Range, thesis, vol. II.

[67] *OS* (1761), 83.   [68] For instance *Ob MS Mus. Sch. d 273*, fos. 4v and 11.

[69] *SJC*, 21 August 1764; Monte Edgel Atkinson, 'The Orchestral Anthem in England, 1700–1775', unpublished DMA thesis, University of Illinois at Urbana–Champaign (1991), 173.

[70] See above, fns. 2 and 49.

[71] 'Unnoticed Works of Dr. Boyce', *Monthly Magazine and British Register* 7 (1799), 103f.

The performance

Not only the composition of the music, but also its performance during the service seems to have been better prepared than at any previous coronation. Like many archbishops after him, Secker was most concerned about timing. On 14 August, he informed Boyce of the king's order that the anthems 'should be as short, & have as little Repetition in them, as conveniently may be'.[72] Boyce replied that 'those anthems with the Organ, shall be as short as possible'; at the same time, however, he argued that some repetition of the words would be necessary in the orchestral anthems, for otherwise 'the performances would appear rather mean than grand'.[73] Boyce promised to inform the archbishop of 'the exact time each of them will require in the performance'. The fact that he sent his list with the times only on the day before the coronation indicates that Boyce did not ask for approval; rather this list was purely for the archbishop's information.[74] Boyce did not include the anthem titles, but simply numbered them. Compared with the numbering in the printed order of service the anthems and their times are:

1. 'I was glad'   3 ½ min.
2. 'The King shall rejoice'   8 min.
3. 'Come, Holy Ghost'   3 ½ min.
4. 'Zadok the Priest' (Handel)   6 min.
5. 'Behold O God, our Defender'   2 min.
6. 'Praise the Lord, O Jerusalem'   3 ½ min.
7. Te Deum   3 ½ min.
8. 'The Lord is a Sun and a Shield'   10 min.
9. 'My heart is enditing'   10 min.
10. 'Let my prayer come up'   1 ½ min.

The length of the anthems to some extent indicates the tempo in which they were sung. It is striking that Boyce scheduled 3′30″ for his short setting of 'Come, Holy Ghost'.[75] Holman has pointed out that it is written in *stile antico*, which might have been perceived as much slower in Boyce's time.[76] For Handel's 'Zadok the Priest', Boyce scheduled 6 min., whereas most

---

[72] *Llp MS 1130* (38).   [73] For this and the following see *Llp MS 1130* (40).

[74] *Llp MS 1130* (77): 'D.ʳ Boyce's Account of the Length of the several Anthems at the Coronation of Geo. 3 and his Queen, sent to the Archbishop the Day before. &'

[75] Cf. *Coronation Anthems*, dir. Edward Higginbottom, track 2, where the anthem takes only 2′37″.

[76] Private conversation.

modern recordings take between 5'15" and 5'30".[77] However, one has to bear in mind that the unusual size of the performing body together with the acoustics of the Abbey may have led to a slightly slower tempo than usual.[78] As William McKie, Director of Music at the 1953 coronation, pointed out when sending a similar list to Archbishop Fisher, his figures were 'only approximate' and he had 'taken into account that music has to move more slowly in the Abbey than elsewhere'.[79] Indeed, he scheduled a generous seven minutes for 'Zadok the Priest', even though in the end its performance took less than six minutes.[80] Similarly, Boyce's figures also are obviously approximate and it would not be surprising if he had rounded up the times, so as to leave a margin of error.

As could be seen in the discussion of the entrance-anthem, Boyce paid close attention to the details of the performance and the necessary preparations. Three public rehearsals of his anthems are confirmed. The first of these was on Friday, 18 September; the following day the newspapers reported:[81]

Yesterday the several Anthems composed by Dr. Boyce, &c. for the Coronation, were rehearsed before a grand Assembly in the Choir of Westminster Abbey, by Mr. Beard, and the Gentlemen and Children of the Chapel Royal, and the whole Band of Musick; Dr. Boyce and Mr. Howard beat Time; Dr. Nares and Mr. Butler played the Organ. The Execution of it was so extremely just, as to merit great Applause, which was universally expressed by the Audience.

'Mr Howard', who conducted the music together with Boyce, is also mentioned in other sources from which it appears that he was very much involved in the practical arrangements of the performance.[82] This most likely refers to the composer and organist Samuel Howard (1710–1782) who in 1761 was organist at St. Bride's Fleet Street and also helped Boyce in the preparation of his *Cathedral Music*.[83] It is noteworthy that with Howard

---

[77] Robert King's performance matches Boyce's timing with 5'59". See *The Coronation of King George II, 1727*, CDA67286 (Hyperion: 2001), CD 1, 16.

[78] In the recordings of the 1937 and 1953 coronations the anthem takes 5'56" and 5'48" respectively. See *The Coronation of Their Majesties King George VI and Queen Elizabeth*, CD 1, track 7, and *The Coronation Service of Her Majesty Queen Elizabeth II*, CD 1, track 17.

[79] McKie to Fisher, 31 October 1952 (*Lwa Library, McKie Papers*).   [80] See Ch. 1, fn. 79.

[81] *SJC*, 19 September 1761. The same text in *PL*, 22 September 1761.

[82] *Lna LC* 2/32: 'D.ʳ Boyce to W. Ely 13.ᵗʰ Sept.ʳ 1761.' See also below, fn. 86.

[83] For biographical details see Roger Fiske, 'Howard, Samuel', NG 11, 767f; see also Donovan Dawe, *Organists of the City of London 1666–1850. A Record of One Thousand Organists with an Annotated Index* ([Purley:] By the author, 1983), 111.

there was a musician involved in the coronation music who was not a member of the Chapel Royal nor of Westminster Abbey; this is the first instance of such a cooperation before the twentieth century.

A second rehearsal seems to have taken place the very next day, as indicated by a hand-dated ticket for an 'Abbey Rehearsal of the Coronation Music'.[84] A third, probably final, rehearsal took place on the day before the coronation; this is referred to by Leake:[85]

Monday the 21st. [...] as had been appointed, the Officers went together to the Abbey to rehearse the parts they were to act the next day, but were disappointed, as they had been the Saturday before, Upon Account of the Rehearsal of the Musick for the Benefit of the Earl Marshals Secretary, by which means they were prevented that previous and necessary Instruction.

First of all it is noteworthy that according to this report the whole cere-monial of the service should have been practised – at least by the heralds, the 'Officers' of the College of Arms. It was not before the twentieth century that rehearsals of the full ceremony became standard. In any case, as the rehearsal of the music was 'for the Benefit of the Earl Marshals Secretary' this also seems to have been a public rehearsal for which tickets could be purchased. However, in how far these public rehearsals were simply events of public entertainment to make money was a matter of argument:[86]

Dr Boyce & Mr Howard who had the direction of the Music prevented the Rehearsal being at Vauxhall which was much desired by Mr Tyers and great interest he made, but as it was an improper place to carry the Clergy to, to perform it and as they must be better Judges of any thing wrong in the performance in the place it was done in, they exerted themselves and prevented its being by interest to Vauxhall.

Boyce and Howard not only took into account that the pleasure gardens of Vauxhall would be an 'improper place' to take the clergy for rehearsal; rather it appears as though they wanted to judge the effect of the music in the building for which it was written and where it was to be performed. This implies that they considered the rehearsals mainly as an opportunity to practise for the service, not as a means of making additional money; this again indicates the special care and attention paid to the music at this coronation. It may have been at one of these rehearsals that Boyce timed the music: his timings would then have been taken in the actual place of performance, under similar conditions.

---

[84] *Lca Coronation George III*, vol. I, p. 186.   [85] *Lca MS S.M.L. 65*, p. 297f.
[86] *Lca Coronation George III*, vol. I, p. 223.

The performance body in 1761 was at least as big as at the previous coronation:[87]

The anthems of the coronation on Tuesday last were performed with the utmost grandeur by upwards of three hundred hand [. . .] The vocal parts were performed by Mr. Beard, and the Gentlemen of the King's Chapel; and the band was led by Mr. Dabourg (first violin) and Mr. Brown. Several eminent performers, as Signiors G[i]ardini, Pinto, Marella, Carbonelli, &c. assisted at this grand performance.

It is difficult to determine who the mentioned 'Several eminent performers' were.[88] As already seen, the surviving performing-parts are possibly incomplete and therefore provide only insufficient information on the performing body. For the choir, details are known for the Chapel Royal only.[89] For the orchestra, the Office of the Wardrobe provided 'Scarlet Cloth for [. . .] The Master and thirty six Musitions [sic]' which probably refers to the permanent royal musicians only.[90] The number of additional musicians would have had to be rather high so as to achieve a performing body of 'upwards of three hundred hands', which probably refers to both the orchestra and the choir combined. Intriguingly, one newspaper, which otherwise printed more or less the same text, reported of only 'upwards of one hundred and fifty Hands and Voices'.[91]

There is clear evidence regarding the distribution of the musicians in the Abbey. Leake reported that 'The Organ and Musick was over the Altar'.[92] Two hand-drawn plans of the galleries in the Abbey at the coronation are preserved in the College of Arms. In one of them a gallery is scribbled in over and around the High Altar, with the explanation 'Band of Music in No [blank] ' (see Illustration 6.1). In the other copy of this plan the gallery is not scribbled in, but 'Music' is written on the three sides around the altar.[93]

Thus, overall the main gallery of the music was at the east end of the quire, on top of St Edward's Chapel, with two further galleries to the side. This arrangement of the musicians is also indicated by Boyce in a note to the Lord Chamberlain. Boyce explained that

---

[87] *PL*, 25 September 1761; *LEP*, 24–26 September 1761.

[88] For details on Giardini, Pinto, and Marella see Range, thesis, vol. I, 174.

[89] See the list of the 'Several Members of His Majestys Chapel Royal' at the coronation of George III and Queen Charlotte in Ashbee and Harley, vol. II, 112f.

[90] *Lca Coronation of George III 1761*, vol. III: 'A List of Particulars necessary to be provided against the Coronation by the Office of Great Wardrobe.', p. [4]. See also *Lna LC 2/32*: 'D.ʳ Boyce to W. Ely 13.th Sept.r 1761 / Including a List of Musicians [. . .] who are entitled to Scarlet Mantles for Coronation'.

[91] *SJC*, 22–25 September 1761.   [92] *Lca MS S.M.L. 65*, p. 299.

[93] *Lca Coronation of George III 1761*, vol. I, drawing between pp. 161 and 162, and vol. II, drawing between pp. 106 and 107.

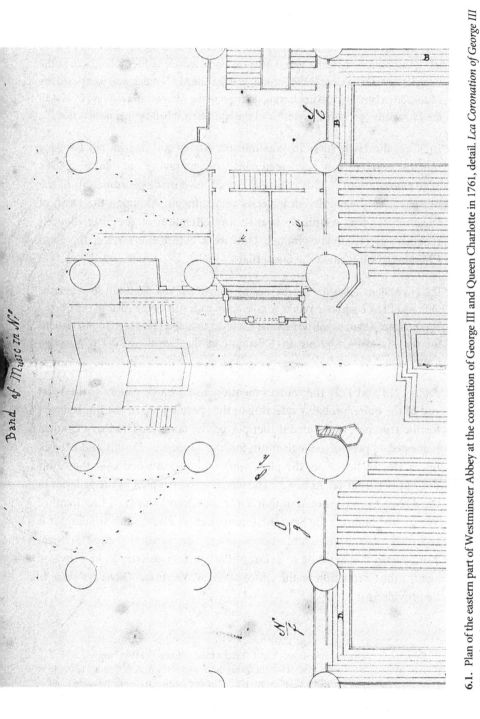

6.1. Plan of the eastern part of Westminster Abbey at the coronation of George III and Queen Charlotte in 1761, detail. *Lca Coronation of George III 1761*, vol. I, drawing between pp. 161 and 162. By kind permission of the Chapter of the College of Arms. The musicians' gallery can be seen scribbled in over and around the High Altar.

the upper-part of the Atar [sic] at Westminster Abbey, as it now stands, will be in the middle of the Gallery appointed for the Music, which renders it impossible for the Musicians to join in the Performance as they ought to do, and will intirely spoil the Composition. The first grand Musical Performance in the Abbey, was at the Coronation of King George the Second, and the late M.ʳ Handel, who composed the Music, often lamented his not having that part of the Altar taken away, as He, and all the Musicians concerned, experienced the bad Effect it had by that obstruction.[94]

In 1761, the High Altar in Westminster Abbey still had its tall Baroque reredos which can be seen in an engraving in John Dart's *Westmonasterium*.[95] This naturally would have made coordination of the musicians in their different galleries very difficult. Although the Dean of Westminster was seemingly against any alteration of the altar, Boyce's request was eventually granted. One week before the service, the Lord Chamberlain informed the Dean that

It is His Majesty's Pleasure [words missing, damaged] / your Lordship do permit the Officers of His Board of / Works to take down such part of the Altar in the Choir / Westminster Abbey as will be necessary in order to ma[ke] proper Accommodations for the Musicians who are to / Perform in the Ceremony of His Majesty's Coronation.[96]

As in 1714 and 1727 the sources mention also a music gallery at the West end of the quire, probably referring to the space on top of the quire screen for the trumpets and timpani that played the fanfares. The Privy Council requested to provide enough room for 'the Trumpets, Drums and Musick under Doctor Boyce' in 'the place where the Organ stood over the Choir door in Westminster Abbey'.[97] The aforementioned plan of the galleries in the Abbey has an annotation that 'Over the Choir Door [...] the Board of Works had built for the Serjeant Trumpetter 38 Places', and similarly it is recorded that thirty-eight tickets were delivered to the 'Serjeant Trumpetter'.[98] According to a 'List of Particulars necessary to be provided against the Coronation by the Office of Great Wardrobe', 'Livereys' were to be provided for

[94] *Lna LC 2/32*: 'D.ʳ Boyce / 9 Sep.ʳ 1761.'

[95] Dart, vol. I, engraving between pp. 70 and 71: 'The Inside Prospect of the Church [...]'

[96] *Lwa WAM 61781*: 'Lord Chamⁿ about the taking down part of the Altar at Coron.ⁿ 1761.', from the 'Lord Chamberlain's Office, 14ᵗʰ Sept:ʳ 1761'. The document was slightly damaged in a fire during World War II. For the Dean's reservations see *Lna LC 2/32* (transcr. App. B3b).

[97] *Lna Work 21/1*, fo. 13, no. 30 (transcr. App. B3c). The same in *Lca Coronation George III*, vol. I, pp. 137 and 224.

[98] *Lca Coronation George III*, vol. I, drawing between pp. 161 and 162, and p. 224.

The Serjeant Trumpet Sixteen Trumpetters and four Kettle Drums of the Horse Guards – the light Drummer and eight Hautbois of the Horse Grenadiers Drum Major and four Household Drums and the Hautbois of the first Regiment of Foot Guards.[99]

This makes a total number of thirty-five musicians to which would be added the unspecified number of the oboes from the first Regiment of Foot Guards. Altogether, these could be the thirty-eight musicians for which tickets were provided, a bigger body of musicians than ever reported for this place. If the oboes were indeed placed in the gallery of the State Trumpeters and Drums, they would presumably also have played in the fanfares, which would then probably have been more elaborate compositions, not mere signals.[100] In any case, it is intriguing that the Privy Council order could be read to mean that all of these musicians from the military were 'under Doctor Boyce'. If that was the case, he would have been responsible for every single detail of the music during the service: not only the anthems and liturgical pieces but also the fanfares. This would be a comprehensive authority not documented for any of his predecessors.

As for previous coronations, a new organ should have been built in the Abbey. Boyce reminded the officials about that and explained

the necessity of an immediate Order for an Organ to be erected in the Music Gallery at Westminster, or there will not be time for the providing of a proper one. There can be no dependance upon the use of that in the Chapel of Harry the Seventh, as it has been **detain'd by the Dean &** [bold original, probably because of new ink] Chapter, and may not be deliver'd in proper time to be put in order for the Coronation.[101]

In response it was ordered that this organ, built for the funeral of George II in the previous year, should be repaired and moved to the main body of the church.[102] Incidentally, this is the only pre-twentieth century coronation organ for which the specification survives.[103] With only seven stops this instrument, originally built for the much smaller Henry VII's Chapel, was clearly smaller than the organ built for the previous coronation, which had twenty-one stops.[104] Nevertheless, it was big enough to accompany the choir and orchestra and also to perform some solo music, such as the

---

[99] *Lca Coronation George III*, vol. III, [p. 5 of this list]. The list is dated '20.th July 1761.'

[100] Cf. Ch. 1, fn. 61.   [101] *Lna LC 2/32*: 'D.[r] Boyce to W. Ely 13.th Sept.[r] 1761'.

[102] *Lwa WAM 61782* (transcr. App. B3d).

[103] *Lwa WAM 48097B* (transcr. App. B3e). See also Knight, 'Organs of Westminster Abbey', 117f.

[104] See Webb, 638.

processional that accompanied the king and queen's retiring into St Edward's Chapel at the end of the service.[105]

This appears to be the first coronation for which there is also evidence for an organ at the banquet in Westminster Hall. Thomson reported that

opposite the King's table, was erected a large balcony for the trumpets, kettle-drums, and other music, and in the centre over them was fixed an organ.[106]

This organ, used during the 'secular' coronation celebrations at the banquet, could have been intended to emphasize the overall sacred character of the occasion. In any case, no details about this instrument or generally the music during the banquet are known.

The music at the coronation of George III and Queen Charlotte in 1761 was probably better planned and executed than at any previous coronation. This was in striking contrast to the rest of the ceremonies, which have been described as having been badly organized.[107] Garter King of Arms himself stated that 'all the Proceedings' at the coronation 'were so Irregular and ill Conducted, they ought to be buried in Oblivion'; indeed, he gave these irregularities as the reason why he opposed the proposition of a published account of the ceremony, similar to Sandford's account of the 1685 coronation.[108] At the 1761 coronation it would have been the music that stood high above the rest of the ceremonies with their apparent disorganization. Overall, with every piece written by the same composer, the programme of music of this coronation service must have been more coherent in style and disposition than in both the 150 years before and the 200 years following.

George IV, 1821

Prince George, the Prince of Wales, was created prince regent by Act of Parliament in 1811, but his father George III nominally reigned from 1760 until his death on 29 January 1820.[109] By the time George IV came to the throne he lived in separation from his wife, Caroline of Brunswick; and when she returned to be crowned the king ordered her exclusion

---

[105] *OS* (1761), 86: '[. . .] they proceed in State into the Chapel, the Organs all the while playing.'

[106] Thomson, 26.

[107] See Strong, 372–416, esp. 394 ('a complete shambles') and 407 ('a disaster area').

[108] *Lca MS S.M.L. 65*, p. 309f.   [109] For details on the Regency see Cannon and Griffiths, 520–41.

from the ceremony.[110] Because of these complications the coronation, originally planned to take place on 1 August 1820, was postponed and finally took place on 19 July 1821. Charles Manners-Sutton, the Archbishop of Canterbury, based his order of service on that of 1761, simply omitting the Coronation of the Queen. He entered his changes in both a handwritten and a printed order of service from 1761.[111] Based on these, as for the two previous coronations, a printed order of service was produced.[112] Indeed, at this coronation one copy of the printed order acquired an unexpected constitutional importance, as the archbishop himself noted:[113]

Immediately after His Majesty had taken ye Oath required on this solemn occasion, His Majesty in ye absence of ye proper instrument for ye purpose, was pleased to sign his name at ye foot of ye Oath as printed in this copy [. . .]

George IV's coronation has been described as 'the most extravagant in history'.[114] The magnificence of the event was caught in an extraordinarily lavish account, printed in pure gold and adorned with numerous hand-coloured engravings of the main participants.[115] However, while this volume with its illustrations provides invaluable details on the ceremonial costumes, the description of the ceremonies themselves is rather basic and gives but few details. The purpose of this publication seems to have been to capture the overall grandeur of the occasion rather than to provide a minute record. A slightly less sumptuous, but still impressive volume was the famous printed account prepared by Sir George Nayler, Garter King of Arms. Following Nayler's early death, the unfinished work was combined with the engravings of the aforementioned account and published as one

---

[110] J.R. Miller, *The History of Great Britain, from the Death of George II. to the Coronation of George IV. Designed as a Continuation of Hume and Smollett* (London: Jones and Company, 1825), 440.

[111] *Llp MS 1312* and *Llp Cod. Misc. 1083A*.The former was probably copied specifically to be revised for George IV, since it does not include the Queen's Coronation.

[112] *The Form and Order of the Service* [. . .] *Coronation of His Majesty King George IIII.* [*sic*] (London: Printed by George Eyre and Andrew Strahan, 1821); hereafter *OS* (1821).

[113] *Llp KA 113 1821***, annotation on front flyleaf. The king's signature is on p. 28.

[114] Strong, 374.

[115] *Ceremonial of the Coronation of His Most Sacred Majesty King George the Fourth* [. . .] (West-Minster: Printed by John Whitaker, 1823). The copy used here was *Lbl 1899.e.13*. For details on this publication see Ifan Kyrle Fletcher, 'The Literature of Splendid Occasions in English History', paper read before the Bibliographical Society (18 February 1947), reproduced on http://library.oxfordjournals.org/cgi/reprint/s5-I/3–4/184.pdf (Date accessed: 2 September 2011), p. 195.

comprehensive volume.[116] This publication is reminiscent of Sandford's printed account of the 1685 coronation, by which it may have been inspired. With the inclusion of the hand-coloured engravings, however, Nayler's work is far more extravagant in appearance; at the same time it is much less concerned with narrative details. Very detailed accounts of the coronation, including details of the music, appeared in the *Observer* and in the *Gentleman's Magazine*.[117] Knight states that the *Observer* report 'reads like an eyewitness account of the proceedings and the music performed'.[118] Indeed, Strong has shown that at this coronation 'members of the press were accorded seats [...] which commanded "an excellent view of all the ceremonies"'.[119] Most of the information in these two reports was adopted in Robert Huish's account published shortly after the event.[120]

For the anthem 'O Lord, grant the King a long life' during the procession from Westminster Hall to the Abbey a list prepared by the archbishop scheduled Child's setting 'to be sung alternately all the way after the sounding the Trumpets and Drums'.[121] Similarly, the reports agree that the anthem 'was sung in parts, the intervals being filled up by his Majesty's Band playing, the sounding of trumpets, and the beating of drums, until the arrival in the Abbey'.[122] Thus the anthem was probably sung in different sections, interspersed by music of the band which probably played on wind instruments only. It is possible that this *alternatim* performance practice reflected established custom: as shown above, instrumentalists walking with the choir were mentioned at several previous coronations; given the length of the procession, the anthem would have had to be repeated several times anyway.

A note signed by the Sub-Dean of the Chapel Royal mentions 'A Symphony to be performed from the commencement of the Procession,

[116] Sir George Nayler, *The Coronation of his Most Sacred Majesty King George the Fourth* [...] *Undertaken by his Majesty's Especial Command. By the Late Sir George Nayler* [...] *and since his Decease completed from the Official Document.* (London: 1837). For more details on the history of this publication see Fletcher, 'Literature', 195ff. See also Strong, 415f.

[117] Supplement to *TO*, 16 July 1821, continued in the issue of 22 July. *GM* 91 (1821), part 2, From July to December, 1821, 3–16.

[118] Knight, 'Organs of Westminster Abbey', 124.

[119] Strong, 355; he refers to *Lwa WAM 51292*.

[120] Robert Huish, *An Authentic History of the Coronation of His Majesty, King George the Fourth* [...] (London: Robins and Co., 1821).

[121] *Lca Coronation 1820. 1821. Ceremonials &c Church Service*: 'By Order of His Grace the Archbishop of Canterbury' / 'The Order of performing the several Anthems at the Coronation of His Majesty King George the Fourth' [MS contains two identical copies of this].

[122] Supplement to *TO*, 16 July 1821, [3]. See also *GM* 91 (1821), Part 2, 6; identical in Huish (1821), 207. Nayler, 114, lists 'HIS MAJESTY'S BAND, IN FULL STATE HABITS' following the choirs.

within the Church, till the King arrives at the Great West Door.'[123] This is the earliest evidence of orchestral music before the service. As this 'Symphony' did not accompany any procession or other proceedings it seems to have been pure entertainment for the spectators/congregation waiting for the service to begin, maybe intended to set the 'atmosphere' within the Abbey. The Sub-Dean provided also instructions for the performance of the entrance-anthem which were radically different from previous coronations. He stipulated that 'All the vocal Performers in the Procession to proceed to their Places in the Orchestra, to be in readiness for the Anthem.' Similarly, the *Gentleman's Magazine* reported that, once the procession from the Hall arrived at the Abbey, both the Chapel Royal and the Abbey choir 'immediately proceeded, with his Majesty's band, to the organ gallery; and, on his Majesty's entering the Abbey, the Choirs commenced singing an anthem'.[124] Thus the entrance-anthem was no longer sung by the Abbey choir in procession from the West door to the quire and the choir had lost its privilege of leading the monarch into the church. The Sub-Dean also stated that

As soon as His Majesty enters the church, the Drums and Trumpets in the Old Organ Loft to sound, till he reaches the entrance of the Choir – and then the Anthem "I was glad &cc." to be sung.

The king's procession up the nave to the quire would therefore have been accompanied only by instrumental music, but not by the anthem. In the event, however, the king's entrance into the Abbey was accompanied by more music than usual. Nayler reports the scene as follows:[125]

And on His Majesty's entering the Abbey, the Choirs sang the Hallelujah Chorus in Handel's Oratorio the Messiah, after which a scene from the Oratorio of Saul, followed by the anthem, "I was glad when they said unto me, We will go into the House of the Lord." Immediately after the conclusion of the Hallelujah Chorus, and before the remainder of the music, the King's Scholars of Westminster School, from the platform gallery over the entrance into the Choir, with their Masters, greeted His Majesty with repeated shouts of "VIVAT GEORGIUS REX."

Regarding the 'scene from the Oratorio of Saul', the *Gentleman's Magazine* describes it as a 'selection from *Saul* [...] beginning with *Already see the Monarch of the Lord advance, &c*'.[126] This text is not found in the libretto of

---

[123] Single-leaf note in *Lca Coronation 1820. 1821. Ceremonials &c Church Service* (emphasis original).

[124] *GM* 91 (1821), part 2, 8. For the 'organ gallery' cf. below, fn. 203.   [125] Nayler, 120.

[126] *GM* 91 (1821), part 2, 9, footnote (*).

Handel's oratorio, but it could have been an adapted version of the opening recitative of the third scene in Act I: the original text begins 'Already see, the daughters of the land', leading into the chorus 'Welcome, welcome, mighty king!' which would be most appropriate. It may have been George IV himself who had 'arranged for the singing' of the Handel pieces 'at his entry'.[127] Indeed, according to the *Observer* the inclusion of the Hallelujah Chorus had been the king's express wish, voiced only a few days before the coronation:[128]

A grand rehearsal of the music performed on Thursday took place on the preceding Monday night, upon which occasion his Majesty, whose judgment and taste in these matters are universally recognised, suggested many alterations and improvements. At his Majesty's command the Hallelujah Chorus from the Messiah was added to the selection already made, and was performed on the entrance into the Abbey.

It is not clear if these Handel pieces accompanied the king's procession or if they were listened to *in situ*, with the king simply standing or sitting at the West Door, or even kneeling as in 1661. It is therefore also not clear if 'I was glad' was performed during his procession up the nave or if indeed it started only once the king reached the entrance of the quire, as originally scheduled by the Sub-Dean.

'I was glad' was performed in a newly composed setting by Thomas Attwood, Composer of the Chapel Royal since 1796. No manuscript source for this anthem is known, but the full score was published soon after the event.[129] Attwood's setting is scored for four-part choir and a full orchestra of symphonic dimensions and is thus different from all previous settings of the text. The anthem text was shortened and slightly changed compared to previous coronations.[130] In his setting, Attwood repeats many portions of the text; most notably he repeats the opening line ('I was glad [. . .] house of the Lord') before the Gloria Patri. For a comprehensive analysis of Attwood's anthem one can refer to the detailed review in *The Quarterly Musical Magazine and Review*, which appeared after the publication of the

---

[127] Leeper, 561.   [128] *TO*, Sunday, 22 July 1821: 'Coronation Music (Additional Particulars)'.

[129] Thomas Attwood, *Anthem, I was Glad. Composed by Command of The King and performed as part of the August Ceremonial of His Majesty's Coronation* [. . .] (London: Novello, [1821]). The catalogue of the Bodleian Library, Oxford lists four more editions from '1822, c1840, 1865, and c1875'.

[130] *Llp Cod. Misc. 1083A*, p. 2 (transcr. App. A6). In *Llp MS 1312*, p. 2, the only alteration in the original printed text is that 'Let us' is changed to 'We will'. This, however, is not changed in the other order, but it is in Attwood's setting, suggesting that both annotated orders served as his source for the text.

score.[131] As in the earlier settings of 'I was glad', there is a clear break between 'the house of David' and 'O pray for the peace of Jerusalem'; Attwood puts a fermata over the crotchet rest between these two sections. As already mentioned, it is possible that at earlier coronations the *Vivat*s of the King's Scholars were meant to be inserted at this place.[132] For 1821 there is an informative report by Richard Newcome Gresley, then one of the scholars. Before the coronation he wrote: 'This time, as the anthem will not be over when he [the King] comes in, immediately that it is, we are to sing out as loud as we can "Vivat Georgius Rex," raising our voices at the end in a curious way'.[133] However, at the actual ceremony the boys did not follow this instruction:

When the anthem was over, Goodenough [the headmaster] cleared his voice with a *hem*, and then sang out melodiously. We then shouted, "Vivat Georgius Rex" six times, and we shouted and clapped gloriously at the Recognition and at other times during the ceremony.

From this report it is not clear when exactly the *Vivat*s occurred. As seen above, Nayler states that they were shouted 'immediately' after the Hallelujah Chorus, and it is possible that this is what Gresley referred to as 'the anthem'. Also, it is possible that he referred to the end of the first part of 'I was glad'. Overall, one cannot preclude the possibility that Attwood had initially planned the inclusion of the *Vivat*s in his anthem, especially since it is clear that they should have been sung. The best known feature of Attwood's anthem is that he prominently incorporates the tune of 'God save the King' in the repeat of the orchestral introduction and it was probably this feature that caused one commentator in 1834 to describe the piece as 'the clever anthem'.[134] Interestingly, the number of bars of the repeated orchestral introduction and the first half of the anthem (up to the fermata) is 59; with one step per bar this comes close to the number of steps needed to walk up the nave to the screen and this might indicate that, as in 1685, the anthem had been laid out carefully to cover the king's procession.[135] Attwood's anthem was published in several editions and in 1832 one writer observed that it 'has been constantly performed since [the coronation] at most of the musical festivals and meetings in various parts

---

[131] Vol. 4 (1822), 88–92. See also William J. Gatens, *Victorian Cathedral Music in Theory and Practice* (Cambridge University Press, 1986), 98f.

[132] See above, Ch. 3. Fletcher, *British Court*, 93, states that the custom of the *Vivat*s 'was extended by George IV to include Town Boys as well', without giving further details.

[133] This and the following quoted after Bridge, *Westminster Pilgrim*, 184, which appears to be the earliest reference to this source. See also Carleton, 109, who quotes with slight differences.

[134] *MLMS* 7 (October 1834), 78.   [135] Cf. the considerations in Ch. 3.

of Great Britain'.[136] It became known simply as Attwood's 'Grand Coronation Anthem' and was also repeated at the two following corona- tions; its abandonment in 1902 was going to cause some consternation.

There is conflicting evidence as to whether there was an anthem after the Recognition. In the draft orders of service an annotation next to 'Anthem II' ('The King shall rejoice') reads: 'This Anthem to be omitted'.[137] Indeed, the reports in the *Gentleman's Magazine* and in the *Observer* mention only a fanfare after the last Recognition.[138] In contrast to this, Nayler and Huish both report that an anthem to the text 'Let thy hand be strengthened' (Ps. 89:14) was performed:[139]

and at the last Recognition, the trumpets sounded and the drums beat. This being done, the anthem, Psalm lxxxix. 14, was sung by the Choirs, the King resuming his seat in the Chair of State.

It is possible, however, that in this point both authors simply followed Sandford's account of the 1685 coronation, which lists this anthem at this place. Notably, referring to this account, Huish himself stated that the 1685 coronation served as a model in 1821.[140] At the same time, it is possible that the anthem had been planned to be included at one stage: intriguingly, there is a setting of the text by Attwood which in Myles Foster's catalogue of anthems is described as '2nd Anthem, Coronation of King George IV'.[141] Foster does not give any reference for this ascription, but John Calvert's anthem word- book from 1844 includes the full text with Attwood's name and the remark 'Composed for the Coronation of His Majesty King George IV'.[142] The only known source for the music is an edition from the 1930s, where the piece is headed: 'Composed by Thomas Attwood for the Coronation of Queen Victoria, but not performed owing to [the] composer's death, 1838.

---

[136] 'Review of New Music', *Harmonicon* (1832), part 1, 59. See also Daniel Lysons, John Amott, Lee Williams and Godwin Chance, *Origin and Progress of the Meeting of the Three Choirs of Gloucester, Worcester and Hereford and of the Charity connected with It* (Gloucester: Chance and Bland, 1895). For the editions see above, fn. 129.

[137] *Llp Cod. Misc. 1083A*, p. 5. See also *Llp MS 1312*, p. 5.

[138] *GM* 91 (1821), part 2, 9; and Supplement to *TO*, 16 July 1821 [4].

[139] Nayler, 121, and Huish, *Authentic History*, 218, who includes the full anthem text.

[140] Huish, *Authentic History*, 18.

[141] Myles Birket Foster, *Anthems and Anthem Composers. An Essay upon the Development of the Anthem from the Reformation to the End of the Nineteenth Century* (London: Novello, 1901), 106.

[142] John Calvert, *A Collection of Anthems used in Her Majesty's Chapel Royal, the Temple Church, and the Collegiate Churches and Chapels in England and Ireland* (London: George Bell, 1844), 81. The same wording in Thomas Pearce, *A Collection of Anthems used in Her Majesty's Chapels Royal, and most Cathedral Churches, in England and Ireland*, new ed. with additions (London: Rivingtons, 1856), 357.

Edited from the original Full Score and Parts by Frederic Fertel.'[143] Unfortunately, no further details about the 'original Full Score' are given and it is not clear on what evidence Fertel's ascription of the anthem to the coronation of Queen Victoria is based. Since the piece is complete, and since Attwood's 'I was glad' was performed for Queen Victoria, it is not clear why his 'Let thy hand be strengthened' should not have been performed – 'owing to composer's death'. The idea that Attwood 'had begun a third [anthem] for the coronation of Queen Victoria' was probably first mentioned by Henry Davey in 1895; however, Davey included neither the title of the anthem, nor a reference for his statement.[144] His suggestion was followed in the anonymously published article 'Coronation Music of the Past' in 1902 which stated that the title of the anthem is not known.[145]

Following the aforementioned ascription in Calvert's anthem word-book it is possible that Attwood had intended this anthem for the 1821 coronation, but in the end never performed it. Indeed, the music itself points to 1821: the introductory prelude on the organ is more or less identical with the orchestral introduction to 'I was glad'. The incorporated tune of 'God save the King' would fit perfectly to the anthem after the Recognition, immediately following the shouts of nearly the same words by the assembled congregation. The theme of the vocal parts is also the same as in 'I was glad'. After all, it could even be that Attwood had first composed 'Let thy hand be strengthened', but reused the material for his 'I was glad' when the anthem after the Recognition was omitted.

The Recognition was followed by the beginning of the Communion Service with the First Oblation and the Litany. In his corrections in the orders of service Archbishop Manners-Sutton had scheduled the Litany to be read, although in one source he curiously stipulated that the choir should be 'reading ye responses unaccompanied to ye Organ'.[146] In any case, musically, there was a significant innovation at this part of the service. The *Gentleman's Magazine* reported that the 'fourth [anthem], previous to the communion service was sung with the organ accompaniment only, or Sanctus music by Jomelli, and responses to the Communion in like manner'.[147] While the archbishop's earliest draft did not include any music at

---

[143] Curwen Edition 80686. (London: J. Curwen and Sons, [1933]). Gatens, 84, also mentions that Attwood 'had been planning an anthem' for Queen Victoria's coronation, but he does not give any details.

[144] Henry Davey, *History of English Music* (London: Curwen and Sons, [1895]), 435.

[145] *The Athenaeum*, no. 3871 (1902), 25–7, here 27.

[146] *Llp Cod. Misc. 1083A*, p. 9. See also ibid., p. 6; *Llp MS 1312*, p. 9; *OS* (1821), 7; and Nayler, 122.

[147] *GM* 91 (1821), part 2, 9, footnote (*).

this place, the final, printed order of service stipulates 'A Sanctus'.[148] The Sanctus would normally follow much later in the service, and its introduction at this place, directly before the 'responses to the Communion', that is before the Responses to the Commandments, was a novelty for the coronation service. However, this merely followed the custom common in English cathedrals at the time.[149] Moreover, referring to the altered position of the Sanctus, Macleane pointed out that 'the early nineteenth-century use was an unconscious return to the Byzantine rite in St. Sophia, in which the hymn *Trisagios* was sung early in the Coronation'.[150]

The 'Sanctus music by Jomelli', together with the Responses to the Commandments, survives in several manuscript sources.[151] These pieces are not original compositions by Niccolò Jomelli, but arrangements based on his music, made by John Spencer under whose name they were included in the Chapel Royal part-books.[152] Little is known about Spencer, except that he was a 'composer and organist', 'pupil of Dr Dupuis', and Boyce's successor as Organist and Composer of the Chapel Royal in 1779.[153] It is yet to be ascertained on which piece(s) of Jomelli's the arrangements are based.[154]

The Nicene Creed before the Sermon was read by the archbishop.[155] He thus did not follow the reintroduction of its singing from the previous coronation. Even the *Veni Creator* before the Anointing had at one point been considered to be read.[156] However, Nayler reports that 'The King returned to his chair; and the hymn, "Come, Holy Ghost, our souls inspire," was then sung by the Choir'.[157] According to Huish, the archbishop began the hymn and the choir 'sang it out' and the *Gentleman's Magazine*

---

[148] See *Llp MS 1312* and *OS (1821)*, 18.

[149] Legg, *Three Coronation Orders*, 138. See also Paul Bradshaw 'Coronations from the Eighteenth to the Twentieth Century', in Bradshaw (ed.), *Coronations. Past, Present and Future*, 22–32, here 27; and Perkins, 99.

[150] Macleane, 85.   [151] For details and a transcription see Range, thesis, vol. II.

[152] *Lbl R.M. 27 g. 1–5*; 'Jomelli' added in pencil.

[153] Only short references to Spencer are found in Bumpus, 321; Maggie Humphreys and Robert Evans, *Dictionary of Composers for the Church in Great Britain and Ireland* (London: Mansell, 1997), 316; and in James D. Brown and Stephen S. Stratton, *British Musical Biography* (Birmingham, 1897), 386.

[154] Knight, 'Organs of Westminster Abbey', 125, states that one source describes the pieces as arrangements 'from Jomelli's overture'. For a copy in the library of St George's Chapel, Windsor, the catalogue entry states that the piece was arranged from Jomelli's 'Requiem Mass'. See Clifford Mould, *The Musical Manuscripts of St. George's Chapel Windsor Castle*. Historical Monographs relating to St. George's Chapel, Windsor Castle, 14 (Windsor: Oxley and Son, 1973), 21.

[155] *Llp Cod. Misc. 1083A*, p. 26. And see for example Huish, *Authentic History*, 220.

[156] *Llp MS 1312*, p. 34: 'May not this be read?'.   [157] Nayler, 122.

provided another detail and reported that the *Veni Creator* was 'sung to the grand chaunt'.[158] This most certainly refers to the Grand Chant by Pelham Humfrey which 'was used at Westminster Abbey for special festivals' and which was also sung at the coronation of Queen Victoria in 1838.[159]

'Zadok the Priest' was performed during the king's robing before his Anointing.[160] At least from this coronation onwards, the anthem did not any more accompany the actual Anointing, as is reported for the seventeenth century. Even though further details are not known, the king's favouring of Handel's music would certainly have ensured this setting a place at his coronation. However, it may be assumed that the anthem was not sung in its original version, but in an arrangement for the bigger forces available. Two contemporary prints suggest that this was produced by Johann Baptist Cramer.[161] Cramer (1771–1858) was a successful and popular composer, pianist and publisher at the time and had been one of the founders of the Philharmonic Society.[162] Furthermore, it is possible that he was involved with leading the band at the coronation.[163]

The anthem 'Behold, O God' after the Anointing was omitted.[164] It had been introduced by Archbishop Sancroft in 1685, probably for the special circumstances of that coronation, and had afterwards been retained without obvious reason. Nevertheless, whilst this cut reverted to the pre-1685 arrangements, from a ceremonial point of view it also meant that the Anointing, the spiritual climax of the service, lost a distinct marker and thus some emphasis.

The text for the anthem following the Crowning was changed in the order of service for the first time since 1689: 'Praise the Lord, O Jerusalem' was replaced by 'The King shall rejoice', with the text as in Handel's setting from 1727.[165] The reason for this change could be that this text had been omitted

---

[158] Huish, *Authentic History*, 226; GM 91 (1821), part 2, 9, footnote (*).

[159] Knight, 'Organs of Westminster Abbey', 125. For further details and a transcription of the version used at the 1838 coronation see Ch. 7.

[160] Miller, 445.

[161] *April Fools. Country Musicians Celebrating a Reginal Coronation.* Dedicated to all Lovers of Social and Domestic Harmony. Drawn and Engraved by I. Sawthem. Performed in Anticipation at C____ April 1, 1821, [London, 1821]: '[. . .] a fine Coronation Anthem improved from Handel by J. Crammer'. *Wednesday Night for Thursday Morning, or the Last Rehearsal of the Coronation Anthem.* Drawn and engraved by 'I. Sawthem' and published for the author [c. 1821]. This print depicts musicians around a music stand; their music is inscribed '[. . .] Coronation Anthem improved from Handel by J. Crammer'.

[162] For biographical details see Jerald C. Graue and Thomas B. Miligan, '(2) Johann [John] Baptist Cramer', NG 6, 640–3.

[163] See below, fn. 183.   [164] *Llp MS 1312*, p. 39 and *Cod. Misc. 1083A*, p. 39.

[165] *Llp MS 1312*, p. 56. See also *Llp Cod. Misc. 1083A*, p. 50, and OS (1821), p. 42. Nayler, 124, gives the title only.

from the anthem after the Recognition, where the orders of service at the four previous coronations had placed it. The aforementioned anthem word-book by Calvert contains the text as in the order of service with the annotation 'Composed for the Coronation of His Majesty King George IV. / W. Knyvett'.[166] Indeed, the *Gentleman's Magazine* reported that the anthem 'was composed by Mr. William Knyvett, whose duty it was (with Mr. Attwood) to provide new compositions'.[167] Knyvett (1779–1856) had been one of the Composers of the Chapel Royal since 1808, when he succeeded his father Charles (1752–1822).[168] Knyvett is also named as composer of this anthem in the archbishop's aforementioned list of anthems; the text of the anthem here is the same as in Handel's setting, but without the verse 'Glory and great worship'.[169] Knyvett's setting of 'The King shall rejoice' seems to be lost. The otherwise very detailed accounts in Huish and in the *Observer* describe this as a 'short anthem', without giving further details, although the latter states that the king 'particularly complimented Messrs. Attwood and Knyvett, the composers of the two new anthems, on the talent which they had displayed'.[170] However, from an anonymous report about a later performance at the Birmingham Festival it can be deduced that the anthem made use of 'the full orchestra'.[171] This latter report points to the fact that Knyvett's anthem appears to have become a popular composition after the coronation: not only in the capital, and not only in chapels and cathedrals which used Calvert's word-book, but also in concert halls. For instance, in 1823, it was performed not only at the aforementioned Birmingham Festival, the biggest music festival outside London, but also at a service at the Gloucester Music Festival.[172]

As at previous coronations, the Te Deum accompanied the king's procession from St Edward's Chair to 'the chair on which his Majesty first sat, on the East side of the Throne'.[173] In one of the annotated orders of service the words 'Boyce in A full' are written next to the Te Deum and according to the *Gentleman's Magazine* Boyce's setting 'composed for the last coronation' was used.[174] This report states also that it was 'accompanied by the organ and band', although Boyce's setting is for choir and organ only

[166] Calvert, 51. The same ascription in Pearce, 357.   [167] *GM* 91 (1821), part 2, 9, footnote (*).

[168] Nicholas Temperley, 'Knyvett, William', *NG* 13, 705.   [169] See above, fn. 121.

[170] Huish, *Authentic History*, 232; Supplement to *TO*, 16 July, 1821, [5]; and *TO*, 22 July 1821, [p. 8].

[171] Clio. [*sic*], 'The Birmingham Festival / To the Editor', in *Harmonicon* (1823), part I, 182f., here 182.

[172] *Harmonicon* (1823), part 1, 148f.   [173] *GM* 91 (1821), part 2, 12.

[174] *Llp Cod. Misc. 1083A*, 56 and *GM* 91 (1821), part 2, 9, footnote; quoted in full in Knight, 'Organs of Westminster Abbey', 124.

and he had scheduled it to be performed like that in 1761. Assuming that the Te Deum was Boyce's setting, it is noteworthy that both Nayler and Huish report that it was 'chanted'.[175] As seen earlier, the term was at the time used not only for chanting as in the modern sense ('Anglican chant'), but also as a synonym for singing in general.[176]

The 'Final Anthem' saw significant changes compared with previous coronations. In the manuscript draft order of service, the text of the Homage anthem, 'The Lord is a Sun and a Shield' is crossed out and that of 'Blessed be Thou, Lord God of Israel' is entered.[177] The *Observer* reported that this was '[James] Kent's celebrated anthem', which was a 'peculiar favourite with the King'.[178] Similarly, Robert Murray stated that it was George IV himself who proposed the inclusion of Kent's anthem.[179] However, the anthem was not sung in its original form, which has organ accompaniment only: the report in the *Observer* indicates that it was sung in an arrangement by 'Mr Kramer', describing him as 'the composer of the music to Kent's celebrated anthem'.[180] According to this report 'Kramer' was 'the master of the King's Band of wind instruments' and it thus refers to 'Christian Kramer', who was the director of the prince's own private (wind) band which became known as the 'Household Band' after his accession to the throne.[181] There is generally little information on Kramer, but a short entry is found in the so-called Sainsbury's dictionary.[182] For the coronation the *Observer* reported that 'Mr. Cramer was appointed to lead the band upon this memorable occasion'; and similarly, it has been observed that 'Stephanoff's drawings of people present at the coronation [1821]' include a 'Mr Cramer, Leader of the King's Band'.[183] These could be referring to the

---

[175] Nayler, 125; Huish, *Memoirs*, vol. II, 316.   [176] See Ch. 5, fn. 95.

[177] *Llp Cod. Misc. 1312*, p. 70.   [178] This and the following *TO*, 22 July 1821, [8].

[179] Robert Murray, *The King's Crowning*, with an introduction by Foxley Norris (London: John Murray, [1936]), 191.

[180] See also Murray, 191; and Crowest, 34. The first edition of Kent's anthem was published by W. Randall in 1773. An edition by Preston and Son had been reissued in 1811 (seen as *Ob Mus. 32c. 101* (1)).

[181] See Peter Holman, 'London (i), §II, 2 (v): Music at court: The decline of secular music', *NG* 15, 107–8.

[182] [J. S. Sainsbury], *A Dictionary of Musicians, from the earliest Ages to the present Time*, 2 vols. (London: Printed for Sainsbury and Co., 1842), vol. II, 24. The text on Kramer must be of an earlier date: he is described as having 'the sole direction of his majesty's band', even though Queen Victoria had come to the throne in 1837. Kramer's lifespan is unknown.

[183] *TO*, 22 July 1821 [8]; and Fletcher, *Splendid Occasions*, 79. The drawings are from the collection of the Victoria and Albert Museum.

aforementioned Johann Baptist Cramer, but also to Christian Kramer. In a letter to Hummel, dated 'Carlton House, London, Nov. 25th 1821', Kramer signed as 'Director of the Music to his Majesty' even though he was formally appointed Master of the King's Musick only in 1829.[184]

It is possible that Kent's anthem was not actually performed during the Homage but rather later on in the service. The otherwise very detailed report in the *Gentlemen's Magazine* does not mention an anthem or any music during the Homage and it mentions Kent's anthem after the communion.[185] This description tallies curiously with a manuscript order of service preserved in the College of Arms. This states that, after communion,

His Majesty will then return to His Chair on the South side of the Area; and the last anthem "Blessed be thou, Lord God of Israel" &c will be sung; and, at the conclusion, and amidst the acclamation of the Assembly, the King will put on his Crown, and, taking the two Sceptres in His Hands, again ascend the Throne, and sit there until the conclusion of the Post-Communion Service and the Blessing.[186]

Similarly, the *Observer* reported distinctly that Kent's Homage anthem was 'the last piece performed in the Abbey' at the coronation.[187] It could be that the anthem was an additional feature at the end of the service similar to the Handel pieces at the beginning.

It is then possible that there was no music during the Homage. Indeed, the way in which the Homage was performed seems to have changed for this coronation. The printed order of service still stipulated that, after the first peer of each rank had paid homage, 'every Peer one by one, in Order, putting off their Coronets, singly ascend the throne again, and stretching forth their hands [...]'[188] This second ascending of the peers to touch the crown and kiss the king's cheek was retained in the official orders of service until 1937. However, for 1821 most descriptions state that once the first of each rank had paid homage all the others of his rank ascended immediately, before the next rank paid homage.[189] A cut of the music during the Homage would have ensured that the vows of the senior peers could still be heard.

---

[184] *Lbl RPS MS 350*: letters of the Royal Philharmonic Society, vol. XVIII, 'Jo-Lan', fo. 135v. See also Michael Joe Budds, 'Music at the Court of Queen Victoria: A Study of Music in the Life of the Queen and her Participation in the Musical Life of her Time', 3 vols., unpublished Ph.D. thesis, University of Iowa (1987), vol. III, 806: Table VIII–23, and vol. III, 808.

[185] *GM* 91 (1821), part 2, 12.

[186] *Lca Coronation 1820. 1821. Ceremonials &c Church Service*, manuscript order of service towards the end of the volume, headed 'The King'.

[187] *TO*, 22 July 1821, [p. 8].   [188] *OS* (1821), 50f.

[189] See the descriptions in *Lca Coronation 1820. 1821. Ceremonials &c Church Service*.

In contrast to all the musical pomp surrounding the king's inauguration ceremonies, the liturgical music of the service appears to have been rather bleak. According to the order of service, the anthem 'Let my prayer come up' was omitted and the Sanctus and Gloria were simply read.[190] Indeed, the Sanctus had already been sung earlier in the service and the Gloria could have been simply read in order to leave time for Kent's anthem which seems to have followed it more or less immediately.

George IV's coronation is the only one for which choral music is reported for the banquet in Westminster Hall and again a personal wish of the king could be the explanation for its inclusion. The *Observer* reported that 'By his Majesty's desire too, "God save the King", and "Non Nobis Domine" were rehearsed preparatory to the banquet'.[191] Generally, it appears that 'God save the King', the National Anthem, had a special role at this coronation. The tune was prominently incorporated by Attwood in the entrance-anthem and the song itself was heard several times. The first documented performance on the day was during the king's entrance into Westminster Hall before the service, when it was played by 'the trumpets'.[192] For the service in the Abbey, the *Gentleman's Magazine* reported that the song was performed 'after the Sacrament, and at the conclusion'.[193] Similarly, Leeper states that the king had 'arranged for the singing of [it] at his departure' from the Abbey.[194] According to Nayler

the King again ascended the throne, and sat there [. . .] until the conclusion of the Post-Communion Service and the Blessing. The Choirs then sang the National air of "GOD SAVE THE KING".[195]

Thus the National Anthem was probably sung during the king's procession into St Edward's Chapel, which at all previous coronations had been accompanied merely by organ music. Whereas Nayler states it was sung by 'the Choirs', according to the *Gentleman's Magazine* it was 'chorused by all the nobles of the land male and female' and 'accompanied with the whole orchestra'.[196] In any case, the end of the service saw a grave mishap. The *Observer* reported that, as soon as the king had gone into St Edward's Chapel, the

musicians and principal singers abruptly left the choir; and when the King returned he had empty benches, covered with dirt and litter [. . .] This mode of clearing the

---

[190] *Llp Cod. Misc. 1083A*, 70, 78, and 83. This is confirmed by Huish, *Authentic History*, 234.
[191] *TO*, 22 July 1821, [8].
[192] Supplement to *TO*, 16 July 1821, [3]. See also Huish, *Authentic History*, 203.
[193] *GM* 91 (1821), part 2, 9, footnote (*).   [194] Leeper, 561.   [195] Nayler, 126.
[196] *GM* 91 (1821), part 2, 9, footnote (*).

Abbey may probably have been found necessary as a measure of convenience, but it certainly was a most unpicturesque arrangement. It had the appearance of a want of due respect to the Sovereign.[197]

This mistake not only raises questions about the rehearsal of the service, since the processions had apparently not been practised; but it also implies that no elaborate orchestral music was performed during the Recess. It is possible that the organist improvised after realizing that the musicians had started to leave. Finally, 'God save the King' was also sung in Westminster Hall after the service. According to Nayler, the combined choirs of the Chapel and the Abbey together sang it following the toast to the king after the second course.[198] The *Gentleman's Magazine* goes into more details and reports that 'God save the King' was sung

in fine style by the whole Choir, the chorus being swelled by the whole company, all standing, who seemed to be electrified by the stanza – "Scatter his enemies, And make them fall."[199]

The enthusiastic singing of this verse of the National Anthem may have been a reference to Britain's success during the Napoleonic campaign a few years previously. Afterwards the king drank to the people and the choirs sang 'Non nobis Domine', which marked the end of the dinner. This most probably refers to the canon formerly ascribed to William Byrd.[200] Interestingly, the use of this piece in such a prominent place at the banquet coincides with the Hanoverians' fascination with the Elizabethan era that has been observed.[201] Furthermore, it is 'Non nobis' that Shakespeare's Henry V invokes to be sung after the Battle of Agincourt;[202] and this gives this text a further poignancy for the coronation of the king who, as prince regent, had fought and won against Napoleon's French Empire. After all, in this context one may wonder if the scene from Saul at the beginning of the service was not included for the same reason: the 'Mighty King' might easily be understood to refer to the victor against the French emperor; the probably adapted line of 'David his ten thousands slew,

---

[197] Supplement to *TO*, 16 July 1821, [5]; the same in Huish, *Authentic History*, 246.
[198] Nayler, 130.   [199] *GM* 91 (1821), part 2, 16.
[200] A late seventeenth-century manuscript copy is found in the Royal Music Library, now *Lbl R.M. 24.c.11.* (11). In addition, the piece had been available in print. See, for instance, *Non Nobis Domini* [sic], *a favourite Canon for Three Voices* (London: Printed for Culliford, Rolfe & Barrow, [*c.* 1798]), and *Non nobis Domine, Composed by W. Bird, 1590* (Liverpod: Hime & Son, [*c.* 1810]). For the ascription to Byrd see David Humphreys, 'Wilder's hand?', *MT* 144 (Summer 2003), 4.
[201] Strong, 367.   [202] *Henry V*, Act IV, sc. viii, 128.

ten thousand praises are his due' from Handel's original text would have been a similarly fitting choice.

The musicians and performance

The performance conditions in 1821 were probably different from those at previous coronations. The *Observer* reported:[203]

Above the altar, and over the traverse, was situated the music gallery, the two front rows of which were devoted to spectators; – behind these were the seats for the choristers, and behind them again seats for the instrumental performers. The organ was in the centre [. . .]

Thus all the singers and musicians were placed in one large gallery, at the east end of the quire, on top of St Edward's Chapel (see Illustration 6.2). Musicians had already been placed here at the two previous coronations, but they were then also placed in other galleries at the side, in front of the altar. Placing all the musicians in one single gallery certainly would have facilitated coordination of the massed forces. It is likely that this arrangement was influenced by the experience of the Handel Commemoration concerts that had been held in the Abbey in 1784; at these all the musicians had been placed in one big gallery over the West entrance of the church.[204] It is noteworthy that in 1821 the singers were placed in front of the orchestra, not behind it. This arrangement, too, was similar to the 1784 concerts, where the principal singers had been placed in front of the orchestra and the choir at the sides; and according to Burney this scheme conformed with contemporary oratorio performance practice.[205] Incidentally, it is not known how Handel himself had placed the musicians in his oratorio performances; apart from the Handel Commemoration the first pictorial evidence dates from the 1790s, and this also shows the choir in front of the orchestra.[206]

[203] Supplement to *TO*, 16 July 1821, [2].

[204] See Charles Burney, *An account of the musical performances in Westminster-Abbey, and the Pantheon* [. . .] *In commemoration of Handel.* (London: Printed for the Benefit of the Musical Fund, 1785), *passim.* For a modern study of these concerts see William Weber, 'The 1784 Handel Commemoration as Political Ritual', *The Journal of British Studies*, 28, no. 1 (1989), 43–69.

[205] Burney, *Musical performances*, 1: 'as at Oratorios', and [23]: 'Plan of the Orchestra and Disposition of the Band'.

[206] Donald Burrows, 'Handel's Oratorio Performances', in Donald Burrows (ed.), *The Cambridge Companion to Handel* (Cambridge University Press, 1997), 262–81, here 266f.

6.2. 'The Recognition at the coronation of George IV in 1821', print, 1824 (detail). © Dean and Chapter of Westminster.

There was again an exceptionally huge number of musicians. The *Observer* summarized that there were 'a hundred instruments, and twice a hundred voices',[207] which may have been a very rough estimate. Indeed, for the instrumentalists, the *Observer* lists in another issue '29 wind-instrument performers' and the organist, as well as twenty-two string players (six first violins, seven second violins, three violas, three cellos, and three double basses), who are named individually.[208] This gives a total number of only fifty-two players, but there is the possibility that the account is incomplete and that it mentions only the main players. This account also states that 'Mr. Shield the master of the King's State Band [William Shield (1748–1829)]' was the conductor, who might thus have shared this position with the aforementioned Cramer or Kramer.[209] The organ in the music gallery was newly built by 'Elliot, of Tottenham-court-road' and was played by Charles Knyvett, Organist of the Chapel Royal and father of William Knyvett.[210] Its specification is not known, but judging from a contemporary depiction (see Illustration 6.2) it seems to have been a larger instrument than that of 1761, which had had a mere seven stops.

All the reports mention the combined choirs of the Chapel Royal and of Westminster Abbey only, but these two choirs would not have amounted to the 'twice a hundred voices' mentioned. It is possible that the choir of St Paul's was also involved, as it was at the following coronation.[211] Moreover, there could again have been other additional singers. The king's meticulous interest in the music extended to its performance and he was concerned about the balance between choir and orchestra:[212]

During the rehearsal, his Majesty found that the instrumental part of the band was too powerful for the vocal – his Majesty therefore commanded that the voices should be increased, and this took place as far as the extent of the orchestra would permit.

Whatever the exact numbers were, a huge performing body of several hundred would have followed the fashion of the time. Claudia Johnson has shown that during the eighteenth century 'gigantic performances' of Handel's music developed and that the musical sublime was associated with voluminousness: it was common perception that 'large forces realize the

---

[207] Supplement to *TO*, 16 July 1821, [4].

[208] *TO*, 22 July 1821: 'Coronation Music. – Additional Particulars'.   [209] Cf. above, fns. 181–4.

[210] *TO*, 22 July 1821 (as in fn. 208). For further information on this organ see *Lna LC 2/50*: 'Coronation Bills George IV.', p. 7. For the organist see Sir George Smart, *Leaves from the Journals of Sir George* Smart, ed. by H. Bertram Cox and C.L.E. Cox (London: Longmans, Green, 1907), 58.

[211] See Ch. 7, fn. 44.   [212] *TO*, 22 July 1821, [8].

sublime properties of Handel's music'.[213] A reviewer in the *Court Magazine* wrote about a performance of Handel's 'Zadok the Priest' at the 'Amateur's Festival' in London on 30 October 1834: 'Though not the best of Handel's coronation anthems, yet the immense mass of harmony given out by the combined efforts of the singers and the orchestra, kindled a powerful emotion in the audience.'[214] However, others questioned whether the huge performing body and Westminster Abbey as a building were suitable for the performance of Handel's music at all, 'with so many people in so large a space'.[215] For instance, Felice Giardini, who had performed at the 1761 coronation, 'disapproved of the colossal forces employed' at the Handel Commemoration in 1784.[216] Unfortunately, there are no reports of how the large performing body at the 1821 coronation was perceived.

George IV's coronation in 1821 was altogether one of the most elaborate in history and in terms of its ceremonial dimensions it may be seen as the apogee of the British coronation spectacle. It is not surprising that for such a display of grandeur the music was also on an unprecedented scale. As a result of the changes demanded by the king, Handel's compositions had a prominent role in the musical programme. Such extensive deployment of Handel's music together with the choice of Kent's anthem and the canon ascribed to Byrd indicates a preference for music of the past; this had probably not been distinct at earlier coronations at which almost all the music had been newly composed.

Overall, the prominent role taken by the music at the 1761 and 1821 coronations contributes to the perception of them as 'concert coronations'. The music not merely accompanied the ritual proceedings, but it stood alone for much of the time and had furthermore become one of the service's main attractions. Indeed, in 1761 the music appears to have been the only part of the service that was rehearsed properly. George IV followed his two predecessors in becoming personally involved in the musical arrangements for his coronation. However, in contrast to George II and George III, he not only chose the composers and pieces, but was also very much concerned with the quality of the performance. His explicit wishes regarding the music turned George IV's crowning into a rather personal 'concert coronation'.

---

[213] Claudia L. Johnson, '"Giant HANDEL" and the Musical Sublime', *Eighteenth-Century Studies* 19 (Summer 1986), 515–33, here 532.

[214] 'C.', 'The Amateur Festival', *The Court Magazine* 6 (January–June 1835), 22–8, here 25.

[215] See Weber, *Musical Classics*, 231, who refers to Claudia Johnson, [here 515].

[216] Simon McVeigh, *Concert Life in London from Mozart to Haydn* (Cambridge University Press, 1993), 168. And see above, fn. 88.

The two coronations of 1831 and 1838 form a small group that followed a 'reformed model' of the overall proceedings. Regarding the music, they still followed the previous 'concert coronations' and at the same time marked the end of centuries of development before significant changes were introduced in the twentieth century.

William IV and Queen Adelaide, 1831

George IV reigned longer as prince regent than as king. He died on 26 June 1830, a mere ten years after his accession to the throne, and was succeeded by his brother, who was crowned as William IV together with his wife, Queen Adelaide, on 8 September 1831. Interestingly, one of the reports of this coronation stressed the fact that this day was the seventieth wedding anniversary of William IV's father; even though not explicitly mentioned, this might well be a subtle allusion to the old analogy of the coronation to a wedding.[1] However, there was a general lack of interest in the coronation, even from the king himself, as was pointed out by contemporaries:[2]

[...] the ceremonial of a public inauguration, according to ancient usage, was neither intended by his Majesty, nor by his ministers, till the subject, as a constitutional one, was brought before the House of Lords by the Duke of Wellington. On the 4th of July, his grace asked the Earl Grey, whether he had received any instructions on the subject of the coronation? The answer being in the negative [...]

It has been argued that the king was 'resolved' to forego a coronation and merely to take the oath before the two Houses of Parliament; according to Golby and Purdue it was the ministers who acknowledged the propagandistic importance of a state occasion such as a

---

[1] See *GM* 101 (1831), part 2, 221; and cf. Ch. 6, fn. 31.

[2] John Watkins, *The Life and Times of "England's Patriot King," William the Fourth. With a brief memoir of Her Majesty, Queen Adelaide, and her Family* (London: Fisher, Son, and Jackson, 1831), 700. See also Strong, 374.

coronation.[3] While the coronation could not be dispensed with altogether, much less money was to be spent on it than had been on the previous coronation and in the end only an eighth of the 1821 sum was spent.[4] Indeed, because of this curtailment the 1831 coronation was mockingly nicknamed from early on. According to the *Gentleman's Magazine*, it was a 'very high legal functionary, if report may be trusted' who 'designated the proceeding as a "half-crownation"' and Jenkyns has explained that the term was 'a play on the half-crown coin'.[5] Overall, approximately half of the 'usual' ceremonies of the day were cut: the ceremonies in Westminster Hall before and after the service were abolished altogether. Thus there was no procession either to the Abbey or back to the Hall, and no banquet was held. It was in respect to these omissions that the 1831 coronation was afterwards described as a *'reformed* model'.[6]

The omission of the processions, however, did not diminish the public character of the overall ceremony. On the contrary, it extended it: the foot processions from Westminster Hall to the Abbey and back were replaced by carriage processions from and to St James's Palace, which resulted in far more people having the opportunity to watch them.[7] While the ceremonies in Westminster Hall and the processions to and from the Abbey may have been abolished in order to decrease the elaborateness of the event, the introduction of the carriage processions answered to a criticism of the spectacle that had been around for at least seventy years. Before the coronation of George III and Queen Charlotte in 1761, one publication specifically criticized the fact that the shortness and narrowness of the processions from the Hall to the Abbey and back gave but a relatively small number of people the opportunity to see their king.[8] The carriage processions introduced in 1831, and widely expanded in the twentieth century, were, intendedly or not, certainly a most appropriate answer to this complaint. Referring to the cavalcade through the City of London – the procession from the Tower to Westminster on the evening before the coronation – it was noted at the time that the 1831 carriage processions meant a 'partial revival of one

---

[3] Golby and Purdue, 39: 'His ministers were wise enough to realize that crowds love bread and circuses and that society and the London crowd must not be deprived of such an occasion.' See also Crowest, 35.

[4] Golby and Purdue give the figures as £30,000 for 1831 and £240,000 for 1821.

[5] *GM*, new series 8 (1838), 198; Jenkyns, 165.

[6] *GM*, new series 10, (1838), 188 (emphasis original).   [7] See Strong, 400f.

[8] [John Gwynn], *Thoughts on the Coronation of his present Majesty King George the Third, or Reasons offered against confining the Procession to the usual Track, pointing out others more commodius and proper* (London: Printed by the proprietor, 1761).

of the ancient ceremonies'.[9] Furthermore, the necessity of such processions to please the public was openly acknowledged:[10]

In order that the public may not be disappointed, from the ceremony in the Hall being dispensed with, it is in contemplation that all the officers and official persons shall accompany the King and Queen in procession to Westminster Abbey.

It was pointed out that both the king and queen were wearing their crowns during the carriage return procession from the Abbey, and in one report this was interpreted as 'proof that they had studied the gratification of the people beyond the programme of the day'.[11] Interestingly, the same report mentions that the rest of the regalia was 'returned to the robing-rooms, adjoining the new Portico'. This first of all points to the temporary annexe that has been built for coronations at the West door of the Abbey from this coronation onwards. The omission of the Westminster Hall proceedings had made it necessary to have such a location to arrange the ceremonial entries into the Abbey and 'The Office of Works hit upon the idea of creating a temporary annexe of wood and canvas outside the west door of the Abbey.'[12] Moreover, this leaving of the rest of the regalia behind also marks a clear contrast to the carriage processions at all the following coronations: Queen Victoria reports in her diary that she carried the orb and sceptre during the return procession from the Abbey, and this was what all the monarchs did in the twentieth century.[13] Not much is known about the music that was played during these processions in 1831, but one report mentions that 'the bands, which were stationed at different points, played, "God save the King."' when the procession passed.[14]

The Service

Despite the overall severe cuts at this coronation, the service proper in the Abbey saw no significant changes. As in 1821 the order of service was clearly modelled on that of 1761: a copy of that order of service containing

---

[9] *GM* 101 (1831), part 2, 219.   [10] *GM* 101 (1831), part 2, 169.

[11] For this and the following see *MLAI* 18 (1831), 188f.

[12] Bury, 528; details of the design, with the reference to the original documents, in fn. 770. For the following coronations see William John Loftie, *The Coronation Book of Edward VII* (London: Cassell [1902]), 128; Tanner, 13; and Brian Barker, *When the Queen was Crowned* (London: Routledge & Kegan Paul, 1976), 89.

[13] Victoria, Queen, *The Girlhood of Queen Victoria. A Selection from her Majesty's Diaries between the years 1832 and 1840*, ed. Viscount Esher, 2 vols. (London: John Murray, 1912), vol. I, 360.

[14] Watkins, 701f.

corrections by William Howley, the Archbishop of Canterbury who officiated at the 1831 service, survives in the Library of Lambeth Palace.[15] The
final order of service was again printed.[16] As for the previous coronation, a
detailed account was published in the *Gentleman's Magazine*, and some
additional details are found in John Watkins's contemporary biography of
the king.[17]

It is not clear who was responsible for organizing the musical programme
of the service. According to the *Gentleman's Magazine* the music was
conducted by 'Sir George Smart, Knt. Organist of his Majesty's Chapels
Royal'.[18] Intriguingly, Thomas Attwood and William Knyvett, the senior
Composers of the Chapel who had been responsible for the music at the
previous coronation, were both not mentioned in the report. There seems to
be no reason why they should not have been in charge this time, too. In fact,
Attwood contributed an elaborate new anthem and Knyvett probably
repeated an earlier composition.

The first anthem, 'I was glad', was sung in Attwood's setting from the
previous coronation, with the text in the 1761 printed order altered accordingly. Watkins confirms that the anthem was performed during the king's
procession 'up the nave into the choir'.[19] In the draft order of service the
traditional instruction that the choir should wait in the nave and then go
before the king in the procession while singing was crossed out.[20] This
officially acknowledged the changed performance conditions of the choir
being placed in the musicians' gallery during the entrance-anthem. No
report mentions the point at which the *Vivat*s were sung – whether they
came before the anthem, as at the previous coronation, or after it; or even
during it, as possibly intended by Attwood.[21] In fact, one report states that
they were sung only after the Recognition; however, as this report does not
mention the entrance-anthem at all there may well be some confusion in
this statement.[22]

In contrast to the previous coronation, it is clear that this time the
Recognition was followed by a fanfare only and that the anthem was
omitted.[23] Such an omission is remarkable: simply to cut one of the main
anthems clearly affected the structure of the whole service and this rite,

[15] *Llp Cod. Misc. 1083B.*

[16] *The Form and Order of the Service* [. . .] *Coronation of their Majesties King William IV and Queen Adelaide* [. . .] (London: George Eyre and Andrew Strahan, 1831); hereafter OS (1831).

[17] GM 101 (1831), part 2, 219–230. For Watkins, see fn. 2.

[18] GM 101 (1831), part 2, 169 and 223. Smart had held this position since 1822.

[19] Watkins, 703.   [20] *Llp Cod. Misc. 1083B*, p. 2.   [21] See Ch. 6.   [22] *MLAI* 18 (1831), 182.

[23] OS (1831), 4, and Watkins, 705.

originally one of the main parts of the service, was degraded to a mere show and prelude to the following ceremonies of the service.

According to the printed order of service, the Litany was read, not sung, by the bishops and the choir.[24] As at the previous coronation, the ensuing beginning of the Communion Service was marked by 'a Sanctus', as Archbishop Howley first noted in his draft order of service.[25] It has been assumed that this Sanctus, as in 1821, was 'sung to an arrangement from Jomelli'.[26] The music at this part of the ceremony would thus have been the same as at the 1821 coronation. As at that event, the archbishop scheduled the Nicene Creed to be merely read.[27]

The next music was presumably also performed as at the previous coronation: the *Veni Creator* sung to the Grand Chant, possibly by Humfrey, and 'Zadok the Priest' in an arrangement of Handel's setting.[28] As in 1821, the anthem 'Behold, O God' after the Anointing was omitted.[29] For the anthem after the Crowning, Archbishop Howley followed his predecessor and stipulated 'The King shall rejoice'.[30] No details on the music survive, but it is plausible that Knyvett reused his setting from 1821. Similarly, while no details of the Te Deum are known it is very likely that Boyce's setting in A was repeated, since it was also sung at the next coronation.

The 'Final Anthem' ceased to be a separate section in the order of service and became part of the Homage.[31] This may have been a reaction to the possible changes at the last coronation: it was now made clear that the anthem had to be part of the Homage, and not performed separately as a 'Final Anthem'. For 1831 the anthem was originally scheduled to be the same as at the previous coronation: the archbishop's preparatory order of the service stipulates Kent's 'Blessed be thou Lord God of Israel'.[32] However, the final printed order of service gives 'O Lord, grant the King a long life' as the anthem. This is one of the most traditional texts for a coronation anthem: it had previously been sung during the procession from Westminster Hall to the Abbey, prior to the service. Since this procession was abolished in 1831, the text would have disappeared with it and this may have been the reason for using it for the anthem during the Homage.

---

[24] *OS* (1831), 7–17.   [25] *Llp Cod. Misc. 1083B*, p. 20.

[26] Anselm Hughes, 95; See also 'Music at the Last Coronation', *MT* 43 (1902), 18–21, here 20.

[27] *Llp Cod. Misc. 1083B*, p. 26.

[28] Schultz, 50, suggests that the *Veni Creator* was sung in Attwood's popular setting, but there is no evidence for this.

[29] *Llp Cod. Misc. 1083B*, p. 39.   [30] *Llp Cod. Misc. 1083B*, p. 50.

[31] Legg, *Three Coronation Orders*, 155.   [32] *Llp Cod. Misc. 1083B*, p. 62.

Moreover, since the text refers explicitly to the person of the king, this anthem seems generally more appropriate for this ceremony than Kent's anthem.

'O Lord, grant the King a long life' was set in a grand manner for choir and full orchestra by Attwood; and, as with his setting of 'I was glad' from the previous coronation, the full score was afterwards published.[33] In his anthem Attwood again makes use of the tune of a popular patriotic song. 'O Lord, grant the King a long life' begins with an instrumental 'prelude', allegro maestoso, which is 'to be repeated Piano, except the last Eight Bars which are to be Forte, with the annexed Air for the Horn & Trumpet'. This 'air' is taken from the patriotic song 'Rule Britannia', originally the final chorus to Thomas Arne's masque *Alfred*: one verse and the beginning of the refrain of Arne's song are quoted.[34] However, 'Rule Britannia' is not only quoted in the introduction, but also serves to develop the musical material of the rest of the anthem (see Example 7.1). For instance, in the second half of the anthem, the 'Amen' is set as an elaborate fugue, and Attwood uses the tune of the verse prominently on the word 'Amen' (b. 26). As in Attwood's 'I was glad', the opening words ('O Lord, grant the King a long life') are restated after the 'Amen' to open the finale. They first appear *piano* to the main theme of the opening chorus (b. 40), but shortly afterwards they are rendered *forte*, this time quoting the nautical tune (b. 48).

Such open musical reference to 'Rule Britannia' was obviously well calculated by Attwood; as pointed out at the time 'the allusion was, no doubt, to the profession of the King before he ascended the throne'.[35] William IV had previously had a splendid naval career, fighting with Lord Nelson against Napoleon; indeed, he later became known as the 'Sailor King'.[36] With reference to this musical link in Attwood's anthem it was judged that the 'thought was as happy as the execution is masterly'.[37] In any case, the incorporation of 'Rule Britannia' in 1831 could have been more than just a reference to the king's past; it could

[33] Thomas Attwood, *Anthem, O Lord, Grant the King a Long Life. Composed as part of the August Ceremonial of the Coronation of His Most Gracious Majesty William the Fourth* [...] (London: Novello, [1831 or 1832]). This edition received a detailed discussion in the 'Review of New Music', in *Harmonicon* (1832), part 1, 59–60.

[34] For Arne's original see *Alfred*, ed. by Alexander Scott, MB 47 (1981), p. 145.

[35] 'Review of New Music', *Harmonicon* (1832), part 1, 59.

[36] See also 'Dotted Crotchet' [F.G. Edwards], 293: 'Attwood played a pretty compliment to the Sailor King (William IV) by introducing 'Rule Britannia,' into the instrumental introduction of the anthem.'

[37] 'Review of New Music', *Harmonicon* (1832), part 1, 59.

Example 7.1   Th. A. Arne, theme of 'Rule Britannia' from *Alfred* (as in *MB* 47, p. 145), and Th. Attwood, 'O Lord, grant the King a long life' ([1831/2] edition): A. Main theme of opening chorus; B. Theme in bb. 26–29 of the 'Amen'; C. Theme in bb. 48–52 of the finale.

also be seen as an indication of the growing awareness of national identity. Indeed, this awareness is well illustrated in the discussion of Attwood's preface in *Harmonicon*:[38]

Having mentioned the dedication [to the king], we feel it almost a duty to devote a few lines to a part of it, wherein Mr. Attwood, speaking with great modesty of himself, throws out a hint concerning the importance of royal countenance to native artists, which we are persuaded will not pass unheeded; for no sovereign of the present dynasty ever evinced so much national feeling, so little disposition to prefer foreigners to his own countrymen, as the patriotic sovereign who now sways the British sceptre.

Attwood's anthem for the Homage is very different from all previous such anthems. At the coronations in the seventeenth and eighteenth centuries, the Homage anthem had stressed the king's divine right as well as illustrated his heavenly protection (most strikingly with the words 'The Lord is a Sun and a Shield'). Thus, it was most likely addressed to the peers who showed their allegiance while the anthem was sung, and also to possible 'enemies' (whom God's 'right hand shall find out', according to one text). The music was appropriately grand and stately. At the previous coronation, in 1821, the anthem chosen was simply a favourite of the king's, possibly without having further significance. However, in 1831 the Homage anthem had, through its music, much gained in symbolism: with its open allusion to the

---

[38]   Ibid.

king's past, it showed not only a reference to the king in general, but to William IV in particular. At the same time, the obvious quotations of 'Rule Britannia' stressed that the anthem further alluded to the whole of the British Nation – the 'Blessed Nation', according to the lines of the second verse.[39] Thus Attwood's anthem combines the exaltation of a single person with the recognition of national identity. The Homage of the Peers became an act of truly national dimensions, with the whole nation musically paying tribute to the new king, who himself had become the personification of Britain. Even though Attwood's anthem was published soon after the coronation it is not known if it ever became as popular as his 'I was glad' from 1821.

The anthem following the Queen's Coronation underwent a drastic change; at the three previous coronations of a queen consort there had been anthems to the text 'My heart is inditing', but in 1831 this was replaced by Handel's Hallelujah Chorus. The replacement of the queen's 'own' text meant that she was no longer represented musically, and this undermined her overall status within the ceremony. What had previously been the function of the ending of the queen's anthem was now adopted by the whole anthem: it served to mark the end of the coronation part of the service. Nevertheless, as already seen, the queen consort may at this coronation have received an unexpected ceremonial elevation of her status in so far as 'immediately that the chorus was over' there was 'a loud shout of "God save the Queen"'.[40]

As in 1821, the remaining part of the Communion Service was read throughout. It cannot be determined if there was any instrumental music accompanying the processions between the thrones, altar and St Edward's Chapel. As at the previous coronation, this part of the service overall appears to have been ceremonially rather plain and austere compared to the earlier musical elaboration.

It has been suggested that Handel's Overture to the *Occasional Oratorio* was played before the Te Deum.[41] However, this would be a most unusual place; if Handel's overture was played at all, then this was more likely during the Recess, as this is how it is reported to have been performed at the subsequent coronation in 1838.[42]

---

[39] 'The nations, not so blessed as thee, must, in their turns, to tyrants fall [...]'
[40] *MLAI* 18 (1831), 188. See also above, Ch. 3, fn. 126.
[41] See Knight, 'Organs of Westminster Abbey', 127, who refers to a list compiled by Sir George Smart, which was later used by Lawrence Tanner but is now lost.
[42] For details see below.

Musicians and performance

Even though this coronation was, from a ceremonial point of view, much less lavish than the previous one, the arrangements of the musical forces appear still to have been rather impressive. Indeed, it has been pointed out that the scoring of Attwood's 'O Lord, grant the King a long life' is 'for a slightly larger orchestra' than 'at the previous coronation when he composed "I was glad"'.[43] During the preparations for the next coronation, Smart noted that the choir in 1831 had consisted of thirty-two singers from the Chapel Royal, twenty-two from Westminster Abbey, fourteen from St Paul's, eight from St George's Chapel in Windsor, and forty-two 'Extra Vocalists' about which no details are known; the same list includes a 'Band' of sixty-nine instrumentalists, which makes a total number of a hundred and eighty-seven performers.[44]

The most important change relative to the previous coronations probably concerned the musicians' position within the Abbey (see Illustration 7.1). The reports in the *Gentleman's Magazine* and by Watkins state that all the musicians were 'placed near the ordinary organ of the Abbey at the entrance of the choir'.[45]

Contrary to previous coronations, this time the Abbey organ was used and no special organ was built. The reason for this may have been the wish to save the money that would have been spent on a new instrument. In the end, this decision was probably the main reason for the change in the positioning of the musicians:[46]

As it was determined to make use of the organ of the Abbey in its usual situation, (not, as on the last occasion, to place the music gallery over the altar,) it was considered desirable to raise the organ screen, in order that the performance of the vocal and instrumental musicians might not be lost in the vast open space. On the beautiful new stone screen which has been recently erected by Mr. Blore, the Abbey architect, was raised a wooden erection of about the same height, so as to inclose the music within the choir [. . .]

The gallery above the altar was now filled with members of the House of Commons.[47] At the same time, the trumpeters for the fanfares were also

---

[43] Knight, 'Organs of Westminster Abbey', 128.

[44] *Lca MS Ceremonials 94*, p. 35f. See also Knight, 'Organs of Westminster Abbey', 127, who states that all the names 'are recorded by Smart in his account of the expenses of the coronation (WAMS 56,779*(4); ii/399).'

[45] *GM* 101 (1831), part 2, 219; Watkins, 704.   [46] *GM* 101 (1831), part 2, 220.

[47] Ibid., 221, reported that 'four hundred and ten members were present'.

7.1. 'The Coronation of their most Excellent Majesties King William the IV & Queen Adelaide, on the 8th of September 1831' print, 1831 (detail). © Dean and Chapter of Westminster.

placed in this gallery, behind the Commons.[48] This meant that the situation was exactly the reverse of that at the previous three coronations: the musicians' gallery had moved from the East end of the quire to the West end, and the trumpeters had moved from the quire screen in the West to the gallery over the altar in the East. This must have changed the sound considerably: being placed more in the centre of the Abbey, the musicians in 1831 would have been better able to fill the whole of the space with sound, not just the quire and the area around the Theatre.

It seems that a grand final rehearsal of the music had by now become customary. A surviving ticket confirms one rehearsal at ten o'clock in the morning of the day before the coronation.[49] Thus, despite cuts in the ceremonies and a desire to save resources, much care was taken for a well-prepared performance of the music at the service. Indeed, there are no reports of any notable mishaps during the ceremony, as at previous such events.

Although William IV's coronation was sarcastically described as the 'Penny Coronation',[50] such a dismissal would not seem to be valid for the music of the service. On the contrary, the music, and especially its grand performance, very well illustrate the trend towards a more elaborate royal ceremonial.

Queen Victoria, 1838

William IV died on 20 June 1837 and was succeeded by his niece Victoria, who was crowned on 28 June 1838 by Archbishop Howley. His order of service for the coronation essentially followed the one he had prepared in 1831.[51] Much material concerning the musical arrangements of the service survives, and the music was also discussed extensively in newspapers and journals.[52] Following the precedent set at the previous coronation, the service followed again the 'reformed model': there were again no processions from or to Westminster Hall and no banquet afterwards.[53] However,

---

[48] Ibid., engraving between 228 and 229: looking east after the Inthronization of both king and queen. This mentions explicitly 'The eastern extremity of the Church, where the Trumpets were placed'.

[49] *Lwa WAM 60017 (14)*. Sir George Smart refers to the tickets for the rehearsal in some letters. See *Lwa Library, 4.c.5*.

[50] See Strong, 374.

[51] *The Form and Order of the Service* [. . .] *Coronation of Her Majesty Queen Victoria* [. . .] (London: George Eyre and Andrew Spottiswoode, 1838).

[52] Interestingly, Felix Mendelssohn was present at the service, but no report by him is known. See Bevan, 157.

[53] For more details about the changes see John Plunkett, *Queen Victoria. The First Media Monarch* (Oxford University Press, 2003), 23.

even though these ancient ceremonies were not revived, overall there was a desire for a greater spectacle than in 1831 and it was pointed out that 'general wishes [were] expressed for a Coronation more stately than the last'.[54]

The music

This is the earliest coronation for which the full musical programme can be reconstructed with certainty. Besides much supporting evidence, the programme of the music was printed.[55] As in 1761, there was only one musician responsible for the music: Sir George Smart. Having been Organist of the Chapel Royal since 1822, Smart succeeded Attwood as Composer in March 1838.[56] Even though Smart would therefore have been the obvious choice for the coronation, his appointment was somewhat marred. One newspaper reported sarcastically that the queen had first appointed Henry Bishop, but that 'the intrigues of another Bishop (Charles of London) and Sir George Smart, procured the latter the situation *despite her Majesty's wish*'.[57] No details are known about this appointment of Bishop by the queen; after all he had no connection with the Chapel Royal or the Abbey and was a well-known theatre and opera composer. In addition to these speculations about the appointment, a dispute arose over the question of who should play the organ at the coronation. Smart recorded many details about this: James Turle, the organist of the Abbey at the time, had 'sent in a claim to the Council to be appointed as organist, because Purcell at a former coronation presided at the organ'.[58] In a letter to the Earl Marshal, Turle supported his claim with the fact that no special, new organ was built for the coronation, but that the Abbey organ was to be used, of which he was the organist.[59] Turle's claim was denied and Smart noted that 'Mr. Turle forgot to mention that Purcell was then also the organist at the Chapel Royal and that in years past the organist of that chapel was the one appointed at the coronations.' In fact, until the death of William Croft in 1727 the organist of the Chapel Royal was often also organist of the Abbey. A similar claim to

---

[54] *GM*, new series 10, (1838), 188.

[55] *The Order of the Music, &c. to be Performed at the Coronation* (London: Printed by Joseph Mallet, [1838]).

[56] The possibility that Attwood may have begun an anthem for this coronation has been discussed in Ch. 6.

[57] *The Spectator*, quoted in *MW* 121 (5 July 1838), 158, (emphasis original).

[58] For this and the following see Sir George Smart, *Leaves from the Journals of Sir George Smart*, ed. by H. Bertram Cox and C. L. E. Cox (London: Longmans, Green, 1907), 291f.

[59] *Lca MS Ceremonials 94*, no. 29 (transcr. App. B4a).

play the organ by Smart's Chapel colleague 'Mr. Sale' was likewise denied. From Smart's point of view, Sale's claim was made only because he was resentful that Smart would receive the fee for both conducting and playing the organ. In the end, the Bishop of London stopped all such claims and informed the Privy Council that he alone was responsible for all the musical arrangements in his capacity as Dean of the Chapel Royal: Smart was appointed to play the organ and to conduct the music.[60] Such dual performance of playing the organ and conducting at the same time reflected the established standard way of directing oratorios and large choral concerts.[61] However, Smart may not have played during the whole service: one report, published shortly before the next coronation, states that William Knyvett played the organ part in the anthem that he had composed for the ceremony.[62]

In any case, the fact that Smart played the organ at all was hugely criticised in one journal. The *Musical World* dedicated a full article to the matter and described Smart's appointment as organist as

a projected arrangement which the sober and right-thinking part of the musical profession regard with feelings of grief and indignation, involving, as it does, an act of injustice towards a most worthy and talented member of the profession [Turle], and exhibiting a shameless disregard of the proprieties of a musical solemnity.[63]

A week later, however, the same journal hailed Smart in a report about the rehearsals of the coronation music in the Abbey:[64]

Great praise is due to the director, Sir George Smart, for the symmetrical disposition of the orchestra, for the order and regularity with which the compositions were executed [. . .] As the orchestra includes the *élite* of the metropolis, it is unnecessary to say more than that there is every probability of the whole ceremony going off with great *éclat*.

Nevertheless, after the event, the initial critique was harshly reinforced in the review of the music of the service:[65]

There was, strictly speaking no conductor; but Sir George sat at the organ. We regret he had not retained that office, in which he certainly has a reputation, and

---

[60] 'Music at the Last Coronation', 18–21, 18. Smart was paid £300 as organist; a further £80, which he claimed 'in compensation for the time spent fulfilling his role as the official Director of Music, which he contended was a separate appointment' was denied. See *Lna PC 22/2*, quoted in Wright, 121.

[61] See, for instance, Samuel Wesley's comments on directing oratorios made in an 1827 lecture, quoted in McVeigh, 217. Cf. also Burrows, 'Handel's Oratorio Performances', in Donald Burrows (ed.), *The Cambridge Companion to Handel* (Cambridge University Press, 1997), 262–81, here 266f. Burrows refers to an oratorio performance in Covent Garden in the 1790s.

[62] 'Music at the Last Coronation', 20.   [63] *MW* 119 (21 June 1838), 125–7, here 126.

[64] *MW* 120 (27 June 1838), 155.   [65] *MW* 121 (5 July 1838), 162–4, here 164.

deservedly well so; but in undertaking to play the organ, he has greatly lowered his reputation, not simply as an organist, but as a professor. Sir George, we believe, lays no claim to the character of being much of an organ performer; and as there is a wide difference in being a mere accompanist and a professor of the instrument, we were prepared to listen to his efforts with no very high standard in view by which to judge him. But after hearing him call the band together, and accompany the simple chant of Pelham Humphrey, we shall decline to offer any opinion on his attainments in the character of either organist or musician. We have heard her Majesty is not so constant in her attendance at the Chapel, St. James'; if the singing be in any way like the playing, we think a casuist might suggest the reason.

The sharp discrepancy of the reports raises questions about their reliability on both sides.[66] Whatever questions there are concerning his appointment and proficiency as a performer, it is Smart's thorough documentation that provides very valuable information on the music at the coronation. He entered many detailed annotations in his copy of the order of service thus giving a meticulous record of the whole ceremony.[67]

The entrance-anthem was once again Attwood's grand setting of 'I was glad'. Smart noted:[68]

By the Consent of the Archbishop of Canterbury the Anthem was not to commence until Her Majesty entered the Choir, therefore I commenced when the Queen ascended the steps into the Choir.

This statement implies that the anthem accompanied not the whole of the queen's procession, but only the end.[69] This schedule ties with the performance that had been planned for the 1821 coronation, but in 1838 the change was still significant enough to require the 'Consent of the Archbishop'.[70] Smart does not report what music accompanied the beginning of the procession, when the queen walked up the nave. In fact, his annotation at the end of the order of service seems to imply that there was none.[71] In contrast to that, one report of the coronation published, with some claim to authenticity, forty-five years later states that the choir and orchestra

---

[66] For an early discussion of this issue see also 'From My Study. Music at the Queen's Coronation', signed 'X.', *MT* 38 (1897), 302–5, here 302f.

[67] *Lwa Library, 4.c.9*. Smart's annotations are transcribed in App. B4b.

[68] *Lwa Library, 4.c.9*, p. 1.

[69] This is also supported by other reports. See, for instance, *The Sun*, London, 28 June 1838: 'On her Majesty's entering the Choir, the cheering was again renewed, and was indeed only put a stop to by the opening of the Coronation Anthem.'

[70] For the 1821 schedule see Ch. 6, fn. 123.

[71] *Lwa Library, 4.c.9*, p. 67: '3 HH 48 M. From Her Majesty's entering and leaving the Choir, that is from the 1st to the last Note of the Music.'

performed the National Anthem when the queen entered the Abbey. The same report also mentions the *Vivats* of the 'Westminster boys' performed 'at the close of the anthem'.[72] It is intriguing that Smart does not mention the *Vivats* at all, since he was otherwise so concerned with all the details; he simply may not have regarded them as part of 'his' music for the service. The *Gentleman's Magazine* reported that they were sung 'as the procession passed up the choir to the theatre'.[73] That would in fact have been before the queen 'ascended the steps into the Choir', with which Smart seems to refer to the steps leading up to the Theatre under the crossing; the *Vivats* would thus have been sung before Smart 'commenced' the anthem. According to another eyewitness report they came rather unexpectedly once the queen was 'seated on the platform' thus after the anthem or at its close; the same report describes them as 'highly disgusting', explaining that they 'marred the proceedings'.[74] This indicates that there was not yet a sense of esteem for this supposedly ancient tradition, which was to become important in the twentieth-century coronations. The same report states also that the National Anthem was played only after these *Vivats*, and this seems overall the most likely position for it.

Following the shortening of the previous coronation, there was no anthem after the Recognition but again merely fanfares. Smart reports:[75]

The Trumpets sounded by Signal given from W. Gwilt to me and from me to them immediately after the Archbishop said the 1ˢᵗ time "Sirs, I here present &c." probably they should not have sounded until after the 4ᵗʰ presentation from the Archbishop.

From Smart's wording it cannot be deduced if, after the 'mishap' of playing too early, the trumpets played after each of the four acclamations. Ironically, this was going to become the custom in the twentieth century. Smart had noted that 'God save the Queen' should be played by the 'trumpets' at the end of the Recognition, after the last acclamation.[76] The printed order of the music states similarly:[77]

At the Recognition, after the general Acclamation "God save Queen Victoria", then the Trumpets sound – ("God save the Queen" to be played).

[72] *A Diary of Royal Movements and of Personal Events and Incidents in the Life and Reign of Her Most Gracious Majesty Queen Victoria, Compiled from Official Documents and Public Records*, vol. I (London: Elliot Stock, 1883), 75–105, here 91.

[73] *GM*, new series 10 (July–December 1838), 195.

[74] Quoted in 'The Musical Service of the Coronation (From the Court Journal)', *MLAI* 32 (1838), 28–9, here 29.

[75] *Lwa Library*, 4.c.9, p. 4.   [76] Note written by Smart on a loose leaf in *Lwa Library*, 4.c.9.

[77] *Order of the Music* [1838].

Therefore it is possible that Smart in his report above refers to the playing of the National Anthem, and not to a mere trumpet fanfare. According to Frederick Crowest 'God save the Queen' was 'rendered by band and people'.[78] In contrast to that, from a report of Harriet Martineau, who was in the Abbey, it seems as though the National Anthem was performed 'merely on the organ', but not sung.[79] However, given the strong evidence by Smart it may be assumed that the National Anthem was played by the 'trumpets', implying a full brass band. The *Musical World* reported that the 'national air' was played in 'the vilest arrangement [. . .] that we think we ever heard, the work of Mr. Kramer'.[80] This refers probably to the aforementioned Christian Kramer, who had been involved in the music at the 1821 coronation.[81] Like most of the actual performing material from coronations, this arrangement seems to be lost and the journal's critique can therefore not be assessed.

According to Smart the Responses to the Litany were only read by the choir, as scheduled in the printed order of the music.[82] As in 1685, a plan of the Abbey at the coronation shows a 'Litany Desk' between the two most eastern pillars of the crossing, and such a desk may have been used at all the other coronations in between as well.[83] After the Litany came the Sanctus and the Responses to the Commandments, all of which were sung in settings by Smart himself.[84] Walter Coward's handwritten catalogue of music of the Chapel Royal from 1917 lists a Communion Service in F and a full service in G under Smart's name.[85] These pieces appear to be lost. However, from a contemporary report it can be deduced that Smart's Sanctus was accompanied by the orchestra. The writer in the *Musical World* provokingly asked:[86]

Does Sir George imagine [that] the melo-dramatic style of the Coburg Theatre, the trombones, followed by clarionets, flutes, and a few bars on the organ (not in organ disposition or phraseology) was a proper introduction to a sanctus, performed in an English cathedral, at the most imposing and august ceremonial his assembled countrymen could expect to witness?

---

[78] Crowest, 35.

[79] See Percy A. Scholes, *God Save the Queen! The History and Romance of the World's First National Anthem* (Oxford University Press, 1954), 209.

[80] *MW* 121 (5 July 1838), 163.   [81] See above, p. 121f.   [82] *Lwa Library*, 4.c.9, p. 7.

[83] *Lca MS Ceremonials 94*, item no. 72.

[84] *MW* 121 (5 July 1838), 163. See also *Lwa Library*, 4.c.9, p. 18.

[85] The catalogue is still kept in the practice room of HM Chapel Royal in St James's Palace, London.

[86] *MW* 121 (5 July 1838), 160.

Smart noted that even the simple response 'Glory be to Thee, O Lord' after the naming of the Gospel was sung 'By the full Band and Chorus'.[87] At the coronation of George III and Queen Charlotte in 1761, this response had been accompanied by the organ alone, and overall it appears that Smart had a preference for a grand style with full orchestral accompaniment. Indeed, in this he may have followed a fashion of the time for embellishing short liturgical pieces with heavy orchestration. At a morning service that was part of the 1834 Hereford Musical Festival, for instance, the Gloria Patri after each of the appointed psalms was 'accompanied by the whole band'.[88]

Despite this tendency for musical elaboration, the Nicene Creed was probably simply read, as in the two previous coronations. The *Veni Creator* was again chanted, the archbishop reading the first line and the choir continuing.[89] Smart noted: 'Grand Chant in D / Organ and Choir only'.[90] The music-folders of the Chapel Royal that were used at the coronation have survived, and in some of the treble and bass folders the respective part is entered on a piece of manuscript paper fixed inside the cover (for a transcription see Example 7.2).[91] Some of these extra sheets bear the name 'Humphrys', identifying it as Pelham Humfrey's Grand Chant, which had presumably been used at the 1821 and 1831 coronations.

The fact that only trebles and basses had the parts entered into their folders implies either that only these two parts, and not the full harmonies, were sung by the choir, or that the alto and tenor parts were improvised.[92] Smart notes that he played through the chant on the organ before the choir sang it.[93] Thus there would have been a full organ verse between the archbishop's beginning the first line and the choir's continuation, creating a considerable gap in the flow of the text.

Handel's 'Zadok the Priest' was probably again performed in an arrangement for the large forces available, possibly by Kramer.[94] Queen Victoria herself reported in her diary that 'at the beginning of the Anthem where I've made a mark' she went to St Edward's Chair for the changing of her robes in preparation for the Anointing.[95] This indicates that the anthem covered the

---

[87] *Lwa Library, 4.c.9*, p. 18.   [88] *MLMS 7* (October 1834), 78.   [89] William Jones, 258.

[90] *Lwa Library, 4.c.9*, p. 29.

[91] I am grateful to Andrew Gant, the Organist, Choirmaster and Composer at Her Majesty's Chapel Royal, who discovered the thirty-two folders in a cupboard in the Chapel's practice room.

[92] Cf. Ruth Wilson, 90f.   [93] *Lwa Library, 4.c.9*, p. 29.

[94] *MW 121* (5 July 1838), 163. This mentions simply 'the anthem of Handel' without giving the anthem title. For a full quotation see below, fn. 143.

[95] Queen Victoria, vol. I, 357. It appears that the Queen had an order of the service which she annotated; this seems to be lost.

Example 7.2 Transcription of Pelham Humfrey's 'Grand Chant', treble and bass part, reproduced by gracious permission of Her Majesty The Queen from Chapel Royal music folders used at Queen Victoria's coronation. Archive of Her Majesty's Chapel Royal. The chant had been printed, without composer's name, in Boyce's *Cathedral Music*, vol. I, 289. Alto and tenor parts are here added following Boyce's edition. (In that edition the 'e' in the bass part, bar 4, beat 2 is dotted.)

monarch's short walk to St Edward's Chair and the clothing in the robes for the Anointing, thus matching the report from the 1821 coronation.[96]

Smart notes that the queen was crowned at '25 M to 2_o'Clock'.[97] The music of the customary fanfare, or 'Flourish' that may have been played at this and at other parts in the ceremony was included in an article published on the occasion of the next coronation.[98] One report explained that such fanfares 'in military language are termed "flourishes", but in musical, would be considered a strange medley of odd combinations'.[99]

After the acclamations and fanfare came 'The Queen shall rejoice', an adaptation of Handel's setting from 1727. The change of text in this anthem followed the precedent of the coronation of Queen Anne in 1702. It may be assumed that, similar to the other pieces, the instrumentation of Handel's setting was arranged for the occasion. The inclusion of this anthem is noteworthy. In the same way as Handel's 'Zadok the Priest', this anthem may at the time have been a 'kind of musical ritual to the house of Hanover'.[100] The second of the 'Concerts of Ancient Music' in 1836, was attended by Queen Adelaide and other members of the royal family. Handel's 'The King shall rejoice' was performed at the beginning of the

[96] See Ch. 6, fn. 160.   [97] *Lwa Library*, 4.c.9, 39f.   [98] 'Music at the Last Coronation', 20.
[99] 'The Musical Service of the Coronation', 30.   [100] See Ch. 1, fn. 105.

concert while the royal party entered, and a commentator observed that 'the Queen and all the company' kept standing during the opening chorus.[101]

As in the previous coronations, the Te Deum in 1838 was sung in Boyce's setting in A from 1761.[102] As in 1821, it was probably sung in an arrangement, incorporating at least some instruments of the orchestra: Smart specifically noted that one trumpet and one trombone player returned for the Te Deum from the gallery where they had played in the fanfare after the Crowning.[103]

The anthem during the Homage was the most elaborate new composition for the coronation: 'This is the Day' by William Knyvett.[104] Knyvett was composer of the Chapel, although the *Gentleman's Magazine* curiously referred to him as 'the Organist to the Abbey' – a position he never held.[105] Thanks to Smart's meticulous notes, there is precise information as to when the anthem was performed. Smart calculated that the Homage would take about 40 minutes and that the anthem was to begin '<u>Before it is over</u>'.[106] Similarly, in his final annotation he emphasized:[107]

N.B. This Anthem was performed during the Performance of the Homage, just before the Homage was concluded.

Another report confirms this by stating that the anthem was performed 'at the conclusion of the homage'.[108] Knyvett's anthem is about twenty minutes in length.[109] If Smart's aforementioned estimate was right and the Homage took about 40 mins, that would mean that only the second half of the ceremony was covered by the anthem. This might indicate that the peers' second approaching the throne could have been restored, allowing for a better understanding of the senior peers' vows before the music started.

The choice of text for the anthem is noteworthy: although the opening verse 'This is the day', Ps. 118:24, had not been used as the text of any previous coronation anthem, it had been the text for the sermon at the coronation of George I in 1714.[110] Furthermore, this had been the text of two other significant anthems for royal occasions: Croft's anthem for the state thanksgiving service in St Paul's Cathedral to celebrate the Peace of

[101] 'Concerts of Ancient Music', *MLMS* 25 (April 1836), 66–7, here 66.

[102] *MW* 120 (27 June 1838), 155.   [103] *Lwa Library, 4.c.9*, pp. 30 and 44. For details see below.

[104] Autograph full score in *Cambridge, University Library (Cu) Add. MS 9491*, transcribed in Range, thesis, Part 2.

[105] *GM*, new series 10 (July–December 1838), 198.

[106] Loose leaf in *Lwa Library, 4.c.9* (emphasis original).   [107] *Lwa Library, 4.c.9*, p. 49.

[108] *Diary of Royal Movements*, 98.

[109] The first movement *c.* 7 mins, the second *c.* 6'30", and the third *c.* 4'30".

[110] William Jones, 245.

Utrecht in 1713, and Handel's wedding anthem for Princess Anne and William, Prince of Orange in 1734 (HWV 262).

Knyvett's 'This is the Day' also incorporates the text 'O Lord, grant the Queen a long life', and the use of this text in the anthem for the Homage creates a neat parallel with Attwood's Homage anthem from the previous coronation. Knyvett wrote on the same grand scale as Attwood, making use of the full forces available. The orchestration is very well balanced and all instruments are used to good effect. Indeed, one report insinuated that

judging from the sound of the orchestra, and in the absence of positive information on the point, we conjecture that some one [*sic*] of more experience in such matters than Mr. Knyvett, has had the arrangement of the instrumental part of the work.[111]

The anthem has three distinct movements. The outer movements draw on the full forces, with a predominantly jubilant tone. In the middle movement, however, to the text 'O Lord, grant the Queen a long life', Knyvett employs a reduced scoring, omitting the trumpets and timpani. He divides the movement into three parts: an orchestral introduction, a quartet, and a chorus, all based on the same musical material of the catchy opening motive. The opinions on Knyvett's anthem at the time were divided. A short overview was included in the report about the coronation music in the *Musical World*.[112] It is striking that the other comments that are quoted in that report are rather positive; for instance the *Court Journal* described the anthem as 'an excellent composition'. The commentary of the *Musical World* itself, however, is full of criticism and complaints, pointing out that Knyvett was a writer of glees and an 'amateur unaccustomed to *think through a long composition*'.[113] With such discrepancy in judgment the *Musical World* review seems to have been stimulated more by some personal animosity than by objectivity.

For the remaining music of the Communion Service, the *Musical World* reported that 'Dr. Boyce's service had also been given to Mr. Kramer' to be arranged.[114] As seen above, the Sanctus and Responses had been sung in settings by Smart, and Perkins observed that 'the Credo and Gloria were merely said instead of being sung'.[115] Therefore it is not clear to what pieces 'Dr. Boyce's service' refers; it could be that this refers to his setting of the Te Deum and maybe also to his communion anthem 'Let my prayer come up'. After the taking of communion, once the queen had gone back to the

---

[111] *The Atlas* (1838), quoted in 'Music at the Last Coronation', 20. The same is found in 'Coronation Music of the Past', 27.

[112] *MW* 121 (5 July 1838), 157–61.   [113] Ibid., 159 (emphasis original).

[114] *MW* 121 (5 July 1838), 163.   [115] Perkins, 23f.

throne, Handel's Hallelujah Chorus was sung.[116] The Queen, in her diary, reports that 'at the commencement of the Anthem [Hallelujah Chorus]' she descended from her throne and went into St Edward's Chapel to prepare for the Recess.[117] One commentator at the time pointed out that the Hallelujah Chorus was 'given in a way peculiar to England, and to the astonishment of the many foreigners present'.[118] With its 'crisp, brilliant, and spirit-stirring grandeur with which our professors are accustomed to give it' it made a most appropriate finale for the coronation service. After having been performed in 1821 and in 1831, the Hallelujah Chorus was now sung at the third coronation in succession. Interestingly, none of the reports mentions the people standing during this chorus, a custom that had probably existed already in Handel's own lifetime and was prominently displayed at the 1784 Handel Commemoration.[119] However, this may not have seemed noteworthy, as the entire congregation should probably have been standing anyway at the respective parts of the service at which the Chorus was performed at these coronations: on the king's entrance into the Abbey (1821), the inthronization of the queen consort (1831), and during the queen's procession into St Edward's Chapel (1838).

From a ceremonial point of view it is curious that Queen Victoria in her diary reports that, after changing into the royal robe for the Recess, she again ascended to the throne, returned again into St Edward's Chapel, and only then left the Abbey in procession.[120] Such an additional inthronization is not part of the scheduled ceremonial and may have been due to some confusion. There is no report of any music accompanying these proceedings, but as always the organist could have improvised to cover any embarrassing silence.

For the procession out of the Abbey, the printed order of the music simply lists 'After the Blessing an Instrumental Piece' by 'Handel', probably referring to the overture from his *Occasional Oratorio*.[121] It may not have been a coincidence if it was music from this patriotic, staunchly pro-Hanoverian oratorio that was chosen for the coronation of a queen who nominally was the last of the House of Hanover. In any case, this is in fact the first instrumental piece at any coronation service for which details are known.

---

[116] *GM*, new series 10 (July–December 1838), 199.   [117] Queen Victoria, vol. I, 359.

[118] This and the following 'The Musical Service of the Coronation', 30.

[119] Donald Burrows, *Handel: Messiah* (Cambridge University Press, 1991), 28f. and 37. See also Tim C. W. Blanning, *The Triumph of Music. Composers, Musicians and their Audiences, 1700 to the Present* (London: Penguin, 2009), 91.

[120] Queen Victoria, vol. I, 359.   [121] 'Music at the Last Coronation', 20. See also below, fn. 143.

Foster states that 'O Lord, grant the Queen a long life' by John Goss was also composed for the coronation.[122] However, there is no evidence that this anthem was performed in the service, and Foster may refer merely to the fact that it was composed on the occasion of the coronation.

Performance

In 1838, the layout of the performing conditions was the same in principle as that at the previous coronation, with a huge gallery for the musicians at the west end of the Quire. However, there is conflicting evidence as to the exact number of performers. In a warrant to the 'Commissioners of the Office of Her Majesty's Woods and Works', order was given to remove the organ from the screen and to erect a gallery, 'sufficiently large and commodious for 270 persons'.[123] This number matches roughly with Smart's records. According to him, the choir consisted of the seventy-six singers from the four choirs as at the previous coronation plus eighty-one 'Extra Vocalists', and the number of instrumentalists was eighty, which makes a total of 237 musicians.[124] Smart later requested fifty more tickets, since he had not included the 'fourteen Household Trumpeters' and other musicians.[125] This brings the total up to 287 musicians. However, it appears that the performing body was further increased. Smart's total of 287 falls short of the 383 musicians that are mentioned in another list of musicians' tickets for the Abbey: seventy-seven members of the four choirs and 306 of 'Sir George Smarts Performers'.[126] Indeed, the *Musical World*, in its report of the rehearsal, listed more than 350 performers.[127] According to this there were 288 singers as well as over seventy instrumentalists: seventy-two sopranos, sixty-four altos, sixty-eight tenors and eighty-four basses and 'thirty-six violins, eighteen tenors, fagotti, six corni, three trombae, three tromboni, one serpent, one ophecleide, and one pair of drums'. This account, however, does not include instruments such as the bass strings and woodwinds. Hence, the number of instrumentalists could have been much higher than seventy and the overall number of performers might have come closer to the 383 persons for whom tickets were provided. This would then come close to the number corroborated by the *Gentleman's Magazine*, which reported that the musicians' gallery was 'to contain 400 performers, more than double the number engaged at the Coronation of William the

---

[122] Foster, 173. An annotation implies that it was printed by 'Cramer', but this edition could not be found.

[123] For this and the following, see *Lca MS Ceremonials 94*, no. 32.   [124] Ibid., no. 35.

[125] Ibid., no. 51.   [126] Ibid., no. 44.   [127] *MW* 120 (27 June 1838), 155.

Fourth'.[128] As a reason for such a drastic increase in the numbers of performers, it was observed that

the constant repetition of choral music, performed *en masse* by the many amateur societies in the metropolis, has rendered it necessary on all great occasions to make the musical arrangement on a much larger scale than in former times.[129]

Thus, since audiences had become used to regularly grand performances, for 'great occasions', such as royal and state ceremonies, the music had to be even grander still to have an impact.

However, it is also important to note that at least for the orchestra the number of performers recorded is not necessarily the same as the number of musicians who actually played during the service. The *Spectator* reported with a sarcastic undertone that

The band, nominally, consisted of four hundred performers, but not really. We know not the terms on which a number of persons, not even in the profession, were admitted into the orchestra, there to personate performers, but no inconsiderable number of such were to be seen.[130]

The *Musical World* similarly observed that the orchestra included 'a number of persons, some of whom were misplaced, and others had no business there'.[131] Thus it appears that the musicians' gallery contained also some non-musicians; indeed, when Smart had initially requested to erect a gallery for 400 people, he had explained that 'this will give much more room for Visitors'.[132] After all, the officials probably cared more for the general spectacle than for the execution of the music. The Earl Marshal is reported to have had the opinion 'that at all events, "the orchestra ought to look well" and accordingly, with the aid of his excellent regulations, it was a gorgeous spectacle'.[133] William Gardiner provides an enthusiastic description of the scene:[134]

The orchestra was magnificent; the crowd of desks were in the form of angels, on whose golden wings lay the crimson music-books: the whole surmounted by an organ of gold, aspiring to the roof. Every instrumental performer was in a full-dress

[128] *GM*, new series 10 (July–December 1838), 191. See also William Gardiner, *Music and Friends; or, Pleasant Recollections of a Dilettante*, 3 vols. (London: Longman et al., 1838–53), vol. II [1848], 871, who reported of 'a band of one hundred and fifty instrumental performers, and nearly three hundred voices'.

[129] 'The Musical Service of the Coronation', 29.

[130] Quoted in *MW* 121 (5 July 1838), 158. 'The band' may refer to the whole of the performing body.

[131] *MW* 121 (5 July 1838), 162.   [132] *Lca MS Ceremonials 94*, no. 30.

[133] *MW* 121 (5 July 1838), 162. See also Hayes, 12, who refers to non-musicians among the orchestra who played on dummy violins.

[134] Gardiner, vol. II, 869.

uniform of scarlet and gold; the men singers in surplices, and the young ladies in white stiff muslin robes.

It was demanded that the musicians' gallery should be constructed in such a way 'as not to project beyond the face of the present Organ Screen next the Choir'.[135] In the end, the gallery was built over the quire screen and two and a half bays of the quire stalls.[136] The reason for this restriction is certainly the custom that 'legally' only the quire of the Abbey turns into a Chapel Royal for the coronation, and thus only this part of the Abbey can easily be managed by the Chapel personnel; jurisdiction over those parts beyond the screen, in the nave, however, remains with the Chapter of the Abbey, causing administrative complications.[137] As seen above, Abbey organist Turle had supported his claim to play the organ at the coronation with the statement that the Abbey organ was to be used at the ceremony. In the end, however, the Abbey organ was removed to make room for the musicians' gallery on the screen and was re-erected after the coronation.[138] Following the precedent of earlier coronations, a new instrument for accompanimental use was erected. In 1902, the *Musical Times* reported that this in 1838 was 'a large pedal organ, on the German scale' with 'six stops'.[139] The adjective 'large' might refer to the pedal only, meaning a full compass, which was then still a novelty for English organs.

There was again a clear preference for a more massive style without soloistic singing. Even though the middle movement of Knyvett's 'This is the Day' begins nominally as a quartet, it was nevertheless sung by several singers per part.[140] This corresponds with the doubling of verse sections known from earlier coronations.[141] Nevertheless, there was probably a striking innovation regarding the vocal parts: this appears to be the first coronation at which female singers were included in the choir.[142] It is to be noted, however, that the women sang only the soprano line; the altos were all male.

---

[135] *Lca MS Ceremonials 94*, no. 32.

[136] See a plan of the Abbey, showing the 'organ gallery' in *Lca MS Ceremonials 94*, no. 73.

[137] See Strong, 385f., and cf. Baldwin, 259, who refers to a 1715 state thanksgiving service in St Paul's Cathedral, at which the Chapel Royal took precedence over the Dean and Chapter of the Cathedral.

[138] *Lca MS Ceremonials 94*, no. 30. For details of this organ see also 'From My Study', esp. 303.

[139] 'Music at the Last Coronation', 18. For more details about the organ see *MW* 127, 155.

[140] Gardiner, vol. II, 871: 'The parts usually sung by a single voice were performed by six of the most eminent English singers to each part. This was a delicious treat; under no circumstances could such a rich mixture of voices have been heard.' According to *MW* 127, 157, the parts were just 'doubled'.

[141] See, for instance, Ch. 5, fn. 71.

[142] *GM*, new series 10 (July–December 1838), 198. See also above, fn. 134, and Lindsay, 260: 'This female quire was an innovation, and a charming one.'

In general, all the music was arranged for the forces available. As seen above, it was again Kramer who was responsible for many of these arrangements and his appointment did not meet with unanimous approval. The *Musical World* complained sharply:[143]

We have no Chapel-Royal men it appears who can dress up the composition of their predecessor. Dr. Boyce's service had also been given to Mr. Kramer, or ought we not to write Mr. Harding the clarionet player in Mr. Kramer's band. So also had the anthem of Handel and the occasional overture, all of which had been instrumented and re-instrumented in the style of the Palace Yard.

The 'style of the Palace Yard' certainly refers to the style of a military band, and it may therefore be assumed that the scores were enriched by additional wind instruments, in particular brass. Indeed, Smart noted that after the fanfares that followed the Recognition, one trumpet and one trombone player 'came down from Gall^y: to play in the orchestra'.[144] This must refer to the trumpeters' gallery which was 'over the large upper gallery at the east end of the choir'.[145] Smart's note implies that these instruments played in Handel's 'Zadok the Priest'. However, after the anthem they went back to the 'Trumpeter's Gallery' to play in the fanfare after the Crowning, returning only for the Te Deum, as seen above.[146] Incidentally, that would mean that these two musicians did not play in Handel's 'The Queen shall rejoice'. After having played in the Te Deum they went back into the trumpeters' gallery again, presumably to play in the fanfares of the Homage.[147] In short, these two musicians had to move from one gallery to the other several times during the service.

Generally, the arranged scores of earlier music are lost for every coronation before the twentieth century. These were probably intended as mere 'one-offs' and therefore not preserved; it may have been conceived as normal practice that the arrangements were made anew for each coronation. Furthermore, the arrangers were normally not acknowledged at all. As seen above, the anthem during the Homage in 1821 was still referred to as 'Kent's anthem', although it was heavily arranged by Kramer, and in the same way 'Zadok the Priest' was normally simply 'by Handel'. One might obtain an impression of the nature of such a 'Palace Yard' arrangement from the performance of 'Zadok the Priest' at the 1937 and 1953 coronations, of which sound recordings exist.[148]

[143] *MW* 121 (5 July 1838), 163.

[144] *Lwa Library*, 4.c.9, p. 4: 'Mess: Harper (Trumpet) and Albrecht (Trombone)'.

[145] *MW*, 120, 155. This would mean they were in a special gallery on top of that over the High Altar.

[146] *Lwa Library*, 4.c.9, p. 30.   [147] *Lwa Library*, 4.c.9, p. 45.

[148] See *The Coronation of Their Majesties King George VI and Queen Elizabeth*, CD 1, track 7, and *The Coronation Service of Her Majesty*, CD 1, track 17.

The difficulties of the performance in the Abbey as seen in earlier coronations still prevailed in 1838. According to Perkins 'a functionary, Mr. Gwilt by name, stood beside the Bishops who *said* the Litany, with a flag, and signalled the moment for each response to the choir!'[149] Indeed, this method of communication was still used fifty years later, at the thanksgiving service for the queen's Golden Jubilee; furthermore, Jeffrey Lant observed that on this occasion 'despite a massed choir and the full use of the Abbey's organ by Dr. Bridge, there were considerable difficulties in hearing what was going on'.[150] As a means of coping with the performance problems, the music for the 1838 coronation was rehearsed several times. There was a private rehearsal on a Saturday morning before the coronation 'at the residence of Mr Hawes, 7 Adelphi Terrace, Strand, 11 o'clock'.[151] A public rehearsal took place in the Abbey on 26 June, at 10.30 in the morning.[152] As in 1727, the public was also able to hear some of the coronation music after the event: a charity concert held in the Abbey on 2 July included three of the anthems from the coronation service.[153]

Murray summarized that the music at Queen Victoria's coronation

> was all that it was not in 1831. It was impressive, and compelled all to realize that they were taking part in a religious service – not merely in a pageant.[154]

However, it is notable that the programme of the music and its performance were in many respects the same as at the previous coronation. Smart's choice in 1838 of full orchestral accompaniment, even for the Responses, was indeed 'impressive'. But such a preference of the full forces over a simple organ accompaniment could rather have enhanced the impression that the ceremony was a grand pompous pageant, not a 'religious service'.

Queen Victoria's coronation marks the end of several traditions in the development of the British coronation service. It was the last for over sixty years, and many things would be very different in the coronations of the twentieth century – especially with regard to the music.

---

[149] Perkins, 23f. (emphasis original). See also above, fn. 75.

[150] Jeffrey L. Lant, *Insubstantial Pageant. Ceremony and Confusion at Queen Victoria's Court* (London: Hamish Hamilton, 1979), 6f.

[151] *Lwa Library, 4.c.8*, no. 5.

[152] *Lwa WAM 60017*, no. 70. See also *Lca MS Ceremonials 94*, no. 47: a list of tickets for this rehearsal.

[153] *GM*, new series 10 (July–December 1838), 201. The rehearsal for that had been on 30 June.

[154] Murray, 192.

8 | The 'marriage of tradition and innovation': the twentieth century

The music at the four twentieth-century coronations is generally very well documented, with outstanding primary sources including sound and film recordings for the two most recent ones. A version of the order of service including the music was printed for each of them, and at least for the 1953 coronation it is known that this was used by the singers during the service.[1]

There were significant changes at these coronations: some features of the service were ultimately removed, while others were reintroduced after centuries of absence and some new ones were added. Regarding the music Strong befittingly summarized that the arrangements in the twentieth century 'fully accorded with the desire that each Coronation should marry tradition with innovation'.[2]

Edward VII and Queen Alexandra, 1902

Queen Victoria's reign was the longest in British history and the coronation of her successor took place a full sixty-four years after hers: Edward VII was crowned together with his wife, Queen Alexandra, on 9 August 1902. One of the leading figures in the planning of the event was Viscount Esher, who had been responsible for organizing Queen Victoria's Diamond Jubilee in 1897 and was very much one of the main architects of the 'ceremonial monarchy'.[3] The musician in charge at the coronation was Sir Frederick Bridge, who himself provides much detailed information in his autobiography.[4] His responsibility for the music is generally noteworthy: Bridge did not hold a position in the Chapel Royal but had been organist of Westminster Abbey since 1882 (deputy to James Turle from 1875). In fact, his appointment is in striking contrast to Smart's argument of 1838 that the organists of

---

[1] See Kenneth and Valerie McLeish (eds.), *Long to reign over us... Memories of Coronation Day and of Life in the 1950s* (London: Bloomsbury, 1992), 139–42, here 140.

[2] Strong, 467.

[3] For details see Kuhn, ch. 3 (57–81): 'Lord Esher: Empire Theatre', and p. 92. See also Olechnowicz, 27; and Strong, 473.

[4] Bridge, *Westminster Pilgrim*. He devotes two full chapters to this coronation (pp. 177–95).

Westminster Abbey never contributed to the coronation music, but only musicians of the Chapel Royal.[5] The Executive Coronation Committee appointed Bridge as 'chief musician' for the service relatively early, in December 1901.[6] While he himself emphasized that this 'was not at all a foregone conclusion', there is no evidence of any dispute over his leadership; after all he had already been responsible for the music at Queen Victoria's Golden Jubilee service in the Abbey in 1887. It seems that it had become more or less accepted that at the great occasions of state the Abbey's own organist was the leading musician. Nevertheless, up until 1953 the issue was reconsidered for each coronation.[7]

The 1902 coronation had originally been scheduled to take place on 26 June, but it had to be postponed as the king had to undergo an operation. John Bodley pointed out that it had already been decided that the service should be shorter than that of Queen Victoria but that after the postponement the Archbishop of Canterbury, Frederick Temple, was asked to abridge it even further due to the king's fragile health.[8] These second cuts resulted in several drastic changes, such as the removal of the sermon.[9] Regarding the music, the Privy Council suggested that 'the Anthems be so arranged that they be sung only while processions or ceremonies are going forward'.[10] On 12 June, before the postponement, Bridge had prepared a list providing the timings for the core pieces of the service:[11]

Te Deum 4 ½ minutes / Creed 3 ½ / Sanctus 1 / Gloria in Excelsis 2½ / Veni Creator 2 ¼ / Zadok the Priest 5 ¼

He offered that 'Other Anthems can be arranged to suit the time at disposal'. After the postponement, however, he seems to have been less willing to accept any cuts in the music. After all, as Bridge himself recorded, 'the King was *most explicit* in declaring his Command that there should be no curtailment of the musical part of the service'.[12]

For the first time a copy of the order of service was published that included the music.[13] This publication, at the time heralded as 'an

[5] See above, p. 210.
[6] For details see Bridge's own report in Bridge, *Westminster Pilgrim*, 177–9. See also Wright, 116.
[7] See, for instance, *Llp Lang 21*, fos. 7–8 (for 1937) and *Lwa WAM 63352–63358* (for 1953).
[8] Bodley, 243.   [9] Ibid.
[10] Minutes of 10 July 1901. See *Llp Temple 57*, fos. 96–97v, here 97v.   [11] *Lwa WAM 58378*.
[12] Letter by Lord Esher to Bridge, 8 August 1902, quoted in Bridge, *Westminster Pilgrim*, 192 (emphasis original). See also below, fn. 37.
[13] *The Form and Order of the Service* [. . .] *in the Coronation of Their Majesties King Edward VII. and Queen Alexandra* [. . .] *With the Music to Be Sung*, ed. by Sir Frederick Bridge (London: Novello, 1902) [hereafter *FOM* (1902)].

important innovation', is an invaluable source.[14] It provides evidence not only for the anthems and liturgical music, but also, for instance, for the smaller items such as the choral responses and Amens throughout the service. However, it is noteworthy that this was published before the postponement of the service, showing the original date of 26 June on the front page. Overall therefore, this publication reflects only what was planned to be performed, but not what actually happened on the day.[15] Moreover, it does not fully represent the music as it was performed in any case: the fanfares and instrumental pieces are not included, and the remainder of the music is arranged for choir and piano or organ accompaniment, with at best marginal indication of the use of the orchestra. This publication was probably intended less to document the actual service than to provide a score for the singers and perhaps a collection of coronation music to be used elsewhere.

The main innovation at this coronation was Bridge's development of a programmatic idea that united all the musical pieces of the service in an overall scheme, as he explained:[16]

In selecting the music for the service I finally determined upon a scheme which would embrace a period of five centuries of English Church music, from 16th century Marbeck and Tallis to composers of the present day; the 17th century being represented by the honoured names of Orlando Gibbons and Henry Purcell; the 18th by Handel, with his masterly Coronation anthem, "Zadok the Priest;" and the 19th century by Samuel Sebastian Wesley, Arthur Sullivan, John Stainer, and Charles Villiers Stanford. In addition to these names special anthems were composed by Sir Hubert Parry, Sir Walter Parratt, and by myself.

According to Wright, Bridge's plan was a 'way that helped represent this contemporary imperial occasion as a climax of the glories of the British past'.[17] Indeed, even though Bridge referred explicitly only to 'English Church music' there was also a clear 'British' aspect in his choice of programme. In the preface to the order of service with the music, he explained that the Threefold Amen at the end of the service was taken from Orlando Gibbons's anthem 'Great King of Gods' and he pointed out that

---

[14] E[dwards], 'Coronation of Edward the Seventh', 578.

[15] The revised order was never printed, but manuscript corrections were entered in the copies of 'the principal participants'. See Bradshaw, 27. For the music that was eventually performed see App. D.

[16] Bridge, *Westminster Pilgrim*, 182.

[17] Wright, 117. For the other important innovation – that the music was 'only to be performed when something was going on' – see Ch. 1, fn. 67.

the manuscript, in the Library of Christ Church, Oxford, records that this anthem was 'made for the King's being in Scotland'.[18]

With emphasizing the piece's origins, Bridge managed to incorporate at least a subtle reference to the Scottish coronation service.[19] Provenance and origins of the coronation music could be very much imbued with direct 'political' significance. Bridge later recalled that he had wanted to include a fanfare for trumpets from Germany of which, however, he could not obtain the music; with obvious reference to the Great War he concluded that 'I need hardly say now that my want of success was very fortunate'.[20]

It may generally have been expected that there would be a repeat of Attwood's grand setting of 'I was glad' for the entrance-anthem. Not only had it been performed at the previous three coronations, it was also put on one level with Handel's 'Zadok the Priest':[21]

In addition to the time-honoured Coronation anthems of Handel and Attwood, some musical novelties (such is commonly the case) may be expected [...]

Bridge seems to have scheduled Attwood's setting at an early stage of the preparations.[22] However, in the end the entrance-anthem was performed in the new, now famous setting by C.H.H. Parry. Bridge, commenting on the coronation music, explained, without going into detail, that 'one or two reasons weight with me in omitting' Attwood's anthem.[23] At the same time, he admitted that some people would regret its not being included. According to a letter from Bridge to Parry, it was the king who wished Parry 'to write something for the Coronation service', although this was rather unspecific.[24] Parry's anthem was to be performed at all the twentieth-century coronations and in 1953 one of the singers pointed out that it 'had become a tradition: this was its fourth Coronation'.[25] Overall, this anthem has by now become one of the 'classics' of royal ceremonial music and is also performed at Jubilees and other services – such as the wedding of Prince William of Wales to Catherine Middleton in 2011. However, Parry's anthem did not achieve its fame immediately. For its performance at the 1911 coronation Parry himself relates the anecdote that Sir Henry Irving,

[18] *FOM* (1902), vi.

[19] This idea seems to be alluded to in Jeffrey Pulver, *A Biographical Dictionary of Old English Music* (New York: Franklin, 1929, repr. Ayer Publishing 1969), 208.

[20] Bridge, *Westminster Pilgrim*, 179f.

[21] Charles Eyre Pascoe, *The Pageant and Ceremony of the Coronation of Their Majesties King Edward The Seventh and Queen Alexandra* (New York: Appleton, 1902), 245.

[22] *Lwa WAM 58307*: Scheduled list of coronation music [1901/1902].   [23] See Shedlock, 157.

[24] *Lcm MS 7281*, no. 2 (transcr. App. B1c).   [25] Harry Coles, quoted in McLeish (eds.), 141.

who sat next to him during the service and was not aware of the fact that Parry was the composer of the entrance-anthem, said to him he did not 'think much of the music so far!'[26] One point of Irving's criticism could have been that Parry's setting, in all its imperial grandeur, is slightly unclear in its rhythm and difficult for a processional piece. One eyewitness reported of the entrance procession at the 1953 coronation that 'nobody *marched* up the aisle, and the music was seldom rhythmical enough to cause everyone to walk in step'.[27] Furthermore, in contrast to all its predecessors, Parry's setting does not conclude with the Gloria Patri – a noteworthy discontinuity of established tradition.

The Litany, which at the three preceding coronations had been merely read, was in 1902 again sung. However, in order 'to spare the convalescent forces of the King' during the postponed coronation, it was eventually removed from the actual service and was sung 'on the steps of Henry VII.'s chapel before the arrival of the royal processions'.[28] This decision was indeed remarkable: the removal of the Litany from the actual service, even from the main body of the Abbey, was a striking break with liturgical tradition. Armitage Robinson, the Dean of Westminster, pointed this out in a letter to the Bishop of Winchester:[29]

I think that you will feel with me that the English Order being the oldest surviving in the world, it would be a very grievous & perhaps irreparable breach of historical continuity to omit it [the Litany]. It is moreover part of the parallel between the Consecration of Kings & the Consecration of Bishops.

While this change would probably not have been introduced had the king not fallen ill, the music at the 1902 coronation overall served to confirm and even revive old traditions, supporting the initially seen idea that there was a 'renovation of tradition', rather than an 'invention'.[30] For instance, a plan for the 'Curtailment of the Service' refers to 'The Anthem after the Crowning. A short Anthem of two lines (part of the old <u>Confortare</u>) is all that is needed here', observing that 'something has always been sung'.[31] Thus, first of all, the anthem at this place was included very much for tradition. Secondly, the specific text of the *Confortare*, 'Be strong and of a good courage', had not been sung since the early seventeenth century, and at

---

[26] Bridge, *Westminster Pilgrim*, 233.   [27] Charles Heriot, quoted in McLeish (eds.), 138.

[28] Bodley, 243. See also Bryon Bevan, 163; Bridge, *Westminster Pilgrim*, 193.

[29] Robinson to Bishop of Winchester, undated (1902), (*Lwa WAM 58308*). The archives of Westminster Abbey and Lambeth Palace (esp. the Davidson and Lang papers) hold a great deal more material on the issue of the Litany at this and the next coronations.

[30] See above, p. 21. For details of the 'revived traditions' at this coronation see Bradshaw, 27.

[31] *Lwa WAM 58425* 'Curtailment of the Service' [1902].

best read as a prayer; in 1902 this very traditional coronation text was sung to a new setting by Sir Walter Parratt. The *Confortare* was to remain part of the service throughout the century, with new settings by Walford Davies (1937) and George Dyson (1953). As for previous coronations, there was a new, elaborate anthem for the Homage. Bridge recorded that

In choosing the music I had to follow exactly the form of service prepared by the Archbishop of Canterbury; but the words of the "Homage" anthem were not in the official programme, and these I myself selected.[32]

Bridge chose a text beginning with Isaiah 49:7, 'Kings shall see and arise', which had not been used for a coronation anthem before. The printed editions include organ accompaniment only.[33] However, as in previous centuries, the Homage anthem would have included orchestral accompaniment and Bridge described that 'in the last section a march, played by the orchestra, is accompanied by the chorus'.[34]

The Homage had been abridged significantly even before the postponement of the coronation: following established custom homage was to be paid by the Archbishop of Canterbury, as a representative of all the Lords Spiritual, and by the senior representative of each degree of the Lords Temporal, with the rest of the bishops and peers kneeling in their places accordingly; however, 'for the shortening of the ceremony' after this only the first of each degree was to approach the throne again to touch the king's crown and kiss his cheek, not each of the peers individually as had been done at previous coronations.[35] This drastic shortening of the ceremony meant that there was also less time to be covered by the Homage anthem, and Bridge's anthem is much shorter than the anthems for this ceremony at previous coronations. Bridge also provided for a 'cut' in the music 'should it be necessary'.[36] Nevertheless, as one of the performers reported:[37]

Word is passed along that we are not to cut short Bridge's homage anthem, as our conductor at rehearsal wished. The King's command is that all of it must be sung, a special and deserved compliment.

---

[32] Bridge, *Westminster Pilgrim*, 180. His proposal probably survives as *Lwa WAM 58471*: 'Words suggested for a short Anthem during the Homage'.

[33] *FOM* (1902), 81–91. The anthem was later also republished separately: Frederick Bridge, *Kings shall see and arise. (The Homage Anthem).* Novello's Collection of Anthems, no. 894 (London : Novello, [1907]).

[34] *FOM* (1902), v.

[35] *FOM* (1902), 80. See also Bodley, 243, and Bridge, *Westminster Pilgrim*, 186. For the earlier practice see above, esp. Chs. 2 and 3.

[36] Bridge, *Westminster Pilgrim*, 186 and 193.   [37] 'In the Choir at the Coronation', here 265.

Another significant change during the Homage was that the scattering of medals was abolished; instead the 'Royal Largesse' took 'the form of the gift of Osborne House to the nation'.[38] It has been suggested that this ancient custom had to be omitted simply because the Royal Mint could not produce new medals with the amended date in time. In any case, ceremonially this change was to be of great advantage as it meant that all the accompanying noise and confusion disappeared, removing 'all possibility of the irreverence which marred some former Coronations'.[39] This new situation also allowed the music to be better heard. In connection with its place in the ceremony, the 1902 Homage anthem has been interpreted as 'a reminiscence' of the General Pardon proclaimed at this stage at earlier coronations, since it contained the line 'That thou mayest say to the prisoners, Go forth!'[40] As a closer link to the political situation of 1902, Richards has pointed out the allusions to the Empire in the anthem's text; these could be interpreted as symbolizing that the whole Empire paid Homage to the new ruler.[41]

With the crowning of Queen Alexandra the service included again the coronation of a queen consort. However, the aforementioned plan for the 'Curtailment of the Service' stated that 'The Anthem at the close of the Queen's Coronation may well be omitted', without giving any reason apart from the implied saving of time.[42] The queen's procession to her throne was presumably not accompanied by any music. Thus the ceremonial quality of this part of the service, indeed of this 'coronation', was further reduced, after the queen's specific 'own' anthem, introduced in 1685, had already been replaced by the more neutral Hallelujah Chorus in 1831. In fact, ceremonially the cutting of this anthem at this and the following coronations must have made the Queen's Inthronization seem rather bizarre: while previously she would have been sitting on her throne during the remainder of the music, she now got up again as soon as she was seated in order to go down to the altar with the king to take communion.[43]

The programmatic approach to the coronation music was reflected also in details. The anthem after the Recognition had disappeared during the nineteenth century, but in 1902 each of the presentations was to be followed by a different fanfare:[44]

For the Recognition [...] a new musical feature was designed by Sir Frederick Bridge. For the cadence of the four State trumpeters, after each Asking, employing

---

[38] Fletcher, *British Court*, 100. For this and the following see also Bury, 568f.   [39] Perkins, 119.
[40] Macleane, 172.   [41] Richards, 105, who refers to Bodley.   [42] *Lwa WAM 58425.*
[43] Cf. the considerations in 1953; see below, fn. 166.   [44] Macleane, 217.

the same passage each time, he substituted a fanfare of four varying sections, adapted from the trumpet calls in *Lohengrin*.

In the end, however, this scheme had to be abandoned: due to the king's ill health there was only one presentation, not four.[45]

Regarding the liturgical music, a heightened awareness of the history and propriety of the service became apparent, with further 'revived traditions' similar to the aforementioned *Confortare*. The Sanctus at the beginning of the Communion Service, which had 'long been improperly used for this purpose in English cathedrals' and had been introduced to the coronation in 1821, was replaced by an introit anthem.[46] The text chosen for this introit was 'O hearken thou', which had not been sung at a coronation since 1661, but which had been the 'Offertory in "Liber Regalis"', as either the Dean of Westminster or Bridge noted in the printed order of service with the music; it was 'Let my prayer come up' that was again sung as the Offertory.[47] Both of these were sung in arrangements by Bridge: the former based on music by Arthur Sullivan, the latter on music by Henry Purcell. The Creed, which at the previous coronations had been merely read, was sung in a setting by Wesley, also arranged by Bridge. This is the first coronation for which there is evidence that the Lord's Prayer was sung: it was to be begun by the archbishop and then recited by the choir on one note, ending with a choral Amen.[48] Overall, the number of breaks with tradition and newly introduced or reintroduced features balanced out against each other.

Notwithstanding the extraordinary wealth of sources for this coronation, uncertainty surrounds the actual performance of the music. Most importantly, during the preparations there seems to have been a change in the way the entrance-anthem was performed. Bridge later recalled that 'the entrance of their Majesties was to be made to the singing in procession of the Psalm, "I was glad"'.[49] Before the service, he explained that following tradition 'certain parts of the anthem' were to be sung by the Abbey choir, to be 'answered by the large choir and orchestra'.[50] Bridge had informed Parry about this scheme for the performance and Parry had laid out his anthem along these directions.[51] In his autograph draft of the anthem the first part is scheduled to be begun by the 'Abbey Choir' in procession and Parry goes on to

---

[45] Strong, 477.   [46] Bradshaw, 27.

[47] *Lwa Library n.s.*: Annotated, printed order of service with the music (1902), 23 and 94.

[48] *FOM* (1902), 104.   [49] Bridge, *Westminster Pilgrim*, 182.

[50] [Sir Frederick Bridge?], 'Notes on the Coronation Music', *MT* 43 (June 1902), 387–8, here 387. Similar in *FOM* (1902), iii; and 'In the Choir at the Coronation', 265.

[51] See Ch. 3, fn. 47.

write in two systems assigned to a 'Small Marching Choir' and the 'Big Choir on Screen'.[52] At the end of the anthem's first part, ending 'that is at unity with itself', Parry also includes the instruction: 'The Choir in the Procession must reach the Screen by then, & move towards their places with the rest Of the Choir'.[53] The following *Vivat*s should be sung by the Westminster Scholars and taken up by the full choir. For the beginning of the section 'O pray for the peace' is again noted 'small choir', only later to be joined by the full choir.[54] However, in the end, the entire anthem was sung with the singers already in their gallery, as is confirmed in an account by William Harvey Bourne, one of the Abbey choristers.[55] The change of the performance may have been a result of the postponement of the service which allowed for many more rehearsals.[56] Indeed, Bodley explained that this 'had given time for the procession to be organised with a perfection of detail rarely achieved in an English spectacle, so that nothing marred the impressive beauty of the scene'.[57] Nevertheless, at the actual ceremony the music of the procession was indeed 'marred'. Bourne recalled that 'a bad mistake was made now by Sir Frederick Bridge in mistaking a peer for the King and signed to the Westminsters to yell "Vivat [...]"'.[58] Parry, too, reports in his diary that by accident the procession began too early; Alcock, the organist, consequently had to improvise so as to cover the royal procession: the *Vivat*s and the remainder of the anthem were repeated.[59]

Overall, there was a big change in the performing conditions. Contrary to having one big gallery for the music as at the three previous coronations, the 1902 coronation orchestra was placed on the quire screen but the 430 singers of the choir 'were split in galleries between the north and south choir aisles'.[60] These performance conditions remained basically the same throughout the twentieth century. A seemingly new solution was found to handle the problem of the musicians' being so separated: the music was conducted by Bridge from the centre of the screen, while 'in the fashion of the opera house his beat was communicated to the singers and musicians by

[52] *Ob MS Mus c. 125*, fos. 120–8, here fos. 120 and 125r.   [53] *Ob MS Mus c. 125*, fo. 125v.

[54] 'Abbey Choir' and 'General Choir' are also distinguished in the edition of the piece in *FOM* (1902).

[55] *Lwa WAM 58489**, p. 5.   [56] Strong, 490–2.   [57] Bodley, 286.

[58] *Lwa WAM 58489**, p. 6f.

[59] See Bridge, *Westminster Pilgrim*, 182. See also Jeremy Dibble, *C. Hubert H. Parry. His Life and Music* (Oxford: Clarendon Press, 1992), 386f.

[60] Wright, 125. For this and the following see also E[dwards], 'Coronation of Edward the Seventh', 578.

sub-conductors on either side of him'; this resulted in the effect that 'neither could Bridges [*sic*] see his singers and players, nor could they see him!'[61] Indeed, one of the performers reported that 'three conductors are beating time, and many of us cannot see either [*sic*] of them'.[62] Similarly, for the next coronation it was reported that

Few of the choir could see the beat of Sir Frederick Bridge. On the cantoris side Sir George Martin subconducted, and Dr. J.C. Bridge on the decani side, but even their beats were not visible to all. The wonder is that the choir kept together so well.[63]

Overall, there had been little change to the problematic performance conditions since the seventeenth century. Employing sub-conductors was the most practical solution and became the standard up to 1953.[64] In fact, a sub-conductor was still employed at the royal wedding in the Abbey in April 2011 in order to coordinate the choral forces in the choir stalls with the orchestral players in the organ loft.[65]

Changing traditions

The observations about the 1902 coronation invite another discussion of the initially mentioned topic of traditions in the coronation music. Apart from the two aforeseen newly introduced ideas – the programmatic approach and the fact that the music should always accompany the ceremonies – there were other significant innovations. The most important and lasting change introduced in 1902 concerned the position of the Te Deum. By ancient tradition the Te Deum had been sung at the heart of the service, following the Benediction after the Crowning, and during the monarch's procession to the throne for the Inthronization: this was its place in the Second Recension and also in the *Liber Regalis*.[66] In 1902, the Te Deum had initially been kept in this place.[67] However, for the postponed coronation it was moved to the very end of the service, when the king and queen walked in procession from their thrones into St Edward's Chapel to prepare for the

[61] Montague Calman, 'The Music in the Abbey', *Music and Musicians* (June 1953), 8; See also Macleane, 213.

[62] 'In the Choir at the Coronation', 266.

[63] 'Music in the Coronation Service. By our Representative in Westminster Abbey', *MH* (1911), 213–15, here 214.

[64] James Wilkinson, 'A Chorister remembers 1953', *The Court Historian* 7, 1 (May 2002), 69–73, here 71. For performing problems and the issue of sub-conductors see also Barker, 121f.

[65] For this information I am grateful to James O'Donnell, Organist and Master of the Choristers of Westminster Abbey.

[66] Strong, 45 and 88.   [67] *FOM* (1902), 65–78.

Recess. As it was sung after the final blessing and Threefold Amen, in this new position the Te Deum was, strictly speaking, not part of the service any longer. The removal of the Te Deum to the end left a gap in the music and it is not known what music eventually covered the king's procession to his throne. It is possible that this became just a quiet spectacle: it was not accompanied by music in 1937 and 1953. This procession thus lost a good portion of its ceremonial impetus, being reduced to a mere change of location.

It is not quite clear what caused the drastic change of the Te Deum's position in 1902. Perkins states it was done 'in order to save time'.[68] He might be referring to the fact that the procession from St Edward's Chair to the throne is much shorter and takes less time than the procession from the throne into St Edward's Chapel, followed by the monarch's robing, which was thus better suited to be covered by the long Te Deum. Similarly, the *Musical Herald* correspondent who sang in the choir stated that the Te Deum was 'transferred to the "recess", where it does not interrupt the "action"'.[69] However, Perkins criticised the relocation of the Te Deum heavily:[70]

Instead of the Church's great Hymn of Praise and Thanksgiving being solemnly rendered with all proper dignity, it has degenerated into the performance of a piece of music to fill up a gap, in fact, it has become little more than a cover for conversation during the retirement of the Sovereign and his attendants to St. Edward's Chapel.

His concerns were confirmed by Sir William St. John Hope who reported:[71]

During the temporary absence of the King and Queen all restraint was gone, and conversation at once became general; and although the choir had meanwhile begun to sing Te Deum, it received as little attention as a mere voluntary.

Nonetheless this reflects merely the problems of the practical handling of the new scheme. Musically, the relocation of the Te Deum to the end of the service was certainly appropriate, as it gave this 'great Hymn of Praise' more weight than when it had been surrounded by all the other ceremonies; it could now expand as a truly triumphant climax to the service. Also, this change turned out to be a great improvement from a ceremonial point of view. At the previous coronations the monarchs' procession into St Edward's Chapel had been accompanied merely by 'the organs playing all the while', according to the customary wording in the orders of service. However, in 1902 it was accompanied by Charles Villiers Stanford's setting

[68] Perkins, 124.   [69] 'In the Choir at the Coronation', 265.   [70] Perkins, 124.
[71] Quoted in Perkins, 206.

of the Te Deum, taken from his 1879 first service and orchestrated for the coronation.[72] Although with a little more than six minutes a relatively short setting, this was still an impressive composition. Overall, the replacement of the organ music by a grand orchestrally accompanied Te Deum continued a development that had begun at the coronation of Queen Victoria, when the Hallelujah Chorus was sung at the end of the service. There was now an accumulation of elaborate music at the very end of the ceremony, as the Te Deum followed the Gloria, which in 1902 was performed in a grand setting by John Stainer. From 1689 until 1761 the Gloria had accompanied the monarch's procession back to the throne after receiving communion at the altar. From 1821 onwards it had been only read. In 1902 and thereafter, however, the reintroduced singing of the Gloria took place at the same position as reported for 1661, only once the monarch had arrived back at the throne, and it did not cover anything else; thus it was indeed 'a lot of music' that he listened to.[73]

After the Te Deum, when the king and queen returned from St Edward's Chapel for the procession out of the Abbey, the National Anthem was 'given by choir and congregation with thrilling effect'.[74] The order of service did not mention this and, indeed, the fact that it was performed at all is note-worthy. Although, as seen above, the National Anthem had been performed at several coronations before, during the late Victorian era the general frequency of its performance had notably declined. Bridge later recalled that the anthem had not been performed at Queen Victoria's Golden Jubilee service in 1887, which he found 'a curious thing'.[75] He went on to explain:

It may be said in passing that there seemed for many years [before the 1887 Jubilee service] to be a shyness, if I may use the term, in singing the National Anthem in Church, and particularly did this seem to apply to the Abbey. Of late years, especially since the recent terrible war, this diffidence has happily disappeared, and at the time of writing I am playing the National Anthem daily at the close of the afternoon service.

Bridge's reference to the Great War could be taken to imply that in 1902 there may still have been some of the observed 'shyness', even though one of the performers at the coronation reported confidently 'the National

[72] For Stanford's contribution to the 1902 coronation music in general see Jeremy Dibble, *Charles Villiers Stanford: Man and Musician* (Oxford University Press, 2002), 338f.

[73] *FOM* (1902), 103. Cf. Ch. 1, fn. 67.

[74] E[dwards], 'Coronation of Edward the Seventh', 582.

[75] For this and the following Bridge, *Westminster Pilgrim*, 134. For Edwardian critique of the National Anthem see also Richards, 93.

Anthem (two verses) is of course sung'.[76] It is not known in what setting it was performed, but the fact that it was described as rendered with a 'thrilling effect' most probably indicates that the National Anthem was accompanied by the full orchestra. It was followed by Richard Wagner's *Kaisermarsch*, or Emperor's March (WWV 104), originally written to commemorate the German victory over France in the war of 1870–1 and the ensuing proclamation of the King of Prussia as German Emperor.[77] This *Kaisermarsch* must have been a striking choice. Not only may it point to the close links of the British and the German Empires at the time – Kaiser Wilhelm II being Edward VII's nephew – but it may also hint at Britain's own Imperial claims. Even though Edward VII was in Westminster Abbey crowned only as a king, he was nonetheless also Emperor of India from his accession; Sir Edward Elgar had pointed out this imperial claim of the British monarchy in his own *Imperial March* for the 1897 Diamond Jubilee. For the 1902 coronation Wagner's march was rearranged to include a choral section to the words 'Hail Lord and Master' by A.C. Benson, the author of 'Land of Hope and Glory'.[78] However, the imperial effect may have been somewhat decimated. Benson afterwards complained that his 'own little contribution, the words of the Kaiser-marsch, was spoilt because the Choir were so anxious to see the King depart that they did not attend or sing, and the result was awfully feeble'.[79]

On the broader scheme, the musical climax that resulted from such an accumulation of elaborate music at the end of the service gave also more emphasis to the preceding communion. At many earlier coronations, where it was not followed by any larger piece of music – at least not by anything that was noteworthy enough to be mentioned in contemporary reports – the communion had seemed like a mere appendix to the coronation ritual.

The 1902 coronation was truly an imperial affair in so far as it was celebrated not only throughout the country, but also throughout the Empire with services appointed for the occasion. The specially produced orders of service often included at least some of the music of the actual coronation service in Westminster Abbey, and there were also special

---

[76] 'In the Choir at the Coronation' 266.

[77] For details see Michael Fischer, '"Heil, Heil dem Kaiser!" Der Kaisermarsch Richard Wagners als nationalprotestantisches Symbol', in Michael Fischer, Christian Senkel and Klaus Tanner (eds.), *Reichsgründung 1871. Ereignis-Beschreibung-Inszenierung* (Münster: Waxman, 2010), 104–18.

[78] Macleane, 218. The text is reproduced in Lindsay, 273 and Range, thesis, vol. I, 243.

[79] A. C. Benson, *Edwardian Excursions, From the Diaries of A.C. Benson 1898–1904*, selected, edited and introduced by David Newsome (London: John Murray, 1981), 72.

collections of appropriate music.[80] It was through such publications that the coronation music became disseminated on an unprecedented scale. At the same time, these special services caused a good amount of new music to be specially written in commemoration of the event.[81]

1911–1953

It has been observed that the 1902 coronation 'has formed a precedent for royal ceremonies down the rest of the century' and that it 'became the sacred icon upon which all that followed had to be modelled'.[82] Indeed, the order of service became more or less standardized in the form of 1902. This extended also to the music, with the programme becoming more established: apart from Handel's 'Zadok the Priest', there were other pieces that were sung at each of these coronations: Parry's 'I was glad' and, from 1911 onwards, Stanford's Gloria in B flat, written for that occasion. Furthermore Gibbons's Threefold Amen had its undisputed place at the end of the service. This 'Amen' had generally a special status: by the late 1920s it was known as the 'Abbey Amen'.[83] It seems to have become a favourite for royal occasions in particular and was, for instance, also sung at the wedding of the Prince of Wales to Lady Diana Spencer in St Paul's Cathedral in 1981.

However, despite such continuity from 1902 onwards, there were still some important changes introduced right up to 1953, and no two coronations were the same. Even though the 'programmatic approach', the idea that the music should represent English church music of all centuries, was followed at all the twentieth-century coronations, this did not mean that there was not a significant amount of new music.[84] In fact, in 1953 the scheme was explicitly reiterated only for the Homage anthems and the rest

---

[80] *The Form and Order of Service recommended for Use in the Churches of the Church of England throughout His Majesty's Empire on Thursday, 26th June, 1902, being the Coronation Day of their Majesties King Edward VII and Queen Alexandra* (London: Novello, [1902]). Without including the actual music of 'I was glad' and 'Zadok the Priest' it instructs them to be sung, or hymns instead. For the music see *A Selection of Music for use at Coronation Services in Churches and Chapels throughout the British Dominions on [. . .] the Coronation Day of their Majesties King Edward VII. and Queen Alexandra.* (London: Novello, [1902]).

[81] See, for instance, *The Music for an Order for Special Services authorized By the Most Reverend The Archbishop of Capetown for Use in his Diocese and, With the Consent of his Suffragans, Throughout the Province of South Africa on the Day of the Coronation of His Majesty King Edward VII. Composed by Charles Macpherson (Sub-Organist of St. Paul's Cathedral),* (London: Novello, [1902]).

[82] Wright, 155f.; and Strong, 473.   [83] Pulver, 208.

[84] For a comparative table of the music see App. D.

of the music was almost all from the twentieth century. As one commentator observed, the composers of the day 'were, exceptionally, not outnumbered or obscured by the great dead'.[85] Indeed, as initially observed, the twentieth-century coronations coincided with the English Musical Renaissance.[86] Overall these coronations included a substantial amount of contemporary music. At the same time, however, one could argue that this merely continued an old custom: for, as seen in the foregoing chapters, most coronations had included a good deal of specially composed new music.

Little is known about the orchestral music during the processions before and after the actual service up to the coronation of Queen Victoria in 1838. For the twentieth-century coronations, however, there are a significant number of specially composed 'Coronation Marches' that were played during the various processions, including works by Elgar (1911), Arnold Bax (1953), and the two famous marches by William Walton: *Crown Imperial* (1937) and *Orb and Sceptre* (1953).[87] Indeed, public competitions were organized, with a prize for the best march, but few of these have made it into the repertoire.[88]

George V and Queen Mary, 1911

At the coronation of George V and Queen Mary on 22 June 1911 again Bridge was the musician responsible and he followed his own 1902 precedent; regarding the musical programme it was observed that 'the choice on this occasion [. . .] shows a wide knowledge of English Church Music and a due care for the necessities of the great Service'.[89] This time the published order of service would have been followed.[90] The idea of a procession of the Abbey choir during the entrance-anthem was fully abandoned and Parry's setting was performed as in 1902, but with a new instrumental introduction.[91] There were few innovations at this service, but Archbishop Randall Davidson reversed some of the 1902 cuts: the coronation sermon was

---

[85] 'Music for the Coronation', *MT* 94 (July 1953), 305–7, here 305. [86] See Ch. 1, fn. 90.

[87] For a fuller discussion of these marches see Richards, 105, 109, 113–15, and 119. For the Walton marches see Frank Howes, *The Music of William Walton* (Oxford University Press, 1973), 119–21, and Neil Tierney, *William Walton. His Life and Music* (London: Robert Hale, 1984), 202f.

[88] See Richards, 105.   [89] Alcock, iii.

[90] *The Form and Order of the Service [. . .] in the Coronation of Their Majesties King George V and Queen Mary [. . .] With the Music to Be Sung*, ed. by Sir Frederick Bridge (London: Novello, 1911); hereafter 'FOM (1911)'.

[91] For details see Dibble, *Parry*, 384–6.

reintroduced and the Litany was moved back to its traditional place at the beginning of the Communion Service, following the Recognition. As in 1902 the Lord's Prayer was sung, but this time to the plainchant tune by John Merbecke.[92] The introit that marked the Communion Service was changed in 1911 from 'O hearken thou' to 'Let my prayer come up'. As H.C. Colles noted on the occasion of the next coronation this change meant a return to 'the "Gradale" [*sic*] of the "Liber Regalis"'.[93] 'O hearken thou', in turn, was performed as the Offertory in the second part of the Communion Service.

Bridge again produced a new anthem for the Homage: 'Rejoice in the Lord, O ye righteous'.[94] Again the published scores contain only organ accompaniment, but the anthem at the coronation would most probably have included the full orchestra. The printed edition indicates at least 'Trumpets', 'Trombones' and 'Tymp'. It is an interesting side-note that Bridge states that his 1911 anthem 'has been reproduced on the gramophone'.[95] Thus this anthem has the distinction of being one of the first coronation anthems ever to be recorded. Bridge prominently quotes the German hymn tune 'Ein feste Burg'. This tune had already been heard at the previous coronation, as part of Wagner's *Kaisermarsch*. More significantly, however, the hymn itself was also sung earlier on the day during the Regalia Procession to the West door and it was observed that 'its employment in the Anthem follows naturally and effectively'.[96]

At the end of the Homage there came the customary fanfare before the people once again acclaimed the monarch. In 1911 for the first time the music of this fanfare survives. It was an especially composed piece by John Borland, a prolific musician and writer, and orchestral secretary at both the 1902 and 1911 coronations.[97] Borland's 'Homage Fanfare' is scored for brass ensemble with drums and full organ. The passages for organ are 'based on the Scottish Psalm Tune "Montrose"' as Borland himself notes on the autograph score.[98] This tune had first appeared in print in 1793, in

---

[92] 'Coronation of King George the Fifth', 433.

[93] H.C. Colles, 'Preface' to *The Form and Order of the Service* [...] *in the Coronation of Their Majesties King George VI and Queen Elizabeth* [...] – *with the Music to Be Sung* (London: Novello and Company, 1937) [hereafter '*FOM* (1937)'], iii–vi, here iv.

[94] Like his 1902 Homage anthem, this was afterwards published separately: Frederick Bridge, *Rejoice in the Lord, O ye Righteous. Homage Anthem composed for the Coronation of their Majesties King George V. and Queen Mary* [...] Novello's Octavo Anthems, no. 992 (London: Novello, 1911).

[95] Bridge, *Westminster Pilgrim*, 234.   [96] Alcock, v.

[97] E[dwards], 'Coronation of Edward the Seventh', 584; and 'Coronation of King George the Fifth', 434.

[98] Private collection of Brian Watkins, Cambridge. The first page of the manuscript is reproduced on www.manuscripts.co.uk/stock/22842.HTM (accessed on 31 August 2011).

Robert Gilmour's *Psalm-singer's Assistant.*[99] While not much is known of the history of the tune, its name alone presented a befitting reference to the Scottish part of the United Kingdom. The Montroses had been an important Scottish family of much relevance to the monarchy: James Graham, 1st Marquis of Montrose (1612–1650) had been a Scottish general and during the Civil War became a Royalist hero with a series of victories for Charles I, fighting the Covenanters in Scotland. Furthermore, James Graham, 4th Marquis of Montrose (1682–1742) was an important figure during the arrangements for the Act of Union in 1707, raising its support in the Northern kingdom, for which he was created 1st Duke of Montrose.[100] Even if all these background details may not have been in the public awareness at the time, the simple fact that this was a Scottish tune made it a good choice for the Homage fanfare, stressing the unity in loyalty of all of the United Kingdom.

For his fanfare Borland suggested the inclusion of the choir, entering the text of 'All hail the power of Jesus' name!' under the hymn sections. His 'fanfare' would thus have been more of a short anthem for full forces, reminiscent of the '*Drums* [...] *Trumpets*', and shouting of the people reported by Ogilby for the coronation of Charles II.[101] Indeed, for the 1902 coronation one of the performers, referring to the end of the Homage, had reported 'and we sing during the fanfare "God save King Edward [...]"'.[102] It is not known if the choir in 1911 eventually sang in the fanfare. From a compositional point of view, the incorporation of hymns in ceremonial music seems to have been popular at the time. Similar to Bridge and Borland, Parry too included hymn quotations in his new setting of the Te Deum for the 1911 coronation; he used the well-known St. Anne's tune as well as 'an allusion to the 'Old Hundredth Psalm-tune'.[103] It was Parry's Te Deum that provoked an interesting comment when its performance, near the end of the service, was described as 'not so effectively presented as were other items earlier'.[104] The explanation given was that 'the performers were wearied after their five hours' confinement in a limited space'. The problem of simple physical exhaustion of the performers during such a long service must certainly also have applied

---

[99] Robert Gilmour, *The psalm-singers's assistant. Being a collection of the most approved psalm and hymn tunes: Mostly in four parts. Selected from the best authors* [...] (Glasgow: Printed by J. Neilson and sold by the author, 1793).

[100] For details see the respective entires by David Stevenson and by Ronald M. Sunter in the *Oxford Dictionary of National Biography online* (www.oxforddnb.com, accessed on 25 August 2011).

[101] Ogilby, 183. See also Ch. 1, fn. 129.   [102] 'In the Choir at the Coronation', 266.

[103] Alcock, vi.   [104] 'Coronation of King George the Fifth', 433.

to earlier coronations, and it might, in fact, be one reason for some of the mishaps at those ceremonies.

As in 1902, the National Anthem was sung during the Recess. For the first time it was included in the order of service with the music; however this included only the first verse, and not two verses as reported for the previous and following coronations and for earlier royal events.[105] The omission of the second verse (beginning 'Thy choicest gifts in store') may have been meaningful on this occasion. As Strong has pointed out, the coronation took place 'simultaneously with the passing of the Parliament Act, which neutered the power of the House of Lords and in effect ended the aristocratic age'.[106] It may have seemed inappropriate, if not impossible, under these circumstances, to ask the assembled peers to sing 'with heart and voice' a verse that had so little relevance to them: they could not easily proclaim the included line 'May he defend our laws' when the king himself was so heavily involved in reducing their established powers with the threat of creating more peers to support the Liberal government.

George VI and Queen Elizabeth, 1937

Due to the 1936 abdication crisis there may have been a special effort to stress continuity and tradition at the coronation of George VI and Queen Elizabeth; they were crowned by Archbishop Cosmo Gordon Lang on 12 May 1937, the very day that had been scheduled for Edward VIII.[107] However, regarding the music there were some notable departures from precedent and tradition.[108] As at the preceding two coronations, the Director of Music was the organist of Westminster Abbey, now Ernest Bullock. For this coronation he collaborated closely with the Master of the King's Music, Walford Davies. This was the first time that the musician responsible for the coronation service did not contribute any notable, major piece of his own to the service; apart from writing some fanfares Bullock was most concerned with compiling the overall programme and arranging its performance.[109] The Director of Music at the coronation had thus become

---

[105] *FOM* (1911), 143: 'At the Conclusion of the Service'. See also above, fn. 76, and the considerations below.

[106] Strong, 428.   [107] Cf. Cannadine, 'Context', 152.

[108] *FOM* (1937). For detailed information on the instrumental music to accompany the various processions before the service, and also a full list of the performers see 'The Coronation Music and Musicians', *MT* 78 (1937), 497–501.

[109] 'Coronation Music and Musicians', 497.

mainly an organizer and coordinator – in striking contrast to all previous coronations.

Again, much effort was put into shortening the lengthy service. This led to some perhaps unexpected ideas as seen in the suggested shortening of Handel's 'Zadok the Priest'.[110] Ceremonially, it is striking that most of the choral 'Amens' after the various prayers were cut and replaced by the simple spoken word. Most notably the lavish Sevenfold Amen after the Prayer of Consecration, which had been included at the two previous coronations, was fully omitted; in fact, it was specifically observed that Gibbons's Threefold Amen was the only choral Amen of the service.[111] These cuts must have altered the overall impression of the service as a choral service. It is not clear by what this change was motivated, but it may have been part of a general attempt to increase the devotional character of the ceremony. In the preface to the order of service with the music, Colles observed that 'Unnecessary musical elaborations have been eliminated from the central act of Eucharistic worship.'[112] Nevertheless, despite such emphasis on the propriety of the 'Eucharistic worship' the Litany, which had been restored to its place within the service at the previous coronation, was again removed. According to Archbishop Lang this had been suggested by Edward VIII himself during the preparations for the coronation.[113] In the end, the Litany was sung before the actual service. This followed the proceedings of the 1902 coronation; however, in 1937 the Litany was not sung far away at the steps of Henry VII's Chapel, but Lang suggested it to be sung during the Regalia procession to the West Door before the royal couple's arrival.[114] He expressed his hope that this new place 'will be very impressive and serve to recall the great congregation to the religious solemnity of the Service'.[115] However, at the same time this change also resulted in the cutting of the congregational hymns that had previously been sung during this procession and which had furthered the congregation's active participation in the service.[116]

The sermon was again removed from the service and was not to return.[117] With the sermon cut, all that remained was a service that consisted of nothing but ceremonies. The sermon had always been the place that offered

[110] See Ch. 1, fn. 102.   [111] 'Music at the Coronation', *The Record* (Friday, 7 May 1937), 291.

[112] Colles, v.   [113] Lang to Ratcliffe, 21 July 1936 (*Llp Lang 21*, fo. 23).

[114] Lang to Dean of Westminster, 17 December 1936 (*Lwa WAM 58579*). The positioning of the Litany was accompanied by much discussion and there is a great deal of material about this in *Llp* and *Lwa*. See also Bradshaw, 27f.

[115] Lang to Wickham Legg, 27 March 1937 (*Llp Lang 22*, fo. 35).

[116] See above, fn. 96, and below, fns. 141–2.   [117] Tanner, 42.

the possibility to link the ancient rites to the present day, explaining the monarch's role in Church and State. Without the sermon, the coronation service had become a timeless ceremonial removed from everyday life.

Musically and ceremonially the most significant innovation affected the Homage: Bullock and Davies proposed 'to introduce here, several short anthems (each lasting about 2 minutes), instead of one long work as done previously'.[118] They explained that 'the advantage of this is that the anthems can be representative of various periods, and any can be omitted without artistic loss as the ceremonial demands'. Archbishop Lang, otherwise very much a traditionalist, approved of this radical change of established custom.[119] In his later recollections he referred to the service music in general and explained that 'our plan was to include representatives of English Church Music from Tudor Times to the present day'; he declared enthusiastically that 'in order to get a wider choice, we agreed to substitute for one long anthem during the Homage six short "Homage anthems"'.[120] During the preparations Lang pointed out that 'there is bound to be a good deal of criticism [...] partly on the ground that it seems like a programme of selected English music'.[121] He later confirmed this and reported that

one or two competent critics such as the good Colles have wondered whether our proposal does not seem to look like a short concert programme of English Church Music.[122]

Nevertheless, Lang insisted that he was 'so much attracted by the idea of the short Homage Anthems illustrating English Music that I should be reluctant to fall back upon' the alternative of having only one, long anthem. Intriguingly, the 'Englishness' of the selection would initially have been even stronger: originally 'one of the first ideas' that Bullock and Davies had regarding the Homage music was 'to suggest such things as Parry's "England" and "Jerusalem", and Holst's "I vow to Thee" and "Earth might be fair"'.[123] This selection was also the reason why they suggested the use of the term Homage 'songs' rather than 'anthems', which was, however, firmly rejected by Lang.[124] Eventually, six anthems were chosen, representative of five centuries, although two

[118] Bullock to Lang, 23 October 1936 (*Llp Lang 21*, fo. 94).

[119] Archbishop's secretary to Bullock, 24 October 1936 (*Llp Lang 21*, fo. 97).

[120] 'Notes on the coronation of King George VI and Queen Elizabeth', in *Llp Lang 218* (Archbishop Lang's diary/notebook), fos. 23–52, here 43.

[121] Lang to Bullock, 26 November 1936 (*Llp Lang 21*, fo. 140).

[122] Lang to Davies and Bullock, 9 January 1937 (*Llp Lang 21*, fos. 192–3).

[123] Bullock to Lang, 29 November 1936 (*Llp Lang 21*, fo. 143).   [124] *Llp Lang 21*, fos. 140 and 143.

of them were cut and not performed, as four anthems turned out to be enough to cover the ceremony. The report of one of the lay vicars of the choir illustrates how improvised the performance of the music was:[125]

The order in which they were to be sung was decided at the service and the Choir informed which they were to sing by Ernest Bullock's son, Michael, who lay stretched out on top of the organ console, holding up cards with the numbers on.

It is interesting to note that, despite all the meticulous preparations and rehearsals, the actual length of the Homage on the day could not be accurately predicted. The reason could be a change in the ceremonial. The order of service still demanded that the senior peers, 'having done their Homage', come to the throne a second time to touch the crown and kiss the king.[126] In the end, however, they did this immediately after their vows which must have shortened the ceremony a good deal.

The new Homage music affected also the overall scheme considerably. Up to the coronation of Queen Victoria, the anthem during the Homage had been one of the most elaborate pieces of the service, performed 'with Instrumental Musick of all sorts as a solemn Conclusion of the Coronation', as the orders of service stated from 1689 onwards. In the twentieth century this anthem became less important: since it was still followed by the now elaborate liturgical music, especially a grand Gloria and the Te Deum, it became one piece among many. Finally, from 1937 onwards, the Homage anthem was reduced to a mere collection of several shorter works. Nevertheless, these Homage anthems were noteworthy in that they were the first and only pieces of music for which the printed order of service included the composers' names.[127] The idea for this inclusion seems to have come from Lang himself, who gave as the reason 'the special character of these Homage Anthems'.[128] Furthermore, at least from 1937 onwards the music accompanied the peers' actual paying of the homage: this certainly increased the aura of solemnity during their vows, but at the same time it meant also that their voices could be heard less clearly. In a way, therefore, the public declaration of loyalty became more of a private act between peers and sovereign.

---

[125] 'Coronation Fever – But Would Their Voices Last?', *WAC* 3, no. 6 (Winter 1996/97), 32–6, here 34f.: from a report by Harry Abbott.

[126] *FOM* (1937), 60.

[127] *The Coronation of Their Majesties King George VI and Queen Elizabeth, May 12th 1937. Official Souvenir Programme* (London: Odhams Press, [1937]), 29.

[128] Lang to Bullock, 21 January 1937(*Llp Lang 21*, fo. 273).

The Homage was concluded by Borland's 'Homage Fanfare' from the previous coronation, which he revised as he noted on the autograph score. With Queen Elizabeth being of Scottish descent the incorporation of the 'Montrose' tune in this fanfare was now particularly appropriate, aptly acknowledging the smaller part of Great Britain before the first coronation of a queen from Scotland for centuries.

The Te Deum, sung as the king and queen retired into St Edward's Chapel to prepare for the Recess, was sung in a specially composed setting by Ralph Vaughan Williams. He based it on traditional tunes, a fact of which he himself seems to have been rather proud.[129] However, the probably more striking aspect of this Te Deum is the fact that it incorporates a great number of very martial fanfares as well as a distinct march-like theme that gives the whole a firm structure, from its first appearance at the beginning of the choir entry to its triumphant repeat in the final section. The overall tonality is a curious mixture of glorious minor modes in a bright orchestration with only occasional excursions into obvious major. In total, this piece leaves the impression of very rough and martial music. In the wider historical context it is tempting to interpret Vaughan Williams' use of such a style as a response to the militaristic ceremonial of the fascist powers on the continent at the time, especially in Germany and Italy. Elaborate martial music was very much part of their public spectacles. With their open references to the imperial splendour of ancient Rome, the continental dictatorships clearly challenged also the ceremonial of the British Empire. Indeed, one year before the coronation, J.M. Keynes had concluded that

The failure of the twentieth-century democracies is in part attributable to their failure to invest the state with ceremonial.[130]

Therefore, there was motivation to ensure that British royal ceremonies would stand the comparison with those of the continental regimes.[131] The music at royal occasions had to compete with such works as for instance Richard Strauss' recent *Olympische Hymne* for the 1936 Olympic Games in Berlin. Furthermore, it is worth remembering that the 'public mood' at the time was already set for the reality of an impending war.[132] Vaughan

[129] See Michael Kennedy, *The Works of Ralph Vaughan Williams*, 2nd edn (Oxford: Clarendon Press 1980, repr. Oxford University Press, 2002), 277, esp. fn. 1.

[130] J. M. Keynes, 'Art and State', *The Listener*, 26 August 1936, quoted in Cannadine, 'Divine Rites', 20.

[131] Cf. also the observations by Philip Williamson, 'The Monarchy and Public Values 1910–1953', in Olechnowicz (ed.), *The Monarchy and the British Nation*, 223–57, esp. 235–8.

[132] Kenneth O. Morgan, 'The Twentieth Century (1914–2000)', in Kenneth O. Morgan (ed.), *The Oxford History of Britain*, rev. edn (Oxford University Press, 2001), 582–679, here 618.

Williams's Te Deum, with its conspicuously martial tone, could be seen as a direct reaction to this context. With a remarkable 'special effect' the final verse of the Te Deum, 'Let me never be confounded', is not the triumphal climax of the piece using the full forces. Vaughan Williams's Te Deum does not end with a lavish proclamation of trust in God; rather, he reduces the scoring to a capella choir and the piece literally finishes on a quiet note, with a calm affirmation of the individual's trust in Divine protection and guidance. This might have been intended to symbolize a simple, straightforward trust in God amidst all the clamour of pomp, majesty, and, perhaps, even foreshadowings of war.

At this coronation an old custom was revived, which had been abandoned over a hundred years previously: a new organ was installed in the Abbey; however, contrary to previous centuries, this organ was built as a permanent instrument and stayed in the Abbey afterwards.[133] Overall, the performance practice reflected a growing historical awareness: as a consequence of the English Musical Renaissance the Tudor music was rendered without orchestral accompaniment.[134] For Byrd's Creed the commentator of *The Times* pointed out that the unaccompanied voices 'conveyed the feeling of presenting the faith of the Church as a matter of fact without undue ornament, but with the vision of sincere belief'.[135] In fact, this fashion was taken so far that even Purcell's 'Hear my Prayer' during the Homage was sung a cappella. At the same time, however, in S.S. Wesley's 'Thou wilt keep him in perfect peace', the last of the Homage anthems, the original simple organ accompaniment was heavily reinforced by the orchestra, thus producing a rich, almost 'Edwardian' sound.

Elizabeth II, 1953

Like her parents' coronation, that of Elizabeth II in 1953 very much followed the patterns established at the beginning of the century. Nevertheless, at this coronation especially there were some salient innovations. The musician appointed with overall responsibility was again the Abbey organist, now William McKie.[136] Although he had composed an anthem for Princess Elizabeth's wedding in 1947 ('We wait for thy loving kindness'), for the coronation he did, like his predecessor Bullock in 1937, not contribute any major work and concentrated solely on the organization and performance

---

[133] Webb, 638f.   [134] See Richards, 114, who refers to Colles.

[135] 'Music in the Abbey', *The Times*, 13 May 1937.

[136] For his appointment see the letter from the archbishop in *Llp Fisher 123*, fo. 113.

of the music. Unlike his predecessor Davies, Sir Arnold Bax, the Master of the Queen's Music, had not much of an impact at the coronation; in his own words he was 'supposed to be consulted' but was in fact merely 'in the position of a yes-man'.[137]

Musically, the most significant innovation was certainly the introduction of a congregational hymn: 'All people that on earth do dwell', taking the place of the Offertory, sung while the queen went in procession from her throne down to the altar for communion. The idea to include a congregational hymn came from the composer Vaughan Williams; he is reported to have 'thought it was a great weakness that there had been no hymn for the congregation to sing' in 1937, and whereas McKie's advisory committee was 'not at all convinced that the congregation should join in a hymn', Geoffrey Fisher, the Archbishop of Canterbury, 'was delighted with the idea' and noted 'The Queen thought well of this'.[138] C.B. Mortlock commented that the hymn was introduced 'with the object of relieving the tension in a vast congregation concentrating on a supreme religious dedication'.[139] Whatever the motives for it were, according to Michael Kennedy, Vaughan Williams was 'extremely proud of introducing this democratic musical reform into the service'.[140]

Even though this was indeed the first 'congregational hymn' in a coronation service, the singing of all people present was not altogether that new: as already seen, they may have joined in singing the National Anthem from as early as 1821 onwards. However, one could argue that the difference between the National Anthem and a congregational hymn is clearly that the former is a direct prayer for the monarch whereas the latter concerns the entire congregation. In addition to the National Anthem, there may have been other possibilities for the Abbey congregation to join in the music: already at the 1902 coronation 'hymns were played and sung as various processions entered'.[141] And it is known that the whole congregation joined in singing the last verse of 'O God our help in ages past' during the procession of the regalia to the West Door before the service – 'producing an unrehearsed climax of overwhelming majesty that will never be forgotten

[137] Lewis Foreman, *Bax: a Composer and His Time*, rev. edn (Woodbridge: Boydell Press, 2007), 395.

[138] 'New Music, and a Hymn for the Coronation', *WAC* 2, no. 8 (Winter 1992–3), 23–4, here 23; Fisher to McKie, 10 November 1952, incl. a typed list of music for the service, approved by the Queen, with annotations by Fisher (*Lwa Library, McKie Papers*).

[139] C.B. Mortlock, 'New Music's Part in Ancient Coronation Rite', *DT*, 18 March 1953, 6.

[140] Kennedy, *Vaughan Williams*, 326. For this innovation's being 'fully in accord with the new democratic age' see also Strong, 468.

[141] Richards, 105.

by those present'.[142] Also, for the 1911 coronation Joceylin Perkins observed that 'an attempt was made [. . .] to produce a congregational effect by the substitution of Merbecke's setting of the Nicene Creed for that of S. S. Wesley'.[143] The Lord's Prayer, which had been sung at the previous three coronations, in 1953 was again merely said: this may have been another means to increase the congregation's joining in.

In any case, while the introduction of 'All people that on earth do dwell' may after all not have been too much of a 'democratic musical reform', it nevertheless, intendedly or not, musically helped point out another important innovation at the 1953 service. From 1603 up to the twentieth century the coronations had been an entirely Anglican affair, with no place for any other denomination in the ritual. It had been only since 1902 that non-Anglican religious representatives were invited and in 1937 there had been for the first time 'six representatives of the Free Churches and three of the Church of Scotland'.[144] However, only in 1953 was a representative of a different denomination also given a concrete role in the service when the Moderator of the General Assembly of the Presbyterian Church of Scotland delivered the Bible to the queen after the Oath. Indeed, as early as 1951, while George VI was still alive, Archbishop Fisher had generally observed that, being both a national and an established church, the Presbyterian Church 'feels acutely that [. . .] it ought to have a special and prominent place in the Coronation of a Sovereign and not just be lumped in with the Free Churches'.[145] In this context, the 1953 hymn 'All people that on earth do dwell' was a subtle, indirect, and perhaps even unrecognized, but nonetheless strong reference to the Presbyterian Church of Scotland: its text, which is based on Ps. 100, was probably written by to the Scottish clergyman William Kethe and its tune, known as the 'Old Hundredth', comes directly from the 1551 Genevan Psalter.[146]

McKie assured Archbishop Fisher that he had asked Vaughan Williams to arrange the hymn in a way so that 'the congregation may sing in all verses, and will not at any time be left unsupported by the Choir'.[147] Vaughan Williams made use of his setting of 'The hundredth psalm' written in 1929 for the Leith Hill Festival chorus and orchestra.[148] Furthermore, he

---

[142] Bridge, *Westminster Pilgrim*, 194.   [143] Perkins, 24.   [144] Bury, 595. See also Strong, 427.

[145] 'Memorandum on conversation with the Dean of Westminster concerning the Church of Scotland and the Coronation Service', dated 9 October, 1951 (*Llp Fisher 80*, fos. 275–6).

[146] Diana Poulton, *John Dowland* (Berkeley: University of California Press, 1982), 325. Text and tune were first printed in the English and Anglo-Genevan psalters of 1561 (ibid.).

[147] McKie to Fisher, 12 December 1952 (*Lwa Library, McKie Papers*).

[148] See Ralph Vaughan Williams, *Letters of Ralph Vaughan Williams 1895–1958*, ed. by Hugh Cobbe (Oxford University Press, 2008), 511.

incorporated John Dowland's faux-bourdon in verse 4, thus adding yet another English composer to the programme of music, reinforcing the overall scheme. At previous coronations, the procession from the throne to the altar had been accompanied merely by the singing of the Gradual, or offertory anthem, which was not an especially grand piece. In 1953, however, it was accompanied by Vaughan Williams' stately hymn setting, beginning with a jubilant introduction and overall making use of the full orchestral accompaniment, including the full plethora of fanfare trumpets. Such a grand opening consequently also elevated the ensuing taking of communion from a quiet, contemplative act to a solemn ritual of Church and State.

Vaughan Williams was generally a prominent and indeed innovative composer at this coronation. Apart from the hymn, he contributed also a short anthem or motet to be sung during the actual taking of communion: 'O taste and see' (Psalm 34:8). This piece draws attention to the fact that it is not known what music was performed during the receiving of communion at earlier coronations. As already seen, according to the *Liber Regalis*, the choir should have sung the anthem 'O hearken thou', although this may have been sung only after the actual communion.[149] As always, the organist could have improvised, as is reported for 1902.[150] As with the congregational hymn, the idea to include 'a short unaccompanied anthem' somewhere in the service came from Vaughan Williams himself and it was McKie who suggested that this could be used during the communion.[151] Although the 1953 communion motet was in fact a confirmation of the *Liber Regalis* tradition, it was probably nonetheless perceived as an innovation. This may be indicated by Claude Jenkins' tentative formulation in a memorandum to the archbishop: 'If the suggestion of music during the Queen's Communion be adopted [...]'.[152] Jenkins continued that 'an effort might be made to ensure that it should be pianissimo', explaining that 'there is nothing that can be more distracting' than loud music. He dismissed the argument that quiet music might focus too much attention on the queen as 'not really substantial'. In the end, Vaughan Williams' motet was indeed pianissimo, but it may have been 'distracting' all the same. For 'O taste and see' is, in all

[149] See Ch. 2, fn. 63.

[150] 'In the Choir at the Coronation', 266: 'During the taking of the bread and wine, Mr. Alcock produces beautifully soft effects on the celestial organ.'

[151] See 'New Music, and a Hymn for the Coronation', 23; Typed account by McKie in *Lwa Library, McKie Collection of Material Related the Coronation, 1953* [in the following 'McKie Account'], p. 2.

[152] 'Some Practical Considerations humbly submitted by the Lambeth Librarian', 10 September 1952, in *Llp Fisher 123* , fos. 125–33, here fo. 133.

its modesty, an outstanding composition, if alone for its scoring: at the beginning of the piece Vaughan Williams prominently scores for a solo treble part, which is then taken up by the choir singing a cappella.[153] His wife afterwards commented:[154]

The boy's solo at the beginning of Ralph's anthem was a perfectly calculated dramatic effect; after so much richness of texture and grandeur, the unaccompanied treble voice held the listeners in its soaring tranquillity.

Besides these two very innovative items Vaughan Williams contributed also the settings of the Creed and the Sanctus, taken from his 1923 *Mass in G minor*.[155] Frank Howes commented that these pieces were 'arranged for Anglican use by Maurice Jacobson' and have been 'liturgically sung not only in the Roman, but also in the Anglican communion ever since'. This 'arranged for Anglican use' is an interesting statement, as it must refer to the fact that the original Latin settings were translated into English. Similarly, William Walton's Te Deum written for this coronation was afterwards also published in an adaptation to the Latin text.[156] Overall, the coronation music was becoming multi-confessional.

Among all these innovations, however, there was also again a revived tradition at the 1953 service. The ancient text of the introit, 'Behold O God', which in the seventeenth century had been moved to different places in the service and after 1761 been dropped altogether, was reintroduced at the beginning of the Communion Service with a new setting by Herbert Howells. As in the coronations since 1902, again the *Confortare* followed the Crowning. Its composer, George Dyson, suggested 'an "a capella" setting', explaining that 'It seems that after Zadok and all the shouts[,] fanfares and artillery, a minute or two of voices only would be a relief.'[157] This is a rare example of a composer's considerations regarding the overall context of the music. In the end, however, this suggestion was abandoned and Dyson set his short anthem for the full forces, thus incidentally complying with Archbishop Secker's directive from 1761.[158]

---

[153] This solo was in fact sung by three choristers. See the choristers' reports in *WAC* 37 (Winter 2003/04), 32–4, here 33.

[154] Ursula Vaughan Williams, *R.V.W.: A Biography of Ralph Vaughan Williams* (London: Oxford University Press, 1964), 334.

[155] For this and the following see Frank Howes, 'Preface' to *The Music with the Form and Order of the Service* [...] *at the Coronation of Her Most Excellent Majesty Queen Elizabeth II* [...] (London: Novello, 1953) [hereafter '*FOM* (1953)'], iii–vi, here iv.

[156] Howes, *Walton*, 177.

[157] Dyson to McKie, 9 December 1952 (*Lwa Library, McKie Papers*).   [158] See Ch. 6, fn. 43.

As in 1937, the Litany was again sung during the clergy's procession to the West door before the service. It was sung in Tallis' setting, which is thus likely to be the one piece of music that has been sung at most coronations since the Reformation. Also following the 1937 precedent was the new 'scheme' for the Homage music: again a selection of anthems from different epochs was to be performed. For the first time the order or service omitted the peers' second approach to the throne, explaining that they should touch the crown and kiss the queen's cheeks immediately after their vows. Probably based on the experience from the previous coronation, where two anthems had to be omitted, this time only five anthems were scheduled; however, in the end only three were performed.[159] Wesley's 'Thou wilt keep him in perfect peace' was again performed as the last of the Homage anthems and this position seems to have been of special importance. McKie wrote to the archbishop that

If only four anthems are required [during the Homage], the Byrd will be omitted. Whatever happens, "Thou wilt keep him" will come last.[160]

When this anthem had been performed at the 1937 coronation, its text from Isaiah 26:3 could still be understood as referring directly to the king, to George VI, just as had the texts at coronations in previous centuries. When the anthem was performed at the coronation of Elizabeth II, however, this possible association was at least obscured if not lost. Despite the very obvious clash of the male pronoun and the female monarch, one commentator curiously recalled that 'everyone found [Wesley's anthem] exquisitely appropriate without being able to say why'.[161] From a performance point of view it is interesting to note that, in contrast to the previous coronation, in 1953 there was organ accompaniment only, reflecting a preferred straightforwardness in musical style while at the same time emphasizing the noble simplicity of the setting. Indeed, the fact that this anthem was now 'sung with organ accompaniment only' was noteworthy enough for McKie to point it out in his account of the coronation music.[162]

Despite the simultaneous performance of music during the Homage the peers' vows could now be heard more easily: a microphone was hidden beneath the queen's throne to magnify the peers' voices above the music.[163]

[159] For this and the following see 'Music for the Coronation', 306.
[160] McKie to Fisher, 3 December 1952 (*Lwa Library, McKie Papers*).
[161] 'Music for the Coronation', 306.   [162] McKie Account, p. 21.
[163] Barker, 186. For a plan of the microphones and cameras in the Abbey see also *The Year that made the Day – How the BBC Planned and Prepared the Coronation Day Broadcast* (London: BBC, [1954]), 36.

In 1937, when the service was radio-broadcast, they could be heard only faintly among the music: two microphones had been hidden not in the throne, but 'in the arms of the Coronation Chair'.[164] The ability to hear the vows clearly may in all likelihood have been a return to the pre-twentieth-century custom. The Homage ended with a fanfare by Bullock who also wrote all the other fanfares of the service.[165] He modelled his Homage Fanfare heavily on Borland's piece from 1911/37, following the same structure of trumpet flourishes interspersed with the organ playing the 'Montrose' tune. Having been performed at least at the third coronation in a row, the use of this tune may have appeared like a new tradition.

After the celebration of communion with the afore-discussed congregational hymn and communion motet the queen returned to her throne while the organist improvised. Once she was seated on the throne, the Gloria followed. This part of the ceremonial caused some concern for Garter King of Arms who worried that 'she would not be long enough on the Throne to justify her return by a dignified period seated there'; however Archbishop Fisher reassured him that the queen's return to her throne was justified 'now that we know the Gloria will take 5 ½ minutes'.[166] Indeed, Fisher reminded McKie of the new, twentieth-century custom that 'the Gloria in excelsis is not to begin until the Queen is in her Throne'.[167] In a striking way this piece was therefore not merely music that the monarch listened to, 'sitting in the crown'; moreover it was the length of the music that justified the ceremonial proceedings.

The Gloria was again performed in Stanford's setting as in 1911; this had become one of the traditional coronation pieces, in the same way as Gibbons's 'Threefold Amen' after the final blessing. After this, however, followed the most elaborate new composition of the service: Walton's *Coronation Te Deum*. Walton's setting, which he himself described as 'rather splendid' was indeed a 'thrilling climax to what had in any case been a musically distinguished service'.[168] In the words of his wife, Walton had been asked by McKie to write the Te Deum for the coronation and 'could not resist the opportunity to use the Queen's Trumpeters, so he agreed'.[169] However, in the end McKie thought that using all of the Queen's Trumpeters 'might be overstaffing too much!'[170]

[164] 'Coronation Fever', 35.

[165] 'Music for the Coronation', 305. Watkins Shaw, 'Coronation Fanfares', *MT* 94 (1953), 273.

[166] Fisher to Garter King of Arms, 14 January 1953 (*Llp Fisher 124*, fo. 25).

[167] Fisher to McKie, 30 March 1953 (*Llp Fisher 124*, fos. 159–61, here fo. 161).

[168] For this and for more details see Michael Kennedy, *Portrait of Walton*, first publ. in 1998, corr. paperback edn (Oxford University Press, 1998, repr. 2002), 166f. See also Tierney, 126f.

[169] Susanna Walton, *William Walton. Behind the Façade* (Oxford University Press, 1988), 130.

[170] McKie to Walton, 18 November 52 (*Lwa Library, McKie Papers*).

It had originally been planned to abridge the Te Deum text so as to keep the piece shorter. It is astonishing that a shortening was suggested for such an ancient, time-honoured text as that of the Te Deum. Walton himself asked McKie to interfere with the archbishop to be allowed to 'set the whole of the Te Deum', as his setting would otherwise be 'too short – about 5 ½ mins & slightly undignified'.[171] After the coronation, Archbishop Fisher is reported to have commented that the Te Deum

was in the wrong place and was bound to be an anti-climax. But after considering other possible places for it he wrote, 'I think the only possible thing to do is to omit it from the service altogether.'[172]

While it is not clear why Fisher considered the Te Deum to be an 'anti-climax', it is astonishing that he suggested a complete omission. If the Te Deum had indeed been shorted, or even omitted, for the purpose of a shorter service, that would have been the ultimate trimming of a musical item to match the ceremonial. In March 1953, Mortlock had still observed that 'in modern times it has become tradition for the Te Deum [...] to be specially composed for each Coronation' and he had reproduced part of the first page of Walton's score.[173] Therefore, a complete cut of the Te Deum might have caused some public furore. After all, a lengthy piece of music was required anyway so as to cover the time of the queen's robing in St Edward's Chapel and the arranging of her leaving procession. Eventually, even after the full Te Deum there was a lengthy organ improvisation to cover the beginning of the procession.

The opening of Walton's Te Deum which accompanied the queen's stately procession into St Edward's Chapel is set in a grand, straightforward way scored for the full forces. After this processional section, however, the music becomes much more complex, with the singers being divided into two choirs and further into semi-choruses. It has been observed that Walton made sure that the piece would fit well to its performance location, with the musicians placed all around the gallery on the screen. He kept it in a traditional style so as to 'suit the acoustic conditions of a high vaulted church' and visited the Abbey 'frequently beforehand [...] listening from various parts of the building to the effects of organ and choir'.[174] Indeed, the special acoustic effects determined the structure of Walton's piece in that he used much antiphonal writing. His setting is reminiscent of the seventeenth

---

[171] Walton to McKie, 17 December 1952 (*Lwa Library, McKie Papers*). See also Walton, 130; and Tierney, 126.

[172] 'New Music, and a Hymn for the Coronation', 24.   [173] Mortlock, 6.

[174] For this and the following see Howes, *Walton*, 176–9.

and early eighteenth-century coronation music, written for a performing body scattered around the Theatre in several smaller galleries.

In one striking conceptual point Walton followed Vaughan Williams' 1937 setting: Walton too did not use the final phrase 'Let me never be confounded' to finish his Te Deum in the probably more traditional way of a great climax in all the forces. Instead, in Walton's setting the choir sings this phrase as a 'choral-recitative' to orchestral accompaniment without trumpets and timpani, all marked *pianissimo*. The Te Deum ends with the organ alone holding the final chord. This 'quiet' moment at the end of the Te Deum may have been intended to be in contrast to the following musical pomp; for the next musical item to follow was the fanfare before the National Anthem. Indeed, similarly to Dyson, Walton was concerned about the context of his piece; McKie recalled that Walton 'also wanted to know what would be happening in the ceremonial just before the *Te Deum* was to be sung, and what music would precede the *Te Deum*'.[175] Walton would certainly have cared in the same way about what happened *after* the Te Deum, and what music was to follow it.

As at the previous coronations the National Anthem was sung as the monarch emerged from St Edward's Chapel for the Recess. As seen above, the National Anthem had probably been sung at some place at more or less every coronation since at least 1821. However, no details of the arrangements of these earlier performances survive and as seen above only from 1911 onwards is the actual music extant, when it was included in the edition of the order of service with the music.[176] That music is an anonymous simple, four-part setting and while there is a drum roll at the beginning there are no other details about the instrumental accompaniment. It is notable that the tune is then in the key of B flat major and thus includes many high notes, which may have made it difficult for congregational singing. By 1937, the publication of the order of service with the music included a full arrangement of the National Anthem; transposed down to G major it was, as Colles explained, 'put into a key which brings the tune within the compass of every voice'. Indeed, Colles not only welcomed the fact that the Abbey congregation joined in the singing, but also suggested that listeners on the wireless might join in:[177]

The Coronation ends, therefore, with an opportunity for all, whether they are in Westminster Abbey or listening in the most distant parts of the Empire, "To sing with heart and voice GOD SAVE THE KING."

---

[175] Undated letter (December 1970) from McKie to Dr Stewart Craggs, quoted in Tierney, 126.
[176] *FOM* (1911), 143.   [177] Colles, vi.

Nevertheless, it was only in 1953 that for the first time the National Anthem was included in the actual text of the order of service.[178] Archbishop Fisher informed McKie that it would become a new rubric and explained that 'two verses, the first and third [...] shall be sung, and those verses will be printed'.[179] In the end, the verses were not printed, but the rubric indicated simply 'the National Anthem'. This was still a significant innovation: even though the National Anthem had been included in the orders of service with the music from 1911 onwards, these earlier performances were mere tradition or custom, but not encoded in the written ceremonial.

In 1953 the National Anthem was sung in a new arrangement by Gordon Jacob who had also re-orchestrated 'Zadok the Priest' in 1937 and 'I was glad' in 1953.[180] Jacob's arrangement very much follows the model of Walford Davies' from 1937. After a fanfare the first verse is sung a cappella in simple four-part harmony; the second one, however, is accompanied by the organ and full orchestra, including a trumpet descant. It is at first surprising that the National Anthem, the musical epitome of the link between Church and State, should begin with a plain a cappella verse, instead of making full use of all the forces available throughout. Notwithstanding that Jacob had merely adopted Davies' 1937 structure one commentator has argued that Jacob's arrangement was 'symbolic of the new kind of seriousness with which the piece was to be taken: less superficial pomp, but real music'.[181] One eyewitness described the effect in 1953:[182]

The new setting of the National Anthem caused a slight hesitation [...] There was a moment of brief uncertainty when people accustomed to the slow style of the familiar anthem paused before joining in the lighter and more majestic rendering in four-square harmony by Dr Gordon Jacob. The fifth [*recte* second] verse, sung 'with all available trumpets', did, however, fill the abbey with a surging wave of triumphant sound.

Jacob himself explained to McKie: 'As you can see I've kept it absolutely plain', when he sent him the score; and McKie replied that it was 'exactly right for the occasion'.[183] In fact, this way of setting the National Anthem

---

[178] *The Coronation of Her Majesty Queen Elizabeth II, 2 June 1953. Approved Souvenir Programme* (London: Odhams Press, [1953]), 39.

[179] Fisher to McKie, 18 February 1953 (*Lwa Library, McKie Papers*).

[180] The scores of these are preserved in *Lwa Library*.

[181] Erik Routley, *An English-speaking Hymnal Guide*, ed. and expanded by Peter Cutts (Chicago: GIA Publications, 2005), 65.

[182] Barker, 121.

[183] Jacob to McKie, 5 February 1953 and McKie to Jacob, 6 February 1953 (*Lwa Library, McKie Papers*).

could claim a strong historic precedent. It is very similar to the arrangement that had been performed at the state thanksgiving service for the victories of the navy held in St Paul's Cathedral in 1797.[184] In this the first stanza was 'Play'd by the Organ', whereas the second was 'Play'd by the Milaray [sic] band'.

Regarding the ceremonial it is intriguing that a coronation is the only royal occasion at which the National Anthem is sung as a processional. At all other events, such as jubilees or weddings, it is performed with all the people standing in their places. One curious, singular exception was the service for the Golden Wedding Anniversary of the Queen and Prince Philip in Westminster Abbey in 1997, when two verses of the National Anthem were sung as the royal couple and the clerics left the Abbey. The fact that at the coronation the monarch with his/her entourage is the only one to move during the Anthem, makes it a great deal more purposeful: this visually points out that the congregation is singing the text for that one person, clad in ceremonial robes and bearing the royal insignia.[185] With everybody simply standing *in situ* this effect is lost and is only partly caught by modern television broadcasts showing the monarch in close-up, being the only person not to sing.

After the National Anthem came, as at the previous coronation, Elgar's *Pomp and Circumstance* March no. 1.[186] The performance, however, was slightly marred: first there was an unusually big gap between the two pieces and then, at the beginning of the Elgar, the orchestra was not together. As Bernard Baboulene, one of the choral singers, put it:[187]

For the first few bars of what thereafter settled down as Elgar's famous march, some of the orchestra evidently had the wrong music before them.

Indeed, in a printed list of music the piece scheduled for this place was Bax's new *Coronation March*, to be followed by Elgar's fourth *Pomp and Circumstance* March and only then the first one.[188] This list was obviously intended for the performers at the service as it includes also instructions for when to shout during the various acclamations. McKie reports that the Earl

---

[184] See *A Complete & exact delineation of the Ceremony from S.ᵗ James's to S.ᵗ Pauls; on Tuesday the 19.ᵗʰ Dec.ʳ 1797* [...] *to which is added, the form of the Church Service with part of the Vocal Music sung at that Celebrity* [...] ([London, Edinburgh: Printed for Corri, Dussek, & Co., [1798]), 19.

[185] At modern-day state banquets the National Anthem accompanies the entrance of the monarch with the guests; however, it is then merely performed by the orchestra, but not sung.

[186] For the 1937 performance see Richards, 115.

[187] 'Coronation Reprise', *WAC* 2, no. 9 (Summer 1993), 19–21, here 21.

[188] *Lwa WAM 63361B*: Printed list of music, 1953 coronation.

Marshal after his final rehearsal found the texture of Bax's march 'rather thin' and asked to have the first Elgar march instead.[189] It is possible that some of the performers still followed the printed programme and were ready for the Bax, while others knew about the last-minute change and had the Elgar on their music stands. Moreover, there was one other fact that may have contributed to the unsmooth transition: McKie reports that after the National Anthem he handed over the conductor's baton to Sir Adrian Boult.[190]

Musical arguments aside, the choice of Elgar's march, with its slow middle section known to the text of 'Land of Hope and Glory' certainly one of the most patriotic pieces of British music, perfectly illustrated the general mood at the time. It underlined the hopes for an era of achievements and the expectations of renewed grandeur. Such a spirit had been present right from the beginning of the queen's reign, when Prime Minister Winston Churchill famously invoked a 'New Elizabethan Age' in his radio broadcast on the occasion of the late king's departing.[191] In his 1952 Presidential Address to the English Association, A.L. Rowse also discussed this idea; he referred explicitly to music and observed:[192]

English music in the twentieth century – the age of Elgar and Delius, Vaughan Williams and Walton and Benjamin Britten – is more distinguished than at any time since the death of Purcell, or perhaps since the Elizabethans themselves.

Elgar's march was but one of several such pieces played before and after the service. Whereas in 1937 it was still observed that the music accompanying the 'arrival of Royal guests and representatives of foreign Powers' was of a 'cosmopolitan character', including pieces by Saint-Saëns and Moussorgsky, for 1953 McKie reported that he and his committee 'decided that the programme [before and after the service] should be all English'.[193] As Strong summarized, the selection in 1953 created 'a national musical mythology which entwines the crown with nostalgia and pride in an heroic past, with pride in the splendour of an imperial present'.[194] The new queen herself explained that she was sure her coronation was 'not the symbol of a power and a splendour that are gone, but a declaration of our hopes for the

---

[189] McKie Account, p. 22.   [190] Ibid.

[191] Chris Wrigley, *Winston Churchill: a Biographical Companion* (Santa Barbara: ABC-CLIO, 2002), 173f. See also Wendy Webster, *Englishness and Empire 1939–1965* (Oxford University Press, 2005), 93 and 98.

[192] A.L. Rowse, 'A New Elizabethan Age?', *The English Association Presidential Address* (1952), 13.

[193] 'Music in the Abbey', *The Times*, 13 May 1937; McKie Account p. 12.   [194] Strong, 468.

future'.[195] Indeed, all this became very apparent in the lavish programme of earlier and especially also contemporary British music at her coronation.

A changing 'character'

During the three and a half centuries considered in this study, the music at coronations was subject to several changes. The anthems grew in length and form, following the general development of music.[196] At the same time, however, the liturgical pieces did not follow that development in such a straightforward way; in fact, up to the twentieth century they were further and further reduced, with the Litany and the Creed often only read. With generally little information on the remaining pieces, these appear to have been unspectacular, simple settings. It was not before the twentieth century that the emphasis on the liturgical aspect of the service increased. From 1902 onwards, the liturgical pieces became more prominent, if not more elaborate, and at the same time the dominance of the anthems in terms of length and elaboration decreased. By 1937, this had led to a situation in which Vaughan Williams's Te Deum was the most elaborate new composition at the coronation, and the same was the case with Walton's Te Deum in 1953. The increased emphasis on the liturgical pieces may illustrate an important shift in the perception of the ceremony as a whole, a heightened awareness of the religious aspect following the so-called Catholic Revival in the Anglican Church.[197] In the wake of the Oxford Movement, High Church aspects were strengthened on a broader scale and it has been observed that there had been a 'reinvention of church music' during Queen Victoria's reign.[198] Since the Reformation, and especially since the later seventeenth century, the coronation had turned more and more into a spectacle, losing in spiritual significance. The newly prominent liturgical music in the twentieth century drew attention to the fact that this was a devotional church service. Although as the century proceeded the coronation was turned ever more into a mere ceremonial occasion, there was at the

[195] Elizabeth II, 'Her Majesty's Coronation-Day Broadcast', in *Elizabeth Crowned Queen. The Pictorial Record of the Coronation* (first publ. Odhams Press [1953], repr. London: Bounty Books, 2006), 7–8, here 8.

[196] For the role of festival concerts in the development of 'a ceremonial religious idiom' in the late seventeenth and early eighteenth century see Shapiro, 221f.

[197] See Strong, 469. For a detailed study of these issues see Nigel Yates, *Anglican Ritualism in Victorian Britain 1830–1910* (Oxford University Press, 1999).

[198] John Wolffe, '"Praise to the Holiest in the Height": Hymns and Church Music', in John Wolffe (ed.), *Religion in Victorian Britain*, Volume V: *Culture and Empire* (Manchester University Press, 1997), 59–99, here 83–93.

same time a growing awareness of the actual meaning of the ceremonies – perhaps as a consequence of the new scholarly interest in the coronations.[199]

Bridge's programmatic plan for the 1902 coronation illustrates how the music could be employed to stress both continuity and national identity. Bodley enthusiastically described this coronation as 'the consecration of the imperial idea', pointing out that at the postponed coronation the absence of 'dignified envoys' of other European states highlighted the 'consecration of a great Empire'.[200] Similarly, John Plunkett observed that following Queen Victoria's creation as Empress of India in 1876 'there was an imperial reinvention of the monarchy'.[201] However, despite the fact that the other 'possessions' were distinctly mentioned in the coronation oath, with their representatives being present at the service, the overall limitations of the coronation in terms of imperial representation were soon acknowledged. In 1911, on the occasion of the 'Festival of Empire' just before the coronation of George V and Queen Mary, the commentator of *The Times* stated that

the Coronation itself, albeit the most ancient and hallowed function of our race and State, is all too narrow in its associations, and too circumscribed by the inexorable conditions of time and space, to represent in all their manifold impressiveness the ever-growing complexity in unity, and the ever-quickening self-consciousness of an Empire on which the sun never sets.[202]

The Empire was to take a more prominent role at the next coronation and George VI himself declared: 'I felt this morning that the whole Empire was in very truth gathered within the walls of Westminster Abbey.'[203] Richards observed that at this coronation 'the emphasis on Empire was to be found everywhere'.[204] However, it was notably not found in the music of the service; throughout the twentieth century the music emphasized the particular Britishness, indeed Englishness of the monarchy – if anything, this aspect grew stronger with the incorporation of 'traditional' tunes and a congregational hymn. In 1953 the commentator of the *Musical Times* observed that during the processions before the service Butterworth's 'Banks of Green Willow' 'brought in the air of folksongs and the countryside'; he furthermore pointed out that in the Homage Fanfare 'the old Scottish psalm tune "Montrose" constituted a national element'.[205] The

---

[199] For a more detailed discussion of this idea see Strong, 469–72.   [200] Bodley, 201 and 238.

[201] Plunkett, 10.   [202] Quoted in Richards, 186.

[203] Quoted in David Cannadine, 'Splendor out of Court: Royal Spectacle and Pageantry in Modern Britain, *c.* 1820–1977', in Sean Wilentz (ed.), *Rites of Power: Symbolism, Ritual, and Politics since the Middle Ages* (Philadelphia: University of Pennsylvania Press, 1985), 206–43, here 228.

[204] Richards, 111.   [205] 'Music for the Coronation', 305.

same would apply to the music during the formation of the Recess procession, when the organist extemporized on hymns such as 'Jerusalem'.

The untainted stressing of Britishness in the coronation music evoked the impression of an undisputed Empire under 'British' supremacy right up to 1953.[206] In this sense A.N. Wilson described this coronation sharply as 'a consoling piece of theatre, designed to disguise from themselves the fact that the British had [...] lost an empire and failed to find a role'.[207] At the same time, this coronation marked the high point of a long development and it has been summarized that

Its blend of ceremonial, traditionalism, religion, and music [...] was the apogee in more than a century's refinement of the British monarchy's talent for public display [...] It was the last great moment when the Church of England, patriotism, and Britishness came together [...][208]

It is certainly the accumulation of rousing, patriotic music that enhances such a perception of the ceremony in the modern commentator. Referring to the 1902 and 1911 coronations, Cannadine has pointed out that it was the upsurge in musical quality, following the English Musical Renaissance, that 'made it possible for the great royal occasions to be presented [...] as festivals of native talent'.[209] At least some saw the 1953 coronation not merely as a matter of 'native' British talent, but in fact of 'imperial' talent: McKie, himself Australian, in a newspaper article drew attention to the fact that

the Homage anthem, "O Lord our Governor," by Dr. Healey Willan, of Toronto, was the first example of Coronation music ever included from an Empire composer.[210]

This statement was, however, soon corrected and it was pointed out that 'though established in Canada for 40 years, Dr. Willan is a Londoner by birth', emphasizing once more that the coronation music was 'all British, and all the composers except Handel (who became a British subject) are English-born'.[211]

The music at modern-day, twenty-first century, royal occasions such as weddings or jubilees has so far been predominantly classical, or at least 'classical' in style. Whether these trends will continue in future coronations

---

[206] Cf. Williamson, 245. [207] A.N. Wilson, 528.

[208] Brian Harrison, *Seeking a Role: The United Kingdom, 1951–1970* (Oxford University Press, 2009), 181.

[209] Cannadine, 'Splendor out of Court', 218. For this see also Strong, 467.

[210] *DT*, 18 March 1953, 7. Originally, McKie had the idea also to include Australian composers. See Vaughan Williams to McKie, 19 November 1952 (*Lwa Library, McKie Papers*).

[211] *DT*, 18 April 1953, 8.

it is impossible to say; the many social and cultural changes in Britain since 1953 may lead to radical departures.[212] These changes could be even bigger than those observed at the beginning of the seventeenth and twentieth centuries. On the occasion of the 1953 coronation, Evan Senior, the editor of *Music and Musicians*, proclaimed that

Music is the ultimate in human expression of emotion. Colours fade, memory grows dim, but the great works of music, written for previous coronations by our masters of the art, remain for all to hear and rejoice in.[213]

This seems to imply that coronation music automatically enters the canon. As the previous chapters have shown, however, there is a fair amount of coronation music that has fallen into oblivion. And while a piece such as Attwood's 'I was glad' had a very secure place in the nineteenth-century repertoire, it was completely forgotten in the twentieth century. Although the above comment is appropriate in so far as the music, in contrast to most of the rest of the ceremony, can be reproduced relatively easily, ultimately music shares the same destiny as the remainder of the great event. Only if the music is known, remembered, and performed will it indeed 'remain for all to hear and rejoice in'. It is to be hoped that this study contributes at least something to this remembering and has answered Gerald Hayes' appeal from coronation year 1953:[214]

'The Service of Music to the Coronations of our Sovereigns is worthy of a complete record.'

---

[212] See Colin Buchanan, 'The Next Coronation', in Paul Bradshaw (ed.), *Coronations. Past, Present and Future*, 34–44.

[213] Evan Senior, [Editor's Preface], *Music and Musicians*. Coronation Number (June 1953), 5.

[214] Hayes, 12.

Appendix A: Full texts of anthems discussed in the text

1) Charles II

'Zadok the Priest' (Baker, 813)

Sadoc the Priest, and Nathan the Prophet anointed Solomon King, and all the People rejoyced, and said, God save the King.

2) James II

a) 'Zadok the Priest'

Ob Tanner MS 31, fo. 103	Sandford, 91	Text as set by H. Lawes
Zadock the Priest, and Nathan the Prophet, Anointed Solomon KING, and all the People rejoyced, and said God save the King ^for ever.	Zadock *the* Priest, *and* Nathan *the* Prophet, *Anointed* Solomon KING, *and all the* People *rejoyced, and said,* God Save the KING; Long Live the KING; May the KING Live for ever.	Zadok the priest, and nathan the prophet anointed Solomon King, and joyfully approaching they cried, God Save the King; for ever and ever, God save the King. Hallelujah!

b) 'God spake sometime [sic] in visions' (*Ob MS Tanner 31*, fo. 111) Psalm 89.

20. GOD spake sometime in Visions unto his Saints, and said: I have laid help upon one that is Mighty.
21. I have found David my Servant: With my Holy Oyl have I Anointed him.
22. My hand shall hold him fast: And my Arm shall strengthen him.
23. The enemy shall not be able to do him Violence: The Son of VVickedness [*sic*] shall not hurt him.
24. I will smite down his Foes before his Face: And plague them that hate him.
25. ~~My truth~~ [written above: But my Faithfulness] also, & my Mercy shall be wth him: & in my Name shall his Horn be exalted.
26. I will set his Dominion also in ye Sea: and his right Hand in ye Flouds. (~~or Rivers~~)

27. He shall ~~call~~ [written above: cry unto] me, Thou art my Father: my God, & the Rock of my Salvation.
28. And I will make him my First-born: Higher than the Kings of the Earth.
29. My Mercy will I keep for him for evermore: And my Covenant shall stand fast with him.
30. His seed also will I make to endure for ever: And his Throne as the Days of Heaven.
    AMEN. ALLELUJAH.

3) William and Mary

a) 'I was glad'

1685 (Sandford, 82)	1689 (*Llp 1077*, p. 1)
Psalm 122, Vers I. I was glad when they said unto Me, We will go into the House of the Lord.	I was glad when they said unto me, Let us go into the House of the Lord. Our feet shall stand within thy Gates, O Jerusalem.
Vers 4. For thither the Tribes go up, even the Tribes of the Lord: To testifie unto Israel, to give Thanks unto the Name of the Lord.	For thither the Tribes go up, even the Tribes of the Lord, unto the Testimony of Israel, to give thanks unto the name of the Lord.
Vers 5. For there is the Seat of Judgement: Even the Throne of the House of David.	For there are set thrones of Judgment, even the Throne of the House of David,
Vers 6. O Pray for the Peace of Jerusalem: They shall prosper that love thee.	O pray for the peace of Jerusalem; They shall prosper that love Thee.
Vers 7. Peace be within thy Walls. And Plenteousness within thy Palaces.	Peace be within thy walls, and Prosperitie within thy Palaces.
Glory be to the Father, &c.	Glory be to the Father &c.
As it was in the beginning, &c.	As it was in the beginning &c.

b) 'Blessed art thou O land' (*Llp MS 1077*, p. 4)

Blessed art thou O Land, when thy King is the son of Nobles: And thy Princes eat in due Season. Eccl. 10. v. 17

Blessed is the People O Lord, that can rejoyce in thee: They shall walk in the light of thy Countenance. Ps. 89. v. 16

Blessed is the Nation whose God is the Lord Jehovah: And blessed are ye Folk whom he hath chosen to him to be his Inheritance. Ps. 33. v. 12.

Happy are the People that are in such a Case: yea blessed are the People, who have the Lord for their God. Alleluiah. Ps. 144. v. 15.

c) 'Zadok the Priest' (*Llp MS 1077*, p. 17f.)

Zadock the Priest and Nathan the Prophet anointed Solomon King; and they blew the Trumpet, and Piped with Pipes, and rejoyced wth great Joy, so that the Earth rent with the sound of them. And they said God save King Solomon, long live the King. May the King live for Ever. Amen.

d) 'Praise the Lord, O Jerusalem' (*Llp MS 1077*, p. 30)

Ps. 147. v. 12 'Praise the Lord O Jerusalem, Praise thy God O Sion'.
Esa. 49. v. 23 'For kings shall be thy nursing fathers, and queens thy nursing mothers.'
Ps. 48. v. 7 'As we have heard, So we have seen, in the City of Our God; God upholdeth the same for ever.'
Ps. 21. v. 13 'Be Thou Exalted Lord in thine own Strength, so will we Sing and praise thy Power.'
Hallelujah

4) Queen Anne, 1702

a) 'Behold, O God, our Defender'

1685 (Sandford, 92)	1689 (*Llp MS 1077*, p. 21)	1702 (*Llp MS 1078*, p. 24)
Ps. 84. 9. Behold, O Lord, Our Defender, and look upon the Face of Thine Anointed.	Ps. 84. 9. Behold, O God, Our Defender: and look upon the face of Thine Anointed.	Ps. 84 v 9. Behold O God Our Defender and look upon the Face of Thine Anointed.
Vers. 12. The Lord God is a Light and Defence, the Lord will give Grace and Glory, and no Good Thing will He with-hold from them that live a Godly Life.	Ps. 18, 51. Great Prosperity givest thou unto thy King: & wilt show loving kindness to thine Anointed for evermore.	Ps. 18. v. 51 Great Prosperity givest thou unto thy Queen, and wilt shew loving kind-nesse to thine Anointed for evermore.
Vers. 13. O Lord of Hosts, Blessed is the Man who putteth his Trust in Thee.	I. Sam. ii. 10. The Adversaries of the Lord shall be broken to Pieces; out of Heaven shall he thunder upon them: But He shall	Allelujah.

give strength unto his
King, and exalt the
Horn of his Anointed.
Amen.'

---

b) 'The Lord God is a Sun and a Shield'

1689 (*Lbl MS 1077*, p. 43)		1702 (*Lbl MS 1078*, p. 46)	
The Lord God is a Sun, and a Shield, The Lord will give Grace & Glory; No good Thing will he withhold from them that walk uprightly. O Lord of Hosts, Blessed is the Man that trust-eth in Thee.	Chorus Ps. 84. v. 11.	The Lord God is a Sun and a Sheild [*sic*] The Lord will give Grace and Glory	Chorus Ps. 84. 11.
Now know I that the Lord Saveth his Anointed, He will hear them from his Holy Heaven, He will hear them and help them with the Saving Strength of his Right hand.	Vers Ps. 20. v. 6.	Now know I that the Lord saveth his Anointed: He will hear her from his holy Heaven, he will hear her & help her with the Saving strength of his Right Hand.	Ps. 20. v. 6.
For the King & Queen trust in the Lord, through the Mercy of the most high they shall not be moved, His hand shall find out all their Enemies.	Ps. 21. v. 7	For the Queen trusteth in the Lord through the mercy of the most High she shall not be moved her Hand shall find out all her Enemys.	Ps. 21. v.7.
Some trust in Chariots & some in Horses, but We will remember the Name of the Lord our God.	Partes Ps. 20. v. 7, 8, 9.		Ps. 20. v. 9.

They are brought down
and fallen, but we are
risen and stand
upright.

His Salvation is nigh them that fear him, That Glory may dwell in Our Land.		His Salvation is nigh them that fear him. That Glory may dwell in our Land.	
Blessed be the Lord God, the God of Israel, who only doth Wondrous Things. And blessed be His Glorious Name for Ever: And let the whole Earth be filled with his Glory, Amen and Amen Hallelujah.	Chorus Ps. 72. v. 18 and 19.	Blessed be the Lord God the God of Israel Who only doth wondrous things. And blessed be his Glorious Name for ever: And let the whole Earth be filled with his Glory. *Amen and Amen. Hallelujah.*	Chorus Ps. 72. v. 18 and 19.

5) George II, 1727

a) 'The King shall rejoice'

1685 (Sandford, 94)	Text as in the Chapel Royal Cheque Book	Text as set by Handel
Psalm 22 [recte 21] Vers. 1. *The* KING *shall rejoyce in Thy strength, O* LORD, *exceeding glad shall* He *be of Thy* Salvation.	The King shall rejoice in thy Strength, O Lord, exceeding glad shall he be of thy Salvation;	Ps. 21, verse1: The King shall rejoice in thy strength, O Lord. Exceeding glad shall he be of thy salvation.
Vers. 2. *Thou hast given* Him *His Hearts desire*, and hast not denied Him *the* Request *of* His Lips.		verse 5: Glory and great worship has thou laid upon him.
Vers. 3. *For Thou hast prevented* Him *with the Blessings of Goodness, and hast set a* CROWN *of Pure Gold upon His* Head.	Thou hast prevented him with the blessings of Goodness, and hast Set a Crown of pure Gold upon his Head.	verse 3: Thou hast prevented him with the blessings of goodness and hast set a crown of pure gold upon his head.
ALLELUIA.	Alleluiah, Ps. 21, v.1.3.	Alleluia.

b) 'My heart is inditing'

Text as in 1685 (Sandford, 102)	Text as in the Chapel Royal Cheque Book and as set by Handel
Psalm 45. Vers. 1. *My heart is Inditing of a good Matter; I speak of the Things which I have made unto the* King.	[Ps. 45, verse 1] My heart is inditing of a good matter, I speak of the things which I have made unto the King;
	[v. 10] ~~Kings Daughters were among thy~~ ~~honourable Women;~~
Vers. 10. *At His Right Hand shall stand the* Queen,	upon thy right hand did stand the Queen in a [Handel: no 'a'] Vesture of Gold;
	[v. 12] and the King shall have Pleasure in thy beauty.
Vers. 14. *all Glorious within, Her Clothing is of wrought Gold.*	
Vers. 15. She *shall be brought unto the* King *in Rayment of Needlework; the Virgins that follow Her shall bear Her Company.*	
Vers. 16. *With Joy and Gladness shall they be brought, and shall enter into the* Kings [*sic*] *Palace.*	
Vers. 11. *Hearken, O Daughter, and consider, incline Thine Ear, forget also Thine own People, and Thy Fathers House.*	
Vers. 17. *In stead of Thy Fathers, thou shalt have Children, whom Thou mayst make Princes in all Lands.*	
Psalm 147. Vers. 12. *Praise the* Lord, O *Jerusalem: Praise Thy* God, O Sion.	
Isaiah 49. Vers. 23. *For* Kings *shall be Thy Nursing* Fathers, *and Their* Queens *Thy Nursing* Mothers	[Isai 49.23] Kings shall be thy nursing Fathers, and Queens thy nursing Mothers.
AMEN. ALLELUIA.	

6) George IV, 1821

'I was glad' (*Llp Cod. Misc. 1083A*, p. 2)

I was glad when they said unto me, Let us go into the House of the Lord. ~~Our feet shall stand within thy Gates, O Jerusalem. For thither the Tribes go up,~~

~~even the Tribes of the Lord, unto the Testimony of Israel, to give thanks~~ ~~unto the name of the Lord~~. For there are set thrones of Judgment, even the Throne of the House of David [changed to: 'is ye seat of Judgment even ye seat of ye House of David.']. O pray for the peace of Jerusalem; They shall prosper that love Thee. Peace be within thy walls, and Prosperitie within thy Palaces. Glory be to the Father, and to the Son: and to the Holy Ghost; As it was in the beginning, is now, and ever shall be: world without end. Amen.

Appendix B: Transcriptions of documents

1) James II

a) *Ob MS Tanner 31*, fo. 31.

James R / James the Second by the Grace of God King of England Scotland France and Ireland Defender of the Faith &c To all to whom these Presents shall come Greeting. We having in Council committed the preparing of the Coronation office to the care of the most Reverend Father in God William Lord Archbishop of Canterbury, With expresse command to leave out the Communion Service, and to abridge (as much as conveniently might be) the extreme length of the rest preserving notwithstanding the forme of the Coronation Oath and other the most essentiall things unaltered & exactly the same as they stood in the Offices of the Coronations of King Charles the first and King Charles the second of blessed memory, and the said Archbishop having with the privity and advice of all the Bishops then in London prepared an Office according to those Directions; We having seen the said Office do hereby approve thereof authorising and commanding the said Archbishop to use the same in the Coronation both of Us and of Our Royall Consort the Queen. Given at Our Court at Whitehall the 21th day of Aprill 1685 [. . .]

b) *Ob MS Tanner 31*, fo. 59.

My Lord: / If I had had time to have waited on your Grace I would have done it. to have acquainted you that the King had signed the warrant for the Publishing the Office. without any alteration. but that his Maj: with his owne hand Blotted out one word over against which I have made a Marke in the Margent. that your Grace May take Notice of it. I am with greate respect. / Your Grace's / Most faithful and most / humble Servant. / Sunderland / Whitehall / May the 2^{d}:

c) *Lcm MS 7281*, no. 2: Sir Frederick Bridge to C. H. H. Parry, 'Littlington Tower, The Cloisters, Westminster Abbey. / Oct 4 [1901]'.

Dear Parry. / The King wishes you to write something for the Coronation service, & I am desired to propose this to you [in] His Majesty's name – You know already how much I hope you will write an anthem 'I was glad'. It will be about[?] the best opportunity & at present we do not know if another anthem (except 'Zadock the Priest') will be wanted[?]– I hope therefore you will be so good as to do this. The words I must furnish you with as soon as they send me the order of service, but I think if you prefer certain verses to others, it can be managed – if you let me know in time. / Yours ever / Frederick Bridge / I suppose you will write to Sir F Knollys [Private Secretary to the King] to say Yes? He wrote to me –

d) *Lbl MS Add. 39864*, fo. 49: Lists of the choir of Westminster Abbey and of the Chapel Royal at the 'Coronation of Ja^s II. April 23. 1685.'

- 'Choir of Westminster Abbey / Boys. Wm Christian, Tho. Price, Geo. Rogers, Wm Morley, John Bates, John Walker, John Howell, W.m Williams / Men. Rev. Chas Green, Rev. Rich. Cherington, Josias Boucher*, Rob. Tanner, Moses Snow, Tho. Jennings, Cha. Taylor, Morgan Harris*, Thos Richardson*, Tho. Blagrave*, Tho. Finell, Edw. Braddock*, Rev. John Charole*, Rev. Tho. Linacre, Rev. John Tynchare alias Littleton, Rev. Stephen Crespion*' [=> altogether 8 boys and 16 Gentlemen]
- 'Choir of the Chapel Royal / Boys Charles Allison, Jeremiah Clark, Thos Richardson, Ja.^{s} Townsend, Simon Corbet, Wm Smith, Jacob Wood, Geo. Rogers, Richd Henmun [*sic*], Chas Husbands, Vaughan Richardson, Wm Norris. / Altos . Michael Wise, / (by Edw. Morton). Tho. Heywood, John Abel, Josias Boucher, Wm Turner, Thomas Richardson, John Goodgroome, Nathaniel Watkins. / Tenors. Morgan Harris, Alphons Marsh, Henry Frost, Rev. Wm Powell, Ja.^{s} Cobb, Eds. Braddock, Rev. Henry Smith, Rev. John Sayer. / Basses. Rich. Hart, Rev. Sam. Bentham, Rev. Leonhard Woodson, Revd John Gostling, Henry Purcell, Nathaniel Vestment, Rev. John Charole, Rev. Andrew Trebeck, Geo. Bettenham, Rev. Ja.^{s} Hart, Rev. Blaze White. Rev. Geo. Yardley, Thos Blagrave (Clerk of the Cheque) [=> altogether 12 boys, 8 altos, 8 tenors, 13 basses; those singing in both choirs are marked with a *, a superscript 'x' in the original.]
- at the bottom of the page: 'Dr Nich. Staggins / Master of the King's Musick | Dr John Blow / M.^{r} of the Children | Dr W.m Child // Rev. Stephen Crespion / Confessor to the Household | Rev. Dr Wm Holden / Sub Dean.
    - 'These are the same names and in the same order as given in Sandford (69f.), who furthermore numbers them. Sandford calls the altos

'Counter-Tenors' and additionally states that Thomas Heywood was 'supplyed by Dr. Uvedal', John Abel by 'Aug. Benford', and Henry Smith by 'Geo. Hart'. Furthermore, in Sandford, Staggins, Blow, and Child are listed among the basses, and he states that John Blow was 'suppl. by *Fra*. [Francis] *Forcer*.'

- In *Lbl MS Harl. 6815*, Henry Purcell and William Child are listed, but no voice is allocated. Child is simply described as 'Eldest Gent', and Blow is titled 'master of yᵉ children', but the same title is given to Edward Braddok, a tenor. This list furthermore states that 'John Sharrol ['Charole' above?]' was 'a french man' and that 'D.ʳ Uvedal' was 'a Stranger', which might simply refer to his status as a deputy.

2) George II

a) *Lna PC 1/15/6*: Preparations for the Coronation, part I. Letter from Archbishop Wake to the Privy Council, dated: 'Tunbridge Wells, Augt: 20ᵗʰ 1727.'

My Lords / I have just now had the Honour to Receive the Order of the Lords of the Committe appointed to consider of their Maᵗⁱᵉˢ Coronation, and beg leave by your Lordship to Return the best and most satisfactory Answer I can to it [. . .] Before I left Lambeth I got into my hands the Original Book of Abp Sancroft, all written by Himselfe, by wᶜʰ He Crown'd Kg James & Queen Mary. I found his Grace had taken very great Care & Pains to examine the antient forms of this Office, & to draw up That wᶜʰ He made use of upon Them. But the Kings Religion obliged Him to omit the whole Communion service [. . .] My immediate predecessor Archbp Tenison, who Crown'd both Q. Anne and his late Maᵗⁱᵉ King George, took great pains to settle this Office in a better method than had ever been done before: And indeed He has succeeded so well in it, that in my Opinion a better Form cannot be framed for the Coronation of his Majestie. But in that there is nothing of the Queens Coronation: That part of the Office therefore may with a very little change of some expressions be taken out of Abp Sancrofts Form: So that taking one of these for the King, the Other for the Queen, the whole may be setled in one Hours time.

b) *Llp Cod. Misc. 1079A*: order of service for the coronation of George II and Queen Caroline, 1727, handwritten by Archbishop Wake, title page.

This book is now made exactly agreeable to that of King Georges Coronation. Wᵗ is here scored with Red lines being wanting in that book, other differences are noted by these letters K.G. The title of that book is / A formulary of that part

of the solemnity wch is performd in the Church at the Coronation of his Mat^{ie}
Kg George at Westm^r Oct^r: 20: 1714. / The Occasion of the Sense & reason in
this book was that wh[en] it was presented to the Committee of Council no
book could be got of the late Kings Coronation: So they orderd this form to be
accommodated to that of Kg James the 2d. Afterwards, by his Maties favour, I
obtain'd his $^+$ Copy of that Coronation office: W^{ch} being found to agree exactly
wth w^t was done at the Coronation of Q. Anne, the Lords order'd this Book to be
made agreeable thereunto, only the necessary Alterations & Additions
excepted, for the Coronation of the Queen. So that the plural number here,
must be Reduced to the Singular in the Book of King George.

    => '+ marked in y^e following book KG' / [in the margin:] '♯ unlesse when
KG is mark'd to shew the Contrary. The – '

c) *Lna PC 2/90*: Minutes of the Privy Council, dated 18 September, p. 88.

His Grace the Arch Bishop of Canterbury informing the Committee that He
had lately obtained from His Majestys Closet a Book containing the Form of
the Service performed in the Abby at His late Majestys Coronation – Their
Lordships reconsidered the Form they had agreed upon for their Majestys
Coronation and Directed that the same should be made agreable thereto,
excepting only such Alterations and Amendments as were necessary to be
made on the Occasion of the Coronation of a Queen Consort.

d) *Lna LC 5/18*: Material relating to the coronation of George II and Queen
Caroline, 1727, p. 16.

These are to pray and require you to pay, or Cause to be paid to
M:r Christopher Smith for the Fifty Seven Supernumerary Performers of
Musick at His Majesty's Coronation each the sum of Three pounds three
Shillings, and for the use of the Instrum.ts and other expenses the sum of
Fifteen Pounds Fifteen Shillings as appears by the Annext Bill Certified by
Mr Handal [sic]. [. . .] 27.th Day of Feb:ry 1727/8 [. . .]

3) George III

a) *Llp MS 1130* (Court Papers), 2 vols, vol. I: numbers in bold = item
numbers in MS

38 'Abp Secker to Dr Boyce'

To Dr Boyce in Quality Court Chancery Lane Aug. 14. 1761.

In the Coronation Service, the first Anthem must not be omitted: for it will enliven the Procession, and the Service will not be the longer for it. The fuller it is, and the more exactly it takes up the Time of the Kings walking through the Church, the better.

His Majesty hath signified his Pleasure, that the 4th Anthem, Zadok the Priest &c should be performed as it was set for the last Coronation: and that the other Anthems should be as short, & have as little Repetition in them, as conveniently may be.

In the 6th Anthem, the Words, For Kings shall be thy nursing Fathers, & Queens thy nursing Mothers, were peculiarly proper at the Revolution, when they were first used, because the King & Queen were both Sovereigns, & both were crowned together.

They were also proper in a lower Degree at Queen Annes Coronation. But they were not so suitable to the Coronation of Geo. I. when there was no Queen, or even of Geo. 2. when there was only a Queen Consort, whose Coronation was not to begin, till the Kings was over: and in whose Coronation these Words come very fitly; and for that reason, amongst others, are better omitted before. It hath therefore been proposed, that the following Words should be used instead of them: Behold, a King shall reign in Righteousness: & Princes shall rule in Judgment. Is. XXXII.1. And his Majesty hath approved this Alteration.

It seems requisite, that the 6th Anthem, since it follows immediately the Principal Act of the Day, setting on the Crown, should be accompanied with the other Instruments, as well as the Organ. And it needs not be much if at all the longer for that.

These things, it is hoped, will not increase Dr Boyces Difficulties. As he hath represented, that the proposed Alterations in the Wedding Anthem would, they are withdrawn & laid aside by / His sincere Friend / Lambeth, Aug. 14. 1761.

40 [William Boyce to Archbishop Secker, 17 Aug. 1761]

My very good Lord / I have received the honour of your Commands, in relation to Zadock the sixth Anthem, and the length of the others, which orders, I will most punctually obey. Those anthems with the Organ, shall be as short as possible, and those with the other Instruments as much so, as is consistent with the Grandeur of the Solemnity; but were the words of these last to be run through without some repetition, the performances would appear rather mean than grand. When I have finished the Anthems, I will inform your Grace of the exact time each of them will require in the performance. Your Lordship has greatly favoured me, by with-drawing the proposed alterations for the Wedding Anthem.

I most humbly propose it to your Grace to give directions to the Dean & Chapter of Westminster, that a proper Space may be reserved in the Isles, for the Choir to perform the First anthem, otherwise, I am apprehensive, that the Scaffolding to be errected within the Abbey, will be a great hindrance to the performers appointed for this particular occasion.

I am with the most profound respect your Grace's most dutiful / humble Servant / William Boyce / Monday Aug.ˢᵗ 17.ᵗʰ 1761.

[on next page] Zadock the Priest, exactly as performed at the last Coronation. / Zadock the Priest, and Nathan the Prophet, anointed Solomon King: And all the people rejoyced, and said; God save the King: Long live the King: May the King live for ever. Amen. Hallelujah.

51 'Dʳ Edward Bentham to Abp' / 'Ch. Ch. Oxford, July 20 1761'

My Lord, I do not recollect any part of ABp Wake's Mss. to bear relation to the Office of Coronation: Neither have I yet met with any printed Copy of that Office excepting that which was used in 1727.

65 'Dr. Boyce to Abp, Sept. 21 1761'

Dʳ Boyce presents his most humble Duty to his Grace, and shall be glad to know his Pleasure concerning the Responses to the Ten Commandments, as likewise the Response after naming the Gospel, viz: Glory be to God on high. If his Grace would have these Responses sung by the Choir, accompanied by the Organ? / Monday, Sep.ʳ 21.ˢᵗ 1761 –

66 [W. Boyce about the Coronation Anthems, undated]

All the Anthems to be performed, as directed / The Second – Fourth – Eigth & Ninth – to be set for Voices & Instruments. All the other Anthems with the Te Deum, to be sung with Voices alone accompanied with the Organ. / The four Anthems for the Voices & Instruments will be considerably the longest: Those for Voice alone will be very short. / Note, The Anthem Zadock the Priest cannot be more properly set than it has already been by M.ʳ Handel. [originally he wanted to write just 'Handel', than he changed it into 'Mr.'] / Note. At the Sacrament [. . .] the Archbishop reads, the Choir begins, and sings Holy, holy holy, &c.'

72 'Anthems. Orderd to be new set. / 36. Zadock the priest / 50. For Kings shall be / Brevity desired' / 'Anthem I. p. 2. & Anthem 8 p. 62 are from the new version'

79 Disposal of the 200 printed copies of the Coronation Office, 1761

'The Subdean of the King's Chapel' 6

'Dr Boyce'   2

81 'A very particular Account of the Coronation of King George 3.^{d} of the Handwriting of Archbishop Secker' [undated]

- [2:] The Anthem, Zadock the priest & p. 36 in the Office of Geo. 2 is neither taken at all exactly from the Place of the scripture named in the margin, nor printed as it was sung. In this last respect, the only one that I could, I have altered it.
- [3:] Instead of, For Kings shall be & p. 50, I substituted Behold a King & because the mention of Queens, though proper in that place at the Coronation of Q. Mary & Queen Anne, was not so afterwards: besides that the same verse is in the anthem p. 69.
- [4:] Dr Boyce told me, that he was orderd by the Committee of Council to set all the Anthems anew: that he could not set that, p. 36, Zadock the Priest & so well as Mr. Handel had done, & must therefore take other words, & proposed some from, Sam. XVI. 13 & other places. I desired him to keep both Handels words & musick. He pleaded the order, unless I would get an Exception made to it. On Examination I found there was no such order, but he had mistaken the Ld Chamberlains Directions. I mentioned the matter to the King: who directed, that Handels Anthem should be used, & that Dr Boyces should be short. See the Length of each in another paper.
- [13:] The petitions after each of the Commandments, & the Nicene Creed, were sung to the Organ.

b) *Lna LC 2/32*, 'Dean of Westminst:^{r} to L.d Chamberlain / rec.^{d} 13.th Septr 1761.'

The Bishop of Rochester, in his Conversation with the Lord Chamberlain in the Abby yesterday, gave no consent to any Alteration of the Altar, except on these two conditions, viz, that no part of the Altar should be taken down except what is above the Pediment, and that no part at all should be touched, till such time as the Bishop had received from the Lord Chamberlain a Letter signifying, that it was his Majesty's Pleasure, that the Alteration above-mentioned should be made. His Grace promised the Bishop to send him such a Letter; and this being not of that kind is therefore sent back again.

c) *Lna Work 21/1*, fo. 13, no. 30.

At the Council Chamber Whitehall the 17:th day of September 1761. / It is this day Ordered by their Lordships, that the Surveyor General of His Majestys Works, do cause such sufficient Room or Gallerys to be prepared in the place where the Organ stood over the Choir door in Westminster Abbey, for the Trumpets, Drums and Musick under Doctor Boyce, as the Earl Marshall shall direct; and that the remaining part of the Organ Loft be appropriated to the use of the Church of Westminster, in such manner as the Earl Marshall shall think proper.

d) *Lwa WAM 61782*: 'Lord. Chamb.^{r} to admit Dr Boyce & Musicians ['&c'?] Coron.^{n} 1761.' => to the Bishop of Rochester/ Dean of Westminster, 'Lord Chamberlain's Office, 14th Sept:^{r} 1761.'

My Lord, / It is The King's Pleasure that your Lordship do permit Doctor William Boyce Master of His Majesty's Musick, by his Workmen to take down the Organ which was used at His late Majesty's Funeral and now stands in King Henry the Seventh's Chapel in Westminster Abbey in order to be put in Order and afterwards to Place it in the Choir of [word missing, burnt: the said church?] be made Use of at His Majesty's Coronation. / I am, My Lord, Your Lordship's most obed^t hum[burnt] serv.^{t} Devon[shire, burnt]

e) *Lwa WAM 48097B.*

The Organ that was used at the Coronation / of his present Majesty, Consist's [*sic*] of the / following Stop's. / A whole Principal of Mettle part / in front, the other in the inside. / An Opendiapason of wood as low as / Cefaut or Gamut, Open; the other Stop'd. / A Stopdiapason of wood all through. / A Twelfth of Mettle Ditto / A Fifteenth of Mettle Ditto / A Bass Mixture of two Ranks Mettle / the treble was taken away. / A Stop't Flute of wood & Mettle all through / [. . .]

4) Queen Victoria

a) *Lca MS Ceremonials 94*: 'Coronation of Queen Victoria 1838', vol. 6:
numbers in brackets = item numbers in MS

(29) William Turle to the Earl Marshall [undated]: 'I beg very respectfully,
to prefer my claim to preside at the Instrument of which I am the
Organist. / On some former occasions, an Organ has been erected in
the Abbey for the express of the Coronation, and it may, sometimes,
have happened under such circumstances, that one of his Majesty's
Organists has occupied that Instrument.'

(30) George Smart to C. G. Young Esqu., May 7. 1838 => about taking
down the organ for the coronation and re-erect it after the ceremony,
and 'to erect the orchestra, commencing at the Screen at the entrance
of the Choir. this will give much more room for Visitors [. . .] I am to
call upon the Archbishop of Canterbury on Wednesday next, to make
the final arrangements for the Music; after this, I shall be enabled to
return the Proof you sent this Afternoon, with a Correct Account of
the Music to be performed.'

b) George Smart's annotations in his printed order of service, *Lwa Library*,
4.c.9.

- 'Her Majesty entered the Choir at 8 M. to 12.', remark about the first
anthem: 'By the Consent of the Archbishop of Canterbury the Anthem
was not to commence until Her Majesty entered the Choir, therefore I
commenced when the Queen ascended the steps into the Choir.'
- 2: 'I was glad': 'Attwood'
- 4: after the Recognition: Then the Trumpets sound.* => 'Immediately
after which Mess: Harper (Trumpet) and Albrecht (Trombone) came
down from Gall^y: to play in the orchestra – see page 30.' => '* The
Trumpets sounded by Signal given from W. Gwilt to me and from me
to them immediately after the Archbishop said the 1st time "Sirs, I here
present &c." probably they should not have sounded until after the 4th
presentation from the Archbishop.'
- 7: Litany: 'The Choir read the Responses by Signal for each from
W. Gwilt. until Page 16.'
- 18: Sanctus: 'Sir George Smart – Organist & Composer to Her Majesty's
Chapels Royal.'
- 23: after the naming of the Gospel: '"Glory be to Thee O Lord" By the Full
Band and Chorus.'

- 25: Sermon: 'By the Bishop of London, begann at 20 M [written on top of that: 19 M] to I.'
- 29: 'Come, Holy Ghost': 'Grand Chant in D / Organ and Choir only.' margin: 'After the Archbishop had read the 1.st line I played the Chant through before the Choir commenced.'
- 30: 'Zadok the Priest': 'Handel' => 'Mess. Harper & Albrecht played in this Anthem in the Orchestra and immediately after it they went up into the Trumpeter's Gallery and returned into the orchestra for "Te Deum" Page 44.'
- 39: Queen crowned: '25 M to 2_o'Clock.'
- 40: 'The Queen shall rejoice': 'Handel'
- 44: Te Deum: 'Dr Boyc.' => 'Mess Harper &' Albrecht, came from the Trumpet Gall:^{y} into the orchestra for this "Te Deum".' [had already left the gallery after the fanfares after the Crowning, p. 40]
- 45: Harper and Albrecht back to gallery after Te Deum
- 49: 'This is the Day': 'W. Knyvett Esq:^{er} / Composer to Her Majesty's Chapels Royal.' => 'N.B. This Anthem was performed during the Performance of the Homage, just before the Homage was concluded.'
- 67: 'FINIS' => '20 M to 4, when the Overture to the Occasional Oratorio, Ended. / 3 HH 48 M. From Her Majesty's entering and leaving the Choir, that is from the 1st to the last Note of the Music.'
- Notes by Smart on loose leaves:
  - 'Signals from Mr Gwilt' (=> handwritten list by G. Smart)
  - 'Page 4 N° I I give the Signal for the Trumpets to play 'God save the Queen' after I receive it from W. Gwilt.' [after the Recognition]
  - 'It is supposed the Homage will take about 40 Minutes – Before it is over Mr Gwilt will give Signal for Mr W. Knyvett's Anthem "This is the day"'

Appendix C: Synoptic table of music at British coronations, 1603–1838

One ? after a piece means that it is not certain if this piece was performed.
Three ??? after a piece indicate that the composer cannot be established.
One ? after a composer's name means that it is not certain that this was the composer of the piece.
For further details, and for details on the two Scottish coronations, see the respective chapters.

Ceremony	James I, Queen Anne, 1603	Charles I, 1626	Charles II, 1661	James II, Queen Mary, 1685	William III & Mary II, 1689	Anne, 1702	George I, 1714	George II, Queen Caroline, 1727	George III, Queen Charlotte, 1761	George IV, 1821	William IV, Queen Adelaide, 1831	Victoria, 1838
Procession from Westminster Hall to the Abbey	omitted?	'O Lord, grant the King a long life'?	'O Lord, grant the King a long life' Child	'O Lord, grant the King a long life' Child	'O Lord, grant the King a long life' Child?	'O Lord, grant the King a long life' Child?	'O Lord, grant the King a long life' Child?	'O Lord, grant the King a long life' Child?	'O Lord, grant the King a long life' Child?	'O Lord, grant the King a long life' Child	omitted	omitted
Entrance into the Abbey	'Behold, O Lord, our protector' ???	'I was glad' ???	'I was glad'? Child? / Child and T. Tomkins?	'I was glad' Blow/H. Purcell?	'I was glad' ??? (perhaps Blow/H. Purcell?)	'I was glad' Pigott	'I was glad' Pigott?	'I was glad', not sung by mistake (planned probably Pigott)	'I was glad' Boyce	Hallelujah-Chorus, Scene from Saul Handel; 'I was glad' Attwood	'I was glad' Attwood	'I was glad' Attwood 'God save the Queen'?
Recognition	'Let thy hand be strengthened' ???	Firmetur manus/ 'Strong is thy hand' ???	'Let thy hand be strengthened' Cooke?	'Let thy hand be strengthened' Blow	'Blessed art thou, O Land' ???	'The Queen shall rejoice' Turner	'The King shall rejoice' Turner?	'The King shall rejoice' Handel	'The King shall rejoice' Boyce	'Let thy hand be strengthened'? Attwood?	'omitted'	'God save the Queen'?
Litany	Litany, in Latin ???	Litany ???	Litany Tallis?	Litany Tallis?	Litany Tallis?	Litany Tallis?	Litany Tallis?	Litany read	Litany Tallis?	Litany read?	Litany read	Litany read
Beginning of the Communion Service					Nicene Creed ???	Nicene Creed ???	Nicene Creed ???	Nicene Creed, read?	Responses Boyce?; Nicene Creed???, 'sung to the organ'	Sanctus and Responses Jomelli; Nicene Creed, read	Sanctus and Responses Jomelli; Nicene Creed, read	Sanctus and Responses Smart; Nicene Creed, read?
Anointing	'Come, Holy Ghost' ??? 'Zadok the Priest' ???	'Come, Holy Ghost, eternal God' ??? 'Zadok the Priest' T. Tomkins?	'Come, Holy Ghost, eternal God' ??? 'Zadok the Priest' H. Lawes	'Come, Holy Ghost, our souls inspire' Turner (chant?) 'Zadok the Priest' H. Lawes	'Come, Holy Ghost' Turner? (chant?) 'Zadok the Priest' H. Lawes?	'Come, Holy Ghost' Turner? (chant?) 'Zadok the Priest?' H. Lawes?	'Come, Holy Ghost' Turner? (chant?) 'Zadok the Priest' H. Lawes?	'Come, Holy Ghost' (not sung by mistake; probably planned to be chanted) 'Zadok the Priest' Handel	'Come, Holy Ghost' Boyce 'Zadok the Priest' Handel	'Come Holy Holy Ghost', sung to 'Grand Chaunt' (Humfrey?) 'Zadok the Priest' Handel (arr. Cramer?)	'Come, Holy Ghost'; (sung to 'Grand Chant', Humfrey?) 'Zadok the Priest' Handel (arr.?)	'Come, Holy Ghost'; sung to 'Grand Chant' by Humfrey 'Zadok the Priest' Handel (arr.?)

	1	2	3	4	5	6	7	8	9	10	11	12
After the Investiture	—	—	'Behold, O God' Blow (5vv)	'Behold, O God' Blow (4vv)	'Behold, O God' Blow? (4vv)	'Behold, O God' Blow? (4vv)	'Behold, O God' (4vv)	'Behold, O God' Blow? (4vv)	'Behold, O God' Boyce	'omitted'	'omitted'	no anthem at this part of the ceremony any more?
Crowning	'Be strong' T. Tomkins? and 'The King shall rejoice' ???	'The King shall rejoice' J. Tomkins?	'The King shall rejoice' Child	'The King shall rejoice' Turner (lost)	'Praise the Lord, O Jerusalem' H. Purcell	'Praise the Lord, O Jerusalem' Clarke?	'Praise the Lord, O Jerusalem' Clarke?	'Praise the Lord, O Jerusalem' Clarke	'Praise the Lord, O Jerusalem' Boyce	'The King shall rejoice' Knyvett (lost)	'The King shall rejoice' Knyvett (lost)	'The Queen shall rejoice', Handel
Inthronization	Te Deum?	Te Deum Child (in F?)	Te Deum Child	Te Deum ???	Te Deum ???	Te Deum ???	Te Deum Gibbons???; 'Let thy hand be strengthened' Handel	Te Deum ???	Te Deum Boyce in A (full)	Te Deum Boyce in A (arr.)	Te Deum Boyce in A (arr.?)	Te Deum Boyce in A (arr. Kramer?)
Homage	perhaps: 'O Lord, grant the King a long life' T. Tomkins	'Behold, O God, our defender' T. Tomkins?	'Behold, O God, our defender' Cooke	'God spake some time in visions' Blow	'The Lord God is a Sun and a Shield' Blow	'The Lord God is a Sun and a Shield' Blow?	'The Lord God is a Sun and a Shield' Croft	'The Lord is a Sun and a Shield'? Croft	'The Lord is a Sun and a Shield' Boyce	'Blessed be Thou Lord God of Israel' Kent, orch. by Kramer	'O Lord grant the King a long life' Attwood	'This is the day' Knyvett
Coronation of the Queen	—	—	'My heart is enditing' H. Purcell	—	—	—	'My heart is inditing' Handel	'My heart is inditing' Boyce	—	—	—	—
Second Part of the Communion Service	Nicene Creed???; 'Lett my prayer be sett forth'???; 'Let my prayer come up', followed by Organ Music???; Sanctus???; Gloria omitted	Nicene Creed, Sanctus and Gloria???	orchestrally acc. Nicene Creed; 'Let my prayer come up', both by Cooke, lost.	omitted	'Let your light so shine' ???; 'Let my prayer', Blow; Sanctus Blow?	'Let your light so shine'???; 'Let my prayer'; Sanctus all Blow?	'Let your light so shine'; 'Let my prayer'; Sanctus all ???	Organ music during Offertory; Sanctus 'sung in Musick'?	'Let my prayer', Boyce; Sanctus; Boyce?	'read'	'said'	'Let my prayer'?; Sanctus; Gloria; if these pieces were sung at all: Boyce?
Procession from Altar to Throne	'O hearken unto the voice of my Calling' ???	'O hearken unto the voice of my Calling', and Gloria, both by Cooke, lost.	omitted	Gloria Blow?	Gloria Blow?	Gloria, ???	Gloria, 'sung in Musick'?	Gloria Boyce?	—	—	—	—
Procession from Throne into St Edward's Chapel	Organ Music	Organ Music	Organ Music	Organ Music	Organ Music	Organ Music	Organ Music	Organ Music	Organ Music	Organ Music	'God save the King'	Hallelujah Chorus Handel
Recess												Overture to Occasional Oratorio Handel

Appendix D: Synoptic table of music at British coronations, 1902–1953

Ceremony	Edward VII, Queen Alexandra, 1902	George V, Queen Mary, 1911	George VI, Queen Elizabeth, 1937	Elizabeth II, 1953
Before the actual service	'Litany', Tallis (version from Boyce's *Cathedral Music*)	'Litany', Tallis	'Litany', Tallis	'Litany', Tallis
Entrance into the Abbey	Parry, 'I was glad'	Parry, 'I was glad', rev.	Parry, 'I was glad', rev.	Parry, 'I was glad', rev. (arr. Jacob)
Recognition	Fanfare (only one presentation due to the king's ill health)	Fanfare (one after each of the four presentations)?	Fanfare (one after each of the four presentations), Bullock?	Fanfares (one after each of the four presentations), Bullock?
Beginning of the Communion Service	- Introit: 'O hearken thou', Sullivan (music from *The Light of the World*, arr. Bridge); - 'Creed', S.S. Wesley (from the Service in E, arr. Bridge)	- 'Litany', Tallis (5vv) - Introit: 'Let my prayer come up', H. Purcell - 'Creed', J. Merbecke (arr. G. Martin)	- Introit: 'Let my prayer come up', Bairstow - 'Creed', Byrd (short service)	- Introit: 'Behold, O God our defender', Howells - 'Let my prayer come up', Harris - 'Creed', Vaughan Williams
Anointing	'Come, Holy Ghost, our souls inspire', sung to the Ancient Plain-song – the voices in unison with organ accompaniment'	'Come, Holy Ghost, our souls inspire', sung to the Ancient Plain-song attributed to Palestrina'	'Come, Holy Ghost, our souls inspire', 'Original VIII Mode Melody'	'Come, Holy Ghost, our souls inspire', arr. Bullock
	'Zadok the Priest', Handel	'Zadok the Priest', Handel	'Zadok the Priest', Handel (arr. Jacob)	'Zadok the Priest', Handel (arr. Jacob)

Crowning	*Confortare*/'Be strong and play the man', Parratt	*Confortare*/'Be strong and play the man', Parratt	*Confortare*/'Be strong and play the man', Davies	*Confortare*/'Be strong and play the man', Dyson
Homage	'Kings shall see and arise', Bridge	- 'Rejoice in the Lord, O ye Righteous', Bridge - *Homage Fanfare*, Borland	'O come ye servants of the Lord', Tye - 'Hear my prayer, O Lord', H. Purcell - ['O clap your hands together', O. Gibbons] - ['All the ends of the world', Boyce] - 'O praise God in his holiness', Dyson - 'Thou wilt keep him in perfect peace', S.S. Wesley - *Homage Fanfare*, Borland (rev.)	- 'Rejoice in the Lord alway' (anon., formerly attr. Redford) - ['O clap your hands together', O. Gibbons] - ['I will not leave you comfortless', Byrd] - 'O Lord, our Governour', Willan - 'Thou wilt keep him in perfect peace', S.S. Wesley – *Homage Fanfare*, Bullock
Coronation of the Queen	no music	no music	no music	no music

Ceremony	Edward VII, Queen Alexandra, 1902	George V, Queen Mary, 1911	George VI, Queen Elizabeth, 1937	Elizabeth II, 1953
Second Part of the Communion Service	- Offertory: 'Let my prayer come up', H. Purcell (to music of middle movement of 'Jehova quam multi sunt hostes') - Sanctus, Stainer (orch. G. Martin) - 'Sevenfold Amen', Stainer (orch. G. Martin) - Gloria, Stainer (orch. G. Martin) - 'Threefold Amen', O. Gibbons (from anthem Great King of Gods)	- Offertory: 'O hearken thou', Elgar - Sanctus, Alcock - 'Sevenfold Amen', Stainer - 'Lord's Prayer', Merbecke - Gloria, Stanford (B flat) - 'Threefold Amen', O. Gibbons	- Offertory: 'O hearken thou', Harris - Sanctus, Byrd (Latin Mass) - 'Lord's Prayer', Merbecke - Gloria, Stanford (B flat) - 'Threefold Amen', O. Gibbons	- congregational hymn: 'All people that on earth do dwell' (arr. Vaughan Williams) - Sanctus, Vaughan Williams - 'O taste and see', Vaughan Williams - Gloria, Stanford (B flat) - 'Lord's Prayer', said - 'Threefold Amen', O. Gibbons
Procession into St Edward's Chapel	Te Deum, Stanford (B flat, arranged for orchestra)	Te Deum, Parry	*Festival Te Deum*, Vaughan Williams	*Coronation Te Deum*, Walton
Recess	- National Anthem (2 verses, ???) - Wagner, *Kaisermarsch* (with chorus) - Wagner, Prelude to Act III of *Lohengrin* - Gounod, 'Marche' (from *La Reine de Saba*) - Elgar, *Imperial March* (1897)	National Anthem (arr. ???), 1st verse	- National Anthem (arr. Davies), 2 verses - Elgar, *Pomp and Circumstance* March no. 1	- National Anthem (arr. Jacob), 2 verses - Elgar, *Pomp and Circumstance* March no. 1

Bibliography and sources

Section one – Musical sources

A *Manuscript music*

Birmingham University: Barber Institute (*Bu*)

MS 5001: Autograph anthems by English Composers, *c.* 1665–1685.

Cambridge, Perne Library, Peterhouse (*Cp*)

'Latter Caroline Set' MS 43 [Cantoris Tenor] and MS 44 [Decani Medius].

Cambridge, University Library (*Cu*)

Add. MS 9491: William Knyvett, 'This is the day which the Lord hath made', autograph score.

London, British Library (*Lbl*)

MS Add. 17784, fo. 177: single chants by Blow, Turner, Tho. Purcell, Humfrey, and anonymous composers, score, 1676.
MS Add. 17840: Sacred Music by early English composers, eighteenth century.
MS Add. 17843: Anthems by William Croft, eighteenth century.
MS Add. 17861: Sacred music by Greene, Croft and Boyce, partly autograph, eighteenth century.
MS Add. 31405: Anthems and odes with English words by William Byrd, Thomas Morley, [William] Mundy, John Bull, John Cooper, otherwise Coperario, Orlando Gibbons, Fiocco, H. Aldrich, W. Turner, H. Purcell, and Croft, *c.* 1700.
MS Add. 33289: Anthems and services, in score, by Dr John Blow. Nineteenth century copies.
MS Add. 33570: 'The Coronation / in / Shakspea's [*sic*] Play / Henry the Fourth / (2d part) / Performed at the Theatre Royal / Covent Garden 1821 / Composed, Selected, & Arranged by / Henry R. Bishop / Originale'.
MS Add. 65477: MS copy by V. Novello of Orlando Gibbons's 'Grant, Holy Trinity'

MS Eg. 3767: Treble part-book of sixteenth- to eighteenth-century services and anthems, early eighteenth-century copies.

MS Harl. 5222: Copy of the order of service for the coronation of Charles I, no date, probably 1626.

MS Harl. 6346: 'The Anthems used in the King's Chapel', *c*. 1665–75, word-book, discussed in Ford, 'Chapel Royal', 101.

MS Harl. 7337–42: Thomas Tudway's MS Collection of 'Services and Anthems', 6 vols.: 1715, 1716, 1716, 1717, 1718, 1720.

MS R.M. 20.h.5: George Frideric Handel Coronation Anthems HWV 258–61, full autograph score.

MS R.M. 20.h.8: Services and Anthems by Henry Purcell, score, partly autograph.

MS R.M. 24.c.11: Vocal music, end of seventeenth century, all in score.

MS R.M. 24.g.2 (1): Anthems by William Croft, copy by James Kent, *c*. 1720.

MS R.M. 27: part-books of the Chapel Royal, 102 vols.; for details see Laurie, 'The Chapel Royal Part-Books'.

London, Gerald Coke Handel Collection (*Lch*)

MS 674: Copy of Handel's Coronation Anthems, formerly in the possession of the Earl of Shaftesbury, *c*. 1740.

London, Lambeth Palace Library (*Llp*)

MS 764: treble part-book of verse and full anthems, probably first half of seventeenth century, donated to the library by Archbishop Tenison.

London, Royal College of Music (*Lcm*)

MS 1066: Anthems by several composers, early nineteenth century.

MS 1067: Anthems by Croft, Humfrey, and the 'Club Anthem' (by Humfrey, Blow, and Turner)

MS 1069: Anthems by Blow, Turner, and Humfrey, eighteenth century.

MS 1097: Sacred and secular music in score.

MS 2043: John Weldon: Te Deum, Jubilate, Cantate Domino and Deus Misereatur in D major, in parts, partly autograph.

London, Westminster Abbey, Library and Muniment Room (*Lwa*)

Library: Score of Parry's 'I was glad', orchestrated by G. Jacob, 1953.

Library: Score of Handel's 'Zadok the Priest', orchestrated by G. Jacob: at end in pencil the Abbey address of Sir Ernest Bullock, indicating that it was written in 1937.

Triforium Music, no. 3: Services and anthems by various composers, part-book for
   Tenor Cantoris.

Oxford, Bodleian Library (*Ob*)

Mus. c. 11 and c. 12: William Boyce's Anthems for the Coronation of George III and
   Queen Charlotte, score, 1761.
Mus. c. 14: Services by Croft (E flat, B flat, and A)
Mus c. 125, fos. 120–8: Charles H.H. Parry, 'I was glad' (1902 coronation), auto-
   graph draft score.
Mus. d. 27: Five Anthems by Croft, second half eighteenth century.
Rawl. Poet. 23: Anthem word-book of the Chapel Royal, copy of *Lbl MS Harl. 6346*,
   probably before *c*. 1645.

Oxford, Bodleian Library (*Ob*): MSS of the College of St Michael, Tenbury

Tenb. 702: Anthems by Croft, first half eighteenth century.
Tenb. 788: Anthems by various composers, early eighteenth century.
Tenb. 1176–1181: TrATB part-books and corresponding organ book (in three
   volumes).
Tenb. 1232: Collection of vocal compositions in score, unknown scribe, early
   eighteenth century.
Tenb. 1382: Anthems and liturgical music, Tenor Cantoris part-book.
Tenb. 1498: Croft, *Birthday Ode* and orchestral Te Deum and Jubilate (1715
   version), and Bassani, *Gaude Alma*; early eighteenth century.

Oxford, Christ Church Library (Och)

Mus. 1220–4: ATB part-books from the cathedral, unknown scribe, begun about
   1643.

Oxford, St John's College (*Ojc*)

MS 181: Bass part-book, services and anthems, early seventeenth century.

Windsor, St George's Chapel Library (*WRch*)

Men's Part Books, vols. I and II (Alto Decani) and vol. III (Tenor Cantoris)

B *Printed music*

Arne, Thomas Augustine, *Alfred*, ed. by Alexander Scott, MB 47 (1981).
Arnold, Samuel (ed.), *Cathedral Music* [. . .] *The whole sel. & carefully rev.*, 4 vols.
   (London, 1790).

Attwood, Thomas, *Anthem, I was Glad. Composed by Command of The King and performed as part of the August Ceremonial of His Majesty's Coronation* [. . .] (London: Novello, [1821]).

Let thy hand be strengthened, ed. by Frederic Fertel. Curwen Edition 80686 (London: J. Curwen and Sons, [1933]).

Anthem, O Lord, Grant the King a Long Life. Composed as part of the August Ceremonial of the Coronation of His Most Gracious Majesty William the Fourth [. . .] (London: Novello, [1831 or 1832]).

Blow, John, *Anthems IV – Anthems with Instruments*, ed. by Bruce Wood, *MB* 79 (2002).

Coronation Anthems and Anthems with Strings, ed. by Anthony Lewis and Watkins Shaw, *MB* 7 (1953; 2nd rev. edn 1969).

Sanctus and Gloria in Excelsis, in D major. Musical Appendix no. 18. *The Choir, and Musical Record* 1 (November, 1863), 197–202.

Boyce, William (ed.), *Cathedral Music: Being a Collection in Score of the Most Valuable and Useful Compositions for that Service by the Several English Masters, Of the last Two Hundred Years* [. . .] 3 vols. (London: printed for the editor, 1760–73).

Cathedral Music [. . .] newly edited and carefully collated and revised, with an Appendix to each Volume [. . .] by Joseph Warren, 3 vols. (London: R. Cocks & Co., 1849).

Services and Anthems, with a separate accompaniment for the organ or piano forte by Vincent Novello, 4 vols. (London: Novello, 1846–9).

Bridge, Frederick, *Kings shall see and arise. (The Homage Anthem)*. Novello's Collection of Anthems, no. 894 (London : Novello, [1907]).

Rejoice in the Lord, O ye Righteous. Homage Anthem composed for the Coronation of their Majesties King George V. and Queen Mary [. . .] Novello's Octavo Anthems, no. 992 (London: Novello, 1911).

Byrd, William, *Non nobis Domine, Composed by W. Bird, 1590* (Liverpool: Hime & Son, [*c.* 1810]).

Non Nobis Domini [sic], *a favourite Canon for Three Voices* (London: Printed for Culliford, Rolfe & Barrow, [*c.* 1798].

A Complete & exact delineation of the Ceremony from S.ᵗ James's to S.ᵗ Pauls; on Tuesday the 19.ᵗʰ Dec.ʳ 1797 [. . .] *to which is added, the form of the Church Service with part of the Vocal Music sung at that Celebrity* [. . .] ([London, Edinburgh:] Printed for Corri, Dussek, & Co., [1798]).

Croft, William, *Musica Sacra: Or, Select Anthems in Score*, 2 vols., (London: J. Walsh, [1724/25]).

The Form and Order of the Service [. . .] *in the Coronation of Their Majesties King Edward VII. and Queen Alexandra* [. . .] *With the Music to Be Sung*, ed. by Sir Frederick Bridge (London: Novello, 1902).

The Form and Order of the Service [...] *in the Coronation of Their Majesties King George V and Queen Mary* [...] *With the Music to Be Sung*, ed. by Sir Frederick Bridge (London: Novello, 1911).

The Form and Order of the Service [...] *in the Coronation of Their Majesties King George VI and Queen Elizabeth* [...] *With the Music to Be Sung* (London: Novello, 1937).

Gilmour, Robert, *The psalm-singers's assistant. Being a collection of the most approved psalm and hymn tunes: Mostly in four parts. Selected from the best authors* [...] (Glasgow: printed by J. Neilson and sold by the author, 1793).

Harmonia Anglicana, A Collection of two, three, and four Part Songs [...] (London: Printed for and sold by John Simpson, [1744]).

Hyde, J., *A New and Compleat Preceptor for the Trumpet and Bugle Horn, with the Whole of the Cavalry Duty* [...] *To which is added a Selection of Airs, Marches and Quick Steps for Three Trumpets, Composed and Compiled by J. Hyde* (London: Printed and to be had of the Author, [1798]).

The Music for an Order for Special Services Authorized By the Most Reverend The Archbishop of Capetown for Use in his Diocese and, With the Consent of His Suffragans, Throughout the Province of South Africa on the Day of the Coronation of His Majesty King Edward VII. Composed by Charles Macpherson (Sub-Organist of St. Paul's Cathedral), (London: Novello, [1902]).

The Music with the Form and Order of the Service [...] *at the Coronation of Her Most Excellent Majesty Queen Elizabeth II* [...] (London: Novello, 1953).

Purcell, Henry, *The Works of Henry Purcell* (London: Novello, 1878–1965; 2/1961– [Stainer and Bell since 2007]).

A Selection of Music for use at Coronation Services in Churches and Chapels Throughout the British Dominions on [...] *the Coronation Day of Their Majesties King Edward VII. and Queen Alexandra.* (London: Novello, [1902]).

Tomkins, Thomas, *Musica Deo Sacra & Ecclesiae Anglicanae* (London, 1668).

    Musica Deo Sacra I, transcr. and ed. by Bernard Rose, *EECM* 5 ([1965]).

    Musica Deo Sacra IV, transcr. and ed. by Bernard Rose, *EECM* 27 (1982).

Weelkes, Thomas, *Collected Anthems* ed. by David Brown, Walter Collins, and Peter Le Huray, *MB* 23 (1966; r. 1975).

Weldon, John, *Divine Harmony, Six Select Anthems* [...] (London: Walsh, [1716]).

Section two – Documentary/ literary/ historical sources

A *Manuscript documentary and archival sources*

Cambridge, St John's College (*Cjc*)

MS L 12: 'The Order of the King's Coronation, as it was observed Feb. 2 1626, at the Coronation of KING CHARLES.', possibly in the hand of John Cosin (1594–1672), later Bishop of Durham; numerous annotations by Archbishop Laud.

MS L 13: 'Order of Coronation of King Charles I; in the handwriting of Archbishop Sancroft', *c.* 1684/5.

MS L 14: 'The Forme of the Coronation Service', written by Archbishop Sancroft, with the signatures of the bishops who officiated with Sancroft [1685]. Given by Thomas Baker.

MS L 15: THE / MANNER / of the / CORONATION / of the /KINGS of ENGLAND; annotation in Abp Sancroft's hand: 'Recovered fro~ Westm~r. upon ye suit[?].', later annotation: 'This probably was the Book, that King Charles the first held in his hand at his Coronation. For wch see ArchBp: Sancroft's note.'

Cambridge, University Library (*Cu*)

Mm. I. 51, fos. 14–16: undated transcription of *Cjc MS L 15*.

London, British Library (*Lbl*)

MS Add. 6284, fos. 36–39v: short version of the order of service, coronation of James I and Queen Anne in 1603.

MS Add. 6286: 'Coronation of King James II' / 'Presented by Lady Banks'

MS Add. 6338: Ceremonials, including the coronations of Charles II, James II, and William and Mary.

MS Add. 14407: 'The Establishm;^{t} / of the Yearly Charge of Our Dyet w:th / Incidents for Housekeeping Also Wages / and Boardwages to the Officers & Servants / of Our House Chamber and Stables with / the Expence of the Chappels & Provisions for Horses Also Allowances Stipends & / Pentions to the Old & Supernumerary Servants / & Widows to Commence the First Day / of July 1702.'

MS Add. 39139, fos. 205–14: order of service, coronation of James I and Queen Anne.

MS Add. 39864, fo. 49: Lists of the choir of Westminster Abbey and of the Chapel Royal at the 'Coronation of Ja^s II. April 23. 1685'.

MS Add. 47184, fos. 4–23: 'A brief out of the Rytes of the coronacion called Liber Regalis', according to catalogue referring to the coronation of Charles I, 1626.

MS Harl. 310: order of service as in *Liber Regalis*.

MS Harl. 4848, fos. 79v–83: 'The maner of Coronations of the Kinges & Queenes / of Englande.', *c.* 1530.

MS Harl. 6117: 'A / Formulary for the / Coronation of His / most Excellent Majesty / King George [. . .]', 1714.

MS Harl. 6118: 'A Formulary for the Coronation of her / Ma~tie Queen Anne.', 1702.

MS Harl. 6336, fos. 16–21: order of service, coronation of Queen Anne, 1702.

MS Harl. 6346: word-book of anthems; discussed in Ford, 'Chapel Royal'.

MS Harl. 6815: Material relating to different coronations.

MS Stowe 580: 'Preparations for the Coronation of King Charles the Second with Accounts of several Preceding Coronations', unknown date and scribe.

RPS MS 350: Letters of the Royal Philharmonic Society, vol. XVIII.

London, College of Arms, also known as Herald's College (*Lca*)

Coronation 1820. 1821. Ceremonials &c Church Service.
Coronation of George III 1761, 3 vols.
Coronation of James II and William and Mary [also up to George II].
Coronations. Queen Anne. George I.
MS Ceremonials 14: Manuscript papers relating to the coronations of James II, William III and Mary II, George I and George II (Steer Catalogue, No. [14]).
MS Ceremonials 18: 'Coronations. Queen Anne. George Ist'. (Steer Catalogue, No. [18]).
MS Ceremonials 94: 'Coronation of Queen Victoria 1838', vol. 6. (Steer Catalogue, No. [94]).
MS L 19: Manuscript orders of the coronations of James II, and of William III and Mary II, not dated; pp. 53–117 (William and Mary) transcr. in Legg, *Three Coronation Orders*.
MS S.M.L. 44: 'Heraldic Annals', vol. I, written by Stephen Martin Leake (in many parts similar to *MS S.M.L. 65*)
MS S.M.L. 65: 'Heraldo Memoriale / Or Memoirs of the College of Arms / Part the Second / From May 1727 to September 1765', written by Stephen Martin Leake, Garter Principal King of Arms.
MS W.Y., fo. 146 'A. Coronacōn of King James'; at the end: 'The Coronation of Kinge James on St James day. July 25 1603.'
MS W.Y., fo. 156: Manuscript order of service, coronation of James I and Queen Anne, 1603.

London, Her Majesty's Chapel Royal, St James's Palace

Manuscript Catalogue of Music at the Chapel Royal, compiled by Walter Coward, dated 'July 1917'.
The New Cheque Book of the Chapel Royal.

London, Lambeth Palace Library (*Llp*)

Cod. Misc. 1079A: 'The Form, and Order, / of the Service that is to be performed, / And of / The Ceremony to be Observed / In the Coronation / of their Mat^{ies} King George the II.^{d} / And Queen Caroline, / In the Abbey Church of St Peter Westm^r / On Wednesday the / 11th of October: 1727.', in the handwriting of Archbishop Wake.
Cod. Misc. 1079B: Printed order of service, coronation of George II and Queen Caroline (1727), with manuscript annotations by Archbishop Wake.
Cod. Misc. 1081A: Printed order of service, coronation of George II and Queen Caroline (1727), with manuscript annotations by Archbishop Wake referring to the coronation of Charles I.

Cod. Misc. 1082: Printed order of service, coronation of George II and Queen Caroline (1727), with manuscript annotations by Archbishop Secker referring to the coronation of George III and Queen Charlotte (1761).

Cod. Misc. 1083A: Printed order of service, coronation of George III and Queen Charlotte (1761), with manuscript changes referring to the coronation of George IV (1821).

Cod. Misc. 1083B: Printed order of service, coronation George III and Queen Charlotte (1761), with manuscript changes referring to the coronation of William IV and Queen Adelaide (1831).

Fisher 80, fos. 275–6: 'Memorandum on conversation with the Dean of Westminster concerning the Church of Scotland and the Coronation Service', dated 9 October, 1951.

Fisher 123, 124, and *125*: Material relating to the 1953 coronation.

*KA 113 1821***: Printed order of service, coronation George IV, with handwritten annotations by Archbishop Charles Manners-Sutton.

Lang 21 and *22*: Material relating to the 1937 coronation.

Lang 218 (Archbishop Lang's diary/notebook), fos. 23–52 (transcr./typed in *Lang 223*, 234–56): 'Notes on the coronation of King George VI and Queen Elizabeth'.

MS 1077: 'A / FORMULARY / of that part of the / SOLEMNITY / which is performd in the Church / at the / CORONATION / of their Mat˜ies / KING WILLIAM / and / QUEEN MARY / AT WESTMINSTER / 11 Apr. 1689.'

MS 1078: 'A / FORMULARY / of that part of the / SOLEMNITY / which is performd in yᵉ Church / at the / CORONATION / of her Majestie / QUEEN ANNE / at / WESTMINSTER / 23. Apr. 1702.'

MS 1130: Court Papers, *c*. 1760–1761, bound in 2 vols., vol. I.

MS 1312: Manuscript order of service, coronation of George III (without the Coronation of the Queen) with corrections for George IV, 1820–21.

MS 1770: Diary of Archbishop Wake, March 1705–25 Jan. 1725.

MS 2797, fo. 143: Letter from Joseph Armitage Robinson, Dean of Westminster, [to Archbishop Frederick Temple], 6 April 1902.

Temple 57: Papers relating to the coronation of Edward VII.

London, National Archives, formerly Public Record Office (*Lna*)

LC 2/15: 'Warrants for Provisions for the Coronation of her Majesty Queen Anne', 1702.

LC 2/32: 'Dean of Westminst:ʳ to L.d Chamberlain/rec.ᵈ 13.ᵗʰ Sept.ʳ–1761'.

LC 2/50: 'Coronation Bills George IV.' (1821).

LC 5/18: Material relating to the coronation of George II and Queen Caroline, 1727.

LC 5/159: Lord Chamberlain's Department: Miscellaneous Records, 1727.

PC 1/3025: Correspondence and papers relating to coronation procedure, 1702, 1714, 1727.

PC 1/14/76: Preparations for the coronation of George I.

PC 1/15/6: Papers relating to the preparation of the coronation of George II and Queen Caroline, 'by the committee of the Council appointed', 3 parts, 1727.

PC 2/85: 'Council Register 1. Aug. 1714–25 Feb. 1716/7'.

PC 2/90: Register of the Privy Council, including the minutes of the meetings, its orders, certain proclamations and the reports of committees with the papers accompanying them, sometimes entered at length, sometimes in abstract only, covering August to October 1727.

Work 21/1: Material relating to the coronations of 1727 and 1761.

London, Royal College of Music (*Lcm*)

MS 7281, no. 2: Sir Frederick Bridge to C. H. H. Parry, [1901].

London, Westminster Abbey, Library and Muniment Room (*Lwa*)

WAM 33741: List of the Abbey choir, 1709.

WAM 48097B: details of the organ used at the coronation, 1761.

WAM 51181: 'The Earl Marshall's Order for Scaffolding in y[e] Abbey.', dated 30 August 1727.

WAM 56760: '1714 / An Account of y[e] Alterations in y[e] Formulatory at y[e] Coronation of King George.'

WAM 56775: Material relating to the coronation of George II and Queen Caroline, 1727.

WAM 58307: Scheduled list of coronation music [1901/1902].

WAM 58308: Armitage Robinson to Bishop of Winchester, undated (1902).

WAM 58362: C. H. H. Parry to Canon Robinson at the Abbey, 12 May 1902.

WAM 58378: Bridge giving times of music, dated 12 June [1902].

WAM 58425: 'Curtailment of the Service' [1902].

WAM 58471: 'Words suggested for a short Anthem during the Homage' [1902 coronation; full text of 'Kings shall see and arise'].

WAM 58489*: account of the 1902 coronation by chorister William Harvey Bourne (letter to his grandfather).

WAM 58579: Archbishop Lang to Dean of Westminster, 17 December 1936.

WAM 60017: 'Papers and Documents Respecting / the Coronation of King George the / 3rd 4th William &. Victoria. down / from William the Conqueror. also / of the Installation of the Kinghts of the Bath. / Collected by R.[d] Clark. / And preserved.'

WAM 61781: 'Lord Cham[n] about the taking down part of the Altar at Coron.[n] 1761.', from the 'Lord Chamberlain's Office, 14th Sept:[r] 1761'.

WAM 61782: 'Lord. Chamb.[n] to admit D.[r] Boyce & Musicians [...] Coron.[n] 1761.'

WAM 63361B: Printed list of music, 1953 coronation.

Library, 4.c.5: Material relating to the 1831 coronation, formerly belonging to George Smart.

Library, 4.c.8 and *4.c.9*: Material relating to the 1838 coronation, 'compiled by Sir George Smart'; printed order of service with handwritten annotations by Smart.

Library, CA 53: 'A / FORMULARY / of that Part of the / SOLEMNITY / which is perform'd / in the Collegiate Church of St Peter / WES^tMINSTER / at the / CORONATION / of his Majesty / King George / 20.th Oct.^ber 1714.'

Library, McKie Papers: Collection of letters and material relating to the 1953 coronation.

Library, McKie Collection of Material related to the Coronation, 1953.

Library, n.s.: Annotated, printed order of service with the music (1902 coronation).

Oxford, Bodleian Library (*Ob*)

Hearne's diaries 124

MS Rawlinson B 40: Order of service for the coronation of James I and Queen Anne, 1603.

MS Rawlinson B 120, fo. 113: 'The maner of Coronations of the Kinges & Queenes of England'

MS Tanner 27, fo. 8: Letter from Henry Compton, Bishop of London, to Archbishop Sancroft, undated.

MS Tanner 31: Material relating to the accession and coronation of James II, 1685.

B. *Earlier printed sources (up to c. 1850)*

The Annual Register, or a View of the History, Politics, and Literature for the Year 1761. The Sixth Edition (London: printed for J. Donsley, 1796).

ANTHEMS To be Sung at the CORONATION of Their Majesties King George III. And Queen Charlotte, in the Abbey Church of St. Peter, Westminster, on Tuesday the 22d September, 1761. All composed for this Occasion by Dr. Boyce, Composer to his Majesty, and Master of the King's Band, except the Fourth, which was composed by the late Mr. Handel (London: Printed by T. Gardner, opposite St. Clement's Church in the Strand, 1761). [Seen as *Lbl RB 31.c.91*]

April Fools. Country Musicians Celebrating a Reginal Coronation. Dedicated to all Lovers of Social and Domestic Harmony. Drawn and Engraved by I. Sawthem. Performed in Anticipation at C___April 1, 1821, [London, 1821].

Ashmole, Elias, *A Brief Narrative of the Solemn Rites and Ceremonies performed upon the day of the Coronation of our Sovereign Lord King Charles II* (n.p., n.d.).

Ashmole, Elias and Sandford, Francis, *The Entire Ceremonies of the Coronations of His Majesty King Charles II. and of her Majesty Queen Mary, Consort to James II. As published by those Learned Heralds Ashmole and Sandford, with the Prayers at full length. To which is prefix'd, An Introduction Historical and Critical; likewise an Appendix, containing many curious Particulars.* (London: Printed for W. Owen et al., 1761).

Baker, Sir Richard, *A Chronicle of the Kings of England, from the time of the Romans Goverment* [sic] *unto the Death of King James* [...] *Whereunto is added, The Reign of King Charles the First, with a Continuation of the Chronicle, in this Fourth Edition, to the Coronation of His Sacred Majesty King Charles the Second that now reigneth* [...] (London: Printed by E. Cotes, 1665).

[Balfour, Sir James], *The Forme and Order of the Coronation of Charles the Second, King of Scotland, England, France, and Ireland. As it was acted and done at Scoone, The first day of Ianuary, 1651* (Abderdeen: Imprinted by James Brown, 1651).

Boyer, Abel, *The History of the Life and Reign of Queen Anne digested into Annals*, vols. I–XI for 1702–1712 (London, 1703–13).

    The Political State of Great Britain [...], 60 vols. (London, 1711–40). [Boyer was author/nominal editor of the series only until October 1729.]

Burney, Charles, *An account of the musical performances in Westminster-Abbey, and the Pantheon* [...] *In commemoration of Handel.* (London: Printed for the Benefit of the Musical Fund, 1785).

    A General History of Music: from the Earliest ages to the present periode: To which is Prefixed, a Dissertation on the Music of the Ancients, 4 vols. (London: Printed for the author, 1789).

'C.', 'The Amateur Festival', *The Court Magazine* 6 (January–June 1835), 22–8.

Calvert, John, *A Collection of Anthems used in Her Majesty's Chapel Royal, the Temple Church, and the Collegiate Churches and Chapels in England and Ireland* (London: George Bell, 1844).

The Ceremonial of the Coronation of His most Sacred Majesty King George II. and of His Royal Consort Queen Caroline [...] *By Order of William Hawkins Esq; Ulster King of Arms of all Ireland.* (Dublin: Printed by and for S. Powell, 1727).

Ceremonial of the Coronation of His Most Sacred Majesty King George the Fourth [...] (West-Minster: Printed by John Whitaker, 1823). [Seen as *Lbl 1899.e.13*]

Ceremonial to be observed at the Baptism of His Royal Highness The Prince of Wales, in the Royal Chapel of St. George [...] *on Tuesday, January the 25th, 1842* (Westminster: Francis Watts [1842]).

The Ceremonies, Form of Prayer, and Services used in Westminster-Abby at the Coronation of King James the First and Queen Ann his Consort [...] *With an Account of the Procession from the Palace to the Abby* [...] *With the Coronation of Charles the first in Scotland.* (London: Randal Taylor, 1685).

Clifford, John, *The Divine Services and Anthems usually sung in His Majesties Chappell, and in all Cathedrals and Collegiate Choires in England and Ireland.* 2nd edn with large additions (London: 1664). [Seen as *Ob Bliss B 274*].

A Complete Account of the Ceremonies observed in the Coronation of the Kings and Queens of England, 4th edn (London: Printed for J. Roberts and D. Browne, 1727).

[Cooke, Edward], *The History of the Successions of the Kings of England. From Canutus the First Monarch* [...] (London, 1682).

Dart, John, *Westmonasterium or the History and Antiquities of the Abbey Church of St. Peters Westminster* [...], 2 vols. (London, 1723).

An Exact Account of the Ceremonial at the Coronation of Their Most Excellent Majesties King William and Queen Mary, The Eleventh Day of this Instant April, 1689. Published by Order of the Duke of Norfolk, Earl-Marshal of England (London, 1689).

The Form and Order of the Service that is to be Performed, and of the Ceremonies that are to be Observed, in the Coronation of Their Majesties, King George II, and Queen Caroline in the Abbey Church of S. Peter, Westminster, On Wednesday the 11th of October 1727 (London: John Baskett, 1727).

The Form and Order of the Service [...] *Coronation of Their Majesties, King George III and Queen Charlotte* [...] (London: Mark Baskett and Robert Baskett, 1761).

The Form and Order of the Service [...] *Coronation of His Majesty King George IIII. [sic]* (London: Printed by George Eyre and Andrew Strahan, 1821).

The Form and Order of the Service [...] *Coronation of their Majesties King William IV and Queen Adelaide* [...] (London: George Eyre and Andrew Strahan, 1831).

The Form and Order of the Service [...] *Coronation of Her Majesty Queen Victoria* [...] (London: George Eyre and Andrew Spottiswoode, 1838).

The Form of Prayers and Services used in Westminster-Abbey at the Coronation of the Kings and Queens of England. With an Account of the Procession from the Palace to the Abbey. (London: Printed for Randal Taylor near Stationers-Hall, 1689).

Gardiner, William, *Music and Friends; or, Pleasant Recollections of a Dilettante*, 3 vols. (London: Longman et al., 1838–53). In *Ob 38.1048* (=vol. 2), the date is corrected by hand to 1848.

Grosse, John, 'God save the King', *MLMS* 7 (Oct. 1834), 75–8.

[Gwynn, John], *Thoughts on the Coronation of his present Majesty King George the Third, or Reasons offered against confining the Procession to the usual Track, pointing out others more commodius and proper* (London: Printed by the proprietor, 1761).

H[awkins], J[ohn], 'Memoirs of Dr William Boyce', in *Cathedral Music* (London: J. A. Novello, 1849), pp. i–vii.

Huish, Robert, *An Authentic History of the Coronation of His Majesty, King George the Fourth* [...] (London: Robins and Co., 1821).

  Memoirs of George the Fourth, Descriptive of the more Interesting Scenes of his Private and Public Life, and the Important Events of his Memorable Reign [...], 2 vols. (London: Thomas Kelly, 1831).

The Life and Reign of Her late excellent Majesty Queen Anne [...] (London, 1738).

Lünig, Johann Christian, *Theatrum ceremoniale Historico-Politicum, oder Historisch- und Politischer Schau-Platz Aller Ceremonien* [...], 2 vols. (Leipzig, 1719–20).

Miller, J. R., *The History of Great Britain, from the Death of George II. to the Coronation of George IV*. Designed as a Continuation of Hume and Smollett (London: Jones and Company, 1825).

The Mirror of Literature, Amusement, and Instruction, vol. 18 (1831).

'The Musical Service of the Coronation (From the Court Journal)', *MLAI* 32 (1838), 29–30.

Nayler, Sir George, *The Coronation of his Most Sacred Majesty King George the Fourth* [. . .] *Undertaken by his Majesty's Especial Command. By the Late Sir George Nayler* [. . .] *completed from the Official Document.* (London: 1837). [The copy used was the one in the Westminster Abbey Muniment Room].

Ogilby, John, *The Entertainment of his Most Excellent Majestie Charles II, in his Passage through the City of London to his Coronation* [. . .] *to these is added, a brief Narrative of His Majestie's Solemn Coronation* (London: Tho. Roycroft, 1662). [Seen as *Ob Johnson b. 56a*].

The Entertainment of His Most Excellent Majestie Charles II in His Passage through the City of London to His Coronation (London: 1662), facsimile with introduction by Ronald Knowles. Medieval and Renaissance Texts and Studies, vol. 43 (Birmingham: Medieval and Renaissance Texts and Studies, 1988).

The Kings Coronation: Being an Exact Account of the Cavalcade [. . .] *Also the Narrative Of his Majesties Coronation* [. . .] *As it was Published by his Majesties Order, with the Approbation, and License of Sir Edward Walker, Garter Principal King at Arms.* (London: William Morgan, 1685).

The Oration, Anthems and Poems, Spoken and Sung at the Performance of Divine Musick, at Stationers-Hall, for the Month of May, 1702. Undertaken by Cavendish Weedon, Esq. (London: Printed for Henry Playford, 1702).

The Order of the Music, &c. to be Performed at the Coronation (London: Printed by Joseph Mallet, [1838]).

Pearce, Thomas, *A Collection of Anthems used in Her Majesty's Chapels Royal, and most Cathedral Churches, in England and Ireland*, new edn with additions (London: Rivingtons, 1856).

Planché, J. R., *Regal Records: Or, A Chronicle of the Coronations of the Queens Regnant of England* (London: Chapman and Hall, 1838).

Playford, John, *An Introduction to the Skill of Music* (London, 1694).

[Sainsbury, J. S.] *A Dictionary of Musicians, from the earliest Ages to the present Time*, 2 vols. (London: Printed for Sainsbury and Co., 1842).

Sandford, Francis, *The History of the Coronation of the Most High, Most Mighty, and Most Excellent Monarch, James II* [. . .] *and of his Royal Consort Queen Mary: Solemnized in the Collegiate Church of St. Peter in the City of Westminster on Thursday the 23d of April* [. . .] *in the Year of Our Lord 1685* [. . .] (London: Printed by Thomas Newcomb, 1687).

The Scots magazine (1761).

[Shakespeare, William], *King Henry IV. (The Second Part,) An Historical Play; Revised by J.P. Kemble, Esq. And printed as it was revived at The Theatre Royal, Covent Garden, On Monday, June the 25th, 1821; with the Representation of the Coronation, as arranged by Mr. Farley* [. . .] (London: Printed for John Miller, 1821).

Sharp, John, *A Sermon preach'd at the Coronation of Queen Anne* [. . .] (London: printed and sold by H. Hills, 1708).

Taylor, Arthur, *The Glory of Regality: An Historical Treatise of the Anointing and Crowning of the Kings and Queens of England* (London: R. and A. Taylor, 1820).

Taylor, William Cooke, *Chapters on Coronations: Comprising Their Origin, Nature and History* (London: John W. Parker, 1838).

Thomson, Richard, *A Faithful Account of the Processions and Ceremonies observed in the Coronation of the Kings and Queens of England: exemplified in that of their late Most Sacred Majesties King George the Third, and Queen Charlotte* [. . .] (London: Printed for John Major, 1820).

Vollständige Beschreibung der Ceremonien, welche sowohl bei den Englischen Crönungen überhaupt vorgehen, Besonders aber bey dem Höchst=beglückten Crönungs=Fest Ihro Königl. Königl. Maj. Maj. [sic] Georgii des II. und Wilhelminae Carolinae [. . .] (Hanover: Nicolaus Förster und Sohn, 1728).

Walker, Edward, *A Circumstantial Account of the Preparations for the Coronation of His Majesty King Charles the Second, and minute detail of that splendid Ceremony* [. . .] (London: T. Baker, 1820).

Watkins, John, *The Life and Times of "England's Patriot King," William the Fourth. With a brief memoir of Her Majesty, Queen Adelaide, and her Family* (London: Fisher, Son, and Jackson, 1831).

Wednesday Night for Thursday Morning, or the Last Rehearsal of the Coronation Anthem. Drawn and engraved by 'I. Sawthem' and published for the author [*c.* 1821].

The Whole Ceremony of the Coronation of His Most Sacred Majesty King George [. . .] *By Order of W. Hawkins Esq; Ulster King of Arms of all Ireland* (Dublin: J. Carson, 1715).

'Y' [anonymous], 'Unnoticed Works of Dr. Boyce' [Letter to the editor], *Monthly Magazine and British Register* 7 (1799), 103–04.

Section three – Secondary works cited or utilized

Adams, Martin, *Henry Purcell: the Origins and Development of His Musical Style* (Cambridge University Press, 1995).

Adamson, John, 'The Tudor and Stuart Courts 1509–1714', in John Adamson (ed.), *The Princely Courts of Europe. Ritual, Politics and Culture under the Ancien Régime 1500–1750* (first publ. 1999 by Weidenfeld and Nicolson, paperback edn, London: Seven Divals, 2000), 95–117.

Alcock, Walter G., Preface to *The Form and Order of the Service* [. . .] *in the Coronation of Their Majesties King George V and Queen Mary* [. . .] *With the Music to Be Sung*, ed. by Sir Frederick Bridge (London: Novello, 1911), iii–vi.

Andrewes, Richard, Osborne, Anne, and Smallwood, Lydia, *A Catalogue of Ascribed Music in pre-1800 Music MSS Deposited in British Libraries*, compiled between 1965 and 1969, prepared for microfilming by Richard Andrewes in 1981 [microfilm].

Arkwright, G. E. P., 'Purcell's Church Music', *Musical Antiquary* 1 (1909–10), 63–72 and 234–48.

Ashbee, Andrew (ed.), *Records of English Court Music*, 9 vols. (Scolar Press, 1991).

Ashbee, Andrew and Harley, John (eds.), *The Cheque Books of the Chapel Royal*, 2 vols. (Aldershot: Ashgate, 2000).

Atkinson, Monte Edgel, 'The Orchestral Anthem in England, 1700–1775', unpublished DMA thesis, University of Illinois at Urbana–Champaign (1991).

Bak, János M. (ed.), *Coronations: Medieval and Early Modern Monarchic Ritual* (Berkley: University of California Press, 1990).

Baldwin, David, *The Chapel Royal – Ancient and Modern* (London: Duckworth, 1990).

Barker, Brian, *When the Queen was Crowned* (London: Routledge & Kegan Paul, 1976).

Barnett, Gregory, 'Handel's Borrowings and the Disputed *Gloria*', *EM* 34 (February 2006), 75–92.

Bartlett, Clifford (ed.), Preface to *George Frideric Handel, Four Coronation Anthems*, full score (Oxford University Press, 1990).

Batchelor, C.G.P., 'William Child: an Examination of the Liturgical Sources, and a Critical and Contextual Study of the Church Music', 3 vols., unpublished Ph.D thesis, University of Cambridge (1990).

Bateman, Stringer, *The Strange Evolution of 'our illiterate National Anthem'... From a Rebel Song* (London: Simpkin, 1902).

Beem, Charles, '"I am her majesty's subject": Prince George of Denmark and the Transformation of the English Male Consort', *Canadian Journal of History* 39 (2004), 457–87.

Bense, Lieselotte, 'Händels Anthems für die Krönung Georgs II. und seiner Gemahlin Konigin Caroline in der Westminster-Abtei am 11. October 1727', *Händel-Jahrbuch* 49 (2003), 307–26.

Benson, A.C., *Edwardian Excursions, From the Diaries of A.C. Benson 1898–1904*, selected, edited and introduced by David Newsome (London: John Murray, 1981).

Bertelli, Sergio, *The King's Body. Sacred Rituals of Power in Medieval and Early Modern Europe*, transl. by R. Burr Litchfield (Pennsylvania State University Press, 2001).

Bevan, Bryan, *Royal Westminster Abbey* (London: Robert Hale, 1976).

Bevan, Maurice, 'A Purcell Coronation Anthem?', *MT* 119 (1978), 938.

Blanning, Tim C. W., *The Culture of Power and the Power of Culture – Old Regime Europe 1660–1789* (Oxford University Press, 2002, paperback edn 2003).

The Triumph of Music. Composers, Musicians and their Audiences, 1700 to the Present (London: Penguin, 2009).

Blumler, J. G., Brown, J. R., Ewbank, A. J., and Nossiter, T. J., 'Attitudes to the Monarchy: Their Structure and Development during a Ceremonial Occasion', *Political Studies* 19 (1971), 149–71.

Boden, Anthony, 'The Life and Times of Thomas Tomkins and his Family', in Anthony Boden (ed.), *Thomas Tomkins: The Last Elizabethan* (Aldershot: Ashgate, 2005), 5–194.

Bodley, John Edward Courtenay, *The Coronation of Edward the Seventh. A Chapter of European and Imperial History* (London: Methuen, 1903).

Bowles, Edmund A., 'Music in Court Festivals of State: Festival Books as Sources for Performance Practices', *EM* 28 (2000), 421–43.

[Bradfield, Harold William] Bishop of Bath and Wells, 'The Significance of the Coronation', in *The Coronation Book of Queen Elizabeth II* (London: Odhams Press, [1953]; repr. London: Bounty Books, 2006), 19–21.

Bradley, Ian, *God Save the Queen. The Spiritual Dimension of Monarchy* (London: Darton, Longmann and Todd, 2002).

Bradshaw, Paul, 'Coronations from the Eighteenth to the Twentieth Century', in Bradshaw (ed.), *Coronations. Past, Present and Future*, 22–32.

   (ed.), *Coronations. Past, Present and Future*. Essays by Henry Everett, Paul Bradshaw, and Colin Buchanan. Joint Liturgical Studies 38 (Cambridge: Grove, 1997).

Bridge, Sir Frederick, *A Westminster Pilgrim. Being a Record of Service in Church, Cathedral, and Abbey; College, University, and Concert-Room, with a Few Notes on Sport* (London: Novello, [1918]).

[Bridge, Sir Frederick?], 'Notes on the Coronation Music', *MT* 43 (1902), 387–8.

Brown, James D. and Stratton, Stephen S., *British Musical Biography* (Birmingham, 1897).

Brown, Keith M., 'The Vanishing Emperor: British Kingship and its Decline, 1603–1707', in Roger A. Mason (ed.), *Scots and Britons. Scottish Political Thought and the Union of 1603* (Cambridge University Press, 1994), 58–90.

Brownlow, James Arthur, *The Last Trumpet: a History of the English Slide Trumpet* (Stuyvesant, NY: Pendragon Press, 1996).

Buchanan, Colin, 'The Next Coronation', in Bradshaw (ed.), *Coronations. Past, Present and Future*, 34–44.

Bucholz, R[obert] O., *The Augustan Court: Queen Anne and the Decline of Court Culture* (Stanford University Press, 1993).

   '"Nothing but Ceremony": Queen Anne and the Limitations of Royal Ritual', *The Journal of British Studies* 30 (1991), 288–323.

Budds, Michael Joe, 'Music at the Court of Queen Victoria: A Study of Music in the Life of the Queen and her Participation in the Musical Life of her Time', 3 vols., unpublished Ph.D. thesis, University of Iowa (1987).

Bumpus, John S., *A History of English Cathedral Music, 1549–1889*, 2 vols. (London: T. Werner Laurie, 1908).

Burrows, Donald, *Handel*. The Master Musicians. (Oxford University Press, 1994, paperback edn 1996).

   Handel and the English Chapel Royal (Oxford: Clarendon Press, 2005).

   'Handel and the 1727 Coronation', *MT* 118 (1977), 469–73.

   Handel: Messiah (Cambridge University Press, 1991).

   'Handel's Oratorio Performances', in Donald Burrows (ed.), *The Cambridge Companion to Handel* (Cambridge University Press, 1997), 262–81.

'Handel's 1738 *Oratorio*: A Benefit Pasticcio', in Klaus Hortschansky and Konstanze Musketa (eds.), *Georg Friedrich Händel – ein Lebensinhalt, Gedenkschrift für Bernd Baselt (1934–1993)* (Halle an der Saale: Bärenreiter, 1995), 11–38.

'Theology, Politics and Instruments in Church: Musicians and Monarchs in London, 1660–1760', *Göttinger Händel-Beiträge* 5 (Kassel: Bärenreiter, 1993), 145–60.

Burrows, Donald and Ronish, Martha J., *A Catalogue of Handel's Musical Autographs* (Oxford: Clarendon Press, 1994).

Bury, Shirley, 'The Coronation from the restoration of the monarchy to 1953', in Claude Blair (ed.), *The Crown Jewels: the History of the Coronation Regalia in the Jewel House of the Tower of London*, 2 vols. (London: Stationery Office, 1998), vol. I: The History, 355–680.

Ceremonial to be Observed at the Investiture of His Royal Highness The Prince of Wales, K.G., Carnavon Castle, 13th July, 1911 ([London:] Harrison and Sons, [1911]).

Caldwell, John, *The Oxford History of English Music*. Vol. I: *From the Beginning to c. 1715* (Oxford University Press, 1991).

Calendar of State Papers and Manuscripts, relating to English Affairs, Existing in the Archives and Collections of Venice, and in other Libraries of Northern Italy, vol. X: 1603–1607, ed. by Horatio F. Brown (London: Printed for Her Majesty's Stationery Office, 1900).

Calman, Montague, 'The Music in the Abbey', *Music and Musicians* (June 1953), 8.

Cannadine, David, 'The Context, Performance and Meaning of Ritual: The British Monarchy and the "Invention of Tradition", *c.* 1820–1977', in Eric Hobsbawm and Terence Ranger (eds.), *The Invention of Tradition* (Cambridge University Press, 1983, repr. 2002), 101–64.

'Introduction: Divine Rites of Kings', in David Cannadine and Simon Rice (eds.), *Rituals of Royalty. Power and Ceremonial in Traditional Societies* (Cambridge University Press, 1987), 1–19.

'Splendor out of Court: Royal Spectacle and Pageantry in Modern Britain, *c.* 1820–1977', in Sean Wilentz (ed.), *Rites of Power: Symbolism, Ritual, and Politics since the Middle Ages* (Philadelphia: University of Pennsylvania Press, 1985), 206–43.

Cannon, John and Griffiths, Ralph, *The Oxford Illustrated History of the British Monarchy*, reissue of the 1st rev. paperback edn 1998 (Oxford University Press, 2000).

Carleton, John Dudley, *Westminster School – A History*, 2nd rev. edn (London: Rupert Hart-Davis, 1965).

Carpenter, Adrian, 'William Croft's Church Music', *MT* 112 (1971), 275–7.

Cheverton, Ian, 'Captain Henry Cooke (*c.* 1616–72) The Beginnings of a Reappraisal', *Soundings* 9 (1982), 74–86.

Chrysander, Friedrich, *G. F. Händel*, vol. II (Leipzig: Breitkopf und Härtel, 1860).

'Henry Carey und der Ursprung des Königsgesanges God save the King', *Jahrbücher für musikalische Wissenschaft* 1 (Leipzig: Breitkopf und Härtel, 1863), 287–407.

Cole, Suzanne, *Thomas Tallis and His Music in Victorian England* (Woodbridge: Boydell Press 2008).

Colles, H. C., 'Preface' to *The Form and Order* [...] *with the Music to Be Sung* (1937), iii–vi.

Colley, Linda, *Britons. Forging the Nation 1707–1837*, first published by Yale University Press, 1992. With a new preface by the author (London: Pimlico, 2003).

Copeman, Harold, *Singing in Latin*, with a preface by Andrew Parrot (Oxford: Harold Copeman, 1990).

'Coronation Fever – But Would Their Voices Last?', *WAC* 3, no. 6 (Winter 1996/97), 32–6.

The Coronation in Pictures – Complete Camera Record of the Mighty Pageant (London: Allied Newspapers Ltd., 1937).

'The Coronation Music and Musicians', *MT* 78 (1937), 497–501.

'Coronation Music of the Past', *The Athenaeum*, no. 3871 (1902), 25–7.

The Coronation of Her Majesty Queen Elizabeth II, 2 June 1953. Approved Souvenir Programme (London: Odhams Press, [1953]).

'The Coronation of King George the Fifth and Queen Mary in Westminster Abbey, June 22, 1911', *MT* 52 (1911), 433–7.

The Coronation of King George VI and Queen Elizabeth (London: Odhams Press, [1937]).

The Coronation of Their Majesties King George VI and Queen Elizabeth, May 12th 1937. Official Souvenir Programme (London: Odhams Press, [1937]).

'Coronation Reprise', *WAC* 2, no. 9 (Summer 1993), 19–21.

Cowdrey, Herbert Edward John, 'The Anglo-Norman Laudes Regiae', *Viator: Medieval and Renaissance Studies* 12 (1981), 37–78.

Cranmer, Damian (ed.), *George Frideric Handel, Zadok the Priest – Coronation Anthem*, miniature score (London: Eulenburg, 1980).

'Handel Borrowings', *MT* 122 (1981), 524.

Crowest, Frederick J., 'Coronation Music', *The Anglo-Saxon Review, A Quarterly Miscellany* 10 (September 1901), 24–37.

Cummings, William H., 'Dr. John Blow', *Sammelbände der Internationalen Musikgesellschaft* 10 (1909), 421–30.

Daub, Peggy E., 'Music at the Court of George II (r. 1727–1760)', unpublished Ph.D. thesis, Cornell University (1985).

Davey, Henry, *History of English Music* (London: Curwen and Sons, [1895]).

Davison, Peter, 'Complete with Orb, Sceptre and Crown – the "Coronation" was repeated 104 Times', *WAC* 42 (Summer 2006), 44–7.

Dawe, Donovan, *Organists of the City of London 1666–1850. A Record of One Thousand Organists with an Annotated Index* ([Purley:] By the author, 1983).

Dean, Winton, 'Handel and the Theatre', in Richard G. King (ed.), *Handel Studies: A Gedenkschrift for Howard Serwer* (Hilsdale, NY: Pendragon, 2009), 244–6.

Sleeve notes to Handel, *Coronation Anthems*, Argo ZRG 5369 (1963).

Dearnley, Christopher, *English Church Music 1650–1750 in Chapel, Cathedral and Parish Church* (London: Barrie & Jenkins, 1970).

Dennison, Peter and Wood, Bruce, 'Henry Cooke', *NG* 6, 385–87.

Deutsch, Otto Erich, *Handel – A Documentary Biography* (London: Adam and Charles Black, 1955).

Dexter, Keri, '*A good Quire of voices*': *The Provision of Choral Music at St George's Chapel, Windsor Castle, and Eton College, c. 1640–1733* (Aldershot: Ashgate, 2002).

'Diadem', *Crowns and Coronation Ceremonies and the Enthronement of King Edward VII.*, illustrated by Percy Reynolds and John Rowlands (London: Illustrated Publications Company, [1901 or 1902]).

A Diary of Royal Movements and of Personal Events and Incidents in the Life and Reign of Her Most Gracious Majesty Queen Victoria, Compiled from Official Documents and Public Records, vol. I (London: Elliot Stock, 1883).

Dibble, Jeremy, *Charles Villiers Stanford: Man and Musician* (Oxford University Press, 2002).

    C. Hubert H. Parry. His Life and Music (Oxford: Clarendon Press, 1992).

Dillon, Patrick, *The Last Revolution: 1688 and the Creation of the Modern World*, first publ. 2006, paperback edn (London: Pimlico, 2007).

Distad, N. Merill, 'Calendar Reform (1751)', in Gerald Newman (ed.), *Britain in the Hanoverian Age, 1714–1837: An Encyclopedia* (London: Routledge, 1997).

'Dotted Crotchet' [F. G. Edwards], 'Westminster Abbey', in *MT* 48 (1907), 293–301.

Duffy, Maureen, *Henry Purcell* (London: Fourth Estate, 1994).

Durost, Barbara J., 'The Academic Court Odes of William Croft (1678–1727)', unpublished DMA thesis, Claremont, California, (1997).

Edie, Carolyn Andervont, 'Succession and Monarchy: The Controversy of 1679–1681', *The American Historical Review* 70 (1965), 350–70.

E[dwards], F.G., 'The Coronation of Edward the Seventh and Queen Alexandra in the Collegiate Church of St. Peter in Westminster, August 9, 1902', *MT* 43 (1902), 577–86.

    'Dr. William Croft (1678–1727)', *MT* 41 (1900), 577–85.

    'Handel's Coronation Anthems', *MT* 43 (1902), 153–5.

Eeles, Francis Carolus, *The English Coronation Service. Its History and Teaching, with the Coronation Services of King Charles I. and of Queen Victoria* (Oxford: Mowbray, 1902).

Elizabeth II, 'Her Majesty's Coronation-Day Broadcast', in *Elizabeth Crowned Queen. The Pictorial Record of the Coronation* (first publ. Odhams Press [1953], repr. London: Bounty Books, 2006), 7–8.

Evelyn, John, *The Diary of John Evelyn*, with an introduction and notes by Austin Dobson, 3 vols. (London: Macmillan, 1906), repr. in 'Great British Diarists' (London: Routlege/Thoemmes, 1996), vol. II: 1647 to 1676.

Field, Christopher D. S., 'Christopher Gibbons', *NG* 9, 830–2.

Fiennes, Celia, *The Journeys of Celia Fiennes*, with an introduction by John Hillaby (London: Macdonald, 1983).

Fischer, Michael, '"Heil, Heil dem Kaiser!" Der Kaisermarsch Richard Wagners als nationalprotestantisches Symbol', in Michael Fischer, Christian Senkel, and Klaus Tanner (eds.), *Reichsgründung 1871. Ereignis-Beschreibung-Inszenierung* (Münster: Waxman, 2010), 104–18.

Fiske, Roger, 'Howard, Samuel', *NG* 11, 767f.

Fletcher, Ifan Kyrle, *The British Court. Its Traditions and Ceremonial* (London: Cassell, 1953).

'The Literature of Splendid Occasions in English History', paper read before the Bibliographical Society (18 February 1947), reproduced on http://library.oxford-journals.org/cgi/reprint/s5-I/3-4/184.pdf (Date accessed: 2 September 2011).

Splendid Occasions in English History 1520–1947 (London: Cassell, 1951).

Ford, Wyn K., 'The Chapel Royal at the Restoration', *The Monthly Musical Record* 90 (1960), 99–106.

'The Chapel Royal in the Time of Purcell', *MT* 100 (1959), 592–3.

Foreman, Lewis, *Bax: a Composer and His Time*, rev. edn (Woodbridge: Boydell Press, 2007).

The Form and Order of Service Recommended for Use in the Churches of the Church of England Throughout His Majesty's Empire on Thursday, 26th June, 1902, Being the Coronation Day of Their Majesties King Edward VII and Queen Alexandra (London: Novello, [1902]).

Foster, Myles Birket, *Anthems and Anthem Composers. An Essay upon the Development of the Anthem from the Reformation to the End of the Nineteenth Century* (London: Novello, 1901).

Fox, Lilla Margaret, *Instruments of Processional Music* (London: Lutterworth Press, 1967).

Franklin, Don Oscar, 'The Anthems of William Turner (1651–1740): an Historical and Analytical Study', unpublished Ph.D thesis, Stanford University (1967).

Fritz, Paul S., 'From "Public" to "Private": The Royal Funeral in England, 1500–1830', in Joachim Whaley (ed.), *Mirrors of Mortality – Studies in the Social History of Death* (London: Europa Publications, 1981), 61–79.

'From My Study. Music at the Queen's Coronation', signed 'X.', *MT* 38 (1897), 302–5.

Gatens, William J., *Victorian Cathedral Music in Theory and Practice* (Cambridge University Press, 1986).

Golby, John M. and Purdue, A. William, *Kings and Queens of Empire. British Monarchs 1760–2000*, rev. edn (Stroud: Tempus, 2000).

Graue, Jerald C., and Miligan, Thomas B., '(2) Johann [John] Baptist Cramer', *NG* 6, 640–3.

Gregg, Edward, *Queen Anne* (first publ. 1980 by Routledge and Kegan Paul, new edn Yale University Press, 2001).

Griffin, Erin, *Henrietta Maria: Piety, Politics and Patronage* (Aldershot: Ashgate, 2008).

Grimwade, Arthur, 'The Plate Catalogue', in Claude Blair (ed.), *The Crown Jewels: The History of the Coronation Regalia in the Jewel House of the Tower of London*, 2 vols. (London: Stationery Office, 1998), vol. II: The Catalogues, 385–501.

Halfpenny, Eric, 'The "Entertainment" of Charles II', *ML* 38 (1957), 32–44.
'Musicians at James II's Coronation', *ML* 32 (1951), 103–14.
'William Shaw's "Harmonic Trumpet"', *GSJ* 13 (July 1960), 7–13.

Hammerton, John (ed.), *The Story of the Coronation* (London: Amalgamated Press, [1937]).

Hanham, Andrew, 'Caroline of Brandenburg-Ansbach and the "anglicisation" of the House of Hanover', in Clarissa Campbell Orr (ed.), *Queenship in Europe 1660–1815. The Role of the Consort* (Cambridge University Press, 2004), 276–99.

Harper, John, 'Continuity, Discontinuity, Fragments and Connections: The Organ in Church, *c.* 1500–1640', in David Maw and Emma Hornby (eds.), *Essays on the History of English Music in Honour of John Caldwell – Sources, Style, Performance, Historiography* (Woodbridge: Boydell Press, 2010), 215–31.

Harper, John and Le Huray, Peter, 'Orlando Gibbons', *NG* 9, 832–6.

Harrison, Brian, *Seeking a Role: The United Kingdom, 1951–1970* (Oxford University Press, 2009).

Harrison, John Fussel, 'The Secular Works of William Croft', unpublished Ph.D thesis, Bryn Mawr College, Pennsylvania (1976).

Hayes, Gerald, 'Coronation Music', in L. G. G. Ramsey (ed.), *The Connoisseur Coronation Book, 1953* ([London, 1953]), 9–12.

Hedley, Owen, *Queen Charlotte* (London: John Murray, 1975).

Hendrie, Gerald, Preface to Georg Friedrich Händel, *Te Deum zur Feier des Friedens von Utrecht, HWV 278 und Jubilate zur Feier des Friedens von Utrecht, HWV 279, HHA*, series III, vol. 3 (Kassel: Bärenreiter, 1998), vii–xvii.

Henze-Döhring, Sabine, 'Händels Coronation Anthems', *Händel-Jahrbuch* 49 (2003), 105–13.

Herbert, Trevor, 'The Sackbut in England in the 17th and 18th Centuries', *EM* 18 (1990), 609–16.

Herissone, Rebecca, *'To Fill, Forbear, or Adorne': The Organ Accompaniment of Restoration Sacred Music* (Aldershot: Ashgate, 2006).

Herrmann, William, Introduction to George Frideric Handel, *Coronation Anthem No. 1 (Zadok the Priest)*, ed. and with keyboard reduction by William Herrmann (New York: Schirmer, [1969]).

Hesketh, Lady Christian Mary, *Charles I's Coronation Visit to Scotland in 1633*, publ. as 'Papers of the Royal Stuart Society' 52 (1998).

Holman, Peter, Booklet notes to *Sound the Trumpet...: Henry Purcell and his Followers*, The English Orpheus 35, CDA66817 (Hyperion: 1996).

Four and Twenty Fiddlers: The Violin at the English Court 1540–1690 (Oxford: Clarendon Press, 1993).

'London (i), §II, 2 (v): Music at Court: The Decline of Secular Music', *NG* 15, 107–8.

'Purcell's Orchestra', *MT* 137 (1996), 17–23.

Holmes, Martin, 'Some Coronation Fallacies', in L.G.G. Ramsey (ed.), *The Connoisseur Coronation Book, 1953* ([London, 1953]), 26–32.

Holst, Imogen, *Henry Purcell, 1659–1695: Essays on His Music* (London: Oxford University Press, 1959).

Hoppit, Julian, *A Land of Liberty? England 1689–1727* (Oxford University Press, 2000; paperback edn 2002).

Howes, Frank, *The Music of William Walton* (Oxford University Press, 1973).

'Preface' to *The Music with the Form and Order of the Service* [...] *at the Coronation of Her Most Excellent Majesty Queen Elizabeth II* [...] (London: Novello, 1953).

Hudson, Frederick, Large, W. Roy, and Spink, Ian, 'William Child', *NG* 5, 607–11.

Hughes, Andrew, 'Antiphons and Acclamations. The Politics of Music in the Coronation Service of Edward II, 1308', *The Journal of Musicology* 6 (1988), 150–68.

'The Origins and Descent of the Fourth Recension of the English Coronation', in János M. Bak (ed.), *Coronations: Medieval and Early Modern Monarchic Ritual* (Berkley: University of California Press, 1990), 197–216.

Hughes, (Dom) Anselm, 'Music of the Coronation over a Thousand Years', *Proceedings of the Royal Musical Association* 79 (1952–1953), 81–100.

Hughes, Meirion and Stradling, Robert, *The English Musical Renaissance, 1840–1940: Constructing a National Music*, 2nd edn (Manchester University Press, 2001).

Humphreys, David, 'Wilder's hand?', *MT* 144 (Summer 2003), 4.

Humphreys, Maggie and Evans, Robert, *Dictionary of Composers for the Church in Great Britain and Ireland* (London: Mansell, 1997).

Hunt, Alice, *The Drama of Coronation: Medieval Ceremony in Early Modern England* (Cambridge University Press, 2008).

Ihalainen, Pasi, *Protestant Nations Redefined: Changing Perceptions of National Identity in the Rhetoric of the English, Dutch and Swedish Public Churches, 1685–1772* (Leiden: Brill, 2005).

'In the Choir at the Coronation ['By the "Musical Herald" Representative']', *MH* (1902), 264–6.

Irving, John, '(1) Thomas Tomkins', *NG* 25, 568–76.

Jackson, Richard A., *Vive Le Roi! A History of the French Coronation from Charles V to Charles X* (Chapel Hill and London: University of North Carolina Press, 1984).

Jacob, Gordon, *The Composer and His Art* (Oxford University Press, 1955).

James, Peter, 'Sacred Music Omitted from *Musica Deo Sacra*', in Anthony Boden (ed.), *Thomas Tomkins: The Last Elizabethan* (Aldershot: Ashgate, 2005), 285–300.

Jenkinson, Matthew, *Culture and Politics at the Court of Charles II, 1660–1685* (Woodbridge: Boydell & Brewer, 2010).

Jenkyns, Richard, *Westminster Abbey* (London: Profile Books, 2004).

Johnson, Claudia L., '"Giant HANDEL" and the Musical Sublime', *Eighteenth-Century Studies* 19 (Summer 1986), 515–33.

Johnstone, H. Diack, 'Coronation Rehearsal', *MT* 118 (1977), 725.

'The Life and Work of Maurice Greene', 2 vols., unpublished DPhil thesis, University of Oxford (1967).

Johnstone, M. F., *Coronation of a King, or, The Ceremonies, Pageants and Chronicles of Coronations of All Ages* (London: Chapman and Hall, 1902).

Jones, Francis, *God Bless The Prince of Wales. Four Essays for Investiture Year 1969* (Carmarthen: Lodwick and Sons, 1969).

Jones, William, *Crowns and Coronations. A History of Regalia* (London: Chatto and Windus, 1883).

Kantorowicz, Ernst Hartwig, *The King's Two Bodies. A Study in Mediaeval Political Theology* (Princeton University Press, 1957).

Kappey, Jacob Adam, *Military Music. A History of Wind-Instrumental Bands* (London: Boosey, [1894]).

Keates, Jonathan, *Handel. The Man and His Music* (London: Gollancz, 1985).

Keay, Anna, *The Magnificent Monarch* (London: Continuum, 2008).

Kennedy, Michael, *Portrait of Walton*, first publ. in 1998, corr. paperback edn (Oxford University Press, 1998, repr. 2002).

The Works of Ralph Vaughan Williams, 2nd edn (Oxford: Clarendon Press, 1980, repr. Oxford University Press, 2002).

Kielmansegge, Friedrich, *Diary of a Journey to England in the Years 1761–1762*, transl. by Countess Kielmansegg (London: Longmans, 1902).

Kilburn, Matthew Charles, 'Royalty and Public in Britain: 1714–1789', unpublished DPhil thesis, University of Oxford (1997).

King, Alec Hyatt, 'The Royal Taste', *MT* 118 (1977), 461–3.

King, Robert, *Henry Purcell* (London: Thames and Hudson, 1994).

Booklet notes to *The Coronation of King George II*, CDA 67286 (Hyperion, 2001).

Kishlansky, Mark, *A Monarchy Transformed: Britain 1603–1714*, first publ. 1996 (London: Penguin, 1997).

Knight, David Stanley, 'The Organs of Westminster Abbey and their Music, 1240–1908', 2 vols., unpublished Ph.D thesis, King's College, University of London (2001).

'Resources for Musicologists in Lambeth Palace Library', *A Handbook for Studies in 18th-Century Music* 14 (2003), 1–15.

Knighton, Charles, 'Random *Vivat*s Threaten Coronation Chaos', *WAC* 3, no. 9 (Summer 1998), 20–2.

Kuhn, William, *Democratic Royalism: The Transformation of the British Monarchy, 1861–1914* (Basingstoke: Macmillan, 1996).

Kumar, Krishan, *The Making of English National Identity* (Cambridge University Press, 2003).

Landon, H. C. Robbins, *Handel and His World* (London: Weidenfeld and Nicolson, 1984).

Lant, Jeffrey L., *Insubstantial Pageant. Ceremony and Confusion at Queen Victoria's Court* (London: Hamish Hamilton, 1979).

Laurie, Margaret, 'The Chapel Royal Part-Books', in Oliver Neighbour (ed.), *Music and Bibliography. Essays in Honour of Alec Hyatt King* (New York: Saur, 1980), 28–50.

'John Weldon', *NG* 27, 265–6.

Lee, Cedric, Foreword to William Croft, *'With Noise of Cannon', from the Ode, for bass, two violins and continuo* ([Richmond:] Green Man Press, [2005]).

Leeper, Janet, 'Coronation Music', *Contemporary Review* 151 (1937), 554–62.

Legg, John Wickham (ed.), *The Coronation Order of King James I*. transcribed from *GB-London, Lambeth Palace Library MS 1075B*, with an introduction and notes by the editor (London: F.E. Robinson, 1902).

Three Coronation Orders (London: Harrison and Sons, 1900).

Legg, Leopold George Wickham (ed.), *English Coronation Records* (Westminster: Archibald Constable, 1901).

Le Hardy, William, *The Coronation Book. The History and Meaning of the Ceremonies at the Crowning*, rev. edn (London: Staples Press, 1953).

Le Huray, Peter, *Music and the Reformation in England, 1549–1660* (first publ. 1967 by Herbert Jenkins/Alden Press, repr. with corrections: Cambridge University Press, 1978).

Le Huray, Peter and Harper, John, 'Anglican Chant', *NG* 1, 672–3.

Liber Regalis Ordo Consecrandi Regem Solum. Ordo Consecrandi Reginam cum Rege. Ordo Consecrandi Reginam Solam. Rubrica de Regis Exequiis, transcribed from the manuscript in Westminster Abbey, printed for the Roxburghe Club (London: Nichols and Sons, 1870).

Lindner, Andreas, 'Zur Intention musikalischer Inszenierung. Die Determination weltlicher Festkonzeption im Umfeld höfisch-geistlicher Institutionen', *Studien zur Musikwissenschaft* 56 (2010), 127–52.

Lindsay, Philip, *Crowned King of England. The Coronation of King George VI in History and Tradition* (London: Ivor Nicholson & Watson, 1937).

Lisle, Leanda de, *After Elizabeth – How James, King of Scots Won the Crown of England in 1603* (London: Harper Collins, 2005).

Loftie, William John, *The Coronation Book of Edward VII* (London: Cassell, [1902]).

Lord Keeper's Speech in Parliament on 6 February 1626, *Journal of the House of Lords:* vol. 3: 1620–1628 (1802), 492–4, reproduced on www.british-history.ac.uk/report.asp?compid=30469&strquery=coronation (Date accessed: 29 August 2011).

Lowerre, Kathryn, *Music and Musicians on the London Stage, 1695–1705* (Farnham: Ashgate, 2009).

Luttrell, Narcissus, *A Brief Historical Relation of State Affairs from September 1678 to April 1714*, 6 vols. (Oxford University Press, 1857).

Lysons, Daniel, Amott, John, Williams, Lee, and Chance, Godwin, *Origin and Progress of the Meeting of the Three Choirs of Gloucester, Worcester and Hereford and of the Charity Connected with It* (Gloucester: Chance and Bland, 1895).

Macek, Bernhard A., *Die Krönung Josephs II. zum Römischen König in Frankfurt am Main. Logistisches Meisterwerk, zeremonielle Glanzleistung und Kulturgüter für die Ewigkeit* (Frankfurt am Main: Peter Lang, 2010).

Macleane, Douglas, *The Great Solemnity of the Coronation of the King and Queen of England According to the Use of the Church of England, with an introduction by the Lord Bishop of Salisbury* (London: George Allen, 1911).

Mann, Alfred, 'Our Handel Image', in Richard G. King (ed.), *Handel Studies: A Gedenkschrift for Howard Serwer* (Hilsdale, NY: Pendragon, 2009), 189–94.

Manning, Robert, 'The Anthems of Henry Cooke', *Royal College of Music Magazine* 88 (1991), 25–33.

'A Purcell Coronation Anthem?', *MT* 120 (1979), 1 and 22.

Review of Bruce Wood (ed.), *A Purcell Anthology: 12 Anthems* (Oxford University Press, 1995), in *ML* 77 (May 1996), 313.

Marx, Hans Joachim, *Händel und seine Zeitgenossen. Eine Biographische Enzyklopädie*, published as 'Händel-Handbuch', ed. by Hans Joachim Marx, vol. I, two parts (Laaber: Laaber-Verlag, 2008).

Mary II, *Memoirs of Mary, Queen of England (1689–1693), together with her letters and those of Kings James II and William III to the Electress, Sophia of Hanover*, ed. by R. Doebner (Leipzig: Veit, 1886).

Mason, Roger A., *Scots and Britons: Scottish Political Thought and the Union of 1603* (Cambridge University Press, 1994).

McGrady, Richard, 'Captain Cooke: A Tercentenary Tribute', *MT* 113 (1972), 659–60.

McLeish, Kenneth and Valerie (eds.), *Long to reign over us... Memories of Coronation Day and of Life in the 1950s* (London: Bloomsbury, 1992).

McVeigh, Simon, *Concert Life in London from Mozart to Haydn* (Cambridge University Press, 1993).

Miserandino-Gaherty, Cathryn J., 'The Rastrology of English Music Manuscripts c.1575–c.1642', unpublished DPhil thesis, University of Oxford (1999).

Monod, Paul Kléber, *The Power of Kings. Monarchy and Religion in Europe 1589–1715* (Yale University Press, 1999).

Morehen, John, 'The English Anthem Text, 1549–1660', *JRMA* 117 (1992), 62–85.

Morgan, Kenneth O., 'The Twentieth Century (1914–2000)', in Kenneth O. Morgan (ed.), *The Oxford History of Britain*, rev. edn (Oxford University Press, 2001), 582–679.

Morris, Timothy, 'Music to Celebrate the Coronation of Elizabeth I', in booklet notes to *Coronation of the First Elizabeth*, CD GCCD 4032 (Griffin: 1994), 4–6.

Mortlock, C. B. 'New Music's Part in Ancient Coronation Rite', *DT*, 18 March 1953, 6.

Möseneder, Karl, 'Das Fest als Darstellung der Harmonie im Staate am Beispiel der Entrée Solennelle Ludwigs XIV. 1660 in Paris', in August Buck et al. (eds.), *Europäische Hofkultur im 16. und 17. Jahrhundert; Vorträge und Referate* [. . .] *in der Herzog August Bibliothek Wolfenbüttel vom 4. bis 8. September 1979*, 3 vols. (Hamburg: Hauswedell, 1981), vol. II, 421–31.

Mould, Clifford, *The Musical Manuscripts of St. George's Chapel Windsor Castle*. Historical Monographs Relating to St. George's Chapel, Windsor Castle, 14 (Windsor: Oxley and Son, 1973).

Murray, Robert, *The King's Crowning*, with an introduction by Foxley Norris (London: John Murray, [1936]).

'Music at the Coronation', *The Record* (Friday, 7 May 1937), 291.

'Music at the Last Coronation [Queen Victoria, 1838]', signed 'One of the Choir', *MT* 43 (1902), 18–21.

'Music for the Coronation', *MT* 94 (1953), 305–7.

'Music in the Abbey', *The Times*, 13 May 1937.

'Music in the Coronation Service. By our Representative in Westminster Abbey', *MH* (1911), 213–15.

'New Music, and a Hymn for the Coronation', *WAC* 2, no. 8 (Winter 1992–93), 23–4.

Newcastle, William Cavendish, *Ideology and Politics on the Eve of Restoration: Newcastle's Advice to Charles II*, transcribed and with an introduction by Thomas P. Slaughter (Philadelphia: The American Philosophical Society, 1984).

Noble, Jeremy, 'Purcell and the Chapel Royal', in Imogen Holst (ed.), *Henry Purcell, 1659–1695. Essays on his Music* (London: Oxford University Press, 1959), 52–66.

Olechnowicz, Andrzej, 'Historians and the Modern British Monarchy', in Andrzej Olechnowicz (ed.), *The Monarchy and the British Nation, 1780 to the Present* (Cambridge University Press, 2007), 6–44.

Oxford Musical Festival, May 5th–12th, 1935: Handel, Bach, Born 1685 (Oxford, 1935).

Pascoe, Charles Eyre, *The Pageant and Ceremony of the Coronation of Their Majesties King Edward the Seventh and Queen Alexandra* (New York: Appleton, 1902).

Passingham, W. J., *A History of the Coronation* (London: Sampson Low, Marston, [1937?]).

Paulu, Burton, *British Broadcasting in Transition* (Minneapolis: University of Minnesota Press, 1961).

Pepys, Samuel, *The Diary of Samuel Pepys: a new and complete transcription*, ed. by Robert Latham and William Matthews. Vol. II: 1661, paperback edn (Berkeley: Harper Collins, 1995, reissued 2000).

Perkins, Jocelyn, *The Crowning of the Sovereign of Great Britain and the Dominions Overseas: A Handbook to the Coronation* (London: Methuen, 1937).

Phillips, Peter, *English Sacred Music 1549–1649* (Oxford: Gimell, 1991).

Pierce, Kathryn, 'The Coronation Music of Charles II', unpublished MA thesis, Bowling Green State University (2007).

Plunkett, John, *Queen Victoria. The First Media Monarch* (Oxford University Press, 2003).

Poulton, Diana, *John Dowland* (Berkeley: University of California Press, 1982).

Price, Curtis A., *Music in the Restoration Theatre. With a Catalogue of Instrumental Music in the Plays 1665–1713* (UMI Research Press, 1979).

(ed.), *Purcell Studies* (Cambridge University Press, 1995).

Pulver, Jeffrey, *A Biographical Dictionary of Old English Music* (New York: Franklin, 1929, repr. Ayer Publishing, 1969).

Purey-Cust, Arthur Perceval, *The Crowning of Monarchs* (London: Ibister, 1902).

Quintrell, Brian, 'William Juxon', *Oxford Dictionary of National Biography online* (www.oxforddnb.com, accessed 25 August 2011).

Range, Matthias, 'Francis Pigott's "I was glad" and its Performance at Three Coronations', *Music in Eighteenth Century Britain* 19 (2008), 47–57.

'Music at British Coronations from James I to Queen Victoria, 1603–1838 – a Study and Edition', 2 vols., unpublished DPhil thesis, University of Oxford (2008).

'The 1685 Coronation Anthem *I was glad*', *EM* 36 (2008), 397–408.

'William Boyce's Anthem for the Wedding of King George III', *MT* 147 (Summer 2006), 59–66.

'"With Instrumental Musick of all sorts" – The Orchestra at British Coronations before 1727', *AM* 82 (1/2010), 87–104.

'The Rehearsals for the Coronation ['By our Representative in the Abbey Choir']', *MH* (1902), 202–3.

Richards, Jeffrey, *Imperialism and Music. Britain 1876–1953*. Studies in Imperialism. (Manchester University Press, 2001).

Risk, James C., *The History of The Order of the Bath and Its Insignia* (London: Spink and Son, 1972).

Routley, Erik, *An English-speaking Hymnal Guide*, ed. and expanded by Peter Cutts (Chicago: GIA Publications, 2005).

Rowse, A. L., 'A New Elizabethan Age?', *The English Association Presidential Address* (1952).

Rye, William Brenchley, 'The Coronation of King James I., 1603', *The Antiquary* 22 (1890), 18–23.

Salmen, Walter, 'Der Tanz in der höfischen Kultur des 17. und 18. Jahrhunderts', in Hans Joachim Marx (ed.), '*Beiträge zur Musik des Barock. Tanz – Oper – Oratorium. Bericht über die Symposien 1994 bis 1997, Günter Köneman zum 65. Geburtstag. Veröffentlichungen der Internationalen Händel-Akademie Karlsruhe*, 6 (Laaber: Laaber Verlag, 1998), 17–28.

Sandon, Nick, 'F G A B-Flat A: Thoughts on a Tudor Motif', *EM* 12 (1984), 56–63.

Saussure, César de, *A Foreign View of England in the Reigns of George I. and George II. The Letters of Monsieur César de Saussure to his Family*, transl. and ed. by Madame van Muyden (London: Murray, 1902).

Scarlett, Robert Dalley, 'Coronation Music and Its Problems', *The Canon – Australian Journal of Music* 6 (March 1953), 308–11.

Schaich, Michael, 'Introduction', in Michael Schaich (ed.) *Monarchy and Religion – The Transformation of Royal Culture in Eighteenth-Century Europe* (Oxford University Press, 2007), 1–40.

Schmid, Josef Johannes, *Sacrum Monarchiae Speculum. Der Sacre Louis XV. 1722: Monarchische Tradition, Zeremoniell, Liturgie* (Münster: Aschendorff, 2007).

Scholes, Percy A., *God Save the Queen! The History and Romance of the World's First National Anthem* (Oxford University Press, 1954).

Schramm, Percy Ernst, *A History of the English Coronation*, transl. by Leopold G. Wickham Legg (Oxford: Clarendon Press, 1937).

Schultz, Thomas Robert, 'Music in the Coronations of the Kings and Queens of England (1603–1953)', unpublished MA thesis, Trenton State College (1992).

Schwoerer, Lois G., 'The Coronation of William and Mary, April 11, 1689', in Lois G. Schwoerer (ed.), *The Revolution of 1688–1689. Changing Perspectives*, (Cambridge University Press, 1992), 107–30.

Senior, Evan, [Editor's Preface], *Music and Musicians*. Coronation Number (June 1953), 5.

Shapiro, Alexander H., '"Drama of an Infinitely Superior Nature": Handel's Early English Oratorios and the Religious Sublime', *ML* 74 (May, 1993), 215–45.

Shaw, Watkins, 'Coronation Fanfares', *MT* 94 (1953), 273.

The Succession of Organists of the Chapel Royal and the Cathedrals of England and Wales from c. 1538 (Oxford: Clarendon Press, 1991).

Shaw, Watkins and Beeks, Graydon, 'William Croft', *NG* 6, 713–16.

Shaw, Watkins, Powell, Christopher, and Johnstone, H. Diack, 'Jeremiah Clarke', *NG* 5, 916–18.

Shedlock, J[ohn] S[outh], 'Coronation Music', *Proceedings of the Royal Musical Association* 28 (1901–2), 141–60.

Shils, Edward, and Young, Michael, 'The Meaning of the Coronation', *The Sociological Review*, new series, vol. 1 (1953), repr. (Nendeln, Liechtenstein: 1970), 63–81.

Slatford, Rodney, 'Double Bass', *NG* 7, 19–25.

Smart, Sir George, *Leaves From the Journals of Sir George Smart*, ed. by H. Bertram Cox and C. L. E. Cox (London: Longmans, Green, 1907).

Smith, Ruth, *Handel's Oratorios and Eighteenth-Century Thought*, (Cambridge University Press, 1995, paperback edn 2005).

Smith, William C., *A Bibliography of the Musical Works Published by John Walsh during the Years 1695–1720* (London: Oxford University Press, 1948).

'George III, Handel, and Mainwaring', *MT* 65 (1924), 789–95.

Spink, Ian, *Henry Lawes* (Oxford: University Press, 2000).

Restoration Cathedral Music 1660–1714 (Oxford: Clarendon Press, 1995).

Stanley, Arthur Penrhyn, *Historical Memorials of Westminster Abbey*. 5th edn, with the author's final revisions (London: John Murray, 1882).

Stevens, Denis, *Thomas Tomkins, 1572–1656* (London: Macmillan, 1957).

Strong, Roy, *Coronation: A History of Kingship and the British Monarchy* (London: Harper Collins, 2005).

Sturdy, David, '"Continuity" versus "Change": Historians and English Coronations of the Medieval and Early Modern Periods', in János M. Bak (ed.), *Coronations; Medieval and Early Modern Monarchic Ritual*, (Berkley: University of California Press, 1990), 228–45.

Sullivan, Sandra Jean, 'Representations of Mary of Modena, Duchess, Queen Consort and Exile: Images and Texts', 2 vols., unpublished Ph.D. thesis, University College, London (2008).

Summers, Billy Wayne, 'The Coronation Anthems of William Boyce (1761): A Performing Edition', unpublished DMA thesis, University of North Carolina at Greensboro (2001).

Sutherland, James, *Background for Queen Anne* (London: Methuen, 1939).

Sykes, Norman, *Church and State in England in the XVIIIth Century* (Cambridge University Press, 1934).

 William Wake, Archbishop of Canterbury 1657-1737, 2 vols., (Cambridge University Press, 1957).

Tanner, Lawrence E., *The History of the Coronation* (1952, repr. London: Pitkin, 1953).

Tarr, Edward H., 'Fanfare', *NG* 8, 543–4.

Tassel, Eric van, 'Music for the Church', in Michael Burden (ed.), *The Purcell Companion* (London: Faber, 1995), 101–99.

 'A Purcell Coronation Anthem?', *MT* 120 (1979), 114.

Taylor, Thomas F., 'The Life and Works of Jeremiah Clarke (*c.*1673–1707)', unpublished Ph.D. thesis, Northwestern University (1967).

Temperley, Nicholas, 'Attwood, Thomas', *NG* 2, 150–2.

 'Knyvett, William', *NG* 13, 705.

Thewlis, G. A., 'Coronation of George I', *MT* 78 (1937), 310–11.

Tierney, Neil, *William Walton. His Life and Music* (London: Robert Hale, 1984).

Titcomb, Caldwell, 'Baroque Court and Military Trumpets and Kettledrums: Technique and Music', *GSJ* 9 (1956), 56–81.

Tomlin, E.W.F., 'Charles II to William IV: Magnificence and Muddle, Seventeenth to Nineteenth Century', in John Hammerton (ed.), *The Story of the Coronation* (London: Amalgamated Press, [1937]), 227–34.

Towndrow, Kenneth Romney, 'Coronation Engravings', *Apollo* (1953), 178–82.

Turner, F. C., *James II* (London: Eyre and Spottiswoode, 1948).

Van Nice, John Robert, 'The Larger Sacred Choral Works of William Boyce (1710–1779): A Study and Edition of Selected Compositions for Choir and Orchestra', 3 vols., unpublished Ph.D. thesis, Iowa State University (1956).

Vaughan Williams, Ralph, *Letters of Ralph Vaughan Williams 1895-1958*, ed. by Hugh Cobbe (Oxford University Press, 2008).

Vaughan Williams, Ursula, *R.V.W.: A Biography of Ralph Vaughan Williams* (London: Oxford University Press, 1964).

Victoria, Queen, *The Girlhood of Queen Victoria. A Selection From Her Majesty's Diaries Between the Years 1832 and 1840*, ed. by Viscount Esher, 2 vols. (London: John Murray, 1912).

Wagner, Anthony Richard (ed.), *Heraldo Memoriale Or Memoirs of the College of Arms from 1727 to 1744* (London: Printed for presentation to the Roxburghe Club, 1981).

Waller, Maureen, *Sovereign Ladies. The Six Reigning Queens of England*, first publ. 2006, paperback edn (London: John Murray, 2007).

Walpole, Horace, *The Letters of Horace Walpole Fourth Earl of Orford*, chronologically arranged and edited with notes and indices by Mrs Paget Toynbee, 16 vols., Vol. V: 1760–1764 (Oxford: Clarendon Press, 1904).

Walton, Susanna, *William Walton. Behind the Façade* (Oxford University Press, 1988).

Ward, P. L., 'The Coronation Ceremony in Medieval England', *Speculum* 14 (1939), 160–78.

Webb, Stanley, 'The Westminster Abbey Organs', *MT* 124, (1983), 637–41.

Weber, William, *Music and the Middle Class: The Social Structure of Concert Life in London, Paris, and Vienna Between 1830 and 1848*, first publ. 1975, 2nd edn (Aldershot: Ashgate, 2004).

  The Rise of Musical Classics in Eighteenth-Century England. A Study in Canon, Ritual, and Ideology, paperback edn (Oxford: Clarendon Press, 1996).

  'The 1784 Handel Commemoration as Political Ritual', *The Journal of British Studies* 28, no. 1 (1989), 43–69.

Webster, Wendy, *Englishness and Empire 1939–1965* (Oxford University Press, 2005).

Weir, Alison, *Britain's Royal Families. The Complete Genealogy*, first publ. The Bodley Head 1989, 3rd edn (London: Pimlico, 2002).

Westrup, Jack A., *Purcell*, first published in 1937, with a new foreword by Curtis Price. The Master Musicians (Oxford University Press, 1995).

Wilkinson, James, 'A Chorister Remembers 1953', *The Court Historian* 7, 1 (May 2002), 69–73.

  The Queen's Coronation: The Inside Story (London: Scaba Publishers, 2011).

  Westminster Abbey. 1000 Years of Music and Pageant (Leighton Buzzard: Evolution Electronics, 2003).

Williamson, Philip 'The Monarchy and Public Values 1910–1953', in Andrzej Olechnowicz (ed.), *The Monarchy and the British Nation 1780 to the Present* (Cambridge University Press, 2007), 223–57.

Wilson, A[ndrew] N[orman], *After the Victorians* (London: Hutchinson, 2005).

Wilson, Ruth M., *Anglican Chant and Chanting in England, Scotland, and America 1660 to 1820* (Oxford: Clarendon Press, 1996).

Windsor, [Edward], Duke of, *The Crown and the People 1902–1953* (London: Cassell, 1953).

Wolffe, John, '"Praise to the Holiest in the Height": Hymns and Church Music', in John Wolffe (ed.), *Religion in Victorian Britain,* Volume V: *Culture and Empire* (Manchester University Press, 1997), 59–99.

Wood, Bruce, Booklet notes to *Coronation Anthems,* CD 470 226-2 (Decca, 2002).

   Booklet notes to *Coronation Music for James II,* Archiv Produktion CD-447 155-2 (Hamburg: Polydor International, 1987).

   Booklet notes to *Music for Queen Mary,* CDSK 66243 (Sony: 1995).

   'Cavendish Weedon: Impresario Extraordinary', *The Consort* 33 (1977), 222–4.

   'A Coronation Anthem. Lost and Found', *MT* 118 (1977), 466–8.

   'John Blow's Anthems with Orchestra', 5 vols., unpublished Ph.D thesis, University of Cambridge (1977).

Woolley, Reginald Maxwell, *Coronation Rites* (Cambridge University Press, 1915).

Wordsworth, Christopher (ed.), *The Manner of the Coronation of King Charles the First of England at Westminster, 2 Feb., 1626* (London: Harrison and Sons, 1892).

Wright David, 'Sir Frederick Bridge and the Musical Furtherance of the 1902 Imperial Project', in Rachel Cowgill and Julian Rushton (eds.), *Europe, Empire, and Spectacle in Nineteenth-Century British Music* (Aldershot: Ashgate, 2006), 115–29.

Wrigley, Chris, *Winston Churchill: A Biographical Companion* (Santa Barbara: ABC-CLIO, 2002).

Yates, Nigel, *Anglican Ritualism in Victorian Britain 1830–1910* (Oxford University Press, 1999).

The Year That Made the Day – How the BBC Planned and Prepared the Coronation Day Broadcast (London: BBC, [1954]).

Zaller, Robert, 'Breaking the Vessels: The Desacralization of Monarchy in Early Modern England', *Sixteenth Century Journal* 24 (1998), 757–78.

Ziegler, Philip, *Crown and People* (London: Collins, 1978).

Zimmerman, Franklin B., *Henry Purcell – An Analytical Catalogue of His Music* (London: Macmillan, 1963).

   Henry Purcell, 1659–1695: his Life and Times, 2nd rev. edn (Philadelphia: University of Pennsylvania Press, 1983).

Section four – Recordings

Coronation Anthems. Choir of New College Oxford and the Academy of Ancient Music, dir. Edward Higginbottom, CD 470 226-2 (Decca, 2002).

Coronation Music for James II, Westminster Abbey Choir and Orchestra, dir. Simon Preston, Archiv Produktion CD-447 155-2 (Hamburg: Polydor International, 1987).

Coronation of the First Elizabeth, A Musical Recreation of the Original State Occasion, CD GCCD 4032 (Griffin: 1994).

Music at the Coronation of James II, 1685, Choir of the Chapel Royal and The Musicians Extra-Ordinary, dir. Andrew Gant, SIGCD094 (Signum, 2006).

Music for Queen Mary, Westminster Abbey Choir and New London Consort, dir. Martin Neary, CDSK 66243 (Sony: 1995).

The Coronation of King George II, Choir and Orchestra of the King's Consort, dir. Robert King, CDA 67286 (Hyperion, 2001).

The Coronation of Their Majesties King George VI and Queen Elizabeth, Westminster Abbey, 12 May 1937, 2 discs, FL 1001–2/FL 1002–2, digitally remastered (New York: Fleur de Lis Recordings, 2010); first published on fifteen 78rpm records (London: The Gramophone Company Limited: 1937; HMV Album No. 281, RG 1–15).

The Coronation Service of Her Majesty Queen Elizabeth II, 2 June 1953. 2 discs, CD 7243 5 66582 2 6, digitally remastered (EMI, 1997); first published by EMI on a 3-LP set: ALP 1056–8.

The Coronation Service of Queen Elizabeth II, 1953 (BBC live coverage), *Lwa Library DVD nos 43a and 43b*.

Index

Printed in the United States
by Baker & Taylor Publisher Services